SUPPORTING LEGAL CAPACITY IN SOCIO-LEGAL CONTEXT

This collection brings together leading international socio-legal and medico-legal scholars to explore the dilemma of how to support legal capacity in theory and practice. Traditionally, decisions for persons found to lack capacity are made by others, generally without reference to the person, and this applies especially to those with cognitive and psycho-social disabilities. This book examines the difficulties in establishing effective and deliverable supported decision-making, focusing in particular on the impact of the UN Convention on the Rights of Persons with Disabilities. It concludes that approaches to capacity need to be informed by a grounded understanding of how it operates in 'real life' contexts.

With 16 chapters written by contributors from the UK, Canada, Finland, India, Ireland, Spain, Sweden, and Turkey, the collection takes a comparative and interdisciplinary approach. Many of the contributors have been directly involved in law reform processes in their home jurisdictions, and thus can combine both academic expertise and practical, grounded awareness of the challenges of legal change.

Oñati International Series in Law and Society

A SERIES PUBLISHED FOR THE OÑATI INSTITUTE
FOR THE SOCIOLOGY OF LAW

Recent titles in this series

Law and the Precarious Home: Socio Legal Perspectives on the Home in Insecure Times
Edited by Helen Carr, Brendan Edgeworth and Caroline Hunter

Collective Bargaining and Collective Action: Labour Agency and Governance in the 21st Century?
Edited by Julia López López

Fundamental Rights and Legal Consequences of Criminal Conviction
Edited Sonja Meijer, Harry Annison and Ailbhe O'Loughlin

Digital Family Justice: From Alternative Dispute Resolution to Online Dispute Resolution?
Edited by Mavis Maclean and Bregje Dijksterhuis

The Legacies of Institutionalisation: Disability, Law and Policy in the 'Deinstitutionalised' Community
Edited by Claire Spivakovsky, Linda Steele and Penelope Weller

Gender and Careers in the Legal Academy
Edited by Ulrike Schultz, Gisela Shaw, Margaret Thornton and Rosemary Auchmuty

Contesting Austerity: A Socio-Legal Inquiry
Edited by Anuscheh Farahat and Xabier Arzoz

The Right to the Continuous Improvement of Living Conditions: Responding to Complex Global Challenges
Edited by Jessie Hohmann and Beth Goldblatt

Supporting Legal Capacity in Socio-Legal Context
Edited by Mary Donnelly, Rosie Harding and Ezgi Taşcıoğlu

For the complete list of titles in this series, see www.bloomsbury.com/uk/series/oñati-international-series-in-law-and-society

Supporting Legal Capacity in Socio-Legal Context

Edited by
Mary Donnelly
Rosie Harding
and
Ezgi Taşcıoğlu

Oñati International Series in Law and Society

A SERIES PUBLISHED FOR THE OÑATI INSTITUTE FOR THE SOCIOLOGY OF LAW

•HART•
OXFORD • LONDON • NEW YORK • NEW DELHI • SYDNEY

HART PUBLISHING

Bloomsbury Publishing Plc

Kemp House, Chawley Park, Cumnor Hill, Oxford, OX2 9PH, UK

1385 Broadway, New York, NY 10018, USA

29 Earlsfort Terrace, Dublin 2, Ireland

HART PUBLISHING, the Hart/Stag logo, BLOOMSBURY and the Diana logo are trademarks of Bloomsbury Publishing Plc

First published in Great Britain 2022

A catalogue record for this book is available from the British Library.

Library of Congress Cataloging-in-Publication data

Names: Supporting Legal Capacity in Socio-Legal Context (Workshop) (2019 : Oñati International Institute for the Sociology of Law) | Donnelly, Mary (Law teacher), editor. | Harding, Rosie, editor. | Taşcıoğlu, Ezgi, editor. | Oñati International Institute for the Sociology of Law, sponsoring body.

Title: Supporting legal capacity in socio-legal context / edited by Mary Donnelly, Rosie Harding and Ezgi Taşcıoğlu.

Description: Oxford ; New York : Hart, 2022. | Series: Oñati international series in law and society | Includes bibliographical references and index.

Identifiers: LCCN 2021060703 | ISBN 9781509940349 (hardback) | ISBN 9781509959075 (paperback) | ISBN 9781509940363 (pdf) | ISBN 9781509940356 (Epub)

Subjects: LCSH: Capacity and disability—Congresses. | Mental health laws—Congresses. | People with disabilities—Legal status, laws, etc.—Congresses.

Classification: LCC K634 .S87 2019 | DDC 346.01/3—dc23/eng/20220204

LC record available at https://lccn.loc.gov/2021060703

ISBN: HB: 978-1-50994-034-9
ePDF: 978-1-50994-036-3
ePub: 978-1-50994-035-6

Typeset by Compuscript Ltd, Shannon

Acknowledgements

In July 2019, a group of socio-legal and medico-legal academics with an interest in the socio-legal dimensions of capacity law met for a workshop in the small Basque mountain town of Oñati, at the International Institute of the Sociology of Law. This book is the ultimate outcome of that workshop. Given how much the world has changed since the summer of 2019, the workshop that created the foundations of this text looms large in our memories as an exemplary experience of academic exchange, friendship and connection around the world. As we go to press, some 41 per cent of the world population have received at least one dose of a vaccine against COVID-19, which raises hopes that one day in the not too distant future, the face-to-face exchange of academic ideas will again be possible. The global COVID-19 pandemic has meant that pulling this book together has taken rather longer that we, as editors, had originally planned, given delays caused by the unprecedented lockdowns, school closures, infections, and bereavements that have punctuated the years since our workshop.

We, as editors, would like to extend our grateful thanks to all of the contributors to this collection for sticking with the project, for helpful peer reviews, and for finalising your thoughts and contributions in the face of these difficult times. Several workshop attendees (Louise Campbell, Magdalena Furgalska, Caoimhe Gleeson, Claire Murray, Laura Pritchard Jones and Chloe Waterman) were unable to contribute to the collection, and we would like to thank them for their engagement at the workshop and their contributions to peer review of the book chapters.

Bringing scholars together from around the world inevitably requires resources. We are grateful to all of the contributors for securing financial support to enable their attendance. Individually, Mary would like to thank the University College Cork School of Law research fund for financial assistance towards attending the workshop in Oñati. Rosie would like to thank the University of Birmingham International Engagement Fund for financial support for international participants at the workshop, and the Leverhulme Trust for their generous support through a Philip Leverhulme Prize, which has funded her time throughout this project. Ezgi would like to thank Keele University Faculty of Humanities and Social Sciences Research Support Fund for financial assistance towards attending the workshop in Oñati. We would also like to thank Malen Gordoa Mendizabal and the rest of the workshop organisation team at the IISL in Oñati, for hosting our workshop, supporting our scholarship and giving us the opportunity to create this text.

Finally, we are grateful to the Oñati Socio-Legal Book Series editors, Rosemary Hunter and David Nelken, and our editorial assistant at Hart Publishing, Rosie Mearns, for their support of the project and their patience as we slowly edged this book towards publication.

Rosie Harding, Mary Donnelly & Ezgi Taşcıoğlu

Contents

List of Contributors

Patricia Cuenca Gómez is a Lecturer in Philosophy of Law at the University Carlos III in Madrid, Spain. She is a researcher at the Human Rights Institute Gregorio Peces-Barba and an expert on Human Rights and Disability and on the implementation of the CRPD in the Spanish legal system. She has developed several research projects and publications on disability and theories of justice, accessibility, legal capacity, deprivation of liberty and access to justice.

Mary Donnelly is a Professor of Law at University College Cork, Ireland. She researches in the fields of mental capacity/mental health/health law. She is author of *Healthcare Decision-making and the Law: Autonomy, Capacity and the Limits of Liberalism* (Cambridge University Press, 2010) and joint-editor of *Ethical and Legal Debates in Irish Healthcare: Confronting Complexities* (Manchester University Press, 2016). She is the joint chair of the Health Service Executive National Consent Advisory Group and the HSE Assisted Decision Making Commencement Group and Chair of the Multidisciplinary Working Group on Advance Healthcare Directives.

Suzanne Doyle Guilloud is a Senior Research Associate at the Centre for Health, Law, and Society at University of Bristol Law School, UK. Her research broadly spans questions of autonomy, liberty, agency and decision-making across the life course. She has a particular interest in the normative implications of the UN Convention on the Rights of Persons with Disabilities for legal systems which provide for the coercion of people with psychosocial disabilities.

Eilionóir Flynn is an Established Professor of Law and Director of the Centre for Disability Law and Policy at the National University of Ireland Galway. Her research focuses on disability and social justice, with a particular emphasis on legal capacity, advocacy and reproductive justice. She is the Scientific Co-ordinator of the Disability Advocacy Research in Europe Marie Curie Training Network, and has held awards from the European Research Council, Health Research Board, and Wellcome Trust.

Rosie Harding is Professor of Law and Society, at Birmingham Law School, University of Birmingham, UK and Chair of the UK Socio-Legal Studies Association. She is author of *Duties to Care: Dementia, Relationality and Law* (Cambridge University Press, 2017) and *Regulating Sexuality* (Routledge, 2011), and series editor of *Law, Society, Policy* for Bristol University Press. She is a Fellow of the Academy of Social Sciences, and held a British Academy Mid-Career Fellowship (2016–2017) and a Philip Leverhulme Prize for Law (2017).

Margaret Isabel Hall, LLB, LLM, PhD is a Professor and the Society of Notaries Public of BC Chair in Applied Legal Studies at Simon Fraser University (School of Criminology) in British Columbia, Canada. Margaret is also an Adjunct Professor at the Australian Centre for Health Law Research, Queensland University of Technology, in Brisbane. Margaret's research interests include tort law, law and dementia, and medical assistance in dying.

Arjun Kapoor is a Research Fellow at the Centre for Mental Health Law and Policy at Indian Law Society, India. He is a lawyer and psychologist by qualification. At the Centre, he provides capacity-building and technical support to a range of stakeholders for the implementation of the Mental Healthcare Act, 2017. He also co-leads the development of a repository of data on mental health laws, policies, and services in India. Previously, he served as Law Clerk to the Supreme Court of India where he provided research assistance on matters of public and constitutional law.

Amanda Keeling is a Lecturer in Law in the Centre for Law and Social Justice at the University of Leeds, United Kingdom. Over the past decade, her work has explored the tension between autonomy and protection which article 12 of the CRPD throws into stark relief. This work has been both empirical and theoretical, and she continues to investigate how the law can shape environments of support for legal capacity.

Camillia Kong is a Senior Research Fellow at the Institute for Crime and Justice Policy Research, Birkbeck College. Her research focuses on medico-legal conceptualisation of mental capacity, the ethics of psychiatry, and the hermeneutics and phenomenology of mental disorder. She is the author of *Mental Capacity in Relationship: Decision-Making, Dialogue, and Autonomy* (Cambridge University Press, 2017) and co-author of *Overcoming Challenges in the Mental Capacity Act 2005: Practical Guidance for Working with Complex Issues* (Jessica Kingsley, 2019).

Jaime Lindsey is a Senior Lecturer in Law at the University of Essex, UK. She is a socio-legal scholar whose research interests include mental capacity law and adult safeguarding, access to justice, dispute resolution, and healthcare ethics and law. Her first book, *Reimagining the Court of Protection: Access to Justice in Mental Capacity Law* (Cambridge University Press), will be published in 2022 and she is currently working on an edited collection *Grandparents and the Law: Rights and Relationships* (Hart Publishing).

Anna Mäki-Petäjä-Leinonen is professor of Law and Ageing at the University of Eastern Finland, Law School. She is also Director of the Institute of Law and Welfare. Her research has focused on elder law, combining jurisprudence with social and medical sciences. Mäki-Petäjä-Leinonen is a member of the UEF Neuroscience Research Community where her Neuro-Ethics and Law research team focuses on the research related to patients' rights in neurodegenerative diseases and other disabilities. New research approaches are developed by combining empirical knowledge with doctrinal legal analysis.

Titti Mattsson is Professor of Public Law at the Faculty of Law at Lund University, Sweden. She has extensive experience of interdisciplinary and comparative research in law and social work on issues concerning social welfare, health and older persons' rights. Her publication list includes monographs, anthologies, book chapters and articles in international and national journals. She is director for three research groups, ie the Health Law Research Centre (http://www.jur.lu.se/#!healthlaw), the Norma Elder Law Research Group (www.jur.lu.se/elderlaw) and the Law and Vulnerabilities Group (http://www.law.lu.se/#!lawandvulnerabilities).

Shaun O'Keeffe is a Consultant Geriatrician in Galway University Hospitals and a Personal Professor of Medicine in the National University of Ireland, Galway. He graduated from University College Dublin and trained in Internal and Geriatric Medicine in Galway, Dublin, Boston and Liverpool. He is currently co-chair of Ireland's Health Service Executive National Consent Policy revision group. His research interests include cognitive impairment, sleep disturbance, dysphagia and ethical issues in the care of older people.

Soumitra Pathare is a psychiatrist by training and Director of the Centre for Mental Health Law and Policy at Indian Law Society, India. His primary interests are in the areas of mental health policy, suicide prevention, scaling up mental health services, rights-based care and legislation. He has provided technical assistance to the Ministry of Health and Family Welfare, Government of India in drafting India's new Mental Healthcare Act, 2017, which takes a rights-based approach to mental health care and provides for publicly funded universal mental health care. He was also a member of the Mental Health Policy Group appointed by the Government of India to draft India's first National Mental Health Policy, released in October 2014.

Jill Stavert is Professor of Mental Health and Capacity Law at Edinburgh Napier University, Scotland, UK. She is founder and Director of the university's Centre for Mental Health and Capacity Law, a unit of the multi-disciplinary Centre for Mental Health Practice, Policy and Law Research, which she also leads. Her main activity involves mental health and capacity law, human rights and related legislative and policy reform. She is currently a member of the Scottish Mental Health Law Review Executive Team.

Ezgi Taşcıoğlu is a Lecturer in Law at the School of Law, Keele University, UK. Her primary research interests lie in socio-legal studies, the regulation of sex, gender and sexuality, disability law, and social and cognitive justice. She holds a BA in Cultural Studies from Sabancı University (Turkey), an MA from the Oñati International Institute for the Sociology of Law (Spain), and a PhD in Law and Society from the University of Milan (Italy). Following her PhD, she was a Research Fellow at Birmingham Law School, University of Birmingham.

1

Situating the Right to Enjoy Legal Capacity

ROSIE HARDING, MARY DONNELLY AND EZGİ TAŞCIOĞLU

I. INTRODUCTION

THROUGHOUT HISTORY, AND in jurisdictions the world over, disabled people[1] have been routinely denied their rights to make decisions about, and have control over, their own lives. This denial has been especially enduring for people with cognitive and psychosocial disabilities. The traditional Enlightenment-derived normative framework for legal decisions operated on the basis of a simplistic binary distinction based on 'capacity', with decisions for persons found to lack capacity being made by others, generally without reference to the person. Most jurisdictions gave legal effect to this normative framework through substituted decision-making regimes, often implemented through wardship, guardianship or trusteeship laws. The UN Convention on the Rights of Persons with Disabilities (CRPD), adopted in December 2006[2] and in force since May 2008, has provided an international human rights-derived impetus for a shift in how States Parties respond to disability rights, and has sparked innovation in both normative approaches and the legal frameworks that give effect to these.

Of particular importance, and referred to by almost every contribution to this collection, is Article 12 CRPD, which affirms disabled people's rights to equal recognition before the law, including both as full legal persons, and in the enjoyment of legal capacity 'on an equal basis with others in all aspects of life.' The text of Article 12 was contentious during debates leading up to the adoption of the Convention and has remained so ever since.[3] The first General

[1] Although we recognise that there are debates over whether to use disability-first or person-first language, we generally use the formulation of 'disabled people' in this collection, to signal our engagement with and support of the social model of disability, ie that people with impairments are disabled by the barriers constructed by society.

[2] A/RES/61/106/Annex 1.

[3] A Dhanda, 'Legal Capacity in the Disability Rights Convention: Stranglehold of the Past or Lodestar of the Future?' (2006–2007) 34 *Syracuse Journal of International Law & Commerce* 429–62; A Dhanda, 'Conversations between the proponents of the new paradigm of legal capacity' (2017) 13

Comment on the CRPD was issued by the Committee on the Rights of Persons with Disabilities (CommitteeRPD) in 2014 to provide a comprehensive interpretation of the scope of that right.[4] Yet more than a decade after the CRPD came into force, guardianship laws of one form or another continue to be used in almost all jurisdictions, including those that have fully ratified the Convention. More positively, in many legal systems, ratification of the CRPD has led to law reform processes that seek to give greater priority to the will and preferences of disabled people, to recognise a presumption of capacity, and to provide legal mandates for support with decision-making in a range of contexts. Yet the shift to legal frameworks for supporting disabled people to enjoy their legal capacity remains at best only partial. It is not clear that any jurisdiction, as yet, offers a regulatory system which can be considered, both in how it appears in law, and how it is realised in practice, to be fully compliant with the vision of the right to enjoy legal capacity in the CRPD as interpreted by the CommitteeRPD.[5]

There are many reasons for this, including legislative and policy mandates to protect vulnerable people, the challenge of balancing paternalism and empowerment, and the different understandings of supported and substitute decision-making across jurisdictions. Economic factors, and cultural and attitudinal approaches to, and understandings of, disability have also played a role. Designing and implementing a CRPD- and CommitteeRPD-compliant regulatory framework that enables the enjoyment of legal capacity by all on an equal basis are also fraught with conceptual and practical difficulties. These include conceptual tensions around differing understandings of autonomy; tensions between mental capacity and legal capacity; contrasting visions of legal and ethical values surrounding decision-making, support and influence; the place of ideas of equality, justice, fairness and trust; practical challenges of creating non-discriminatory, but effective, safeguards against abuse; and the sometimes tenuous place of international conventions and law reform in social change.

The contributions to this edited volume tackle all of these thorny conceptual and practical problems and more. In this introductory chapter, we seek to provide an overview of the context of the academic debates to which the

International Journal of Law in Context 87–95; E Flynn and A Arstein-Kerslake, 'The Support Model of Legal Capacity: Fact, Fiction, or Fantasy?' (2014) 32 *Berkeley Journal of International Law* 124–43; E Flynn and A Arstein-Kerslake, 'Legislating personhood: realising the right to support in exercising legal capacity' (2014) 10 *International Journal of Law in Context* 81–104; A Arstein-Kerslake and E Flynn, 'The General Comment on Article 12 of the Convention on the Rights of Persons with Disabilities: a roadmap for equality before the law' (2016) 20 *The International Journal of Human Rights* 471–490; A Arstein-Kerslake and E Flynn, 'The right to legal agency: domination, disability and the protections of Article 12 of the Convention on the Rights of Persons with Disabilities' (2017) 13 *International Journal of Law in Context* 22–38.

[4] Committee on the Rights of Persons with Disabilities, *General Comment No 1 on Article 12: Equal recognition before the law* (April 2014), UN Doc CRPD/C/GC/1.

[5] A good deal is expected from recent reforms in Colombia (Ley 1996 of 2019) and Peru (Legislative Decree No 1384 amending the Civil Code): see A Martinez-Pujalte, 'Legal Capacity and Supported Decision-Making: Lessons from Some Recent Law Reforms' (2019) 8 *Laws* 4, doi:10.3390/laws8010004.

substantive chapters contribute, drawing out the points of tension and convergence in our contributors' ideas. We begin with a discussion of the importance of the right to enjoy legal capacity as a cornerstone of the CRPD, explaining why so much academic attention has been directed at Article 12, perhaps at the expense of substantive discussion of the rest of the Convention. This, in turn, helps to explain why tensions in the way autonomy is understood by different scholars have captured intellectual energy so fully, such that this debate has struggled to move forward. In exploring the tensions in these debates, we offer alternative conceptual framings that we hope will help to provide routes out of this quagmire. In seeking to advance debates, we hope that this collection will help to shift academic discourse on legal capacity towards equality, justice and fairness, whilst also being attentive to the importance of trust, protection and safeguards against abuse. We hope, too, to showcase the contribution of socio-legal methodologies in developing an evidence-base for the enhanced delivery of the right to legal capacity.

II. LEGAL CAPACITY AS A CORNERSTONE OF THE CRPD

Despite the wealth of academic commentary on the right to equal treatment for disabled people, it is vital to remember there is much more to the CRPD than Article 12. Article 12 has, however, been the focus of a great deal of socio-legal academic attention because it acts in many respects as a gatekeeper to so many of the other rights set out in the CRPD. The right to equal recognition before the law seems, at first glance, a merely academic exercise; the idea of legal capacity and the enjoyment of it may appear abstract and removed from everyday life. Yet the historical and continuing exclusion of disabled people rests firmly on a denial of these important foundational rights. For example, the right to liberty and security of the person (Article 14), and the right to live independently and be included in the community (Article 19) are meaningless if your decisions about where and with whom to live are overruled in your 'best interests', or you are deprived of your liberty in a locked care facility for your protection. The right to freedom of expression (Article 21) only has meaning if your will and preferences are respected. The right to the highest attainable standard of health (Article 25) can only be realised if your right to equal treatment before the law is also protected, to ensure that your choices about, consents to and refusals of medical treatment have the same force as those of everyone else. At the same time, delivery on the Article 12 right to equal recognition requires that States Parties engage substantively with the positive rights in the CRPD so as to ensure that Article 12 is made meaningful within a comprehensive human rights framework for disabled people.[6]

[6] See Doyle Guilloud, Chapter 6.

Rather than this collection, therefore, being one more contribution to the ever-expanding literature on the interpretation/implementation of Article 12 CRPD, we want to show that by looking at the idea of equal enjoyment of legal capacity across a range of theoretical, jurisdictional and practical contexts, we can find ways through the legal, conceptual and implementation challenges. To do so, there are three conceptual threads that sit across the contributions to this collection. First, we need to be attentive to, but not become bogged down in, the challenges posed by the abstract concept of 'autonomy'. Second, we need to focus law reform and implementation debates away from 'decision-making' and the related concept of 'mental capacity' onto legal capacity (the formal ability to hold and exercise rights and duties). Finally, we need to use the full panoply of socio-legal methodologies to interrogate the barriers to and catalysts for social and legal change for disabled people. We introduce each of these in turn.

A. Challenging Traditional Conceptions of Autonomy

Autonomy is a contested concept. The ideal of the lone, self-governing individual is one of the most persistent stereotypes of the neo-liberal, late capitalist state. The idea that people can and do make choices about their lives in a rational, self-interested, and deliberate way belies the everyday experiences of many, if not most, people. Traditional academic debates on autonomy valorise the legal fiction of the autonomous decision-maker; the person who listens to and digests all of the relevant information before making a reasoned, logical, careful decision.[7] Increasingly, however, autonomy scholarship highlights the relational contexts that shape, guide and limit the decisions that people can make. Relational approaches to autonomy challenge the idea of the self-ruling individual and foreground the significance of relationships, social norms and legal rules in the formation of autonomy.[8] On this understanding, respect for autonomy imposes positive obligations to provide support and create structures which enhance and develop each person's decision-making skills and capacities. The requirement in Article 12(3) that States Parties 'take appropriate steps to provide access by persons with disabilities to the support they may require in exercising their legal capacity' is grounded in this vision of autonomy.

Whilst this collection engages with debates about autonomy, and, we hope, takes them another step forward, the contributions here also make the case for engaging with other theoretical approaches, like vulnerability theory,[9] or the capabilities approach.[10] Vulnerability theory reconceptualises the traditional

[7] See Kong, Chapter 4 for a discussion of some of this literature.

[8] R Harding, *Duties to Care: Dementia, relationality and law* (Cambridge, Cambridge University Press, 2017); see also Donnelly, Chapter 2 and Keeling, Chapter 3 for discussion of this literature.

[9] See Mattsson, Chapter 13.

[10] See Stavert, Chapter 10.

liberal subject to incorporate vulnerability as a fundamental aspect of the human condition, albeit one that is experienced differently by different people at different times.[11] Vulnerability theorists offer various ways to understand and address vulnerability, including identifying the need for structures to enhance resilience and empowerment as well as to protect against exploitation and abuse.[12] The capabilities approach also focuses on structures, in this instance on what is needed for human functioning. Originally conceived as an alternative normative approach to indicators of human development across states,[13] as it has developed, the capabilities approach has come to provide a basis for more wide-ranging understandings of the goal of social justice.[14] In this way, the capabilities approach offers new ways to evaluate states' responsiveness to citizens' needs, including the specific needs of disabled people.[15]

Whether through a more expansive conceptualisation of autonomy or through engagement with alternative theoretical perspectives, the chapters here aim to shift the academic gaze away from individual difficulties with decision-making that disabled people may or may not have, onto the responsibilities of the state to provide the resources, both financial and interpersonal, required to support, and where necessary protect, disabled people.

B. Re-focusing the Debates on Legal Capacity, Rather than Decision-making

Much of the academic debate about legal capacity has cohered around the possibility and limitations of replacing substituted decisions with supported decisions.[16] Here, we seek to broaden that literature, and contribute to the

[11] M Fineman, 'The Vulnerable Subject: Anchoring Equality in the Human Condition' (2008) 20 *Yale Journal of Law and Feminism* 1–23.

[12] R Goodin, Protecting the Vulnerable: A Re-Analysis of our Social Responsibilities (Chicago IL, University of Chicago Press, 1985); MA Fineman (ed), *Transcending the Boundaries of Law, Generations of Feminism and Legal Theory* (Abingdon, Routledge, 2011); C Mackenzie, W Rogers and S Dodds (eds), *Vulnerability: New Essays in Ethics and Feminist Philosophy* (Oxford, Oxford University Press, 2013).

[13] A Sen, 'Informational Bases of Alternative Welfare Approaches: Aggregation and Income Distribution' (1974) 3(4) *Journal of Public Economics* 387–403.

[14] M Nussbaum, 'Capabilities as Fundamental Entitlements: Sen and Social Justice' (2003) 9(2–3) *Feminist Economics* 33–59.

[15] M Nussbaum, *Frontiers of Justice: Disability, Nationality, Species Membership* (Cambridge MA, Belknap Press, 2007).

[16] G Richardson, 'Mental Disabilities and the Law: From Substituted to supported decision-making?' (2012) 65 *Current Legal Problems* 333–54; P Gooding, 'Supported Decision-Making: A Rights-Based Disability Concept and its Implications for Mental Health Law' (2013) 20 *Psychiatry, Psychology and Law* 431–51; K James and L Watts, *Understanding the Lived Experiences of Supported Decision-Making in Canada: Legal Capacity, Decision-Making and Guardianship* (Canadian Centre for Elder Law/Law Commission of Ontario, March 2014); K Del Villar, 'Should Supported Decision-Making Replace Substituted Decision-Making? The Convention on the Rights of Persons with Disabilities and Coercive Treatment under Queensland's Mental Health Act 2000' (2015) 4 *Laws* 173–200; G Davidson and others, 'Supported decision making: a review of the

somewhat smaller (so far) debate that focuses on giving depth to the concept of legal capacity, and how to create systems of law that facilitate appropriate support systems for disabled people to enjoy their legal capacity.[17] In doing so, we discuss a wide range of legal and practical approaches to operationalising support for legal capacity, including formal and informal support schemes from 16 different jurisdictions.[18] These include informal family/carer support, formal and informal forms of advocacy, limited guardianship models, nominated supporters, co-decision-makers, network decision-making, microboards, powers of attorney, and advance decisions. Many of these supports operate alongside contemporary approaches to guardianship and/or enable substitute decisions to be made as a last resort. In prioritising legal capacity, the contributors to this collection primarily focus on the ways that the jurisdiction(s) they explore have legislated for these kinds of frameworks, and the benefits and limitations

international literature' (2015) 38 *International Journal of Law and Psychiatry* 61–67; T Carney, 'Supporting People with Cognitive Disabilities with Decision-making: Any Australian Law Reform Contributions?' (2015) 2 *Research and Practice in Intellectual and Developmental Disabilities* 6–16; G Davidson and others, 'An international comparison of legal frameworks for supported and substitute decision-making in mental health services' (2016) 44 *International Journal of Law and Psychiatry* 30–40; T Stainton, 'Supported decision-making in Canada: principles, policy, and practice' (2016) 3 *Research and Practice in Intellectual and Developmental Disabilities* 1–11; R Harding, 'Care and relationality: supported decision making under the UN CRPD' in R Harding, R Fletcher and C Beasley (eds), *ReValuing Care in Theory Law and Policy: Cycles and Connections* (London, Routledge, 2017) pp 114–30; R Harding and E Taşcıoğlu, '"That's a bit of a minefield": Supported decision-making in intellectually disabled people's intimate lives' in C Ashford and A Maine (eds), *Research Handbook on Gender, Sexuality and Law* (Cheltenham, Edward Elgar, 2019); R Harding, E Taşcıoğlu and M Furgalska, *Supported Will-Making: A Socio-Legal Study of Experiences, Values and Potential in Supporting Testamentary Capacity* (University of Birmingham, 2019).

[17] Dhanda, 'Legal Capacity in the Disability Rights Convention' (n 3); G Quinn, 'Personhood & Legal Capacity: Perspectives on the Paradigm Shift of Article 12 CRPD' (HPOD Conference, Harvard Law School, 20 February 2010); O Lewis, 'Advancing legal capacity jurisprudence' (2011) 6 *European Human Rights Law Review* 700–714; K Booth Glen, 'Changing Paradigms: Mental Capacity, Legal Capacity, Guardianship, and Beyond' (2012) 44 *Columbia Human Rights Law Review* 93–169; R Harding, 'Legal constructions of dementia: Discourses of autonomy at the margins of capacity' (2012) 34 *Journal of Social Welfare and Family Law* 425–42; E Flynn, 'Mental (in)capacity or legal capacity: A human rights analysis of the proposed fusion of mental health and mental capacity law in Northern Ireland' (2013) 64 *Northern Ireland Legal Quarterly* 485–505; Flynn and Arstein-Kerslake, 'The Support Model of Legal Capacity' (n 3); Flynn and Arstein-Kerslake, 'Legislating personhood' (n 3); B McSherry and K Wilson, 'The concept of capacity in Australian mental health law reform: Going in the wrong direction?' (2015) 40 *International Journal of Law and Psychiatry* 60–69; A Mäki-Petäjä-Leinonen and K Juva, 'Of Sound Mind? Dementia and Aspects of Assessing Legal Capacity' (2015) 22 *European Journal of Health Law* 13–37; A Arstein-Kerslake, 'An empowering dependency: exploring support for the exercise of legal capacity' (2016) 18 *Scandinavian Journal of Disability Research* 77–92; Dhanda, 'Conversations between the proponents of the new paradigm of legal capacity' (n 3); C De Bhailis and E Flynn, 'Recognising legal capacity: commentary and analysis of Article 12 CRPD' (2017) 13 *International Journal of Law in Context* 6–21; R Harding and E Taşcıoğlu, *Everyday Decisions Project Report: Supporting Legal Capacity through Care, Support and Empowerment* (University of Birmingham, 2017); R Harding and E Taşcıoğlu, 'Supported Decision-Making from Theory to Practice: Implementing the Right to Enjoy Legal Capacity' (2018) 8 *Societies* 25.

[18] These include: Argentina, Australia, British Columbia (Canada), Colombia, Denmark, England & Wales, Finland, India, Ireland, Norway, Ontario (Canada), Peru, Scotland, Spain, Sweden and Turkey.

that flow from these laws, rather than debating whether or not supporting legal capacity is desirable. This reflects a common commitment among many contributors to exploring and expanding what is possible rather than fixating on questions which, for the moment, remain largely theoretical.

In exploring support for legal capacity across the broad range of jurisdictions discussed here, both in the letter of the law and in the ways that law is operationalised in practice, the patterns of implementation of the right to enjoy legal capacity are brought into view. Placing these multiple and sometimes contrasting jurisdictional approaches together in one text enables socio-legal scholars to see how and where patterns of regulation are emerging on a global scale. It also facilitates ongoing multi-level iterative exchanges between states, NGOs and domestic activists and between the CommitteeRPD and States Parties, contributing to a more dynamic 'experimentalist' approach to CRPD implementation.[19]

From the contributions to this volume, it is clear to see that the early focus of the CommitteeRPD on Article 12, legal capacity and support has begun to make a difference in many jurisdictions and may well be beginning to catalyse some of the regulatory innovation that will be necessary to create the new paradigm of disability rights.

C. Capacity, Law Reform and Social Change

Ongoing research into the implementation and effectiveness of the CRPD is embedded in the text of the Convention. Article 31(1) requires States Parties to collect appropriate information, including statistical and research data, to enable them to formulate and implement policies to give effect to the Convention. In thinking through the implications, benefits and limitations of the ways that the right to enjoy legal capacity has been legislated for across the jurisdictions surveyed in this book, the contributions also provide insights, as a collection, into the patterns of disability law reform in the light of the CRPD. We see jurisdictions where engagement with CRPD requirements has been largely formulaic.[20] We also see jurisdictions that have made significant legal changes since ratifying the Convention, but that have yet to produce significant impacts on disabled people's lives.[21] In other jurisdictions, where support for legal capacity was already embedded firmly into legal frameworks, we see the potential limitations of the CommitteeRPD focus on capacity and choice, in creating conditions for (self)neglect.[22] In seeking routes out of these difficult

[19] G de Búrca, *Reframing Human Rights in a Turbulent Era* (Oxford, Oxford University Press, 2021) 39.

[20] See Taşcıoğlu, Chapter 11.

[21] See, eg, Donnelly, Chapter 2; Flynn, Chapter 7; Pathare and Kapoor, Chapter 8; Mäki-Petäjä-Leinonen, Chapter 12.

[22] See Mattsson, Chapter 13.

dilemmas, some contributions to the collection look to alternative ways of regulating to support those who need more help, through universal approaches to safeguarding,[23] or the expansion of the applicability of common law remedies like undue influence.[24]

Overall, the arguments, contributions and discussions in this book show that the CRPD, the CommitteeRPD's General Comment and even capacity law reform in individual jurisdictions may not be enough to make a difference to disabled people's lives. Instead, law reform agendas need to speak directly to disabled people as well as to the wide range of people whose personal and/or professional lives include disabled people. They need to be backed up with, and responsive to, movements for social change. This is why socio-legal methodologies play a central role. It is only through grounded engagement with law in practice that we can establish what is working and what is not and that we can plot a course to a better future.

III. ABOUT THE BOOK

This book has been concluded in what we hope is the beginning of the end of the Covid-19 pandemic. At this time, we cannot ignore the impact of the pandemic on disabled people. Although we cannot yet (and may never) definitively determine the full impact of the pandemic on disabled people, we have enough data to know that disabled people have disproportionately borne the burden of the pandemic. This is evident in mortality statistics but extends to all aspects of disabled people's lives, including significant reduction in services and support, long periods of isolation and loneliness, and marked decline in the quality of life in institutional settings.[25] It is clear that notwithstanding extensive ratification of the CRPD, there is still a very long way to go to create a society in which the equal right to legal capacity of disabled people is respected. This reinforces the need to find ways to deliver on this right, giving added urgency to this book and to ongoing efforts by activists, law and policy-makers, and scholars across the world.

Finally, before we go on to introduce the contents of the book, we want to provide a quick note about the voices that this book highlights, prioritises and makes visible. Contributors to this collection are all socio-legal and medico-legal academics with an interest in disability law and social justice. These contributors are aware of, and attentive to, the disability rights mantra

[23] See Lindsey, Chapter 14.

[24] See Hall, Chapter 15.

[25] From the growing literature, see G Quinn, 'Covid-19 and Disability: A War of Two Paradigms' in M Kjaerum, M Davis and A Lyons (eds), *Covid-19 and Human Rights* (London, Routledge, 2021); T Shakespeare, F Ndagire and Q Seketi, 'Triple Jeopardy: Disabled People and the Covid-19 Pandemic' (2021) 397 *The Lancet* 1331.

of 'nothing about us, without us' and we are aware of the lack of explicitly disabled voices in the authorship of this text. Many of the contributors to this collection have personal experience of supporting disabled friends and family members, clients, or patients to navigate and break down the barriers that social and legal constructions of disability have created. Others have personal lived experience of mental ill-health, supporting family members and/or of working within mental health services and tribunals. Yet others have worked with and alongside disability charities, NGOs and people with lived experience, for positive social and legal change. In creating this book, our collective endeavour seeks to push forward debates on disability justice, to create space for thinking differently about capacity law, and to provide foundational concepts and analysis that will help others, both disabled and non-disabled, to further agendas for legal and social change.

A. Part I – Charting the Conceptual Contours of Capacity Law

The first part of this collection focuses on the normative debates that underpin theoretical and practical difficulties and possibilities of making Article 12 rights a reality in disabled people's lives. The CRPD forces us to confront the fact that disabled people, especially those with cognitive and psychosocial disabilities, do not enjoy the rights of citizenship that the rest of us take for granted. While restrictions posed by domestic legislation on disabled people's legal capacity are generally acknowledged, how we make the shift to supported decision-making is not yet clear. Lurking behind this is a set of questions about 'autonomy' and what it means as a philosophical, legal and practical concept. Contributions in this part deal with this question, exploring a wide range of normative implications which arise from supporting legal capacity, and deepening our conceptual language.

In Chapter two, Mary Donnelly opens up the debate with an exploration of formal support relationships, their framing, legal fictions and challenges, through the lens of relational autonomy. Reading Ireland's Assisted Decision-Making (Capacity) Act 2015 (ADMCA) alongside Australian and Ontario Law Commission reports, her discussion uncovers three elements that determine the legal framing of support: entering into a support relationship, temporal and structural contexts where the support unfolds, and the attribution of legal responsibility in the context of high-support situations. Donnelly's discussion demonstrates the importance of the recognition of fictions, especially in high-support situations, as well as the role of relationships in enhancing or diminishing legal capacity. The chapter demonstrates how supporting legal capacity necessitates a responsive state that acknowledges, and responds to, the complex and multifaceted nature of relationships beyond capacity-derived boundaries, to strike the right balance between access to support and need for safeguards against abuse and harm.

The potential of relational approaches to autonomy is also highlighted in Amanda Keeling's contribution in Chapter three. Paying close attention to the differing interpretations of Article 12 by academic commentators and the CommitteeRPD, Keeling examines the different conceptualisations of 'autonomy' underpinning these interpretations and the role that the state should play in responding to that autonomy. Keeling identifies a conceptual incoherence in the CommitteeRPD's General Comment No 1 and its adherence to 'will and preferences' – a conflicting retreat to individualism despite its rejection of such traditional conceptualisations of autonomy. Instead of this thin understanding of autonomy that assumes the need for minimal state intervention for the enhancement of autonomy, Keeling argues for a relational model of autonomy that foregrounds the substantive context of decision-making. Approaching legal capacity as a universal but not an absolute right, the chapter charts a careful path for normative evaluations of 'good' and 'bad' influence in relationships and calls for a more active engagement with duties of states to encourage the former, while preventing the latter, through the development of holistic policies to support legal capacity.

Camillia Kong, in Chapter four, maintains the focus on Article 12's evocative phrase that respect should be accorded to the 'rights, will and preferences' of individuals, and in particular, its interpretation by the CommitteeRPD in General Comment No 1. Kong argues that the normative weight given by the CommitteeRPD to 'will and preferences' rests on an extension of negative liberty to disabled people and presents an incoherent conception of human agency based on Sartrean radical freedom. This vision of radical freedom presupposes that agency can be stripped of its deeper evaluative conditions which qualitatively assess the worth of different options, their motivational sources and surrounding self-narratives. Examining cases of conflicting choices, as well as of egosyntonic self-harming disorders, Kong argues that this vision of human agency is unsustainable for the aim of supporting legal capacity. For her, the significance of supporting legal capacity revolves around evaluating and fulfilling positive obligations to intervene in certain narratives. It is only through normative evaluations of substantive and motivational conditions of agency that conflicting intentions and the impact of self-narratives and behaviours premised on oppressive or neglectful relationalities can be critically assessed and navigated.

In Chapter five, Shaun O'Keeffe shifts our focus from the theoretical implications of Article 12 to the practical level of supporting legal capacity in the context of capacity assessments. Although some recent capacity laws, such as Ireland's ADMCA, endorse supported decision-making and eschew the diagnostic threshold in capacity assessments, a functional test remains central to the process. O'Keeffe's contribution explores the challenges of functional capacity assessments by healthcare professionals. Problems include statutory criteria for mental capacity that do not reflect how people make decisions in real life, difficulties in operationalising poorly defined and arbitrary criteria for decision-making capacity, the potential misuse of non-statutory concepts like 'lack of insight' and 'executive brain dysfunction', and the poor reliability of clinical capacity assessments, contributed to by factors like the arbitrariness of thresholds for capacity and the biases and values of assessors. O'Keeffe suggests some strategies for addressing these serious problems and improving capacity assessments in practice by giving non-cognitive factors adequate weight, challenging the use of non-statutory criteria, standardisation of capacity assessment, and ensuring that procedural safeguards are in place to promote fairness. Importantly, the chapter stresses the critical importance that access to independent advocacy has for those faced with the prospect of a capacity assessment to support them in preparing for the assessment.

In the final chapter of this part, Suzanne Doyle Guilloud considers the normative implications of the CRPD for mental health laws that provide for disability-specific involuntary detention. In Chapter six Doyle Guilloud outlines a CRPD-based approach to the elimination of systems of coercive mental healthcare, addressing the tensions and resistance which have arisen at the state level on the right to liberty, taking Ireland as a case study. Using Deleuze and Guattari's 'rhizome' metaphor, the chapter eloquently demonstrates the dynamic and interconnected nature of the rights to liberty, to universal legal capacity, and other relevant provisions of the CRPD, such as the right to live independently and be included in the community, and the provision of healthcare on the basis of free and informed consent. Doyle Guilloud argues that emphasis on the progressive realisation of these rights may make the rights to universal legal capacity and liberty, as interpreted by the CommitteeRPD, appear more realistic and realisable to policy-makers and legislators.

B. Part II – Reforming Capacity Law: Making, Shaping and Interpreting Legal Frameworks

Part II of this collection looks to the ways that Article 12 and associated ideas have been legislated for in a range of different jurisdictions. Contributors to this part take us on an international journey, reflecting on how recent and contemporary law reform processes in Europe, Asia, the Middle East and South America seek to take account of the right to enjoy legal capacity on an equal basis with others, and evaluate their success thus far. This part of the book begins with a chapter by Eilionóir Flynn, who provides a fascinating reflexive account of her involvement with the ADMCA in Ireland. As academic research funders seek to highlight and encourage attentiveness to the non-academic impacts and effects of scholarship, experiences like those Flynn describes will become ever-more prevalent in academic careers. Yet treading the tightrope between academic contribution and social activism, or between facilitating the voices of others and imposing your own academic conceptual and theoretical viewpoints, always poses challenges. Enabling complex arguments to be heard and acted on by politicians, civil servants and other civil society actors takes a great deal of skill and, as Flynn's tale shows, always has multi-faceted and unpredictable effects. The overall impact of the Irish reforms is yet to be felt, or evaluated, as they should come into full operation around the time this book is published. Flynn's experience, no doubt reflected in the experiences of other disability law scholars, serves, however, both as inspiration and as a handbook on how to engage multiple audiences with important legal and social issues.

In Chapter eight, we look at the implementation challenges of the support-focused Mental Healthcare Act 2017 (MHCA) in India. Soumitra Pathare and Arjun Kapoor show how regulatory reform is dependent on both resource allocation and political will, whilst also demonstrating how positive legislative reform cannot alone solve the problems that stem from diametrically opposed positions on support for the enjoyment of legal capacity. They also demonstrate how a range of legislative interventions, from advance decisions through to nominated representatives can work together to provide a full suite of support frameworks for enabling people to have say in, and control over, the decisions that are made in their lives, irrespective of their impairments. As with the recent reforms in Ireland, the law reform trajectory in India has not completely abandoned the potential for and possibility of substitute decision-making when an individual is unable to choose for themselves, a position which these authors support. This means, of course, that the MHCA 2017 falls short of fully implementing the CommitteeRPD's interpretation of Article 12, but Pathare and Kapoor show how this legislation has paved the way for other, deeper, legal changes that prioritise the will and preferences of the individual, acts as a stepping-stone towards more substantial legal change, and enables the progressive realisation of rights.

Chapter nine takes our focus to Spain, a civil law jurisdiction, where the new legislative framework for disabled people provides significantly more support for the enjoyment of legal capacity than the previous law. Patricia Cuenca Gómez argues that the previous Spanish capacity law was operationalised in an essentially status-based way: people with a diagnosis of a capacity impairment routinely had their capacity to act removed from them. This new law builds on the experience of reform in legally similar jurisdictions (including Peru and Colombia) where universal legal capacity has been recognised and legislated for. Cuenca Gómez argues, however, that the new Spanish framework ultimately falls short of full compliance with the CommitteeRPD's vision of Article 12 as, like in Ireland and India, there continues to be recourse to substitute decision-making as a last resort. Indeed, despite legal scholars, disability activists and law reform committees exploring alternative ways to regulate legal capacity, this fall-back position of guardianship/trusteeship as a decision-making status of last resort remains common. In part, this is because, as Cuenca Gómez argues, even when fully recognising disabled people as both holders and users of legal capacity, there remains a need, recognised by the CommitteeRPD and in the text of Article 12, for safeguards to protect against abuse and harm.

Balancing the need for safeguards with the text and intent of Article 12 is also discussed by Jill Stavert in her contribution (Chapter ten), which reflects on the ongoing process of updating mental health and mental capacity law in Scotland. Ultimately, Stavert argues for a shift in conceptual focus towards the capabilities approach,[26] as a way of moving this debate away from the well-trodden ground of supported or substituted decision-making and towards ensuring that the law enables people to do and be the things they want. In making this shift, Stavert's contribution also reminds us of the important justice implications of treating disabled people differently from non-disabled people, and that finding ways to ensure equal enjoyment of legal capacity must be at the heart of law reform projects in this area.

Finally, in Part II, Ezgi Taşcıoğlu explores the ways that disability law in Turkey has evolved since their ratification of the CRPD. Here, we are reminded that there is often a sizable gap between the law as it is written, and as it is experienced in practice. In the Turkish context, this has translated, argues Taşcıoğlu, into a form of 'regulatory ritualism' where the state claims compliance with its international obligations on paper through the reporting processes, but in reality provides only a performance of disability rights and Convention compliance. Full guardianship of disabled adults remains the norm, as do restrictions on the enjoyment of legal capacity by those with sensory disabilities, and the routine removal of rights of democratic participation from disabled citizens.

These five contributions help us to bring the conceptual debates in Part I of the book into practical view. If we cannot move beyond academic debates about individual vs relational autonomy, or substitute vs supported decision-making, the limitations of pre-CRPD disability and capacity law are remade in law reform processes, even as these seek to engage and comply with the Convention. Leaving aside the technical features of these multiple jurisdictional contexts, we see, through the contributions in this part, the consequences of our failure to envision alternative approaches, where disability rights are supported both in theory and in practice.

C. Part III – Supporting Legal Capacity in Everyday Life: Balancing Empowerment and Safeguards

The final Part of the book further refines our interrogation of support for the enjoyment of legal capacity, through its focus on the realities of support in

[26] A Sen, *Commodities and Capabilities* (Oxford, Oxford University Press, 1985); MC Nussbaum, 'The Capabilities of People with Cognitive Disabilities' in EF Kittay and L Carlson (eds), *Cognitive Disability and its Challenge to Moral Philosophy* (Oxford, Wiley-Blackwell, 2010); MC Nussbaum, *Creating Capabilities: The Human Development Approach* (Cambridge MA, Harvard Univesity Press, 2013); S Venkatapuram, 'Mental disability, human rights and the capabilities approach: Searching for the foundations' (2014) 26 *International Review of Psychiatry* 408–14; A Agnello, 'Disability and Justice: The Capabilities Approach in Practice by C Riddle (Lanham MD, Lexington Books, 2014) – Book Review' (2015) 54 *Dialogue: Canadian Philosophical Review* 567–69; R Brunner, 'Disability and justice: the capabilities approach in practice by C Riddle' (2015) 30 *Disability & Society* 310–12.

everyday life. Here too the chapters cover a wide range of jurisdictions, each of which is at a different stage in the transition to delivering supported decision-making. Contributors here use a range of socio-legal methodologies to address the role of supported decision-making in the everyday. Several of the chapters are grounded in empirical research, reflecting the rich body of work which has been emerging in this space since the introduction of the CRPD.

The empirically grounded chapters in this part probe different elements of supported decision-making across several different jurisdictions. In Chapter twelve, Anna Mäki-Petäjä-Leinonen draws on her study of guardianship in Finland to identify dissonances between law and practice. The chapter relies on interviews with public guardians and guardians' secretaries operating in Southern Finland and so the focus is on guardians who have a professional rather than a personal relationship with the person under guardianship. Under Finnish law, the appointment of a guardian does not in itself result in a denial of legal capacity, although provision is made for a formal restriction on the exercise of legal capacity where the person's important interests are found by the court to be endangered. Although formal restrictions are rare in Finland, Mäki-Petäjä-Leinonen shows that in practice guardians have significant powers, especially in respect of financial matters, even where a formal restriction has not been made. Her study uncovers significant differences in practice among guardians in the use of these powers, with some prioritising the client's right of autonomy and others adopting a more protective, even paternalistic, approach. Given that some degree of variation in approach is inevitable, Mäki-Petäjä-Leinonen identifies the need for clear guidance for guardians which prioritises the client's autonomy in line with Finland's commitments under the CRPD.

Chapter fourteen also uses empirical research to interrogate the role of professional supporters, in this case social workers. Jaime Lindsey identifies the untapped potential of social worker support in the operation of the legal framework for adult safeguarding in England and Wales and argues that empowering social workers can help reduce resort to the coercive powers of law. Lindsey identifies the different claims to legitimacy of law and of social work and provides an empirically grounded analysis of the circumstances which lead social workers to seek legal legitimation, usually through an application to the Court of Protection under the Mental Capacity Act 2005. The effect is to diminish the more person-centred and supportive approach which characterises social work. In order to counter this retreat to the law, Lindsey argues that, in a safeguarding context, social workers need to be legislatively empowered to intervene through support. However, she recognises that any such empowerment must be sensitive to the underpinning principle of legitimacy and so she argues that any legislative intervention in this area must be based on five foundational principles, specifically: support; accountability; applicability to all; partnership working; and proportionate harm.

In Chapter sixteen, Rosie Harding goes to the heart of the supported decision-making endeavour, presenting the voices of the people who are most directly affected by supported decision-making. This chapter is informed by interviews with 25 care and support professionals, 19 intellectually disabled people, and six supporters chosen by the disabled participants to help them with participation. Harding's focus reflects the significance of the everyday in the delivery of the equal right to legal capacity. She shows that the complex, stratified approach to support currently operational in England and Wales fails to meet the needs of the people it should serve, for reasons which are conceptual, practical and legal. Harding advocates the legislative introduction of a formal nominated supporter scheme as a way of embedding support and providing an effective alternative to the best interests and substitute decision-making models that permeate current English law.

A recurring insight throughout the chapters in this Part is the difficult balance which needs to be negotiated and re-negotiated between support and safeguarding. The perspectives offered by Titti Mattsson and Margaret Isabel Hall are especially helpful in this regard because they both come from jurisdictions (Sweden and British Columbia respectively) in which supported decision-making regimes are highly advanced. In Chapter thirteen, Titti Mattsson explores the interplay between autonomy, capacity and vulnerability in decision-making in relation to social services for people with dementia in Sweden. This takes place against the backdrop of a general move to home-based care for the elderly which has been happening across all the Nordic states. As Mattsson notes, the Swedish limited guardian model (or *god man*) has long been held out as an exemplar for supported decision-making. However, drawing on a body of empirical work, including some of her own,[27] she shows that operation of this model can make it difficult to deliver a decent standard of living for people with dementia and can result in neglect and sometimes danger. In part, this is due to the quality of the services provided by some limited guardians. However, it also reflects a legal framework that requires that the client's explicit consent must be given for the provision of all services. This creates tension between the individual's right to care and attention when needed and the same person's right to integrity, participation and self-determination in their everyday life. Mattsson draws on vulnerability theory to propose as a solution an institutional framework which addresses the vulnerabilities which are common to all at different stages in our lives.

Margaret Isabel Hall also seeks ways to resolve the tensions between conflicting rights to care/protection and autonomy/self-determination. For Hall, the solution lies in Article 12 of the CRPD, which she argues must be read as an integrated whole, encompassing both support and safeguards, and which she places within the broader context of the Anglo-Canadian common law tradition. Drawing on examples from both the common law and the law of equity,

[27] T Mattsson and L Giertz, 'Vulnerability, Law, and Dementia: An Interdisciplinary Discussion of Legislation and Practice' (2020) 21 *Theoretical Inquiries in Law* 139–59.

she argues that safeguards to prevent the abuse of legal capacity are an intrinsic part of the general law and that these derive from the law's concern for fairness and not from protective or paternalist underpinnings. On this basis, she advocates new legal responses grounded in fairness which apply to all legal subjects and not just to disabled people, so that all people can exercise legal capacity 'in a way that is consistent with fairness, justice and equity'.

IV. CONCLUDING REMARKS

In summary, then, this collection offers those interested in legal capacity and disability social justice an insight into how the rights contained in the CRPD are being implemented across a wide range of jurisdictions. These diverse chapters provide socio-legal analysis of the theoretical, doctrinal and practical challenges of implementing the 'paradigm shift' in disability rights sought by the CRPD and the CommitteeRPD. Taken together, this collection offers a wide-ranging evaluation of contemporary ideas in realising disability social justice through law reform. It provides readers with micro- and macro-level analyses of how capacity law reform can help to improve the lives of disabled people, especially those with cognitive and psychosocial disabilities. In doing so, we hope it offers routes forward, away from normative debates about whether or not disabled people should be granted their right to enjoy legal capacity, and towards the development and evaluation of concrete proposals that strike an effective balance between empowerment and protection.

Part I

Charting the Conceptual Contours of Capacity Law

2

Support Relationships in Law: Framing, Fictions and the Responsive State

MARY DONNELLY[1]

I. INTRODUCTION

THE CONCEPT OF supported decision-making is simultaneously intuitively obvious and profoundly radical. It is obvious because, as feminist moral philosophers have long observed, dependency and the concurrent need for support is an inherently human characteristic.[2] When translated to law, it is radical because it challenges a foundational premise of the common law – specifically, individualised decision-making and individualised responsibility.[3] Supported decision-making occupies a liminal space which challenges this legal understanding in fundamental ways.

One of the great strengths of the United Nations Convention on the Rights of Persons with Disabilities[4] (CRPD) is its conceptualisation of support as a legal right requiring action on the part of States Parties.[5] In General Comment No 1 (GC No 1),[6] the Committee on the Rights of Persons with Disabilities (the Committee) (arguably[7]) goes further, interpreting article 12 to require that all

[1] With many thanks to my co-editors for their hugely helpful comments on earlier iterations of this chapter and for being a joy to work with.

[2] See eg, A Baier, *Postures of the Mind: Essays on Mind and Morals* (Minneapolis MN, University of Minnesota Press, 1985); E Kittay, *Love's Labour: Essays on Women, Equality, and Dependency* (Abingdon: Routledge, 1999); see also A MacIntyre, *Dependent Rational Animals: Why Human Beings Need the Virtues* (Peru IL, Carus Publishing, 1999).

[3] See M Brennan, 'The Lodestar of Personal Responsibility' (2004) 88(2) *Marquette Law Review* 365.

[4] A/RES/61/106/Annex 1.

[5] CRPD art 12(3).

[6] Committee on the Rights of Persons with Disabilities, *General Comment No 1. Article 12: Equal Recognition Before the Law* (19 May 2014), UN Doc CRPD/C/GC/1.

[7] The matter had been (deliberately) left unresolved in the text of the CRPD itself: on the reasoning behind this political choice, see A Dhanda, 'Legal Capacity in the Disability Rights Convention: Stranglehold of the Past or Lodestar for the Future?' (2006–2007) 34 *Syracuse Journal of International Law & Commerce* 429, 448.

forms of substitute decision-making regimes should be abolished and replaced with supported decision-making frameworks.[8] Furthermore, because GC No 1 categorises article 12 rights as civil and political rights subject to immediate realisation, the Committee appears to reject a more gradual transition to support frameworks.[9]

The Committee's political wisdom in advancing this interpretation of article 12 remains to be seen. Theresia Degener (who chaired the Committee in the final stages of the development of GC No 1) describes it as 'perhaps naïve' for the Committee to address the issue of legal capacity in its first General Comment, arguing that

> [t]he stereotype of the unable, because disabled, citizen is so deeply entrenched in our legal tradition, that courts, legislatures, guardians and family members can claim [a restriction on human rights of disabled people] to be a form of protection – a form of caretaking.[10]

This tension means that, while on the one hand, the Committee provided disability rights advocates with a powerful, unequivocal expression of principle with which to challenge deeply ingrained paternalist norms, it also risked diminishing the normative force of this aspect of the CRPD among States Parties who could legitimately point to limited data on the operation of legal frameworks for supported decision-making.[11] This may at least partly explain why quite a number of States Parties have ratified the CRPD subject to interpretative declarations/reservations which retain the possibility of substitute decision-making in some circumstances.[12] The abolitionist perspective raises important normative questions explored in several chapters in this collection.[13] However, it would be unfortunate if this proved to be a distraction from the challenges which arise in giving effect to the support requirement and critical analysis of how these might best be addressed.

As recognised in GC No 1, support 'is a broad term that encompasses both informal and formal support arrangements'.[14] This chapter explores the legal framing of one element of support, specifically the formal appointment of a decision-making supporter/s and asks how this might evolve through expanded conceptual understandings. I argue that this form of supported decision-making, especially in high-support situations, will inevitably involve elements of legal

[8] GC No 1, para 28.

[9] GC No 1, para 30.

[10] T Degener, 'Editor's Foreword' (2017) 13(1) *International Journal of Law in Context* 1, 1.

[11] Prior to the post-CRPD round of reforms, several Canadian provinces/territories and Sweden had supported decision-making legislation in place (in each case operating alongside substitute decision-making mechanisms). However, there was limited empirical evidence regarding the operation of this legislation: see K James and L Watts, *Understanding the lived experiences of supported decision-making in Canada* (Toronto ON, Law Commission of Ontario, 2014), Mattsson, chapter 13, this volume; Hall, chapter 15, this volume.

[12] See reservations lodged by Australia; Canada; Egypt; Estonia; Georgia; Ireland; the Netherlands; Norway; Poland; Singapore; Syrian Arab Republic; Venezuela.

[13] See eg. Kong, chapter 4, this volume; Keeling, chapter 3, this volume.

[14] GC No. 1, para. 17.

fiction. For this reason, support structures cannot be evaluated without reference to counterbalancing safeguards. While the need for safeguards is recognised in the CRPD,[15] the operationalisation of safeguards has as yet received limited attention from the Committee.[16] In fact, I argue here that striking the appropriate balance between support and safeguards is far from straightforward and requires ongoing engagement by a responsive State.

This chapter uses the Assisted Decision-Making (Capacity) Act 2015 (Ireland) (the ADMCA) as an entry point for its analysis of the framing and the fictions of support relationships. After a long gestation, the ADMCA will finally come fully into force in mid-2022.[17] The ADMCA is overtly informed by the CRPD, although, to the disappointment of disability advocates,[18] it retains both capacity-based distinctions[19] and provision for substitute decision-making.[20] Nonetheless, the ADMCA may still fairly be described as progressive legislation in many respects. It avoids the obviously discriminatory use of a diagnostic threshold before the functional test for capacity can be applied[21] and it includes requirements to take 'all practicable steps' to support a 'relevant person'[22] before they are determined to lack capacity.[23] It also includes measure to ensure that substitute decision-making is a step of last resort[24] and it elevates the rights, will and preferences of the relevant person who has been found to lack capacity to make a particular decision.[25] Most significantly for this chapter, it allows for the appointment of two forms of decision-making supporters: decision-making assistants and co-decision-makers.[26] Although (surprisingly) the ADMCA

[15] See in particular art 12(4) and art 16.

[16] The issue of safeguards is one of the least developed aspects of GC No 1: see paras 20–22.

[17] The only elements in force at the time of writing are the provisions allowing for the establishment of the Decision Support Service, which is the operational and oversight body for the ADMCA, provisions relating to the development of codes of practice, and s 7(1) which repeals the Marriage of Lunatics Act 1811.

[18] See Flynn, chapter 7, this volume.

[19] ADMCA s 3(1).

[20] Under ADMCA s 38 the Circuit Court (a non-specialist court which has jurisdiction in respect of most aspects of the ADMCA) may appoint a substitute decision-maker, referred to in the ADMCA as a Decision-Making Representative.

[21] Contrast the Mental Capacity Act 2005 (England & Wales) s 2(1), which provides that a prerequisite for the operation of the functional test for capacity is that the person's inability to make a decision must be as a result of 'an impairment of, or a disturbance in the functioning of, the mind or brain'.

[22] This is the term used in the AMDCA to refer to (a) 'a person whose capacity is in question or may shortly be in question in respect of one or more than one matter'; (b) a person 'who lacks capacity in respect of one or more than one matter' or (c) a person who 'falls within paragraphs (a) and (b) at the same time but in respect of different matters': ADMCA s 2.

[23] ADMCA s 8(3).

[24] A substitute decision-making representative may only be appointed where the Circuit Court has made a declaration that the relevant person lacks capacity, even with the assistance of a suitable person as a co-decision-maker or if there is no suitable person to act as a co-decision-maker: ADMCA s 38(1).

[25] ADMCA s 8(7).

[26] The ADMCA also provides for advance appointment of substitute decision-makers through Enduring Powers of Attorney and Advance Healthcare Directives (although this aspect of the ADMCA is not drawn upon in this chapter).

does not explicitly draw this distinction, it is implicit in the framing of the Act that co-decision-making is intended to apply in more high-support contexts.[27]

The ADMCA is just one example of post-CRPD efforts to provide for supported decision-making, and the analysis here is supplemented with reference to two other law reform projects which recommended legislating for decision-making supporters.[28] These are the Australian Law Reform Commission Report on *Equality, Capacity and Disability in Commonwealth Laws* (ALRC Report)[29] and the Law Commission of Ontario Final Report on *Legal Capacity, Decision-making and Guardianship* (LCO Report).[30] Read together, these efforts provide valuable insights into both the potential for legal support relationships and some of the challenges to which these give rise. The chapter looks first at how support relationships are framed in law, including consideration of the role of fictions in the evolution of law in this sphere and then turns to the obligation of the State to extend support relationships beyond their current boundaries.

II. FRAMING SUPPORT RELATIONSHIPS IN LAW

The basic premise that a person can be supported in making decisions has rich theoretical antecedents as well as growing empirical underpinnings.[31] Its theoretical foundations lie in the recognition of dependency, connectedness and relationality, associated especially with feminist scholarship, which has challenged traditional individualist conceptions of autonomy.[32] Although this scholarship has led in various directions,[33] the conceptual framework

[27] See B Kelly, 'The Assisted Decision-Making (Capacity) Act 2015: What it is and Why it Matters?' (2017) 186(2) *Irish Journal of Medical Science* 351, 355.

[28] These are of course not the only relevant law reform projects: there have been important developments in a range of jurisdictions, including Colombia: see Ley 1996 of 2019; Peru: see Legislative Decree No 1384 amending the Civil Code, and A Martinez-Pujalte, 'Legal Capacity and Supported Decision-Making: Lessons from Some Recent Law Reforms' (2019) 8 *Laws* 4, doi:10.3390/laws8010004; and Spain, see Cuenca Gómez, chapter 9, this volume. However, the jurisdictions chosen here share a common law heritage which allows for easier comparison.

[29] Law Reform Commission of Australia, *Equality, Capacity and Disability in Commonwealth Laws* (ALRC No 124) (November 2014).

[30] *Legal Capacity, Decision-making and Guardianship* Final Report (Toronto ON, Law Commission of Ontario, March 2017): www.lco-cdo.org/wp-content/uploads/2017/03/CG-Final-Report-EN-online.pdf.

[31] From the expanding body of empirical work, see eg. R Harding and E Taşcıoğlu, *Everyday Decisions Project Report: Supporting Legal Capacity through Care, Support and Empowerment* (University of Birmingham, 2017); R Harding and E Taşcıoğlu, 'Supported Decision-Making from Theory to Practice: Implementing the Right to Enjoy Legal Capacity' (2018) 8(2) *Societies* 25; E Flynn et al, *Global Perspectives on Legal Capacity Reform: Our Voices, Our Stories* (Abingdon, Routledge, 2019).

[32] See eg Baier, *Postures of the Mind* (n 2); D Meyers, *Self, Society and Personal Choice* (Columbia University Press, 1989); M Friedmann, *Autonomy, Gender, Politics* (Oxford, Oxford University Press, 2003); A Baier, *Reflections on How we Live* (Oxford, Oxford University Press, 2010).

[33] See eg care-based models advanced in a disability context, most notably by Eva Feder Kittay: see E Feder Kittay, *Love's Labour: Essays on Women, Equality, and Dependency* (Routledge, 1999); 'The Ethics of Care, Dependence and Disability' (2011) 24(1) *Ratio Juris* 49; and *Learning from my Daughter: The Value and Care of Disabled Minds* (Oxford, Oxford University Press, 2019).

provided by relational autonomy is the most helpful in analysing the role of legally appointed supporters.[34] This is because autonomy has been a foundational value in disability rights advocacy,[35] where it provides a necessary counterweight to centuries of paternalist presumptions. Yet, traditional liberal autonomy lacks the sophistication to address the structural and other factors which limit or impede individual decision-making.[36] In contrast, at the heart of relational autonomy is the premise that any individual's autonomy is not a given but rather, as Jennifer Nedelsky describes, 'is made possible by constructive relationships'.[37] This insight provides a foundation from which to engage with support relationships.

As might be expected, given its feminist origins, relational autonomy does not presume that all relationships are constructive. The issues are not just the obvious ones – undue influence and abuse – which are identified in GC No 1.[38] Instead, many (probably most) relationships are complex and multifaceted. The same relationship can simultaneously be both supportive and controlling; loving and restrictive. And all relationships take place against a structural backdrop which includes the participants' economic resources and living conditions. Thus, a key strength of the 'relational project' as an analytic tool is that it is 'intrinsically evaluative and aimed at transformation'.[39] Using relational autonomy as a conceptual compass, this part of the chapter identifies three elements which determine the legal framing of support: first, the entry points for formal support arrangements; secondly, the temporal and functional understanding of legal support; and, finally, legal responsibility in the context of high-support options.

A. Entering a Support Relationship

Most of us rely on supportive relationships to live our lives and so the idea of formally entering into a support relationship may seem counter-intuitive, a legalistic formalisation of something natural and innate. Yet, in an increasingly legalistic world, formalising support relationships provides important clarity in transactions with third-parties, including health professionals, social care

[34] For background, see eg C Mackenzie and N Stoljar (eds), *Relational Autonomy: Feminist Perspectives on Autonomy, Agency and the Relational Self* (OUP, 2000); J Nedelsky, *Law's Relations: A Relational Theory of Self, Autonomy and Law* (Oxford, Oxford University Press, 2011); R Harding, *Duties to Care: Dementia, Relationality and Law* (Cambridge, Cambridge University Press, 2017).

[35] Respect for individual autonomy 'including the freedom to make one's own choices' is one of the general principles of the CRPD and an equal right to autonomy underlies all the substantive articles: see A Arstein-Kerslake, *Restoring Voice to People with Cognitive Disabilities: Realizing the Equal Right to Equal Recognition before the Law* (Cambridge, Cambridge University Press, 2017).

[36] See M Donnelly, *Healthcare Decision-making and the Law: Autonomy, Capacity and the Limits of Liberalism* (Cambridge, Cambridge University Press, 2010), pp 22–41.

[37] Nedelsky, *Law's Relations* (n 34) p 118.

[38] GC No 1, para 22.

[39] Nedelsky, *Law's Relations* (n 34) p 32.

providers, lawyers and financial advisers.[40] From the perspective of the supported person, this clarity opens up possibilities for increased action and engagement in formal legal settings which would otherwise be denied.

It is largely uncontentious that both the choice to enter a support relationship and the designated supporter/s must be freely chosen by the supported person. As recognised in GC No 1, any alternative cannot accurately be described as supported decision-making.[41] It is also uncontentious that a person should not be restricted in the number of supporters they can have. Much more contentious is the requirement in the post-CRPD reforms explored in this chapter that a person must meet a functional standard for capacity in order to appoint a supporter.[42] This requirement clearly departs from GC No 1, which identifies all capacity-based distinctions as discriminatory and contrary to article 12.[43] However, even leaving aside the broader question of whether capacity-based distinctions should be abandoned, there is still an arguable case that entry into a formal support relationship should not necessarily be linked to capacity. This argument derives from the nature of a support relationship. This is not a typical third-party transactional relationship. Instead, it involves the formalisation of a pre-existing relationship/s which is (or should be) based on trust. Trust is a complex concept which has been rather neglected in moral philosophy.[44] Karen Jones describes trust as

> an attitude of optimism that the goodwill and competence of another will extend to cover the domain of our interaction with her, together with the expectation that the one trusted will be directly and favourably moved by the thought that we are counting on her.[45]

Trust, in this sense, is primarily affective rather than cognitive/rational. As Jones explains, trust is 'functionally equivalent to blinkered vision: it shields from view a whole range of interpretations about the motives of another and restricts the inferences we will make about the likely actions of another.'[46] At the same time, Eva Feder Kittay identifies a link between trust and dependency. Trust and trustworthiness can be created and reinforced by the giving of care in situations of dependency.[47] Trust, therefore, is clearly ontologically distinct from autonomy, and autonomy may even, as Onora O'Neill has argued, at times be antithetical to trust.[48] This raises the question of why we should use the standard required to make autonomous decisions (in the traditional sense) in order to create a formal relationship based on trust.

[40] See AHRC Report, pp 96–97.
[41] GC No 1, para 29.
[42] See eg ADMCA, ss 10(1) and 17(1).
[43] GC No 1, para 15.
[44] See A Baier, 'Trust and Antitrust' (1986) 96(2) *Ethics* 231, 232.
[45] K Jones, 'Trust as an Affective Attitude' (1996) 107(1) *Ethics* 4, 4.
[46] Ibid, 12.
[47] Kittay 'The Ethics of Care' (n 33), p 57.
[48] O O'Neill, *Autonomy and Trust in Bioethics* (Cambridge, Cambridge University Press, 2002).

Trust can, of course, be misplaced. Indeed, as Annette Baier identifies, the very act of 'entrusting' involves an element of vulnerability; it leaves the person who trusts open to being let down.[49] This is not just something that arises where the person who trusts has impaired capacity but is inherent in the nature of all trust relationships. Certainly, a person's vulnerability may be increased because their capacity is impaired but this is far from the only relevant factor and it is by no means clear that a determination of capacity is the best way of distinguishing between those who should be permitted to place their trust and those who should not.[50]

The role of trust in support relationships is reflected in the gradated treatment of capacity in the Representation Agreement Act 2000 (British Columbia) (RAA) which was influential in the policy discussions which preceded the CRPD. This Act distinguishes between two kind of 'representation agreements': an agreement with standard provisions and a non-standard agreement. For standard representation agreements,[51] the question of whether a person has capacity to enter the agreement depends on all relevant factors, including whether the person has a relationship with the representative that is characterised by trust.[52] For non-standard agreements,[53] the general functional test for capacity applies.[54]

The British Columbia model is not without difficulties. A particular concern is that while the legislation recognises and respects the supported person's trust 'instinct', it provides limited safeguarding counterbalance to address situations where trust is misplaced. Representation agreements are private arrangements, with limited formalities[55] and no external oversight at the time of creation. Ongoing oversight is provided by two mechanisms. First, any person may raise an objection to the agreement or any changes or revocations with the Public Guardian and Trustee (the relevant oversight body) on a variety of grounds, including incapacity or the use of fraud or undue pressure in respect of the agreement as well as neglect or abuse of the person.[56] Secondly, the representation agreement must appoint a monitor who must make 'reasonable efforts' to determine whether the representative is complying with their legal obligations[57] to act honestly and with reasonable care, skill and diligence and within the authority of the representative agreement.[58] The effectiveness of this

[49] Baier, 'Trust and Antitrust' (n 44), p 235.

[50] See B Clough, 'Disability and Vulnerability: Challenging the Capacity/Incapacity Binary' (2017) 16(3) *Social Policy & Society* 469.

[51] These are agreements which cover decisions about personal care, routine management of financial affairs, most healthcare, and obtaining legal services: RAA s 7.

[52] RAA s 8(2).

[53] The matters covered in non-standard agreements are set out in RAA s 9(1).

[54] RAA s 10: the test here is capacity to understand the nature and consequences of the proposed agreement.

[55] The representation agreement must be in writing and witnessed: RAA s 13.

[56] RAA s 30(1).

[57] RAA s 20(1).

[58] RAA s 16(1).

as oversight is entirely dependent on the effectiveness (and trustworthiness) of the chosen monitor. Research on the legislation in practice does not indicate that the limited oversight has caused difficulties, with the researchers noting that most representatives were 'highly engaged in the lives of the people they were supporting.'[59] However, the perception of inadequate oversight may explain why there has been a very limited uptake on representation agreements outside of the intellectual and developmental disability community.[60]

B. The Scope of Support

Support is multi-faceted and complex and by no means neatly translatable into a legal norm. In thinking about translation, a useful starting point is Michael Bach and Lana Kerzner's taxonomy of support, prepared for the Law Commission of Ontario.[61] Bach and Kerzner identify six elements of support: independent advocacy (helping a person to express his or her will and preferences); communicational and interpretative supports (helping the person express their views); representational supports (representing the person's will and preferences on the basis of a long-standing relationship); administrative supports (addressing formal and procedural requirements); life-planning supports (making decisions in the context of broader values); and, relationship-building supports (helping the supported person to build relationships).[62] I have argued elsewhere that in cases of dementia, support should also include some form of memorial 'holding', balancing the person's past and present preferences and helping them to reach decisions which respect and represent both their past and present selves.[63]

While each element in Bach and Kerzner's taxonomy is important, they speak to different understandings of autonomy. The first four elements are focused on specific decisions and reflect a view (which is also reflected in GC No 1[64]) that the role of support is to facilitate the delivery/operationalisation of a decision which the supported person has already made. In this way, they cohere closely with a traditional, individualistic view of autonomy. The final two elements presume a longer timeline and draw on a more hermeneutic or dialogical approach to

[59] James and Watts (n 11), 50.

[60] James and Watts (n 11), 49–50.

[61] M Bach and L Kerzner, *A New Paradigm for Protecting Legal Autonomy and the Right to Legal Capacity: Advancing Substantive Equality for Persons with Disabilities through Law, Policy and Practice* (Toronto ON, Law Commission of Ontario, 2010). Available at https://www.lco-cdo.org/wp-content/uploads/2010/11/disabilities-commissioned-paper-bach-kerzner.pdf.

[62] Ibid, pp 74–82.

[63] M Donnelly, 'Deciding in Dementia: The Possibilities and Limits of Supported Decision-Making' (2019) 66 *International Journal of Law and Psychiatry*, 101466, p 3, drawing on B Jennings, 'Agency and Moral Relationships in Dementia' and H Lindemann, 'Holding One Another (Well, Wrongly, Clumsily) in a Time of Dementia' in E Feder Kittay and L Carlson (eds), *Cognitive Disability and its Challenge to Moral Philosophy* (Wiley-Blackwell, 2010).

[64] GC No 1, para 17.

decision-making.[65] A person's decisions are not simply waiting to be discovered but rather they are shaped through the support relationship. Thus, life-planning supports are 'a process of identifying values and purpose, making key decisions congruent with those interests, and making and executing the necessary agreements'.[66] While for most people most of the time 'life may not feel very planful', Bach and Kerzner also acknowledge that 'we operate from an assumption that it is a good thing to have some direction in our lives'.[67] Relationship-building is aimed at addressing the consequences of a 'life of discrimination and exclusion' which has left some people with capacity impairments without trusting relationships.[68] As Bach and Kerzner recognise, the development of this form of support 'takes time, intentional relationship building, and community based supports to facilitate the process, identifying individuals who can play this role and provide the person with a support network'.[69]

These final two elements reflect a recognition that the way we make decisions can be enhanced or diminished by context. In this way, they speak to the ideas of constructive relationships advanced by relational theorists and recognise that, as Nedelsky describes, '[a]utonomy can thrive or wither in adults depending on the structures of relationship they are embedded in'.[70] This vision of support is also underpinned by a 'thicker' or more substantive conception of autonomy, which some feminist scholars have advanced.[71] It recognises that'[t]o be autonomous is to find one's own law and live in accordance with it' and that '[t]his is a lifelong process, the individual dimensions of which are embedded in a social context.'[72]

Turning to the legal framings of support explored in this chapter, we see different approaches to the elements of support. The ADMCA tracks the first four elements of Bach and Kerzner's taxonomy. Thus, the support to be provided by a decision-making assistant is: to assist the appointer in obtaining relevant information; to advise the appointer by explaining relevant information and considerations relating to the relevant decision; to ascertain the appointer's will and preferences; to assist the appointer to make and express the relevant decision; and to endeavour to ensure that the appointer's relevant decisions are implemented.[73] This approach to scope is largely replicated for co-decision-makers.[74]

[65] See J McCarthy, *Dennett and Ricoeur on the Narrative Self* (Amherst NY, Humanity Books, 2007).

[66] Bach and Kerzner (n 61) p 75.

[67] Ibid, p 75.

[68] Ibid, p 80.

[69] Ibid, p 80.

[70] Nedelsky, *Law's Relations* (n 34) p 39.

[71] See eg Meyers, *Self, Society* (n 32); M Oshana, *Personal Autonomy in Society* (Aldershot, Ashgate, 1988). It also coheres with a conceptualisation of 'autonomy as achievement' as advanced by Joseph Raz in *The Morality of Freedom* (Oxford, Oxford University Press, 1986): see M Donnelly, *Healthcare Decision-making and the Law* (n 36), pp 41–44.

[72] Nedelsky, *Law's Relations* (n 34) p 124.

[73] ADMCA s 14(1).

[74] ADMCA s 19(1).

Both the Australian and Ontario Law Commissions recognise the need to address the structural aspects implicit in the final two elements of Bach and Kerzner's taxonomy, although they address this in different ways. The Australian Law Reform Commission recommends that the duties of a decision-making supporter include supporting the person, if they wish to do so, to consult with existing appointees, family members, carers and other significant people in their lives in making decisions, and assisting the person to develop their own decision-making capacity.[75] The ALRC recognises both the complexity of the second of these duties and that the imposition of this kind of a duty on a supporter (especially an unpaid family member) raises difficult policy issues.[76] For this reason, it considers that the nature and content of this obligation should vary according to the nature of the appointment.[77] The Ontario Law Commission proposes a more State-based response, recommending that the Government of Ontario develop pilot projects that evaluate autonomy-enhancing approaches to decision-making among people with impaired decision-making capacity and their families.[78]

C. Legal Responsibility and High-Support Options

GC No 1 is clear that '[a] person's level of support needs, especially where these are high, should not be a barrier to obtaining support in decision-making'.[79] In order to deliver on this, States Parties have to address conceptual challenges in allocating legal responsibility in high-support contexts. As noted in the Introduction to this chapter, common law systems are premised on individualised legal (and indeed moral) responsibility.[80] Decisions made with lower levels of support do not challenge this premise; the fact that a decision was made with support does not displace the legitimacy of a legal framework premised on individual responsibility. However, as levels of support increase, the legitimacy of individualised responsibility comes under increased pressure. For this reason, legal framing of high-support options has involved the allocation of joint or shared responsibility between the supported person and the supporter/s. The idea of joint responsibility is of course not alien to the law. However, most of the conceptual work in this regard has been in a commercial context, through the development of corporations, unincorporated associations and partnerships. Joint responsibility for deeply personal decisions raises different issues and presents different challenges.

[75] ALRC Report (n 29), pp 104–5.
[76] ALRC Report (n 29), pp 106–07.
[77] ALRC Report (n 29), p 106.
[78] LCO Report (n 30), p 98.
[79] GC No 1, para 29.
[80] See J Gardner, *From Personal Life to Private Law* (Oxford, Oxford University Press, 2018), p 60.

The attribution of joint responsibility inevitably involves elements of legal fiction, with perhaps the most famous legal fiction of all being the attribution of separate corporate personality to the group of people who come together to make joint decisions in the form of a corporation.[81] Something similar happens when the legal system attributes joint responsibility for a decision made by a supported person and a supporter/s. As noted by the Law Commission of Ontario, 'it is difficult for the law to effectively reach into the essentially private realm of decision-making practice'.[82] This means that the legal system has no way of ascertaining how the parties actually made this decision, the quality of the communication, or the myriad factors (personal and structural) that may have impacted on the decision made.[83] Thus, the complexities of relationality are obscured. In this way, attribution of joint responsibility in a high-support situation can be seen as a legal fiction not because, in the classic sense, it is a 'statement propounded with a complete or partial consciousness of its falsity'[84] but because it is a statement which cannot be verified.[85]

Although the term is sometimes used pejoratively, fictions are necessary elements of a functioning legal system.[86] They can also help the law to develop in particular directions. Karin Knorr-Cetina notes that etymologically, the word fiction is derived from 'fingere' which means 'the act of fashioning and shaping which includes imitating and inventing'.[87] Thus, in a high-support context, joint decision-making is not just a practically useful way for the legal system to get around the need to attribute legal responsibility for decisions; it also has powerful expressive and educational force, serving as a reinforcement of the moral personhood of the supported person.[88] A joint decision made *with* a supported person rather than a decision made *for* a person with impaired capacity has considerable rhetorical and symbolic force. However, difficulties arise where, to borrow Lon Fuller's term, a fiction becomes 'dangerous'.[89] This happens where people stop recognising something as a fiction and start to believe it to be true.[90]

[81] See S Schane, 'The Corporation is a Person: The Language of a Legal Fiction' (1986–87) 61 *Tulane Law Review* 563.

[82] LCO Report (n 30), p 60.

[83] Joint decision-making is a complex (and under-researched) process even outside of high-support situations: see eg, P Osamor and C Grady, 'Autonomy and Couples' Joint Decision-Making in Healthcare' (2018) 19 *BMC Medical Ethics* 3: doi.org/10.1186/s12910-017-0241-6.

[84] L Fuller, *Legal Fictions* (Stanford CA, Stanford University Press, 1967), p 9.

[85] See the use of this broader definition of legal fiction in S Shah, 'Piercing the Veil: The Limits of Brain Death as a Legal Fiction' (2015) 48(2) *University of Michigan Journal of Law Reform* 301, 315.

[86] See Fuller, *Legal Fictions* (n 84), p 21; K Knorr-Cetina, 'Primitive Classification and Post-modernity: Towards a Sociological Notion of Fiction' (1994) 11(3) *Theory, Culture & Society* 1, 8–9; C Leonhard, 'Dangerous or Benign Legal Fictions, Cognitive Biases, and Consent in Contract Law' (2017) 91(2) *St John's Law Review* 385.

[87] Knorr-Cetina (n 86), 7.

[88] On the significance of this, see O Lewis, 'The Expressive, Educational and Proactive Roles of Human Rights: An Analysis of the United Nations Convention on the Rights of Persons with Disabilities' in B McSherry and P Weller (eds), *Rethinking Rights-Based Mental Health Laws* (Oxford, Hart Publishing, 2010).

[89] Fuller, *Legal Fictions* (n 84), pp 9–10.

[90] Ibid, p 10.

While the fictional elements remain to the forefront, the need for safeguards is obvious. Where the fiction is obscured or ignored, as Louise Harmon described in her critique of the use of substituted judgment in the United States, '[s]omething hidden, something potentially dangerous or brutal, can go on beneath the surface'.[91]

Thus, the recognition of the role of fiction in high-support contexts is both liberating and constraining, requiring an intricate layering of access to support and protections. Bearing this in mind, it is instructive to turn to two examples of joint decision-making in post-CRPD reforms: co-decision-making in the ADMCA and network decision-making which is endorsed, in principle, by the Law Commission of Ontario. Because the first of these examples has been legislated for, it allows for a more fine-grained analysis of the policy choices made.

(i) Co-decision-making

The concept of co-decision-making emerged in Canada in the 2000s. In a period of innovative law reform, largely inspired by the Canadian Association for Community Living, two Canadian provinces, Alberta and Saskatchewan, introduced measures for co-decision-making.[92] In both jurisdictions, co-decision-makers are appointed by the court.[93] Under the Alberta legislation, the application for appointment is brought by the person themselves or by someone on their behalf[94] while in Saskatchewan, the application may be brought by any person with sufficient interest in the personal welfare of the person, the public guardian or other designated bodies.[95]

The ADMCA model is inspired by these Canadian examples but is distinct in several ways. Under the ADMCA, a co-decision-maker is appointed by the relevant person. The appointer must be formally certified as having capacity to make a co-decision-making agreement by both a medical professional and another healthcare professional.[96] Capacity must be freshly certified after the first year[97] and thereafter every three years.[98] If this certification is no longer possible, the co-decision-making agreement comes to an end.[99] In addition, any person may make a complaint to the Decision Support Service (the oversight

[91] L Harmon, 'Falling off the Vine: Legal Fictions and the Doctrine of Substituted Judgment' (1990) 100 *Yale Law Journal* 1, 70.

[92] See Adult Guardianship and Trustee Act 2008 (Alberta); Adult Guardianship and Co-Decision-Making Act 2001 (Saskatchewan).

[93] Adult Guardianship and Trustee Act 2008 (Alberta) s 14(1); Adult Guardianship and Co-Decision-Making Act 2001 (Saskatchewan) s 14(1).

[94] Adult Guardianship and Trustee Act 2008 (Alberta) s 13(1).

[95] Adult Guardianship and Co-Decision-Making Act 2001 (Saskatchewan) s 6 (personal decisions), s 30 (property decisions).

[96] ADMCA s 21(4)(f).

[97] ADMCA s 26(3).

[98] ADMCA s 26(1).

[99] ADMCA s 26(6): this decision is made by the Circuit Court following an application by the Decision Support Service.

body established under the ADMCA) on the basis that the appointer no longer has the capacity to make one or more of the decisions covered by the co-decision-making agreement[100] and if this is found to be the case, the co-decision-making agreement is brought to an end by the court.[101]

In order to come into force, the co-decision-making agreement must be registered by the Decision Support Service,[102] which must make several substantive evaluations before completing the registration.[103] These include: that the co-decision-maker is a suitable person;[104] that the co-decision-making agreement is in accordance with the appointer's will and preferences; and that the appointer understands the implications of having entered into a co-decision-making agreement.[105] There is also provision for designated people[106] to object to the registration.[107]

Once the co-decision-making agreement has been registered, all decisions made are legally categorised as joint decisions of the appointer and the co-decision-maker[108] and cannot be challenged on the grounds that the appointer lacks capacity.[109] However, reflecting an awareness of the fictionality of joint decision-making, the ADMCA shifts the balance of authority towards the supported person. Thus, the ADCMA requires that, in reaching joint decisions, a co-decision-maker must 'acquiesce with' the wishes of the appointer and must not refuse to sign any relevant document unless it is reasonably foreseeable that the acquiescence/signature would result in 'serious harm' to the appointer or to another person.[110]

Co-decision-makers are subject to rigorous reporting and oversight requirements. They must submit an annual report to the Decision Support Service,[111] which report must also be approved by the supported person.[112] Any costs and expenses claimed by the co-decision-maker (which must be 'fair and reasonable') must be evidenced and included in the annual report.[113] Complaints about

[100] ADMCA s 30(1)(g).
[101] ADMCA s 30(5).
[102] ADMCA s 21(1).
[103] ADMCA s 22(1).
[104] Some categories of persons are statutorily designated to be ineligible to be a co-decision-maker: ADMCA, s 18(1).
[105] ADMCA s 22(1).
[106] These are the appointer's: spouse/civil partner/cohabitant; children aged over 18 years; decision-making assistant; decision-making representative; attorney; designated healthcare representative; other co-decision-maker for different decisions: ADMCA, s 21(3).
[107] ADMCA s 24(1).
[108] ADMCA s 17(1).
[109] ADMCA s 23(1).
[110] ADMCA s 19(5). There are similar provisions in the Canadian legislation: see Adult Guardianship and Trustee Act 2008 (Alberta), s 18(5); Adult Guardianship and Co-Decision-Making Act 2001 (Saskatchewan), s 17(2).
[111] ADMCA s 27(1).
[112] ADMCA s 27(2). A co-decision-maker's failure to make a report can ultimately lead to the removal of the co-decision-maker (following an application to the court by the Decision Support Service): s 27(5).
[113] ADMCA s 19(2).

a co-decision-maker may be made to the Decision Support Service on a range of grounds, including that the co-decision-maker is acting outside of their authority, is not suitable, or is not acting in accordance with the appointer's will and preferences.[114] Where a complaint is made, the Decision Support Service must carry out an investigation and, if of the view that the complaint is well founded, must refer the determination of any relevant matter to the Circuit Court.[115] The Decision Support Service may also on its own initiative carry out an investigation and refer any matter to the Circuit Court.[116] On any such application, if the Circuit Court finds that the complaint is upheld, it may stop the co-decision-maker from acting as such.[117]

The uptake on the co-decision-making option under the ADMCA remains to be seen. However, on a purely textual analysis, it may be argued that there are better ways to carve out a space for co-decision-making. On the positive side, the protections afforded are robust and extensive. Presuming that the Decision Support Service performs its functions effectively, the potential for abuse may be averted at registration and following annual reviews and through the complaints mechanism. While there can be no absolute protection against abuse/harm, the ADMCA would seem to reduce significantly this possibility.

However, the model looks like falling short on access to support. Some of the difficulty lies in the role of capacity as both an entry and exit point for co-decision-making agreements. This means that the high-support option is not available to the people who most need high support. This also makes co-decision-making a less attractive option for people with a progressive condition such as dementia, who must also set up an enduring power of attorney to deal with the eventuality that they may reach a point when the co-decision-making agreement will no longer apply.[118] If the extensive oversight mechanisms established under the ADMCA are effective, it is not clear why co-decision-making should come to an end when a person loses capacity or indeed why entry into a co-decision-making agreement should require that the appointer meet the generally applicable functional standard for capacity.

A further potential barrier to access lies in the extensive formalities which form part of the protective element of the ADMCA. The role of co-decision-maker is daunting. It involves the assumption of joint legal responsibility as well as opening oneself up to suitability assessments, reporting requirements, and possible complaints. There are of course reasons why someone might choose to do this, perhaps because of their strong commitment to a loved one and a belief in the importance of maximising a loved one's decision-making authority.[119] However, this does require quite a sophisticated understanding of

[114] ADMCA s 30(1).
[115] ADMCA s 30(2)(a).
[116] ADMCA s 30(4).
[117] ADMCA s 30(5).
[118] See Donnelly, 'Deciding in Dementia' (n 63), p 6.
[119] A co-decision-maker may not be remunerated for performing their functions: ADMCA, s 19(3).

the legislation, which in turn is likely to depend on the way in which the Decision Support Service, as well as legal and other advisors, communicate both the potential and the risks of co-decision-making. Ultimately, the success or failure of the co-decision-making project in the ADMCA will turn on whether family member and friends of the relevant person are convinced to become engaged. Without co-decision-makers there can be no co-decision-making.

(ii) Network Decision-making

Network decision-making is identified by the Law Commission of Ontario as a high-support alternative to co-decision-making.[120] The LCO Report sketches network decision-making in outline rather than developing its analysis in depth and so the discussion here is similarly curtailed. Describing the model, the LCO states '[t]he bringing together of a group of people with diverse skills and perspectives to support one individual offers not only some checks against abuse, but also a unique form of decision-making'.[121]

Network decision-making derives from the microboard process, associated especially with the Canadian community living movements.[122] Although there are various models, as Sophie Nunnelly recounts, they all involve 'groups of people coming together on a voluntary basis, with varying levels of formality, to in some way support a single individual through relationships of trust and intimacy'.[123] The formal term 'microboard' is copyrighted by the Vela Microboard Association in British Columbia and may only be used by models which involve an incorporated not-for-profit organisation to support a single individual and which have designated features, including a minimum of five directors.[124] Microboards can hold and administer funds, including acting as an employer and making contracts (although this is not a requirement).[125] They are also expected to participate in person-directed planning.[126] Other support networks adopt different titles (eg, self-directed support corporation; Aroha entity; person-centred society) and adopt the requirements of the microboard model to varying degrees.[127]

The preferred model of the LCO involves a network comprising three or more members, one of whom is not a family member. The person for whom the network is formed is at the centre of the network and the goal of the network is to promote this person's participation in the decision-making process. Decisions

[120] LCO Report (n 30), p 70.
[121] LCO Report (n 30), p 106.
[122] LCO Report (n 30), p 107.
[123] S Nunnelly, *Personal Support Networks in Practice and Theory: Assessing the Implications for Supported Decision-Making Law* (Toronto ON, Law Commission of Ontario, 2015), p 17.
[124] Ibid.
[125] Ibid, p 23.
[126] Ibid, p 24.
[127] Ibid, p 17.

are made by the network and the decision-making entity itself is accountable rather than any single member.[128] While recognising difficulties with the incorporation model, which it describes as 'an uneasy pairing between corporate law and the ultimately private and personal nature of the decision-making at stake', the LCO nonetheless saw the possibility of utilising elements of this model in network decision-making.[129] This would involve a set of formal requirements for the network to commit to, including the purpose, principles and processes of the network; record-keeping requirements; the roles of individual members; and a formal registration process.[130] The LCO identified the potential of this model to 'provide a more flexible and accessible alternative to substitute decision-making where there are great risks associated either with the extent of the individual's decision-making impairment or the nature of the decisions to be made.'[131] On this basis, it recommended further research and consultation towards the development of a statutory legal framework for network decision-making.[132]

Without more detail, it is not possible to evaluate the benefits of network decision-making as a high-support option or to draw reasonable comparisons to co-decision-makers. From the LCO description, it seems that the main safeguarding mechanism is the role of the external member but that this will be supplemented by a registration. Whether this will prove more attractive to a wider range of people than the British Columbia model remains to be seen. Like co-decision-making, however, a key challenge of network decision-making is finding people willing to be members of the network, and here, the bigger the network, the bigger a challenge this is likely to be.

III. UNIVERSAL ACCESS TO SUPPORT

It is clear from the preceding discussion that the legal framing of support relationships involves the formalisation of pre-existing relationship/s. This recognises the essential role which informal support relationships play in 'everyday decision-making' for people with impaired capacity.[133] Yet as relational theorists remind us, not everyone has access to constructive underlying relationships. Indeed, as acknowledged by the Law Commission of Ontario, 'many of the groups profoundly affected by this area of the law, including persons with cognitive, neurological, mental health, or intellectual disabilities, the very old and persons living in long-term care, are disproportionately likely to be socially isolated'.[134] Whether because of social isolation or because pre-existing

[128] LCO Report (n 30), p 107.
[129] LCO Report (n 30), p 108.
[130] Ibid.
[131] Ibid.
[132] Ibid.
[133] See Harding and Taşcıoğlu, *Everyday Decisions Project* (n 31).
[134] LCO Report (n 30), p 39.

relationships are not constructive, there may be no one to call on to act as a decision-making supporter. In this situation, legal mechanisms, however well formulated, are out of reach. This is a structural problem inherent in all support models. Addressing this problem requires attention to be paid to the relationship between the person who needs support and the State. This is a space with which relational autonomy theorists are familiar. As Nedelsky describes, from a relational autonomy perspective, 'the central problem in the modern administrative state' is 'no longer the traditional liberal objective of protecting individual autonomy by keeping the state at bay but how to protect and enhance the autonomy of those who are *within* the (many) spheres of state power.'[135]

Work to date suggests various ways in which the law can be used to address the structural challenges posed by lack of access to supporters.[136] One is the imposition of duties on any party proposing an intervention/providing a service to support (or accommodate[137]) the person who has to make a decision about the intervention or service.[138] Such duties ensure that the party who (besides the decision-maker) has the closest connection to the decision is made responsible for delivering support in respect of the decision. Thus, a healthcare professional has a duty to support the person in making a healthcare decision; a financial professional, in making a financial decision. The efficacy of this lies in both the closeness of the contact and the specialist expertise of the person providing the support. Because this support option is reliant on service providers, the effectiveness of the support provided will depend on the service provider's attitude, approach and abilities. It is inevitable that this will vary. Compliance with the duty can be enhanced through sub-legislative measures, such as codes of practice/professional guidance which can provide further detail regarding the scope of duties. If these are to avoid the usual failings of 'soft' law, sub-legislative measures of this kind must be buttressed by appropriate enforcement mechanisms. This can be achieved by incorporating codes of practice into the legislative framework and making non-compliance a factor to be taken into account in regulatory actions or court proceedings.[139] This 'de-centred' approach places responsibility for delivery of support on a wide range of service providers, and responsibility for compliance on a wide range of regulatory bodies/courts.

Another way of addressing the structural deficit is the provision of personal advocacy support and/or the use of paid supporters.[140] Both of these interventions have the potential to expand the pool of people who can avail themselves of some form of support. However, as elaborated upon elsewhere in this

[135] Nedelsky, *Law's Relations* (n 34), p 118.

[136] There are of course many other ways outside of the law for a State to provide/facilitate the provision of support.

[137] LCO Report (n 30), p 94.

[138] See eg, Mental Capacity Act 2005 (England & Wales) s 1(3); ADMCA s 8(3) (although note that the obligation is limited to 'interveners' only).

[139] See eg. ADMCA, s 103(14).

[140] ALRC Report (n 29), p 100.

volume, both a statutory right to personal advocacy and the provision of paid support present their own challenges and neither provides an all-encompassing solution.[141]

Ultimately, if universal supported decision-making is to become a reality, deeper structural intervention is required. Insights from relational autonomy indicate that this must include engagement with and appreciation of supported peoples' living environments,[142] the multitude of ways in which individuals' voices are heard or not, and the presence or absence of meaningful choices which must include the framing of decisions within broader aspects of the person's life. In this context, the international law obligations under the CRPD are an essential tool in holding States Parties to account, with the advocacy opportunities presented by the reporting process and the Committee's Concluding Observations[143] providing a necessary impetus to ensure that State Parties remain responsive.

IV. CONCLUSION

Support relationships are key to the creation of an inclusive society for people with impaired capacity. Yet, as shown in this chapter, the legal framing of support relationships is not a straightforward process. It involves an array of policy choices and requires a careful balancing of access to support with the need for safeguards, with the level of safeguards increasing with the level of support required. This chapter has argued that useful guidance can be gained by looking at support relationships through a relational autonomy lens. This enables us to see both why safeguards are necessary (and what safeguards should involve) and also how support relationships could be expanded beyond current capacity-derived boundaries. Drawing on relational autonomy also shows why attention needs to be paid to a broader range of temporal and structural contexts and why a view of support as simply eliciting a person's decision is too narrow. It also serves as a reminder that constructive relationships are not a given but need to be created and nurtured.

Given the challenges of framing support relationships in law, it is no surprise that States Parties did not immediately jettison substitute decision-making and replace it with supported decision-making when recommended to do so by GC No 1. Yet this clearly cannot be the end of the matter. All three jurisdictions explored in this chapter issued reservations/declarations retaining the possibility of substitute decision-making but each one also committed to ensuring

[141] See Harding, chapter 16, this volume; Mattsson, chapter 13, this volume.

[142] See eg, analysis of nursing home policies in this respect: S Dodds, 'Choice and Control in Feminist Bioethics' in Mackenzie and Stoljar, *Relational Autonomy* (n 34), p 229.

[143] While not legally binding on States Parties, Concluding Observations nonetheless have 'notable authority' because they are 'outputs of the treaty bodies': M O'Flaherty, 'The Concluding Observations of United Nations Treaty Bodies' (2006) 6(1) *Human Rights Law Review* 27, 36.

that this would be used only as last resort. The challenge now is to ensure continued engagement with the potential of supported decision-making so as to allow States Parties to make good on this promise. Of the post-CRPD law reform projects drawn on in this chapter, only one (the ADMCA) has made it to legislation.[144] In spite of limitations with the ADMCA, its attempt to legislate for support relationships provides an important international exemplar. It may well be that changes to the ADMCA will be needed but the very action of producing a working attempt to deliver on formal support relationships deserves credit, while also requiring careful critical scrutiny.

Moving forward, as the CRPD honeymoon wanes, keeping supported decision-making on political agendas requires a combination of domestic activism and reinforcement by the international community, and in particular by the Committee.[145] In this respect, the Committee's recent turn towards a more granular analysis of States Parties' efforts under article 12 is greatly to be welcomed as providing a more concrete basis for domestic advocates and law- and policy-makers to work from.[146] The conceptual grounding provided by relational autonomy, together with shared analysis of different legal frameworks and focused empirical studies, can provide necessary scaffolding for this ongoing work.

[144] Although there has been legislative change at a State level in Australia: see eg, Medical Treatment Planning and Decisions Act 2016 (Victoria); Guardianship and Administration Act 2019 (Victoria); Guardian of Adults Act 2016 (NT).

[145] Gráinne de Búrca uses the term 'human rights experimentalism' to describe this ongoing iterative exchange: see *Reframing Human Rights in a Turbulent Era* (Oxford, Oxford University Press, 2021), pp 38–47.

[146] See eg, Committee on the Rights of Persons with Disabilities, *Concluding Observations on the Combined Second and Third Reports of Australia*, 15 October 2019, para 24 which recommended that Australia implement a 'nationally consistent supported decision-making framework, as recommended' by the ALRC Report (n 29); *Concluding observations on the initial report of Turkey*, 1 October 2019, CRPD/C/TUR/CO/1, see Taşcıoğlu, chapter 11, this volume.

3

The Problem of Influence: Autonomy, Legal Capacity and the Risk of Theoretical Incoherence

AMANDA KEELING[1]

I. INTRODUCTION

ARTICLE 12 OF THE UN Convention on the Rights of Persons with Disabilities has been the focus of much scholastic energy and for good reason. In challenging a long-held link between legal capacity and mental capacity, it up-ends a model of legal subjectivity which has dominated and defined liberal legal systems, and jettisons an understanding of autonomy as an individual concept, linked to capacities of rationality and reasoning. However, despite moving towards a 'support model' of legal capacity, which appears to both embrace and necessitate an understanding of human relationality, there remain in many interpretations vestiges of an individual approach to autonomy which creates a challenge for defining State obligations with regard to the provision of support for legal capacity.

Within the disability legal studies scholarship, there remains significant disagreement over the interpretation of article 12 – and in particular the extent to which 'substitute decision-making' should be prohibited. The Committee for the CRPD, in General Comment No 1, clearly states that substitute decision-making is prohibited, and that the focus for States should be in providing access to 'support' for legal capacity,[2] but the extent of this prohibition continues to be

[1] This chapter is the result of a thought-provoking workshop at Oñati, Spain, organised by the editors. My thanks to them, and to Rosie in particular, for encouraging me to turn my paper there into this final publication. Many thanks also to Bev Clough and Jaime Lindsey for their useful insights into the ideas. I also realise that this chapter is the result of almost a decade of thinking about this problem, and my thanks must go to Peter Bartlett who has always encouraged me to pursue the nagging feeling I had that something just didn't quite make sense. Hopefully this may provide some clarity.

[2] United Nations Committee on the Rights of Persons with Disabilities, *General Comment No 1, Article 12: Equal Recognition Before the Law*. UN Doc CRPD/C/GC/1 (19 May 2014).

challenged in the literature.[3] This chapter argues that, in seeking a way through this disagreement, we need to recognise what is actually going on under the surface: different understandings of what 'autonomy' is and means, and the attendant obligations this dictates for the State.

The question of autonomy within article 12 is something which has been looked at in the literature. In the early stages of academic analysis, there was exploration of the utility of relational autonomy to explain the basis of the support model of legal capacity which article 12 was outlining, and why decisions resulting from such a process could be considered legally valid.[4] However, in general, relational autonomy has been embraced for its ability to legitimise decisions made in close relationships of support. What has been less examined by the literature is the implication that relational autonomy does not necessarily equate to *universal* autonomy. In general, relational models of autonomy consider that some environments or relationships are not enabling or constitutive of autonomy. This sits uneasily alongside the interpretation of article 12, which calls for a prohibition of substitute decision-making and universal legal capacity led only by the individual's expressed will and preference. This results in a thin 'universal autonomy',[5] where any interventions by the State in the individual's choices are seen as an interference with their autonomy. But this struggles to take account of the interventions that may be oppressive of the individual's autonomy by *private* actors, and what the State can do in terms of protecting disabled people from such exploitation and abuse.[6]

Amita Dhanda states that 'there are two choices […] one recognises that all persons have legal capacity and the other contends that legal capacity is not a universal human attribute'.[7] This chapter argues that legal capacity is a universal right, but not an *absolute* one – that it may be limited where individuals are not autonomous, but that autonomy can be defined in a way which is neither linked

[3] J Dawson, 'A realistic approach to assessing mental health laws' compliance with the UNCRPD' (2015) 40 *International Journal of Law and Psychiatry* 70; M Donnelly, 'Best Interests in the Mental Capacity Act: Time to Say Goodbye?' (2016) 24 *Medical Law Review* 318; MC Freeman and others, 'Reversing hard won victories in the name of human rights: a critique of the General Comment on Article 12 of the UN Convention on the Rights of Persons with Disabilities' (2015) 2 *The Lancet Psychiatry* 844.

[4] P Gooding, 'Supported Decision-Making: A Rights-Based Disability Concept and Its Implications for Mental Health Law' (2013) 20 *Psychiatry, Psychology and Law* 431; L Series, 'Relationships, Autonomy and Legal Capacity: Mental Capacity and Support Paradigms' (2015) 40 *International Journal of Law and Psychiatry* 80.

[5] J Stavert, 'The Exercise of Legal Capacity, Supported Decision-Making and Scotland's Mental Health and Incapacity Legislation: Working with CRPD Challenges' (2015) 4 *Laws* 296.

[6] A Keeling, '"Organising objects": Adult safeguarding practice and article 16 of the United Nations Convention on the Rights of Persons with Disabilities' (2017) 53 *International Journal of Law and Psychiatry* 77; L Pritchard-Jones, 'Exploring the potential and the pitfalls of the United Nations Convention on the Rights of Persons with Disabilities and General Comment no. 1 for people with dementia' (2019) 66 *International Journal of Law and Psychiatry*.

[7] A Dhanda, 'Legal Capacity in the Disability Rights Convention: Stranglehold of the Past or Lodestar for the Future?' (2006–2007) 34 *Syracuse Journal of International Law and Commerce* 429, 457.

to mental capacity nor exclusionary of disabled people. A model of relational autonomy better reflects the situatedness and interconnectedness of all human agents, and the reality of influence in and on all our lives and decisions. Yet it also requires acceptance that not all influence is benign, and that in adhering to their obligations under the CRPD in article 12(4), there will be action required from States to ensure that autonomy is fostered and nourished, and 'good' relationships of support encouraged, and 'bad' ones discouraged.

This chapter first explores the linkages between legal capacity, mental capacity and autonomy, outlining why the concept of autonomy is relevant to the interpretation of article 12. It then outlines what has been rejected by the delinking of mental capacity from legal capacity to allow for a universal model of legal capacity, and the relational model that best explains the concept of autonomy which appears to underpin this new model of legal capacity. It analyses the retention of some vestige of individual autonomy in many interpretations of article 12, including the CRPD Committee's General Comment No 1 (GC1), and outlines why this is problematic. It concludes by arguing that only a relational concept of autonomy can properly explain the 'shared personhood' of the support model of legal capacity, and sufficiently accommodate the issue of influence in support.

II. AUTONOMY, LEGAL CAPACITY, MENTAL CAPACITY, AND ARTICLE 12

Article 12 was one of the most hotly contested provisions in the negotiations on the CRPD,[8] due to its challenging and 'revolutionary'[9] approach to the concept of legal capacity. The impetus for the 'revolution' was the experience of disabled people being consistently denied legal capacity and the recognition of their legal agency and legal personhood.

Article 12(1) states that disabled people have the right to equal recognition before the law, an uncontroversial statement. The element of article 12 that contains the 'revolution' is also the locus of the disagreement: the delinking of mental capacity and legal capacity. The justification for substitute decision-making frameworks has always been, in some shape or form, that the individual was incapable of making the decision themselves due to their mental impairment. Article 12(2) states that all persons with disabilities have legal capacity 'on an equal basis with others'. This has been interpreted by a number of prominent scholars[10]

[8] Ibid; L Series, 'Article 12 CRPD – Equal Recognition before the Law' in I Bantekas, M Ashley Stein and D Anastasiou (eds), *The UN Convention on the Rights of Persons with Disabilities* (Oxford, Oxford University Press, 2018).

[9] T Minkowitz, 'The United Nations Convention on the Rights of People with Disabilities and the right to be free from nonconsenssual psychiatric interventions' (2006–2007) 34 *Syracuse Journal of International Law and Commerce* 405.

[10] A Arstein-Kerslake and E Flynn, 'The General Comment on Article 12 of the Convention on the Rights of Persons with Disabilities: a roadmap for equality before the law' (2016) 20 *International*

and the Committee for the CRPD[11] as 'universal' legal capacity: a right held by everyone by virtue of being human, rather than being based on whether a threshold of required 'mental capacity' is required.

This provision led to questions around the extent to which substitute decision-making could be retained in domestic frameworks, resulting in the Committee issuing a General Comment unusually early in the life of the Convention. General Comment No 1 demands a blanket prohibition of substitute decision-making frameworks[12] – processes where there is often no need to pay heed to the expressed will and preferences of the individual, substituting instead the decision-maker's view of the individual's 'best interests'. Following the wording of article 12(3), the required replacement is a model of legal capacity based around 'support', which does not focus on individual mental ability to make decisions, but rather the support that the individual needs to make them. This support has been broadly conceived and can be intensive to the point that it is hard to understand it as a decision 'made by' the individual themselves.[13] There is recognition both by the Committee[14] and in the literature[15] that for many adults what will be happening is a 'best interpretation' of the individual's will and preferences. It is, in essence, a form of making a decision 'for' someone, which is led as much as possible by what we know they want, or would want, in the relevant situation.

It is this aspect of article 12 which has been the most controversial. There are those who consider that some level of substitute decision-making should be retained in the interests of protecting those who do not 'really' understand the decisions they are making, and are at risk of harm if this model is followed – particularly in the context of acute mental health crises.[16] Others hold valid concerns that such intensive levels of support require relationships that are so close – to the potential exclusion of the rest of the outside world – that they are open to abuse and exploitation, and question the positive benefits of such an approach.[17] Paul Skowron notes that at the very least we should be open

Journal of Human Rights 471; A Dhanda, 'Universal Legal Capacity as a Universal Human Right' in M Dudley, D Silove and F Gale (eds), *Mental Health and Human Rights: Vision, Praxis and Courage*, 1st edn (Oxford, Oxford University Press, 2012); E Flynn and A Arstein-Kerslake, 'The Support Model of Legal Capacity: Fact, Fiction, or Fantasy?' (2014) 32 *Berkeley Journey of International Law* 124.

[11] United Nations Committee on the Rights of Persons with Disabilities, *General Comment No 1, Article 12: Equal Recognition Before the Law* (n 2).

[12] Ibid, para 25.

[13] Ibid.

[14] Ibid.

[15] Arstein-Kerslake and Flynn, 'The General Comment on Article 12' (n 10); P Gooding, 'Navigating the "Flashing Amber Lights" of the Right to Legal Capacity in the United Nations Convention on the Rights of Persons with Disabilities: Responding to Major Concerns' (2015) 15 *Human Rights Law Review* 45.

[16] Dawson, 'A realistic approach' (n 3); Freeman and others, 'Reversing hard won victories in the name of human rights' (n 3).

[17] Donnelly, 'Best Interests in the Mental Capacity Act' (n 3); Pritchard-Jones, 'Exploring the potential and the pitfalls' (n 6).

about what we are doing and recognise that the process of interpretation creates changes in the 'interpreted person', and that 'best interpretation' of will and preferences is not the same as a 'true interpretation'.[18]

This chapter argues that at the root of the interpretive difficulty is an unspoken and unrecognised disagreement about who is autonomous for legal purposes, and how the State should behave in response to that autonomy. Although the word 'autonomy' does not feature in the text of article 12, it is referenced by the Committee in GC1 and in much analysis of legal capacity.[19] This is unsurprising in the way that mental capacity works in legal frameworks: it creates the legal boundaries around whose lives the State can, and cannot, intervene in. An individual without mental capacity is considered incapable of making a decision and so it is appropriate for the State to intervene and make it 'for them'. An individual 'with capacity' is considered capable of decision-making, and so the State should not intervene. Lucy Series notes that there is a close link between mental capacity and autonomy in law; when someone passes the threshold of mental capacity, they are considered autonomous at law and so are left alone.[20] It is important to note that mental capacity is not *the same* as autonomy, but rather operates in an analogous fashion as a gatekeeper. In creating a limit for State intervention in the lives of adults, it operates, de facto, as a legal 'test' for autonomy. In legal systems where autonomy is valued, it creates the 'condition' for legal capacity; by being seen as autonomous, one can be seen as having legal capacity.[21] This creates a conception of legal capacity as an individual who is 'autonomous' in the sense of meeting a particular criterion for cognitive ability. The fact that this is not, itself, 'autonomy' leads to some of the conceptual confusion.

In removing the requirement of mental capacity, the Committee and other commentators are able to create a conception of legal capacity which is universal – no longer does an individual have to pass a threshold of mental ability, and so legal capacity can be inclusive of all people, regardless of impairment. This necessitates a jettisoning the traditional model of autonomy which underpins legal capacity, but in the various interpretations of article 12 there are elements of conflicting models of autonomy. This helps explain the lack of clarity in State obligations about how support should be provided and how any abuse or exploitation should be handled. This chapter argues that while relational autonomy is the better model of autonomy, vestiges of individuality remain in the dominant 'will and preferences' paradigm, which create significant problems.

[18] P Skowron, 'Giving substance to "the best interpretation of will and preferences"' (2019) 62 *International Journal of Law and Psychiatry* 125.

[19] Gooding, 'Navigating the "Flashing Amber Lights"' (n 15); Keeling, '"Organising objects": Adult safeguarding practice' (n 6); C Kong, *Mental Capacity in Relationship; Decision-Making, Dialogue, and Autonomy* (Cambridge Bioethics and Law, Cambridge University Press, 2017); Series, 'Relationships, Autonomy and Legal Capacity' (n 4).

[20] Series, 'Relationships, Autonomy and Legal Capacity' (n 4).

[21] G Richardson, 'Mental disabilities and the Law: From Substitute to Supported Decision-making?' (2012) 65(1) *Current Legal Problems* 333.

III. RETHINKING AUTONOMY AND LEGAL CAPACITY

A. Beyond the Individual and Accepting Influence

In rejecting the link between legal and mental capacity, interpretations of article 12 are implicitly rejecting a model of autonomy which has been criticised by feminist philosophers for the past two decades. In disconnecting legal capacity from mental capacity, there is a rejection of a notion of autonomy as being about individual ability for reason and rationality. Procedural self-governance models of autonomy have been dominant in the ethical literature since the 1980s, and prioritise the way in which a decision is made, rather than the substantive context in which it is made, or the content of the decision itself.[22] This allows for a broad scope of freedom from intervention from the State, and the value-neutrality that liberalism prioritises in pursuit of tolerance.

This self-governance concept of autonomy is about preventing interference with the individual, and their own self-governance and self-determination. This may be interference from the State, but it also presents a challenge in how to take account of other external factors which influence the individual. For self-governance models,

> the notion of autonomy still finds its core meaning in the idea of being one's own person, directed by considerations, desires, conditions, and characteristics that are not simply imposed externally on one, but are part of what can somehow be considered one's authentic self.[23]

In this account, the 'threats' to autonomy come from things internal to the individual; that which may preclude their cognitive ability for reason and rationality, and their ability to engage in the reflection necessary to determine authenticity. These internal threats cannot be overcome by external support, for the individual is not capable of the reason required to determine the authenticity of their decision separate from the influence of the person providing the support. In removing the link between mental capacity and legal capacity, it is this notion of autonomy which article 12 is implicitly rejecting. However, this does not necessarily entail rejection of autonomy as a foundation for legal capacity.

Individual approaches to autonomy do not reflect the reality of human experience – and in particular our social connectedness. The idea that we are able to disentangle our true 'authentic' self from the external influences which surround us – and constitute us – and, as discrete atoms, be separated from the social whole, cannot be anything more than an unachievable thought experiment. A more complete, grounded understanding of autonomy can be found in relational conceptions. Relational approaches to autonomy are much less

[22] J Christman, 'Autonomy, self-knowledge, and liberal legitimacy' in John Christman and Joel Anderson (eds), *Autonomy and the Challenges to Liberalism* (Cambridge, Cambridge University Press, 2005).
[23] Ibid, 23.

interested in the procedure of the decision, or the internal state of the individual. Rather, they are substantive theories of autonomy, taking a stance on the type of environment which is able to constitute or cause autonomous selves, allowing an explanation of 'how structural (social and political) constraints can undermine or impair individual autonomy and to identify the enabling structural conditions for autonomy'.[24]

Rather than having to engage in the abstraction of human experience, trying to determine which of the influences on our decision-making is 'real', relational models simply accept that these influences 'are'. There is a danger, however, that such approaches can be open to accusations of paternalism, where they are strongly substantive. Relational autonomy requires a normative stance to be taken on what types of environments and social relations can be constitutive of autonomy, and models which only look to the socio-relational status of the individual mean that some environments are considered simply too oppressive to allow individuals enmeshed within them to be considered autonomous.[25] Therefore, while one can enter into such relationships autonomously, autonomy is forfeited once the relationship has been entered into, and the individual is effectively 'governed by others'. This position has been subject to criticism because, in seeking to create a less-individualised approach to autonomy, ironically it requires hyper-individualisation of the individual and their reflective processes, in order to extricate themselves from the socio-relational context in which they have found themselves.[26] It is also open to accusations of paternalism, 'rescuing' people from situations they appear to have entered into completely freely.[27]

A better approach incorporates a dimension of 'self-authorisation', which focuses on the ability to account for one's decisions to others when challenged.[28] The skills for doing this do not have to be innate or individual; they can be developed and fostered through empowering social environments and support networks. This approach restores agency to the individual, rather than leaving them trapped in a non-agentive position and provides a riposte to concerns of paternalism.[29]

Relational approaches to autonomy seem to provide a conception which fits more sensibly with the demands of article 12. Understanding autonomy as something which is fostered or enabled by the relationships around us – indeed, seeing them as *essential* rather than a threat – reflects the support model of legal capacity, with its emphasis on relationships of support. The 'traditional' self-governance model which has held sway for the past 40 years excludes many

[24] C Mackenzie, 'Three Dimensions of Autonomy; A Relational Analysis' in A Veltman and M Piper (eds), *Autonomy, Oppression, and Gender* (Oxford, Oxford University Press, 2014) 23.

[25] M Oshana, *Personal Autonomy in Society* (Aldershot, Ashgate Press, 2006).

[26] Donnelly, 'Best Interests in the Mental Capacity Act' (n 3).

[27] J Holroyd, 'Relational Autonomy and Paternalistic Interventions' (2009) 15 *Res Publica* 321.

[28] AC Westlund, 'Rethinking Relational Autonomy' (2009) 24 *Hypatia* 26; Mackenzie, 'Three Dimensions of Autonomy' (n 24).

[29] Westlund, 'Rethinking Relational Autonomy' (n 28).

people with mental impairments for failing to meet thresholds of rationality and reason, and due to the risk of 'influence' from third parties compromising the authenticity of their decisions. In contrast, relational autonomy both accepts the inevitability of influence and positively embraces it, allowing for an understanding of autonomy, and in turn legal capacity, which is less individualised and less focused on individual mental ability.

B. Universal Legal Capacity and 'Universal Autonomy'?

The key question here is whether a right to 'universal' legal capacity, where links to mental capacity are broken, equates to 'universal' autonomy. The central argument of this chapter is that the idea of 'universal autonomy' is a flawed concept and inconsistent with the other values that article 12 puts forward. A coherent interpretation of article 12 requires an overt commitment to relational autonomy, which is not a model whereby 'everyone' is universally autonomous. It is a substantive approach to autonomy, which requires normative evaluation of the environments and relationships in which individuals find themselves. This means that not *every* environment or *every* relationship will be enabling of autonomy. Equally, where an aspect of self-authorisation is added to restore a sense of agency, these relational autonomy models retain some threshold for mental capacity – some awareness of self is required for this process, even when it is a supported one, and it is not clear whether the theory would support a 'universal' autonomy in this sense.[30] In the context of article 12, however, this raises questions concerning the obligations on the State to assess and evaluate the relationships and networks of support as being enabling of autonomy – in a way that traditional, individual approaches to autonomy do not advocate or permit.

Universal autonomy essentially means that no one can be subject to any interference with their will and preferences – but this does not recognise that in the support model of legal capacity there is already 'interference' in the shape of influence from the supporter. This may be in the sense that we all experience influence when we seek advice and support, or it may be more malign influence, designed to manipulate or control. Currently, some interpretations of article 12 call for an idea of 'shared personhood' in the support model of legal capacity which reflects relational concepts, but nevertheless retain a conflicting commitment to individualism in 'universal' autonomy. This creates an incoherence in terms of State obligations, but further, in failing to engage more deeply with the issue of influence, potentially opens disabled people to a high risk of abuse and exploitation.

[30] See, for example, Mackenzie's discussion of this dimension in 'The Importance of Relational Autonomy and Capabilities for an Ethics of Vulnerability' in C Mackenzie, W Rodgers and Susan Dodds (eds), *Vulnerability: New Essays in Ethics and Feminist Philosophy* (Oxford, Oxford University Press, 2014) 46.

IV. (RE)CONSIDERING AUTONOMY IN GENERAL COMMENT NO 1

The interpretation of provisions of international human rights law is often an uncertain field, especially when a Convention is young, such as the CRPD. Authoritative interpretation comes from the UN Committee for the Convention, through jurisprudence and General Comments, but these are not 'binding' in the same way as domestic judgments, and academic and other commentary may come to different conclusions through examination of the *travaux preparatoires* and the interpretation of other, similar, provisions in other treaties. With regards to the interpretation of article 12, General Comment No 1 has been highly influential, and there has been a broad move towards consensus in the academic literature that the 'support model' of legal capacity is the direction of travel for reforms. However, there is still debate over the precise limits of the universality of legal capacity, and in particular the extent to which support for legal capacity is possible for every individual.

Those who critique the approach of universal legal capacity often do so from a retained commitment to an idea of mental capacity at least at some level, and implicitly an understanding of autonomy and decision-making that is still, at essence, both internalist and individual.[31] For these commentators, the retention of substitute decision-making frameworks is required in order to fulfil an obligation to protect individuals from harm resulting from decisions they have not fully understood. In contrast, the model of decision-making outlined in interpretations of article 12 is heavily reliant on support from third parties and a sense of 'shared personhood'.[32] The guiding principle, according to GC1 and a variety of commentators,[33] is that the individual's own 'will and preference' should be the primary (and in most cases only) relevant factor when supporting decision-making. It is the job of the supporter to help determine that will and preference, and where necessary to communicate this to the world. It is clear that the Committee envisions a model of decision-making where the support may be quite intensive, and certainly where it cannot be said to be an 'individual' decision – even if the 'fiction' that is maintained is that it is the disabled individual who is the sole decision-maker. It has been acknowledged by the Committee[34] and others[35]

[31] Dawson, 'A realistic approach' (n 3); Freeman and others, 'Reversing hard won victories in the name of human rights' (n 3).

[32] Series, 'Relationships, Autonomy and Legal Capacity' (n 4).

[33] Arstein-Kerslake and Flynn, 'The General Comment on Article 12' (n 10); Dhanda, 'Legal Capacity in the Disability Rights Convention' (n 7); Flynn and Arstein-Kerslake, 'Legislating personhood: realising the right to support in exercising legal capacity' (2014) 10(1) *International Journal of Law in Context* 81; Flynn and Arstein-Kerslake, 'The Support Model of Legal Capacity' (n 10); E Flynn and A Arstein-Kerslake, 'State intervention in the lives of people with disabilities: the case for a disability-neutral framework' (2017) 13 *International Journal of Law in Context* 39; Series, 'Article 12 CRPD' (n 8).

[34] United Nations Committee on the Rights of Persons with Disabilities, *General Comment No 1, Article 12: Equal Recognition Before the Law* (n 2).

[35] M Bach and L Kerzner, *A New Paradigm for Protecting Autonomy and the Right to Legal Capacity* (Prepared for the Ontario Law Commission, 2010); Gooding, 'Navigating the "Flashing Amber Lights"' (n 15).

that it may be a 'best interpretation' of will and preferences which is required in some cases. Piers Gooding[36] and Jill Stavert[37] have noted that what is actually happening in many cases is essentially still a decision being 'made for' the individual – the difference is that the decision is being based on what we know, or think we know, about the individual's will and preferences in that situation, rather than an objective assessment of their 'best interests'. In a similar vein, Skowron calls for an open acknowledgment that the process of support is not a process of 'discovery' of the individual's will and preferences, but rather a process of interpretation which cannot avoid changing the person being interpreted, particularly when we engage in a 'best interpretation'.[38]

In all cases of support, there will be influence – from the way that information is simplified, to the 'important facts' for basic forms of support, through to situations as above where the supporter is the only person who is able to 'translate' the will and preferences of the disabled person to the wider world. In all these cases, we may be concerned about the authenticity of the decisions: is it really what the individual themselves would have wanted? These concerns, however, only hold if we understand autonomy as an individual concept; one where autonomy is a process of attempting to divine our true, authentic self through rational reasoning. Understood like this, decisions reached through the kind of support model envisioned by article 12 feel non-autonomous. When we understand autonomy through a relational lens, the issue of influence takes on a different weight. Rather than being a threat to our autonomy unless we can rationalise our authentic self as separate from it, relational models accept influence as an inescapable aspect of our humanity. They understand influence as exerting an effect on all of us, shaping our identities, our desires and our choices, both at the micro level of our individual relationships and also at the higher, structural level of societal forces.

Understanding a support model of legal capacity makes no sense without accepting the issue of influence in the process of support. In doing so, however, we must also accept the fact that not *all* influence is of equal value. Some influence will be negative and oppressive. If we adopt a relational model, then the type and quality of the influence in the relationship must be acknowledged. As Mary Donnelly notes, the risk of abuse of power in supportive relationships where the level of impairment and ability to communicate with the outside world is very limited is strong – and there is little acknowledgment from the Committee of this problem, nor any serious attempt to deal with it.[39]

I have argued that the complication in the interpretation of article 12 comes from a continued desire to retain some element of individualisation. This is understandable: the notion of individual autonomy as precluding the

[36] Gooding, 'Navigating the "Flashing Amber Lights"' (n 15).
[37] Stavert, 'The Exercise of Legal Capacity' (n 5).
[38] Skowron, 'Giving substance to "the best interpretation of will and preferences"' (n 18).
[39] Donnelly, 'Best Interests in the Mental Capacity Act' (n 3).

intervention of the State in the private lives of disabled people is a powerful one, given the history of disability. Unfortunately, such an interpretation of article 12 sits uncomfortably – and incoherently – alongside the relational demands of the support model of legal capacity, and further risks the abuse and exploitation of disabled people. The next section explores this continued retention of individualisation in the interpretation of article 12, and the problems that it presents.

A. Continued Individualisation

It is the concept of 'will and preferences', and the way it is interpreted and used, which creates the individualisation found in universal legal capacity. Central to the concept is a demand that the individual's will and preferences should be the sole guiding factor in the decision-making process. No longer should any other objective concerns around the individual's wellbeing or best interests influence the decisions, over what the individual themselves wants. A link between 'will and preferences' and 'autonomy' is frequently made by the Committee. While article 12(4) simply states that the will and preferences of the individual must be respected, the phrase used in GC1 and in Concluding Observations on States Parties is 'autonomy, will and preferences'. The overriding of an individual's will and preference is considered an overruling of their autonomy.

This is not an individual account of autonomy that has anything in common with the 'thick' procedural self-governance approach, which has influenced and to a large extent underpins legal frameworks based on mental capacity, which are rejected by article 12. This is, rather, a 'thin' idea of autonomy; that there should be no interference in the lives of individuals, to allow them what Mill termed the 'moral space' to develop as agents.[40] Such approaches are 'thin' as they make very few demands on the agents themselves, and are focused much more on external threats. The individual themselves is the best judge of what is 'good' for them; therefore what the individual says or does is not open to scrutiny, and should be respected without interference from external forces. In conceptualising autonomy this way, the role of the State in interfering in the lives of disabled people is minimised, and the link between legal capacity and mental capacity is neatly broken. Whereas 'thick' conceptions of autonomy place complex criteria around cognitive functioning, this 'thin' conception appears to open the way for 'universal' autonomy.

This understanding of autonomy can explain the strong 'will and preferences' approach favoured by the Committee in GC1 and some commentators. There are, in GC1, a number of mentions which demonstrate a desire to keep the State out of individual choices. The first mention of autonomy is to reiterate the basic principles of the Convention, but then hints as to how the Committee

[40] JS Mill, *On Liberty and other essays; Edited with an introduction and notes by John Gray* (Oxford, Oxford University Press, 1998).

envision it operating as a concept begin to appear. In paragraph 18, in discussing the idea of support, it is noted that 'at all times, including in crisis situations, the individual autonomy and capacity of persons with disabilities to make decisions must be respected.' This is not elaborated on, but the implication of universal legal capacity is that an individual's will and preference, even in crisis, should be respected – regardless, presumably, of the harm that may result. This is an issue commentators have attempted to grapple with, with frameworks for intervention in the event of 'serious adverse events' being shaped by early draft policies[41] and considerations of the application of a 'doctrine of necessity' by others.[42]

A second mention of autonomy is in the phrasing the Committee has repeatedly used in Concluding Observations: that, in reviewing domestic legal frameworks, States Parties needed to pay heed to the 'autonomy, will and preferences' of the individual. GC1 goes on to discuss that this must be done through the removal of substitute decision-making frameworks, and their replacement with models of 'support' for legal capacity, which *also* must maintain respect for 'rights related to autonomy' (such as legal capacity, equal recognition before the law, etc).[43] The Committee conceptualises autonomy as a removal of interference from the State in decision-making – an understanding which becomes very clear when recommendations of what type of support might be given are discussed, and in particular how a supporter might be appointed. These relationships are ones of close support, and it is understandable that this is often a relationship of a very personal nature. The Committee notes that both who an individual chooses, and indeed whether they choose to enter into a relationship of support at all, is a question of individual autonomy, and that 'the person must have the right to refuse support and terminate or change the support relationship at any time'.[44] Academic commentary is divided on this, with endorsement for Anna Arstein-Kerslake and Eilionóir Flynn in particular,[45] but with questions raised by others.[46]

What is presented by this interpretation is one of disabled people being 'left alone' to make their own decisions, with minimal interference from the State. This is an individualised conception of autonomy, where the agent is considered to be responsible for their own decision-making and to know what is best for them. In this context, external interference is problematic and a violation of

[41] Bach and Kerzner, *A New Paradigm* (n 35).

[42] C de Bhailís and E Flynn, 'Recognising legal capacity: commentary and analysis of Article 12 CRPD' (2017) 13 *International Journal of Law in Context* 6; Flynn and Arstein-Kerslake, 'State intervention in the lives of people with disabilities' (n 33); P Gooding and E Flynn, 'Querying the Call to Introduce Mental Capacity Testing to Mental Health Law: Does the Doctrine of Necessity Provide an Alternative?' (2015) 4 *Laws* 245.

[43] United Nations Committee on the Rights of Persons with Disabilities, *General Comment No 1, Article 12: Equal Recognition Before the Law* (n 2).

[44] Ibid, para 29(g).

[45] Flynn and Arstein-Kerslake, 'The Support Model of Legal Capacity' (n 10).

[46] Bach and Kerzner, *A New Paradigm* (n 35); Pritchard-Jones, 'Exploring the potential and the pitfalls' (n 6).

their individual autonomy. But 'interference' in a support model of legal capacity is difficult to avoid. The expression of the will and preference, for many people who fall within the scope of existing substitute decision-making processes, is not something they can do as atomised social units, free from external influence. They require support, often intense support, which will be difficult to separate from influence.

In rejecting the link between mental capacity and legal capacity, article 12 rejects an individual notion of autonomy – but this interpretation of will and preferences replaces it with another, where the individual's own will and preference must be seen in individual isolation, as entirely binding and absolute. This is in contrast to the demands that a support model appears to make for an acknowledgment of our relationality as humans, and recognition of the fact that our decisions are not made in isolation, and separating out our own views and ideas from the influences of others is almost impossible. Influence is inescapable, and without overt acknowledgement of it, it will act in ways which continue to harm disabled people. As Linda Steele notes, a reversion to a 'doctrine of necessity' will simply reinstate high-level control over disabled people, who will continue to be seen as requiring 'different' levels of necessary intervention.[47] An insistence on individual choice, without considering influence in how those choices are formed, in a model of legal capacity where the individual providing the support has potentially a huge amount of power over the person being supported, opens the potential for unmonitored abuse and exploitation.[48] The support model of legal capacity is a recognition in human rights law of our relationality as humans, but that comes with an acceptance that we cannot retreat to individuality to resist influence. We must accept that there *is* influence, and not all of it is 'good', and that this can only be done through interpreting the autonomy underpinning the right to legal capacity in a relational, not individual, framework.

B. Influence, Relationality and the Regulation of Support

In recognising that disabled people may require support to exercise their legal capacity, article 12 has challenged the concept of the individual autonomous agent. For a fully coherent interpretation of article 12, however, we must let go of other vestiges of individuality, set out above, and accept that we cannot separate our agency from influences on it, but rather take a normative stance on the type of influence. However, it must also be noted that we cannot simply accept that all influence is of equal value. We must acknowledge that there are particular risks associated with the very close relationships of support that some people

[47] L Steele, 'Temporality, disability and institutional violence: revisiting *In re F*' (2018) 26 *Griffith Law Review* 378.

[48] Donnelly, 'Best Interests in the Mental Capacity Act' (n 3).

with mental impairments might require, and the high levels of power over the shape of their lives that some of their supporters might have.[49]

It would be wrong to say that this issue has not been considered with regard to article 12, but it has not been considered in a way that leads to clear conclusions in terms of State obligations. There is a general recognition in the literature that all humans are susceptible to influence, that disabled people should not be considered differently, and they should be permitted the 'dignity of risk'.[50] In GC1, in discussing the safeguards necessary to protect the 'rights, will and preferences' of the individual required by Article 12(4) the Committee briefly consider the issue of 'undue influence', and normative issues around support:

> 22. All people risk being subject to 'undue influence', yet this may be exacerbated for those who rely on the support of others to make decisions. Undue influence is characterized as occurring, where the quality of the interaction between the support person and the person being supported includes signs of fear, aggression, threat, deception or manipulation. Safeguards for the exercise of legal capacity must include protection against undue influence; however, the protection must respect the rights, will and preferences of the person, including the right to take risks and make mistakes.

Here there is a recognition that the relationships required for the support model of legal capacity have the potential for undue influence, exploitation and abuse, and an attempt to define what a 'bad' relationship of support may be – where the 'quality of the interaction' shows signs of fear, aggression, threat, deception, or manipulation. However, the issue is what is then to be done in these situations. The Committee themselves do not elaborate on this point, but it has been discussed in the academic commentary.

Arstein-Kerslake notes that where individuals are in abusive or exploitative relationships of care and support, while a court may demand that the individual be removed from that situation temporarily, ultimately their decision to return must be respected, noting that: 'the state … is [not] permitted to intervene and remove decision-making power from the individual and impose its own decision of what is best for the individual'.[51] Flynn and Arstein-Kerslake together have sought a 'disability neutral' solution to the problem, exploring a way that State intervention can only happen on an equal basis, regardless of impairment.[52] Their concern is that State interventions are disempowering for those who are the subject to them – looking to mandatory reporting of domestic violence as a comparison – and that any disability-neutral position should result in less intervention for everyone overall.[53] In seeking to achieve this, they put forward a framework of 'imminent and grave harm' as a threshold for State intervention – but this does not involve coercive or violent relationships.[54] In this situation, as

[49] Ibid.

[50] Gooding, 'Navigating the "Flashing Amber Lights"' (n 15).

[51] A Arstein-Kerslake, 'An empowering dependency: exploring support for the exercise of legal capacity' (2016) 18 *Scandinavian Journal of Disability Research* 77, 88.

[52] Flynn and Arstein-Kerslake, 'State intervention in the lives of people with disabilities' (n 33).

[53] Ibid, 40.

[54] Ibid, 52.

Arstein-Kerslake argued alone, the State should offer support for the individual to leave, but cannot force them to do so.

This analysis is avoiding the question about what constitutes 'good' and 'bad' support, the answer to which can only be found by engaging properly in the ethics of autonomy. The support model of legal capacity demands a relational understanding of ourselves, and of the limits of our autonomy. In entirely rejecting mental capacity criteria, the strong 'will and preferences' model has something in common with a strongly substantive model of relational autonomy. Marina Oshana argues that it is possible to freely choose to enter an oppressive relationship, but a decision to remain in one cannot be considered an autonomous decision, and that if we value autonomy, we should intervene in these cases.[55] This approach has no recourse to assessments of the individual's ability to reflect on their choices – they are purely substantive. There are no requirements for self-reflection or self-authorisation. Rather, the environment itself is constitutive of the individual's autonomy, and if an individual was to autonomously choose to return to the oppressive situation, it raises questions about whether the State should repeatedly intervene.

In the work discussed above, Arstein-Kerslake and Flynn say no – that the State should not intervene once the individual has shown that their decision to return is 'autonomous'.[56] Unlike Oshana's model, which focuses almost entirely on the external environment, this is a model of autonomy which calls for the acceptance of relationality in allowing decisions made in a relationship of support to be given legal recognition, but retains a level of individuality in determining the authenticity of a decision when there are concerns around influence. Strong substantive relational models of autonomy are open to criticisms of paternalism, requiring repeated intervention and 'rescuing' of people from oppressive situations that they have themselves chosen to enter. I have argued elsewhere that repeated action 'on behalf of' someone simply engenders a sense of disempowerment and opens them to repeated abuse and exploitation – it is better to focus on policies which support them to make decisions for themselves.[57] However, there are still questions here about how this support should be delivered, and by whom, if we are to consider it 'autonomous'. If it is not about mental capacity, then is it not about good and bad relationships?

If we consider Arstein-Kerslake's example, the person with learning disabilities who is being malignly influenced in their family relationship will likely be in need of some support to make the decision on whether or not to return to that potentially abusive relationship when they are removed from it. There are two different forms of influence happening here – it is not that they are experiencing 'undue influence' in the first scenario, and independent reasoning, able to remove themselves from the influence in the second. In weak substantive

[55] Oshana, *Personal Autonomy in Society* (n 25).

[56] Arstein-Kerslake, 'An empowering dependency' (n 51); Flynn and Arstein-Kerslake, 'State intervention in the lives of people with disabilities' (n 33).

[57] Keeling, '"Organising objects": Adult safeguarding practice' (n 6).

relational models, a notion of agency is restored through self-authorisation; an ability to claim the decision as one's own, through reflection.[58] This is a process which can be supported, but importantly that relationship of support has to be enabling of autonomy. Therefore, equally in this model, choosing an abusive or oppressive relationship of support would be incompatible with a notion of autonomy. In such an approach, perhaps the individual might choose to return to the abusive relationship, but what does that mean for any decisions they make with the 'support' of the abusive family member? Should *these* be seen as a valid expression of the supported person's 'autonomous' will and preferences? GC1 is generally silent on this. The guidance on article 12(4) suggests that States should respond in some way where there are concerns of abuse, but that is 'still respectful for their will and preferences'. The question remains as to why the will and preferences that result from oppressive relationships should be respected as autonomous.

This obviously raises challenging questions of State obligations. There have been suggestions from the very earliest days of implementation plans for some level of State oversight and regulation of relationships of support, but it is understandable that this level of oversight in the lives of disabled people may feel invasive and another form of State control. However, the alternative cannot be an individual approach to personal autonomy which in effect abandons disabled people to exploitative and abusive relationships. Universal legal capacity, as a universally *accessible* right, does not equate to *universal* autonomy. The State can intervene where a relationship of support is oppressive, abusive and not facilitative of an individual's will and preferences, and, as Beverley Clough has eloquently argued, the State is *already* intervening, through enacting (or failing to enact) policy, not just at the moment of removing someone from an abusive relationship.[59] The next stage for the project on legal capacity is to consider what these 'interventions' should look like, and will likely require extensive consideration of how disabled people are supported in their legal capacity from early stages of their life where impairments are lifelong, and the building of 'supportive environments' through holistic health, education and social care policy.

V. CONCLUSION

It is not the job of a UN Committee to engage in deep, philosophical debate about the notion of autonomy. But, in retaining a link between legal capacity and autonomy, the debate has been opened, and has generated questions about

[58] Westlund, 'Rethinking Relational Autonomy' (n 28); Mackenzie, 'Three Dimensions of Autonomy' (n 24).

[59] B Clough, 'Vulnerability and Capacity to Consent to Sex – Asking the Right Questions?' (2015) 26 *Child and Family Law Quarterly* 371; B Clough, 'Disability and Vulnerability: Challenging the Capacity/Incapacity Binary' (2017) *Social Policy and Society* 1.

the consistency of the interpretation of the obligations within the right, and the attendant obligations of the State. Once we recognise that where the conflict in interpretation lies is between relationality pulling one way to justify a move away from mental capacity models of legal capacity, and individualism retained to restrict the role of the State on the other, we can begin to create a solution.

The desire to retain an individual notion of autonomy, and seeking recourse to traditional accounts of the individual as free from interference from the State, is understandable. However, the insistence of the Committee on adherence to the individual's will and preference, regardless of the type of relationship in which the expression of this may have been fostered, opens serious questions of the continued utility of autonomy beyond a thin concept which provides little ethical scaffolding for difficult questions around abuse and exploitation, or self-neglect.

Relational autonomy models provide a much better framework for explaining the acceptability of decisions resulting from the support model as autonomous, but also require us to recognise the universality of influence, and the need for normative positions to be taken on what constitutes 'good' and 'bad' support. This, in turn, requires an engagement in the role of the State in facilitating the former, and preventing the latter in fulfilling its obligations under the Convention. In doing this, we recognise that as long as we *have* a State, it is 'intervening' in the sense of shaping the environment around us, and therefore being a partial causative element of our autonomy. The State can, therefore, have a role to play in regulating the normative question of good and bad support – but our focus in terms of State action must go beyond the 'hard' cases of the exact moment of abuse and exploitation. Though we must continue to address this challenge, the literature on the support model of legal capacity must start to look more holistically at the question of what 'good' environments that are facilitative of legal capacity look like, and how we can build them.

4

The Significance of Strong Evaluation and Narrativity in Supporting Capacity

CAMILLIA KONG[1]

I. INTRODUCTION

IN *NOTTINGHAM HEALTHCARE NHS Trust v RC* Mostyn J was charged with determining the capacity of a young man to refuse blood transfusion and self-lacerate.[2] At an earlier hearing Holman J described RC's story as 'desperately sad'.[3] RC was a 23 year old man who had a long history of repeated self-injurious behaviour, including self-strangulation, burning, cutting, and head-butting. He had been formally diagnosed with antisocial and emotionally unstable personality disorder (the latter also known as borderline personality disorder).[4] He had a long history of various institutional interventions: at age four he had been taken into care; his first admission to a psychiatric hospital was when he was 15; at 21 he was convicted of a serious sexual assault and had been given a prison sentence of five years. During his time in prison, two things happened: first, RC embraced the Jehovah's Witnesses faith; second, he

[1] My thanks to the organisers and participants of the *Supporting Legal Capacity in Socio-Legal Context* workshop, held at the Oñati International Institute for the Sociology of Law, 18–19 July 2019, particularly Mary Donnelly, Claire Murray, Rosie Harding, and Ezgi Taşcıoğlu for their comments. Thanks also to Alex Ruck Keene and John Coggon for their feedback on an earlier draft of the chapter. I am grateful to the Arts and Humanities Research Council for its support through the *Judging Values and Participation in Mental Capacity Law* project (AHRC Grant Reference: AH/R013055/1).

[2] *Nottingham Healthcare NHS Trust v RC* [2014] EWCOP 1317.

[3] *Nottinghamshire Healthcare NHS Trust v RC* [2014] EWCOP 1136 [8].

[4] The diagnostic label of borderline personality disorder (and its more recent renaming as emotionally unstable personality disorder) is highly controversial, particularly due to questionable validity, as well as the stigma, pejorative connotations, and attitudes towards those given the diagnosis in psychiatric settings. For my purposes here, I acknowledge this controversy but have used the term borderline personality disorder, to maintain consistency with the therapeutic resources referred to later in the chapter, though it should be emphasised that very little of my analysis hinges on the diagnostic label.

continued to seriously self-harm, to the point where he had slashed his brachial artery (the major blood vessel of the upper arm). At the hospital he refused a blood transfusion. He was then transferred to a secure psychiatric unit where he continued to try and reopen the wound, resulting in his periodic restraint. RC subsequently signed an advance decision to refuse blood transfusion on the basis of his religious faith. According to his counsel's note,

> When asked about the reason for his self-harming, he has described feeling intense emotions which he can only dampen down by self-harm. Although at times in the past he has said he wishes to die, he does not express any wish to die at the present time. The motivation for his self-harm does not appear to his responsible clinician to be to bring about his death.[5]

Holman J put the legal dilemma as follows:

> On the one hand, this young adult has made a clear advance decision, whilst apparently having capacity to do so, that, because of his religious beliefs, he utterly refuses consent and positively directs that he should not be transfused with blood or blood products. On the other hand, he is compulsorily detained, both as a prisoner and now in a psychiatric hospital, where, so far as possible and lawful, the state is under obvious duties to protect him, as the consultant psychiatrist identified in the above passage. He has a right to life under Article 2 of the European Convention on Human Rights; but, under other articles of that Convention, he has a right to freedom of religion and a right to respect for his private life, which includes his own bodily integrity.[6]

RC's conflicting wishes represent a serious conundrum on three fronts: first, what kind of respect should be accorded to RC's preference to self-lacerate and self-harm? Second, his long-term wishes do not necessarily accord with the potential consequences of his preferred method of coping with his strong emotions, since he does not intend to die as a result of his self-injurious behaviour. Third, respect for his religious beliefs precludes any potential life-saving blood transfusion if he inadvertently cuts a major artery in the process of his self-injurious behaviour.

Cases like this reveal the problematic, conflicting normative status that may be accorded to the 'rights, will and preferences' of the person concerned. The normative shift towards automatic deference towards a person's subjective preferences has been expressed through Article 12 of the United Nations Convention on the Rights of Persons with Disabilities, particularly in General Comment No 1 ('GC1') by the UNCRPD Committee.[7] Different interpretations of GC1 allow for some space for interventions, particularly where life, health, or safety are at grave and imminent risk.[8] Yet the normative grounding for these interventions is

[5] *Nottinghamshire Healthcare NHS Trust v RC* (n 4), [8].

[6] Ibid [16].

[7] UNCRPD Committee, *General Comment No 1 (2014), Article 12: Equal Recognition Before the Law*. CRPD/C/GC/1 (Geneva, United Nations, 2014).

[8] A Arstein-Kerslake and E Flynn, 'The Right to Legal Agency: Domination, Disability and the Protections of Article 12 of the Convention on the Rights of Persons with Disabilities' (2017) 13 *International Journal of Law in Context* 22; C De Bhailís and E Flynn, 'Recognising Legal Capacity: Commentary and Analysis of Article 12 CRPD' (2017) 13 *International Journal of Law in Context* 6.

unclear, as is how to resolve the problem of ambivalent, incoherent, or conflicting choices, partly because there has been little sustained theoretical exploration of the unequal normative status that might be justifiably accorded to different preferences and commitments.

This lack of clarity is symptomatic of a deeper issue around the conception of human agency that foregrounds interpretations of 'will and preferences'.[9] Adherence to GC1 cannot help but prioritise the protection of individuals' negative liberty, focused on the right to make choices without external interference. For example, Gerard Quinn's particular formulation of positive and negative freedoms is commonly used to describe legal capacity as 'both a "sword" to promote positive freedom and make one's way through the world in "uncoerced" relations with others; and a "shield" protecting against others who would impose decisions upon you'.[10] Though all scholars and activists in this area acknowledge the necessity of positive obligations to provide accommodations and supports, primacy is nonetheless accorded to the expression, facilitation, and enactment of an individual's subjective preferences due to the rights-protective nature of Article 12.[11] The normative emphasis on acceding to a person's expressed will and preferences is understandable, particular in light of the longstanding disrespect that has been shown to those with disabilities.

However, the picture of human agency that is presupposed warrants critical examination. The purpose of my chapter is to undertake such an analysis and scrutinise the foregrounding vision of agency involved in supporting legal capacity as interpreted by GC1. First, I challenge the overriding emphasis on the deference to and enactment of a person's will and preference, arguing that this presupposes an incoherent model of existential agency premised on radical freedom. This model's incoherence stems largely from the hiving off of any conditions which engage in deeper evaluation, to justify and foreground one's subjective preferences. It is my view that this is deeply problematic, leaving us with a denuded and potentially harmful account of human agency. Instead, I suggest that supporting legal capacity must be grounded in an account of agency that retains substantive evaluative and motivational conditions which help frame the choices we make and constitute our sense of personal identity. More specifically, these conditions include qualitative distinctions which help determine the worth and value of certain preferences, their motivational sources, and their surrounding self-narratives.

[9] C Kong, 'The *Convention for the Rights of Persons with Disabilities* and Article 12: Prospective Feminist Lessons against the "Will and Preferences" Paradigm' (2015) 4 *Laws* 709.

[10] M Bach and L Kerzner, *A New Paradigm for Protecting Autonomy and the Right to Legal Capacity* (Toronto ON, Law Commission of Ontario, 2014) 43.

[11] De Bhailís and Flynn, 'Recognising legal capacity' (n 8); A Arstein-Kerslake and E Flynn, 'The General Comment on Article 12 of the Convention on the Rights of Persons with Disabilities: A Roadmap for Equality Before the Law' (2016) 20 *International Journal of Human Rights* 471.

The structure of the chapter is as follows. Section II explores how the GC1 interpretation of 'rights, will and preference' turns on a Sartrean concept of radical freedom. Using Charles Taylor's distinction between 'weak' and 'strong' evaluation, I argue that this vision of radical freedom cannot sustain the status or weight of choice without likewise assuming the necessity of some kind of evaluative horizon which engages in contrastive distinctions and judgements. This qualitative horizon is often deemed to be overly demanding for persons with disabilities, but I use examples to show its importance in according proper respect to individuals' choices. Section III explores the motivational sources of agency – the importance of intersubjective narratives and their impact on self-interpretations that help express one's personal identity. Cases of egosyntonic self-harming disorders can emerge through oppressive, abusive, and neglectful relational conditions, and thus highlight the importance of considering the genealogy and integration of certain narratives in the formation of agential motivation.

II. AGENCY AND STRONG EVALUATION

According to human rights discussions of disability law, legal agency is associated with the ability to act in the world, to make choices that are of legal consequence, and to have those choices recognised and enacted.[12] Two aspects of legal capacity are highlighted in GC1: first, legal standing recognises persons with disabilities as rights-holders before the law; second, legal agency constitutes the ability to act on one's rights and have those actions legally recognised. The latter dimension is typically withheld in mental capacity regimes and, according to GC1, indicates the discriminatory treatment of individuals with disabilities. Legal capacity, by contrast,

> means that all people, including persons with disabilities, have legal standing and legal agency simply by virtue of being human … both strands of legal capacity must be recognized for the right to legal capacity to be fulfilled; they cannot be separated.[13]

The desire to promote more equitable structures which recognise and respect individuals with disabilities is undoubtedly a laudable and justifiable intention behind the 'will and preferences' paradigm. However, a number of consequences follow from GC1 – not least the purported illegitimacy of mental capacity regimes and substituted decision-making mechanisms. I set aside these practical issues, though I do believe my argument will have implications for these two claims which cannot be drawn out here. Instead, my focus is the vision of agency that this notion of legal capacity presupposes. In denying the contingent link between legal and mental capacity, GC1 effectively presumes that human agency

[12] Arstein-Kerslake and Flynn, 'The Right to Legal Agency' (n 8).
[13] UN CRPD Committee, *General Comment No 1* (n 7), [14].

is separable from three conditions: (i) decision-making abilities; (ii) evaluative capacities; and (iii) motivational sources. How each of these conditions is set aside is explored below: GC1 assumes that it only sets aside condition (i), but what I show here and in the next section are the ways in which its rejection of condition (i), in combination with its focus on acceding to subjective will and preferences, necessarily entails abandoning both conditions (ii) and (iii).

In the first instance, condition (i) is set aside in GC1 through its rejection of the notion of mental capacity. Most functional approaches to the mental capacity threshold uphold certain decision-making criteria, similar to those of the Mental Capacity Act 2005 in England and Wales. Though the exact meaning of their criteria can be debated, broadly speaking, the theoretical basis behind functional tests seems to presume a loose Frankfurtian framework which focuses on the procedural conditions of choice, premised on the coherent ordering of preferences through a hierarchical distinction between first-order desires and higher-order volitions. According to such a model, first-order desires consist in our wants, preferences, cravings, and so on, that can move us. Second-order volitions, by contrast, are those desires that function as the object of one's will. In other words, this framework involves the critical endorsement and reflective identification with certain desires, meaning we choose between different first-order desires, or suppress certain preferences in favour of others in the process of decision-making.[14] Functional accounts of mental capacity, for example, typically demand evidence of some consistency between first-order desires and second-order volitions to some degree, as reflected in whether individuals can logically weigh up their expressed preferences or wishes. Is there evidence of some kind of rational calculus; can they deliberate about things in a coherent fashion?

In denying the contingent link between the concept of legal capacity and mental capacity, proponents of GC1 necessarily reject the claim that agency is bound up with the procedural conditions of decision-making capacity as set out in condition (i). But in fact, conditions (ii) and (iii) are also treated as unnecessary for meaningful agency: to assert the primacy of subjective will and preferences in the manner suggested means we need to presume a model that is stripped of this (or any) criteria. Indeed, its resemblance to the model of existential freedom espoused by Jean-Paul Sartre reveals how GC1 involves not just the eschewal of procedural conditions of decision-making, but also evaluative capacities to qualitatively assess the worth of different options (condition (ii)) and the motivational sources that drive these options (condition (iii)).

In 'Existentialism is a Humanism', Sartre describes radical freedom, where '[m]an … is simply what he conceives himself to be … he is what he wills'.[15] Such freedom is epitomised in the radical choice of the young man faced with

[14] HG Frankfurt, 'Freedom of the Will and the Concept of a Person' (1971) 68 *Journal of Philosophy* 5.

[15] J-P Sartre, 'Existentialism as Humanism', trans P Mairet, in W Kaufman (ed), *Existentialism from Dostoyevsky to Sartre* (London, Plume, 2004) 349.

the option of staying with his mother or fighting in the Resistance, torn by two kinds of moralities: on one hand, he feels the sympathy and personal devotion towards his mother, on the other is his sense of national patriotism. Sartre describes this predicament as a moment of radical choice because no ethical doctrines or a priori frameworks can provide an answer to this predicament. Indeed, 'nothing remains but to trust our instincts',[16] where simply to 'choose between this or that is at the same time to *affirm the value of that which is chosen*; for we are unable ever to choose the worse' (emphasis added).[17] As such, 'feeling is formed by the deed that one does', meaning that 'I can neither seek within myself for an authentic impulse to action nor can I expect, from some ethic, formulae that will enable me to act'.[18]

Freedom therefore excludes traditional goals or frameworks for human beings: it is unsituated within a broader domain of normative significance. Unmoored from any evaluation, the goal of freedom is simply for itself. Sartre declares:

> [F]reedom, in respect of concrete circumstances, can have no other end and aim but itself; and when once a man has seen that values depend upon himself, in that state of forsakenness he can will only one thing, and that is freedom as the foundation of all values. That does not mean that he wills it in the abstract: it simply means that the actions of men of good faith have, as their ultimate significance, the quest of freedom itself as such.[19]

According to the Sartrean view, aspirations of authenticity have no connection with discovering our 'higher purposes'; rather, authenticity involves being alive to the fact of our entirely voluntary existence as humans, of our capacity to invent ourselves and our own judgements, and facing up to the fact that no general morality or criteria can help guide our actions. Any conditions of agency, ranging from the more procedural criteria of decision-making abilities, to more substantive criteria bound up with evaluative capacities and motivational sources (discussed below), represent a violation of our existential freedom. Indeed, adopting Sartre's rhetorical flourishes, we are 'cowards' or 'scum', to turn away from, let alone deprive others of, this primordial condition of absolute choice that is fitting to our dignity.[20]

This vision of human agency resonates strongly with GC1's statements that 'support in the exercise of legal capacity must respect the rights, will and preferences of persons with disabilities and should never amount to substitute decision-making',[21] as well as the assertion of the 'inherent right' of legal capacity to all individuals, regardless of decision-making capacities.[22] Emphasis on the uncontested enactment of subjective choice in this manner makes sense only

[16] Ibid 355.
[17] Ibid 350.
[18] Ibid 355–56.
[19] Ibid 365–66.
[20] Ibid 366.
[21] UN CRPD Committee, *General Comment No. 1* (n 7), [17].
[22] Ibid [14].

through the Sartrean lens of the radical chooser, where the individual is free to judge for themselves, free to move by their instincts or intuitive feel in a situation, free to create their own evaluative language, and it is the obligation of others to acknowledge one's condition of existential freedom. But this represents a deeply problematic account of agency, with its troubling practical implications coming into sharp relief in the RC case: from a Sartrean viewpoint, no evaluative criteria can challenge his preference to self-soothe through self-laceration, even if it imperils his life. The fact that he chooses as he does, based on his instincts, is sufficient for freedom. Equally, we lack the evaluative language needed to navigate the conflicting intentions that are expressed in his actions: we are at a loss as to why some of his commitments, like his religious beliefs, might have overriding importance in comparison to others.

To escape this dilemma, one might argue that at the very least we need to focus on condition (i) to generate a plausible vision of agency. Yet this will get us only so far: we might highlight, for instance, the inconsistencies of RC's purported preferences, or question whether these reflect his own hierarchical ranking. The focus on procedural decision-making conditions does introduce some nominal criteria, but not necessarily of the type that enables us to understand, interpret, and respect evaluation of a deeper kind: standards of consistency provide little scope for explaining and justifying why his advance decisions might trump imperatives towards certain clinical interventions, or why these religious convictions necessarily have a different normative status to that of his self-injurious preferences. Moreover, retaining condition (i) is not an option available to GC1 given its unequivocal rejection of not just functional approaches to mental capacity, but the concept of decision-making capacity as a whole.

Ultimately this signals that the model of agency underlying GC1's 'will and preferences' paradigm is ungrounded in any evaluative conditions, much like Sartrean radical freedom. Following Charles Taylor, evaluative conditions can be thought of in two ways. At times, they are presumed to be reducible to condition (i) – simple or weak forms of evaluation that are focused on the consistent expression of or calculus between preferences of some kind, their logical hierarchical ordering, and the consummation of those preferences through means-end reasoning. Weak evaluation as such posits the sufficiency of a desire (in as much that something is judged to be good simply on the grounds that it is desired or preferred), as well as the contingent incompatibility of alternatives (meaning that alternatives can be set aside based on their contingent or circumstantial conflict with a more desired alternative). As a 'simple weigher', an agent is minimally reflective, capable of evaluating the different alternatives and able to intend and act on that evaluation. The simple weigher therefore has reflection, evaluation, and will. The procedural criterion in condition (i) captures this vision of the simple weigher and as such, is often presumed in functional thresholds of mental capacity. A commitment to condition (i) will therefore necessarily signal a commitment to some kind of evaluative abilities in condition (ii).

Even the simple weigher – constituting what one might assume to be the barebones of agency – must presuppose even the most nominal standards of evaluation.[23]

But what interests me here is Taylor's second sense of evaluation in condition (ii) and how it is dismissed in GC1. In contrast to the weak evaluation undertaken by the simple weigher, strong evaluation is premised on questions of worth through the use of contrastive terms of higher and lower, noble or ignoble, dignity or debased, good or bad. That something is desired is insufficient; indeed, alternatives or preferences may be abandoned, not necessarily because of their contingent incompatibility, but because of a more fundamental, profound conflict that is resolved by appealing to a vocabulary of worth premised on contrastive distinctions. The evaluation of alternatives carries substantive depth, revolving around language which goes beyond a calculus of maximisation, advantage, and logical consequences. Such evaluation cannot be reduced to some subjective attraction or an ineffable gut feeling for one alternative over another. Rather, it involves developing a mode of articulation about ourselves, where acquiring strongly evaluative language engages a broader frame of significance in speaking about our preferences, desires, and so on. Summarising the distinction between these two modes of evaluation, Taylor writes:

> Whereas a reflection about what we feel like more, which is all a simple weigher can do in assessing motivations, keeps us as it were at the periphery; a reflection on the kind of beings we are takes us at the centre of our existence as agents. Strong evaluation is not just a condition of articulacy about preferences, but also about the quality of life, the kind of beings we are or want to be.[24]

Ultimately, condition (ii) in this stronger meaning provides the contrastive language by which RC's conflicting intentions and commitments could be qualitatively distinguished and judged, thereby avoiding the pitfalls of Sartrean radical freedom in discharging the duty to support his legal capacity. Yet, GC1's normative emphasis on the uncontested enactment of subjective will and preferences forecloses these evaluative resources, effectively following a general trend in theory and practice which abandons or relegates contrastive language to the level of implicit assumption when speaking about human agency. Part of this trend is attributable to the strong utilitarian and/or deontological strand in our culture which questions the need for strong evaluation: our choices are reducible to imperatives of maximisation of some kind, or protected through the formal prism of individual rights, where conflicting values are distilled through a more manageable, indeed less contentious lens than that of the contrastive frame

[23] As debates between models of instrumental and more substantive modes of practical reasoning show, it is nonetheless questionable whether the evaluation in condition (i) is strictly 'procedural' in the sense that it can somehow remain focused solely on the process of decision-making as opposed to the substantive content of means and ends.

[24] C Taylor, 'What is Human Agency?' in Taylor, *Human Agency and Language* (Cambridge, Cambridge University Press, 1985) 15, 26.

of qualitative evaluation.[25] Another important reason is its purported inconsistency with liberal commitments which assert the freedom of individuals to pursue the life they wish (so long as their choices do not interfere with the liberty of others).

Arguably, both the liberal imperative and deontological temper underlying the human rights framing of legal capacity help explain GC1's eschewal of weak and strong forms of evaluation: weak evaluation would effectively promote standards of decision-making akin to functional tests of mental capacity; meanwhile, strong evaluation appears to be too demanding and paternalistic, framing choice around substantive conditions of contrastive worth and value. Both conditions purportedly impose normative frameworks that are arbitrary and exclusionary towards individuals with certain impairments. In theory, one isn't left without a vision of agency – just one that is premised on Sartrean radical choice by default.

But is this vision even possible, or do we lose something foundational about what it means to choose? The real cost of adopting a Sartrean vision of radical freedom lies ultimately in the inarticulacy of why agency matters in the first place. Shorn of any criteria, what it means to be an agent is stripped of its significance; its meaning becomes coextensive with the espousal of subjective preferences or instincts disoriented from any evaluative horizon. As Taylor asks, 'a choice made without regard to anything, without the agent feeling any solicitation to one alternative or the other, or in complete disregard of such solicitation: is this still choice?'.[26] Indeed, '[i]n order for us to speak of choice, we cannot just find ourselves in one of the alternatives. We have in some sense to experience the pull of each and give our assent to one'.[27] In other words, choice has to be grounded in some fashion: at the very least one has to appeal to one option over another as a simple weigher would, justified along the lines of an attraction to one option over another as a result of some further reflection. It involves at minimum the coherent registration of preferences and grounding those preferences in reasons.

Yet even this move would be illegitimate through the lens of radical freedom. That one can grasp one's preferences and weigh up the different options is neither here nor there; justification of why one option is chosen over another isn't even required. What matters is the espousal and expression of that choice by individuals. GC1's implicit commitment to radical freedom likewise enables it to tread a delicate line which preserves the intrinsic value of choice whilst disengaging from evaluations that revolve around the desirability of preferences (the simple weigher) or the worth of that choice through contrastive language (the strong

[25] Hence the focus on risk-related assessments which tend to preoccupy professionals in mental capacity and welfare-related legal jurisdictions; see M Hedley, *The Modern Judge: Power, Responsibility and Society's Expectations* (Bristol, LexisNexis, 2016).

[26] Taylor, 'What is Human Agency?' (n 24), 32.

[27] Taylor, 'What is Human Agency?' (n 24) 31.

evaluator). There need not be any sense as to why that preference is favoured over the other or why one choice is superior; an agent can just find themselves in one alternative. Values as such are bound up with the mere espousal of them, selected and created by ourselves. In other words, the force of a person's will and preferences remains rooted in a commitment to choice but without any of its constitutive evaluative criteria, even in a nominal sense. Not only is it possible for agents to decide one way or another independently of their preferences, but these choices are framed in such a way that they purport to possess the gravity of strong evaluation, even as its situating, contrastive horizon is denied through the claim that one's evaluations are themselves the product of radical choice.

This picture of agency ultimately rests on a circular argument: radical choice is valuable because it is based on evaluations which themselves stem from radical choice. Either our choices have evaluative depth and we necessarily acknowledge that such judgements involve evaluations which have little to do with our status as radical choosers, or we hive off all strong evaluation to maintain our status as free choosers, meaning then that our choices lack any depth and effectively become superficial expressions of our de facto preferences, or worse, are removed from those preferences altogether and lack the basic criteria of what it means to choose.[28]

So far, this discussion of strong evaluation in agency has been fairly abstract. But a couple of serious practical consequences also motivate the argument for its significance. First, once agency is stripped of its evaluative conditions we become trapped in misleading equivalencies. Consider the case of RC: through the prism of radical freedom his self-harm could be perceived as a choice on a par with his desire to continue living, and even with his refusal of blood because of his religious faith. There are no grounds to judge his actions in the first sense as lesser than the latter two; instead, we are forced into a meaningless equivalency between choices which involve one's conscience and long-term commitments, and those that involve momentary preference, instinct, or even dysfunctional modes of bodily coping. We cannot help but engage in strong evaluations when faced with such conflicting choices, to distinguish between and hierarchically order them. As noted above, certain interpretations of GC1 permit some third-party judgements to prioritise certain choices over others in cases of conflict, in order to escape precisely the circularity implied in radical choice.[29] But this rests on a distinction between 'will' – representing one's longstanding values and sense of one's life as a whole – and 'preferences' – which signify short-term, more momentary wishes. These moves are only available, however, through an appeal to some qualitative criteria that are separable from the value of subjective choice, and indeed, function as the backdrop from which the presumptive weight of different options could be questioned and evaluated. This backdrop

[28] Ibid 32–33.

[29] Arstein-Kerslake and Flynn, 'The right to legal agency' (n 8); also De Bhailís and Flynn 'Recognising legal capacity' (n 8).

in fact enables Mostyn J's decision to legitimately distinguish RC's religious convictions from his self-harming reactions to emotional distress: regarding the latter Mostyn J concludes that 'it is likely that he does so without the capacity to choose to self-harm',[30] yet RC's Jehovah's Witness faith nonetheless deserves respect, even if one of the unintended consequences might be the refusal of necessary medical treatment for his instinctive, self-injurious behaviour.

Second, there is a risk of disrespecting the very foundation of a person's identity. Agency premised on radical freedom severs the constitutive link between our sense of self and our evaluations. As Taylor writes,

> Our identity is [...] defined by certain evaluations which are inseparable from ourselves as agents. Shorn of these we would cease to be ourselves, by which we do not mean trivially that we would be different in the sense of having some properties other than those we now have – which would indeed be the case after any change, however minor – but that shorn of these we would lose the very possibility of being an agent who evaluates; that our existence as persons, and hence our ability to adhere as persons to certain evaluations, would be impossible outside the horizon of these essential evaluations, that we would break down as persons, be incapable of being persons in the full sense.[31]

The evaluative horizon matters, in other words, because we draw from it as a constant source of self-definition and nourishment, valuing or devaluing various parts of ourselves. It is in this respect that incorporating strong evaluation in our foregrounding concept of agency in supporting legal capacity need not be unduly paternalistic or disrespectful towards individuals with disabilities, but in fact carves out some crucial space for choices that reflect one's identity and valuing in a deep sense, even as they simultaneously defy any rational calculus. For instance, in RC's case, his present capacity and advance decision to refuse blood products were upheld by Mostyn J, who argued,

> There can be no circumstances where a Muslim could 'weigh' the merit of eating pork. It is simply beyond the pale. So too, it would appear, when it comes to Jehovah's Witnesses and blood transfusions. But it would be an extreme example of the application of the law of unintended consequences were an iron tenet of an accepted religion to give rise to questions of capacity under the MCA.[32]

Two other examples illustrate the evaluative basis of personal identity well. First, in the commonly cited case, *Wye Valley NHS Trust v Mr B*,[33] Jackson J decided that it was against the best interests of Mr B to be forcibly treated for his gangrenous leg, the result of type II diabetes. The status accorded to Mr B's religious commitments is notable: whilst expert witnesses described them to be the result of auditory hallucinations or delusions, Jackson J made a point

[30] *Nottingham Healthcare NHS Trust v RC* [2014] EWCOP 1317 [27].
[31] Taylor, 'What is Human Agency?' (n 24) 34–35.
[32] *Nottingham Healthcare NHS Trust v RC* [2014] EWCOP 1317 [34].
[33] *Wye Valley NHS Trust v Mr B* [2015] EWCOP 60.

of clarifying the importance of these religious beliefs to Mr B's sense of self, appealing to Mr B's own evaluations in the process. He stated, 'Mr B's religious sentiments are extremely important to him, even though he does not follow an established religion'.[34] When meeting with him, Mr B stated,

> I'm not afraid of dying, I know where I'm going. The angels have told me I am going to heaven. I have no regrets. It would be a better life than this … I don't want it, I'm not afraid of death. I don't want interference. Even if I'm going to die, I don't want the operation.[35]

Jackson J concluded,

> His religious beliefs are deeply meaningful to him and do not deserve to be described as delusions: they are his faith and they are an intrinsic part of who he is. I would not define Mr B by reference to his mental illness or his religious beliefs. Rather, his core quality is his 'fierce independence', and it is this that is now, as he sees it, under attack.[36]

The second example is the controversial 'sparkly' case, *King's College Hospital NHS Foundation Trust v C & V*,[37] which revolved around C's capacity to refuse life-preserving renal dialysis necessitated by her failed suicide attempt following a number of personally difficult circumstances. C's primary purpose was to live 'unapologetically on her terms … revolving largely around her looks, men, material possessions and "living the high life"… that "sparkles"'.[38] C was adamant she wished to refuse treatment and die, stating that

> I know that I could get better; I know that I could live without a health problem, but I don't want it; I've lost my home; I've lost everything I'd worked for; I've had a good innings; it's what I have achieved.[39]

Describing her mother's position, her daughter, V, stated:

> [M]y mother would never have wanted to live at all costs. Her reasons for trying to kill herself in September and for refusing dialysis now are strongly in keeping with both her personality and her long held values. Although they are not reasons that are easy to understand, I believe that they are not only fully thought through, but also entirely in keeping with both her (unusual) value system and her (unusual) personality … 'Recovery' to her does not just relate to her kidney function, but to regaining her 'sparkle' (her expensive, material and looks-orientated social life) which she believes she is too old to regain. Again, the references in the notes to her talking about being 'sociable, hosting parties and going out with the girls' are fitting: to those who know her well, her entire identity has been built around being a self-described 'vivacious and sociable person who lives life to the full and enjoys having fun'.[40]

[34] Ibid [14].
[35] Ibid [37].
[36] Ibid [43].
[37] *King's College Hospital NHS Foundation Trust v C & V* [2015] EWCOP 80.
[38] Ibid [8].
[39] Ibid [53].
[40] Ibid [63].

Macdonald J came to the conclusion:

> The decision C has reached to refuse dialysis can be characterised as an unwise one. That C considers that the prospect of growing old, the fear of living with fewer material possessions and the fear that she has lost, and will not regain, 'her sparkle' outweighs a prognosis that signals continued life will alarm and possibly horrify many, although I am satisfied that the ongoing discomfort of treatment, the fear of chronic illness and the fear of lifelong treatment and lifelong disability are factors that also weigh heavily in the balance for C. C's decision is certainly one that does not accord with the expectations of many in society. Indeed, others in society may consider C's decision to be unreasonable, illogical or even immoral within the context of the sanctity accorded to life by society in general. … C has capacity to decide whether or not to accept treatment [and] C is entitled to make her own decision on that question based on the things that are important to her, in keeping with her own personality and system of values and without conforming to society's expectation of what constitutes the 'normal' decision in this situation (if such a thing exists).[41]

Both judgments recognise the constitutive connection between the evaluative horizon and one's personal identity as the backdrop of choice. The contrastive distinctions about what kind of life Mr B and C wished to lead, what commitments had overriding value, were recognised as inseparable from who they were as persons and their subsequent decisions to refuse treatment. Vital to Mr B's sense of independence were his religious beliefs and his resistance to being in a care home like his deceased partner; for C, certain evaluations about the kind of lifestyle she deemed worthwhile were essential to how she saw herself, framing her decision to refuse dialysis.

Thus, the evaluative conditions of agency help reveal the ranging depth of qualitative contrasts which frame our decisions, enabling us to avoid the problematic equivalencies and circularity of radical choice. They also bring into sharp relief what is at stake in recognising another as someone who evaluates in this manner, where they help us arrive at a non-trivial sense of how we value and see ourselves, of our very notion of personal identity. Agency pared of its evaluative horizon risks disrespecting the person and their sense of self in deep ways, effectively meaning that individuals are denied the possibility of being recognised as agents who evaluate, contributing to a loss of one's identity or the fundamental misrecognition of another.

III. MOTIVATIONAL SOURCES

The cases I have discussed so far illustrate ways in which the domain of contrastive distinctions is intimately bound up with what it means to be an agent as well as one's self-understanding. Closely related to the evaluative conditions of

[41] Ibid [97].

agency is its motivational basis, or condition (iii), which revolves around the relational and social development of our motivational sources and how these are incorporated in our sense of self. Motivation is constituted by our intentions, desires, and reasons which move us in particular ways. These constituents are formed intersubjectively and relationally, and their crucial link to our sense of selfhood comes through narratives. These narratives are a profound influence on our agency – they impact on how and what we value and disvalue, believe or question about ourselves, leading us to interact with and move about the world in certain ways. Thus, the stories we tell ourselves, the stories we convey to others about ourselves, provide a window into the relational, intersubjective narratives that have surrounded us, shaping and grounding our identity.[42]

Whether these narratives and stories can be critically evaluated by the Sartrean model of radical choice assumed in GC1 is questionable. Dismissal of qualitative evaluations (conditions (i) and (ii)) entails the omission of condition (iii), since our motivational sources, much like our evaluations, emerge from radical freedom. At most, one might permit some nominal story of why one chooses as one does ('I simply prefer this over that'), reducing the motivational question to one's instinctive pull towards one option over another. Whether this really captures radical choice is questionable, however – freedom seems to be epitomised by the prospect of finding oneself on a path, perhaps even irrespective of preference. A choice simply stands: that one moves one way rather than another is all that needs to be told about why we decide in certain ways. Even if a proponent of radical freedom thinks motivations were explicable in a nominal sense of one being moved towards *x* over *y*, their content and genealogy is hollowed out in serious ways. Critical explorations of what these motivations are, and how they have evolved and developed, are unnecessary, maybe even discouraged, because to probe with this depth is to gesture towards the fact that our choices draw upon sources and frameworks that go beyond freedom itself.

In reality, our intentions aren't the product of subjective creation *ex nihilo* but represent a particular genealogy that may not be value-neutral. The motivational conditions of our agency matter especially in situations where choice is closely bound up with oppressive, disempowering, and disabling narratives. Indeed, GC1 acknowledges the possibility of 'undue influence', particularly 'signs of fear, aggression, threat, deception or manipulation'.[43] Yet since its foregrounding concept of agency rejects the evaluative conditions of individuals' will and preferences (as shown above), there are few normative resources to pass judgement on choices that integrate skewed motivations based on internalised oppression, manipulation, and so on. Responses to pernicious narratives will inevitably be superficial: the presumptive weight of expressed will and preferences in GC1 is purchased at the cost of crucial evaluative resources needed to differentiate, not just between varying depths of commitment, but also

[42] DT Meyers, *Self, Society, and Personal Choice* (New York, Columbia University Press, 1989).
[43] UN CRPD Committee, *General Comment No 1* (n 7), [22].

the validity or distortion of certain narratives that feed into our motivational structure.

The case of RC's self-injurious behaviour illustrates the importance of attending to and evaluating the motivational conditions of agency. Multiple reasons lie behind the self-injurious behaviour of conditions like borderline personality disorder, including parasuicidal expression, attempts to regulate and control strong affect or to soothe and diminish pain, as well as self-abnegating motives (such as blaming and punishing the self). Importantly, these reasons are often egosyntonic: both the expressive act and reasons are internally consistent with a highly pernicious sense of self. Self-harming behaviour not only helps achieve a short-term goal (eg control of affect or pain) but also tracks and expresses an individual's personal identity and self-narrative in deep ways.

Consistent as they may be, delving further into the motivational sources of self-harming behaviour raises crucial questions as to how these intentions have been shaped, what status ought to be accorded to those preferences, and what it reveals about the individual's self-conception.[44] Borderline personality disorder is a clear example of why such questions matter, as the condition develops through past experiences of trauma, sexual and physical abuse, deprivation, punishment, and subjugation.[45] The invalidation, fear, and hostility characterising these relational contexts foster the internalisation of disrespect, distrust, and lack of esteem, as well as the endorsement of self-abnegating narratives of inherent worthlessness or badness, and motivations geared towards self-harm and self-punishment. An unstable sense of self emerges due to a distrust of their subjective experience and interpretation of reality, since the relational context encourages individuals to 'bring into play only those aspects of [their] inner experience that fit the inner experience of another'.[46] As one person described, she saw herself as 'not really a whole person, whatever a whole person is, I don't even know. I just know that I look at other people, and I just don't see myself equal to anybody'.[47] Her self-mutilating behaviour led to an incident of attempted suicide, of which she stated, 'I just felt that I was no good, that I was worthless. [...] I was just nobody'.[48]

Cases of borderline personality disorder therefore provide a bald illustration of the myriad of ways in which the genealogy and sources of our motivation bear on how one (dis)values and (in)validates oneself in agency, though

[44] C Kong, 'Nurture Before Responsibility: Self-in-Relation Competence and Self-Harm' (2019) 26 *Philosophy, Psychiatry, & Psychology* 1–18; C Kong, 'The Problem of Mental Capacity in Self-Harming Egosyntonic Disorder' in AM Phillips, TC de Campos, J Herring (eds), *Philosophical Foundations of Medical Law* (Oxford, Oxford University Press, 2020).

[45] JE Young, JS Klosko and ME Weishaar, *Schema Therapy: A Practitioner's Guide* (New York, Guilford Press, 2003).

[46] D Becker, *Through the Looking Glass: Women and Borderline Personality Disorder* (Boulder CO, Westview, 1997) 108.

[47] Young et al, *Schema Therapy* (n 45), 315.

[48] Ibid 316.

this condition is far from an isolated example.[49] Surrounding narratives form the basis of how we envisage our present and our future, how we assess and judge ourselves – and they likewise promote or hamstring our choices. Abusive socialisation and destructive narratives harm so deeply precisely because they encourage the development of internal sources of heteronomy, inauthenticity, and distortive self-narratives. But the impact of destructive narrative sources is ignored if the motivational conditions of agency are superficially construed and we retreat from engaging in the contrastive, evaluative language required to pass judgement. For someone with a deeply self-abnegating egosytonic disorder, this places the responsibility for their motivations and dysfunctional (yet explicable) modes of coping on their own shoulders – we have no means of picking apart their internalisation of intersubjective narratives of disrespect and worthlessness which frame their sense of self and agency within the world.

One might respond that our motivational sources are often so well inculcated within our sense of identity that distinguishing between that which stems from certain relational or social influences and that which is ours is impossible. If absolute clarity or absolute knowledge of ourselves or others was the ultimate aim, this would be a valid point. Instead, gaining critical awareness of the genealogy behind one's intentional action is sought so that one can move towards a *better*, *clearer*, or *more articulate* understanding of self and others. This in turn helps us and others to develop a more nuanced sense of what we are, and are not, responsible for, raising crucial evaluative questions as to whether certain self-interpretations warrant intersubjective validation or contestation.

Ignoring the motivational genealogy underlying one's agency therefore involves high normative stakes. Narratives of self-abnegation go unchallenged and by default, distorted, harmful notions of selfhood are subjectively and intersubjectively endorsed and able to acquire the status of truth. In other words, abandoning the motivational conditions incurs an explanatory and normative cost, not just for the individual, but for others: the absence of insight into the intersubjective and structural genesis of our desires, narratives, and agency as a whole, means, by default, the foreclosure of possible normative responses to pernicious sources and influences internalised by the self. Yet, widespread experiences of institutional and familial abuse, trauma, and neglect amongst individuals with mental impairments highlight the necessity of attending to these structural and intersubjective contexts, without which we fall short of providing the positive legal and ethical supports that are putatively owed to such persons

[49] Studies have shown the impact of self-stigma through pejorative connotations associated with particular diagnoses, eg PW Corrigan, et al, 'Self-stigma and coming out about one's mental illness' (2010) 38 *Journal of Community Psychology* 259–75. Also, Naoki Higashida in *Fall Down 7 Times Get up 8* (London, Sceptre, 2017) writes, 'Whenever I hear the words "Ah, it's because he's autistic", I feel dismay. That word, "autistic" packs a negative punch and this negativity, I think, corrodes the position of people with autism […] The fact is, we have no choice but to live in a society where autism is thought of exclusively as a sorrow and a hardship: a fact that triggers further sorrow and hardship. Even I, as a child, used to think, "Wow, if *only* I didn't have autism, wouldn't life be great?"' (261).

under the CRPD.[50] Only when motivational sources are seen as constitutive of agency does is it become possible to question self-expressions of internalised coercive control, abuse, and neglect. Resistance to disabling self-conceptions will hinge on our willingness and that of others to engage in qualitative evaluations about the vision of self, reflected in and expressed through one's choices.

From this theoretical standpoint, we have a much firmer grounding as to why, when faced with RC's conflicting choices and the imperative to support his legal capacity, we might justifiably query and delve further into the motives behind his self-harming behaviour in ways that differ from his religious convictions. As soon as the question of motivational sources is treated as legitimate, evaluative judgement helps sift out those narratives that foster or inhibit, clarify or distort, a person's agency. Importantly, this will impact on the narratives that are intersubjectively endorsed and validated: RC's advance decision around blood transfusion warrants respect in light of the evaluative capacities revealed in this choice as well as the implicit narratives which motivate it. By contrast, we do and should feel hesitant about indirectly communicating acceptance of his self-harming actions, particularly as they are an instinctive response to emotional distress which also potentially expresses narratives of self-abnegation. His long history of institutionalisation, particularly his early years in care, may well reveal traumatic and destructive roots to self-harming as a coping response. Through the radical choice model presumed in GC1, we have no means of articulating our discomfort here: one has no basis on which to question the value of those narratives or the validity of the self-harming impulse which follows. Rather disturbingly, unquestioned accession to his preferences results in the passive acceptance of RC's self-harming behaviour and its surrounding narratives, effectively reinforcing their truth and legitimacy. But anchoring support for RC's legal capacity in a conception of agency constituted by strong evaluation provides the requisite tools to tease apart the pernicious genesis of self-abnegating narratives and their subjective endorsement. These narratives and their sources would not be viewed as value-neutral when examined through the prism of evaluative and motivational conditions, meaning it may be deemed appropriate to withhold intersubjective validation and endorsement in favour of normative responses focused on supporting damaged agency, such as the process of 'narrative repair' that encourages counter-stories against disabling self-conceptions.[51]

What I am saying here in no way implies that RC's views ought to be dismissed; neither does it sanction coercive interventions or intersubjective blame for his behaviour. Nor is it my claim that choices which stem from problematic motivational sources ought to be immediately disregarded. My suggestion, rather, is that the mere expression of a person's will and preference is insufficient to warrant

[50] See, eg Care Quality Commission, *Out of Sight – Who Cares? A review of restraint, seclusion and segregation for autistic people, and people with a learning disability and/or mental health condition* (October 2020).

[51] H Lindemann Nelson, *Damaged Identities, Narrative Repair* (Ithaca NY, Cornell University Press, 2001). See also Young et al, *Schema Therapy* (n 45).

immediate accession by others. Cases of obvious self-harming behaviour show the import of incorporating assessments of motivational sources in our conception of agency – particularly in order to be attuned and responsive to the complex dynamic between socialised narratives and their internalisation by individuals. As such, we need to be willing to engage in evaluative judgement about them, sanctioning and providing suitable mechanisms of intervention where necessary.

IV. CONCLUSION

In this chapter, I have looked at the question of supporting legal capacity in a roundabout way, by arguing that we need to have a clearer idea of the foregrounding vision of agency that is owed support in the first place. The evaluative and motivational conditions of agency help frame the choices we make and constitute our sense of personal identity. Choice is situated within a horizon of qualitative evaluation, forcing us to move beyond what Frankfurt calls the 'economy of first-order desires'.[52] This tracks some deeply held intuitions about how certain commitments have particular weight, such as those bound up with attachments that resonate with the self in a deep way, beyond temporary whims. Moreover, considering our motivational sources is equally important because even those deep attachments could stem from highly questionable sources which tread a delicate – or not so delicate – line between coercion and support.

Taking into consideration the evaluative and motivational conditions of agency looks highly demanding. This is undeniable in some ways and it is not my suggestion that these conditions ought to be standards of legal or mental capacity. That still requires much more debate which goes beyond my limited scope here. My purpose, rather, has been to elucidate the costs of disregarding these as background conditions in our concept of agency which foregrounds legal capacity. At present, one has to rely on a Sartrean vision of existential freedom to make sense of the priority placed on the unquestioned enactment of subjective will and preferences in GC1. However, the inclusivity of radical freedom is purchased through circularity and incoherence at a conceptual level, and more seriously, through sacrificing the evaluative nuance that bestows human choice its significance. The demandingness of these conditions will need to be balanced with the imperative to foster respect and acceptance for the choices made by individuals with disabilities, but I have indicated how this enriched account of agency takes seriously the expressive and self-interpreting quality of individual narratives, carving out some crucial space between accommodating respect for the expressed choices of individuals, on one hand, and evaluating and fulfilling positive obligations to intervene, challenge, and question expressed choices which stem from self-abnegating narratives, on the other.

[52] Frankfurt, 'Freedom of the Will' (n 14), 12.

5

Functional Capacity Assessments by Healthcare Professionals: Problems and Mitigating Strategies

SHAUN O'KEEFFE

I. INTRODUCTION

IRELAND SIGNED THE UN Convention on the Rights of Persons with Disabilities (CRPD) in 2007 but it was noted that ratification would require reform of the legislative framework on legal capacity which was (and remains) governed by the Regulation of Lunacy (Ireland) Act 1871 and the ward of court system conducted in the High Court. The Assisted Decision Making (Capacity) Act (ADM Act) was signed into law on 30 December 2015 but is not yet fully in force. On 19 April 2018 Ireland became the final EU Member State to ratify and enter into force the UN Convention on the Rights of Persons with Disabilities.

In contrast to an 'all or nothing' process, a functional test of mental capacity is central to the ADM Act and will determine whether a person can access certain supports or have a decision-making representative imposed on them. In general, the functional model of capacity – the idea that decision-making capacity depends on the demands of a particular decision at a particular time and on the person's abilities and those demands[1] – focuses on the specific cognitive abilities relevant to decision-making and on the process of making a decision rather than the decision itself or its consequences. As in the English Mental Capacity Act 2005 (MCA), in the Irish ADM Act a person is treated as unable to make a decision for himself if he cannot 'understand the information relevant to the decision', 'retain that information long enough to make a voluntary choice', 'use or weigh that information as part of the process of making the decision' or 'communicate his or her decision'. Unlike the MCA where the second part of the definition of mental incapacity is that it is 'because of an impairment of, or

[1] T Grisso and PS Appelbaum, *Assessing Competence to Consent to Treatment: A Guide for Physicians and Other Health Professionals* (Oxford, Oxford University Press, 1998).

a disturbance in the functioning of, the mind or brain', the Irish ADM does not have such a 'diagnostic threshold'.

In this chapter I discuss firstly the relationship between legal and mental capacity and whether the functional approach to capacity is consistent with the CRPD.[2] Secondly, I examine some problems in how capacity assessments using the functional approach are conducted and interpreted by healthcare professionals and courts. Finally, I examine what strategies might be helpful to mitigate these problems.

II. FUNCTIONAL ASSESSMENT OF CAPACITY AND THE CRPD

Legal capacity is the formal ability to hold and to exercise rights and duties. The legal effect of the actions and decisions of a person will be recognised if the person has legal capacity; in contrast, actions and decisions will have no legal effect if a person lacks legal capacity. The ADM Act makes legal capacity conditional on legally defined mental capacity, ie the functional decision-making skills and competencies of a person.

Article 12 of the CRPD – equal recognition before the law – states that persons with disabilities have the right to recognition everywhere as persons before the law. The first General Comment (GC1) of the CRPD Committee states that legal systems based on capacity, when determination of capacity is based in whole or in part on disability, are in violation of Article 12.[3]

A. Discriminatory Effect of Functional Capacity Assessments?

Non-discrimination on the basis of disability is a core principle of the CRPD, and it defines 'Discrimination' in Article 2 as 'any distinction, exclusion or restriction on the basis of disability which has the purpose or effect of impairing or nullifying the recognition, enjoyment or exercise, on an equal basis with others, of all human rights and fundamental freedoms.' In Article 5(1), the CRPD goes on to state: 'all persons are equal before and under the law and are entitled without any discrimination to the equal protection and equal benefit of the law.'

Legal systems where the definition of mental incapacity is contingent on impairment or disturbed function of the mind or brain are explicitly discriminatory. The Irish ADM Act, for example, does not have such a diagnostic test. On the face of it, at least, it applies to all citizens rather than making distinctions on

[2] I am co-chair of the revision group for Ireland's Health Service Executive National Consent Policy, charged with ensuring the policy is consistent with the ADM Act. The views expressed in this chapter are entirely personal.

[3] UN Committee on the Rights of Persons with Disabilities, *General Comment No 1, Article 12: Equal Recognition Before the Law* (2014), UN Doc CRPD/C/GC/1.

the basis of disability: anyone may be found to lack capacity to make a particular decision at a particular time if there is a mismatch between the, primarily cognitive, demands of the decision and the person's abilities at that time.

However, according to the CRPD Committee, indirect discrimination under the CRPD denotes situations in which 'laws, policies or practices appear neutral at face value but have a disproportionate negative impact on a person with a disability'.[4] Thus, even if the absence of a diagnostic threshold avoids direct discrimination against those with disabilities that impair cognitive function, it is inevitable that any assessment with a cognitive dimension will disproportionately impact on such people.

It is arguable that a disproportionate impact need not necessarily represent (although it may raise the possibility of) discrimination. The UN Human Rights Committee, in its General Comment on Non-Discrimination, notes that it 'observes that not every differentiation of treatment will constitute discrimination, if the criteria for such differentiation are reasonable and objective and if the aim is to achieve a purpose which is legitimate under the Covenant.'[5]

Does the functional approach serve a legitimate purpose for those with disabilities under the CRPD? The many aims of the CRPD include promoting the effective enjoyment of the right to life (Article 10); protection from exploitation, violence and abuse (Article 16); protection of the physical and mental integrity of the person (Article 17) and ensuring access to health services (Article 25). These aims seem consistent with, and their achievement may be contingent on, a functional approach to capacity which recognises that some people with (or without) disabilities may be unable to decide for themselves, may need protection in situations of significant risk and provides a mechanism for identifying such cases.

B. Is the Functional Approach to Capacity 'Reasonable and Objective'?

In the next section, I will argue that in many circumstances, a functional approach to capacity in practice is unreasonable because the emphasis on rational decision-making and on the need for patients to reason with and balance options does not reflect how people actually make decisions in real life. The reliability of assessments is often poor and influenced by the biases and values of assessors. However, a functional approach is not always unreasonable or lacking objectivity. There is an objective difference between someone with advanced Alzheimer's disease who cannot make financial decisions and someone with mild dementia who can. This is not just a matter of opinion or dependent on social and

[4] UN Committee on the Rights of Persons with Disabilities, *General Comment No 6 on Equality and Non-discrimination* (2018) para 18(b).

[5] UN Human Rights Committee, *General Comment No 18, Non-discrimination* (1989/1994), para 13.

political factors (although the latter may indeed be important biases in practice in some cases). On the other hand, I suggest that in many cases the problems with functional determinations of capacity for those with disabilities are 'hard-wired' into that approach and as a result this constitutes discrimination.

C. Individual Autonomy versus Other Ethical Theories

The normative underpinning of the functional approach to capacity is an emphasis on the importance of individual autonomy, with the individual seen as an independent, isolated decision-maker. 'We live in the time of the triumph of autonomy' as Schneider put it.[6] The goal of giving people maximum liberty in devising and sculpting their own lives and values is on the face of it an admirable one. However, it is also a form of reductionism which ignores the complexity of life and how people often engage with and even rely on others when making decisions. Indeed, to some hardliners, exercising one's autonomy is mandatory: 'It is practically unwise and morally objectionable for the patient to forswear making medical decisions personally.'[7]

Other ethical theories and approaches emphasise the importance of relationships rather than isolation and individualism. Communitarianism is based upon the belief that a person's identity is largely defined by community relationships rather than individualism.[8] The ethics of care emphasises interpersonal relationships and care or benevolence as a virtue. More broadly, relational theorists highlight the importance of emotions and non-verbal communication and the support of others as essential elements of human decision-making.[9] Important relations are not just with family and friends but with healthcare professionals: Onora O'Neill, commenting on informed consent processes, noted the tension between autonomy and trust, with trust linked to relationships and mutual obligations, and individual autonomy to rights and adversarial claims.[10]

A sensitivity to the importance of relationships and societal factors is also helpful in understanding those, often the most vulnerable to neglect and abuse, who are *not* socially embedded. For example, in an Irish series of older 'reclusive' people living alone whose capacity to decide where they should live was called into question, most had one or more of the following: previous, sometimes prolonged, psychiatric admissions; childhood attendance at an industrial

[6] CE Schneider, *The Practice of Autonomy: patients, doctors and medical decisions* (New York, Oxford University Press, 1998) 11.

[7] D Brock, 'Informed consent' in D McLean (ed), *Life and Death: Philosophical Essays in Biomedical Ethics* (Cambridge, Cambridge University Press, 1993) 33.

[8] D Callahan, 'Individual good and common good: a communitarian approach to bioethics' (2003) 46(4) *Perspectives in Biology and Medicine* 496.

[9] ES Dove and others, 'Beyond individualism: Is there a place for relational autonomy in clinical practice and research?' (2017) 12(3) *Clinical Ethics* 150.

[10] O O'Neill, *Autonomy and Trust in Bioethics* (Cambridge, Cambridge University Press, 2002) 30, 83–85.

school (Irish institutions notorious for widespread physical, sexual, and emotional abuse); and previous imprisonment.[11] Many had very good reason to be distrustful and wary of officialdom.

Applied appropriately, a relational approach can enhance rather than override autonomy and support a person's control over his or her life and decision-making while also recognising people as socially embedded and encouraging a supported decision-making model. However, I'm not convinced that it is possible to eliminate *some* requirement for an ability to reason: one can debate where the threshold should lie, but there is arguably a stage where, no matter how much support is provided, one's decision should not have legal effect.

D. The Law as it is versus the Law as it should be

I have concluded earlier that the functional approach to assess incapacity does in many cases amount to indirect discrimination under the CRPD. In practice, of course, a healthcare practitioner is obliged to apply the law as it is, rather than the law that could or should be. The functional approach to capacity is deeply embedded in healthcare practice, in legal and ethical requirements for informed consent. It is important that the flaws and pitfalls in this approach are firstly recognised by practitioners (and courts), and that these are mitigated to the greatest extent possible.

III. PROBLEMS WITH THE FUNCTIONAL APPROACH TO CAPACITY

A. Statutory Criteria for Capacity Do Not Reflect How People Actually Make Decisions

A fundamental problem with the functional approach to capacity and the linking of mental capacity, determined on the basis of medical opinions, to legal capacity is identified by the CRPD Committee who note that 'it presumes to be able to accurately assess the inner-workings of the human mind' and that mental capacity is not 'an objective, scientific and naturally occurring phenomenon.'[12]

The functional approach, and the statutory criteria for capacity, do indeed reflect a crude and reductionist view of decision-making. Economists have long accepted that the model of the rational, calculating '*Homo economicus*' does not adequately reflect how financial decisions are made in real life. The same applies to other decisions such as choosing a spouse or making healthcare decisions. Rather than a cold analysis and weighing of risks and benefits, people

[11] M Brennan and others, 'Indications and outcomes of home visits by geriatricians' (2019) 10(3) *European Geriatric Medicine* 511.

[12] *General Comment No 6* (n 4) at para 14.

also rely on factors such as intuition, emotions, values, goals, experiences and cognitive heuristics (decision-making short cuts).

Different people often have different decision-making styles. Cultural factors may influence preferences for how decisions are made. While some prefer to make decisions on their own, as O'Neill has noted, people do not usually make decisions in a vacuum, and relational decision-making, involving other people such as family and friends, is common in real life. To increase the complexity further, individuals may have different decision-making styles depending on the nature and context of the decision. When people are very unwell, they may not want to, and may be in poor condition to, engage in a 'demanding exercise of individual autonomy' with a menu of complex options but may prefer to have somebody they trust recommend what seem the most appropriate option.[13]

Decision-making styles and preferences may also change with time. Older people without any cognitive disorder, for example, are slower at processing information processing and have more difficulty handling large amounts of information, and they may show a less reflective and more automatic and emotion-influenced style of decision-making than their younger selves.[14]

B. Poorly Defined and Arbitrary Criteria for Decision-making Capacity

There is a hierarchy of increasing difficulty in the statutory cognitive criteria as follows: communicate, retain, understand, use or weigh. 'Difficulty' applies in two ways: the extent of the mental 'hurdle' for the person; and difficulty in operationalising the criteria so they can be reliably assessed. There is empirical support for this contention. A review of 23 mental capacity disputes before England's Court of Protection found no case where inability to communicate a decision or to retain information was cited by a judge as the sole reason for a finding of lack of capacity.[15] In contrast, lack of understanding was the sole reason in two cases, inability to use or weigh information the sole reason in seven cases and both were cited in 13 cases.

In general, it is straightforward to determine whether someone can express a choice (using whatever means is necessary for the individual). 'Retaining information long enough' is also usually easily (and reliably) determined, and 'long enough' should suffice to ensure that capacity is not reduced to a test of short-term memory. 'Understanding' is more challenging. How much understanding is needed? What is the relevant information?

[13] O O'Neill, *Autonomy and Trust in Bioethics* (Cambridge, Cambridge University Press, 2002) 30 10) at 38.

[14] TR Bashore, KR Ridderinkhof and MW van der Molen, 'The decline of cognitive processing speed in old age' (1997) 6(6) *Current Directions in Psychological Science* 163; E Peters and others, 'Adult age differences in dual information processes: Implications for the role of affective and deliberative processes in older adults' decision making' (2007) 2(1) *Perspectives on Psychological Science* 1.

[15] AR Keene and others, 'Taking capacity seriously? Ten years of mental capacity disputes before England's Court of Protection' (2019) 62 *International Journal of Law and Psychiatry* 56.

'Use or weigh' is more difficult again to operationalise, especially considering the importance of the inability to 'use or weigh' in determinations of incapacity in dispute cases. The Law Commission in England noted three categories of case where an individual could understand information but could not use it and where their final decision was, as a result, divorced from their understanding of information: (1) 'compulsive conditions' such as anorexia nervosa; (2) where a mental disability meant they were 'unable to exert their will against some stronger person who wishes to influence their decisions or against some *force majeure* of circumstances'; and (3) where the person is prevented by their disability from being able to believe information.[16]

C. Use of Non-statutory Criteria in Capacity Determinations

Understand, retain, use or weigh, and communicate are the statutory functional abilities. However, there are other abilities that frequently feature in professional and judicial judgements regarding capacity, in particular the often-overlapping concepts of 'appreciation', 'insight' and 'executive brain function'.

(i) Appreciation (Belief)

Although appreciation, or belief, of the personal relevance of relevant information is not explicitly noted as a criterion in Irish and English legislation, in *Fitzpatrick v K*, Laffoy J. noted that:

> The patient's cognitive ability will have been impaired to the extent that he or she is incapable of making the decision to refuse the proffered treatment if the patient [...] has not *believed* the treatment information and, in particular, if it is the case that not accepting the treatment is likely to result in the patient's death, has not believed that outcome is likely (emphasis added).[17]

Similarly, in the seminal case of *Re C (Refusal of Medical Treatment)*, Thorpe J broke down the decision-making process into three stages: comprehending and retaining treatment information, believing it and, finally, weighing it in the balance to arrive at choice. He noted: 'Although his general capacity is impaired by schizophrenia [...] I am satisfied that he has understood and retained the relevant treatment information, that *in his own way he believes it*' (emphasis added).[18]

It might be argued that appreciation and understanding are closely related conceptually (and this was the approach taken by the Law Reform Commission in England).[19] Thomas Grisso and Paul Appelbaum acknowledged this but

[16] Law Commission of England and Wales, *Mental Incapacity* (Law COM No 231) (February 1995) para 3.17.
[17] *Fitzpatrick & Anor v K. and Another* [2008] IEHC 104.
[18] *Re C (Refusal of Medical Treatment)* [1994] 1 WLR 290.
[19] Law Commission, *Mental Incapacity* (n 16).

suggested that separation is useful, not least because it makes explicit the need for the patient to believe that the information provided is relevant to his own situation and that it is their future that is at stake.[20] Appreciating information also implies that people need to be able: 'to appreciate the nature and meaning of potential alternatives – what it would be like and "feel" like to be in possible future states and to undergo various experiences – and to integrate this appreciation into one's decision making'.[21]

It should be noted, however, that requiring 'appreciation' as part of understanding is often to raise the standard required of the person: it is easy enough to define a small amount of relevant information that the person must be able to comprehend. Requiring appreciation is to ask in effect: do you *really* understand this information? It is also possible for a person and for an assessor to differ in what they think it might 'feel' like to be in some possible future state (that neither has experienced) and for the latter to judge incapacity on the basis of that difference. For example, one third of people over 70 years have a fall each year: a person who has had several falls without serious injury may, perhaps over-optimistically, see their luck holding out, while those assessing them may foresee their death from a fall.

(ii) Insight

'Lack of insight' is a complex phenomenon that is regarded as a core feature of schizophrenia but can occur in other mental and neurological disorders. It has been argued that insight is the clinical concept that is most closely associated with the legal concept of capacity, and that it deserves a significant role in determination of decision-making capacity.[22] In practice this is what happens, and lack of insight is commonly reported, by psychiatrists in particular, as a cause of lack of capacity. This occurred, for example, in a third of 57 health and welfare judgments identified in Britain from 2007 to 2015.[23]

However, 'lack of insight' has been described as easier to use than to define,[24] and it has been argued that it can be misused in determining capacity. Some people will, for whatever reason, deny the undeniable, and lack of insight may be a reasonable description of this. However, extending 'insight' to its vernacular use as a form of self-knowledge that anyone may be judged to lack or possess to varying degrees in general (rather than as an indication of a serious illness)

[20] Grisso and Appelbaum, *Assessing Competence to Consent* (n 1) at 43.

[21] AE Buchanan and DW Brock, *Deciding for Others: The Ethics of Surrogate Decision Making* (Cambridge, Cambridge University Press, 1989) at 23.

[22] R Cairns and others, 'Prevalence and predictors of mental incapacity in psychiatric in-patients' (2005) 187 *British Journal of Psychiatry* 379.

[23] P Case, 'Negotiating the domain of mental capacity: Clinical judgement or judicial diagnosis?' (2016) 16(3–4) *Medical Law International* 174.

[24] KWM Fulford, 'Insight and delusion: from Jaspers to Kraeplin and back again via Austin' in X Amador and A David (eds), *Insight and Psychosis*, 2nd edn (Oxford, Oxford University Press, 2004).

risks its misuse in capacity assessments. Lack of insight might then operate as a facile label for someone who doesn't comply with recommended interventions or has different values to an assessor. As Paula Case has noted:

> There are a number of implications of allowing psychiatry to dominate this terrain, not least that [...] clinical discourse, which makes reference to non-statutory terminology such as 'lack of insight' and 'non-compliance' are imported into the business of capacity assessment. This terminology, if used lazily and without clear reference to the statutory criteria, has the potential to muddy the waters of assessing P's capacity. At its worst, it can mask value judgements.[25]

The case of the trial for murder of the Unabomber, Theodore Kaczynski, provides an example of the circular arguments generated by reliance on 'insight'. He refused an insanity defence – by which his anti-technological manifesto would be seen as a sign of madness – and accepted a life sentence. His legal team had argued that he suffered from an impairment of insight caused by schizophrenia: thus, by denying his madness, he only confirmed it. Alston Chase, noting the comparison with the novel *Catch 22*, where claiming to be too ill for combat only proved one's fitness, wrote: 'a refusal to admit to being insane or to cooperate with people who are paid to pronounce one insane cannot be taken seriously as proof of insanity.'[26]

(iii) Executive (Frontal Lobe) Dysfunction

'Executive functions' of the brain, meaning cognitive functions involved in planning and directing complex goal-directed behaviours, may be especially relevant to decision-making. Executive functions are held to reside primarily in the frontal lobes of the brain, and in brain damage to this area (including 'frontal lobe dementias') there may be profound disturbance of behaviour and judgement with relative preservation of other cognitive functions. However, tests also identify sizeable proportions of patients with conditions such as diabetes mellitus and lung disease as having abnormal tests of executive function, potentially bringing them into the lack of capacity net (especially if they do not follow treatment recommendations).[27]

It is not uncommon in practice to find a circular argument: if you are making 'bad' decisions, it is probably because you have frontal lobe or executive dysfunction; this in turn justifies – and provides a scientific (or pseudoscientific) justification and jargon – for a finding of lack of capacity. Thus, in *NCC v PB and TB*, one expert witness stated that the person 'has compromised executive function stemming from her frontal lobe' and another that she had 'frontal lobe

[25] Case, 'Negotiating the domain of mental capacity' (n 23) at 200.

[26] A Chase, 'Harvard and the making of the Unabomber' (2000) 285(6) *Atlantic Monthly* 41.

[27] JE Schillerstrom, MS Horton and DR Royall, 'The impact of medical illness on executive function' (2005) 46 *Psychosomatics* 508.

damage', which he described as 'mild brain damage'.[28] One may well conclude reading the facts of this case that the relevant person had great difficulty making decisions in her own interest, but linking this to the frontal lobes seems entirely speculative. Ultimately, a deficit in executive functioning was tied to the inability to 'use or weigh' information in the judgment, but the reason for linking these was unclear.

The reasoning in another case relied on the person's decline in 'executive functioning' sufficient to interfere with 'complex abstract thinking' and with the person's ability to manage his business affairs.[29] Again, the facts in this case would suggest that the person had great difficulty managing his affairs, but the language of the statutory criteria was not used, and one might argue, in any event, that complex abstract thinking is difficult for most people and an unfair standard to apply.

D. Poor Reliability of Clinical Capacity Assessments

If clinicians are to be given an important role in assessing decision-making capacity, and given the potentially important consequences of a legal judgment that someone lacks capacity to make a decision, one might hope that clinicians, judging according to the same legal standard, would show good agreement in their judgements of capacity. However, there is substantial evidence for poor agreement between clinicians in many cases.[30] This is not just a matter of ignorance of the appropriate legal standard (although this occurs, and misuse and misinterpretation of brief mental-function tests, as providing definitive evidence about capacity, remain common). Even experts who are knowledgeable about, and trained in, the appropriate standard show poor agreement. For example, a major study examining competency judgements of people with mild dementia to make their own decisions found no greater than chance agreement – the equivalent of tossing a coin.[31]

The English MCA (but not the Irish legislation) has a diagnostic threshold – an identifiable impairment or disturbance of mental function usually (but not always) constituted by the diagnosis of a condition (such as a mental disorder, learning disability or brain damage) – as stage 1 in the process of assessing capacity and separate from the functional criteria. However, what is a 'mental disorder'? A recent large survey including psychiatrists and non-psychiatric physicians showed how little agreement there is.[32] Although psychiatrists are

[28] *NCC v PB and TB* [2014] EWCOP 14.

[29] *A, B and C v X and Z* [2012] EWHC 2400 (COP).

[30] SYH Kim and others, 'Current state of research on decision-making competence of cognitively impaired elderly persons' (2002) 10 *American Journal of Geriatric Psychiatry* 151.

[31] DC Marson and others, 'Consistency of physician judgments of capacity to consent in mild Alzheimer's disease' (1997) 45 *Journal of the American Geriatrics Society* 453.

[32] KAO Tikkinen and others, 'Public, health professional and legislator perspectives on the concept of psychiatric disease: a population-based survey' (2019) 9(6) *BMJ Open* 1.

more inclined to consider mental health-related states of being as diseases compared with other physicians, even among psychiatrists a substantial minority were unconvinced that, for example, personality disorder or attention-deficit disorder, were psychological diseases.

There are a number of (related and overlapping) possible contributors to this alarming finding: lack of clarity about appropriate thresholds; lack of standardisation of assessment; and intrusion of the personal values of assessors.

(i) Arbitrariness of Thresholds for Capacity

From a clinical and indeed a logical perspective, capacity and relevant cognitive abilities exist on a continuous scale such that one may have more or less capacity or of its constituents. However, legal competence requires a yes or no decision as to whether a patient's mental capacity is sufficient to entitle them to decide for themselves. What threshold is to be applied by an assessor (or court for that matter)? If the standard is high, many people will fail and be found incapable of making a decision; if low, many will pass but might risk suffering the consequences of poor – and perhaps poorly understood or reasoned – decisions.

Decisions vary in their complexity, their nature and in their possible consequences. If more complex decisions require greater cognitive abilities, this will inevitably mean a higher effective threshold for capacity. Similarly, different types of decisions may have different cognitive burdens: financial decisions, in particular, present challenges to those with any significant cognitive difficulties. It also seems reasonable that someone's threshold for capacity should be placed higher if their decision may place others at risk (such as driving a commercial vehicle) or if benefit to themselves is likely to be minimal (such as participating in a clinical trial).

One approach is for the threshold for decision-making capacity to be adjusted depending on the consequences of that decision – a sliding-scale or risk-relative approach. In a medical setting, the standard would effectively depend on whether or not a person was agreeing with the recommended treatment. A lower threshold could be set if a patient were accepting a treatment with a high likelihood of benefit and relatively low risk of harm, but a higher threshold set if he or she were refusing the same treatment. For a high-risk treatment with less certain benefit, the higher threshold would be set for accepting the treatment. This approach has been taken in several legal judgments including, for example, *Re M.B. (Medical Treatment)* where Butler-Sloss LJ noted '[t]he graver the consequences of the decision, the commensurately greater the level of competence is required to take the decision.'[33]

The sliding-scale approach is superficially appealing and logical. However, as Tom Beauchamp and James Childress have noted, making a person's competence contingent on the decision's outcome or importance 'is conceptually and

[33] *Re M.B. (Medical Treatment)* [1997] 2 FLR 427.

morally perilous.'[34] Allowing an assessor to juggle the standard and judging capacity by whether or not the decision is a 'good' one or not represents a return 'through the back door' to paternalism and to an outcome model of capacity. The consequences of making the 'wrong' decision *might* be serious but it would also be easy to manipulate the threshold for capacity based on 'what ifs' rather than certainty of a poor outcome.

(ii) Biases of Assessors and Judges in Making Capacity Determinations

Provision (and consumption of) healthcare is a value-laden affair. Patients' values influence their preferences and decisions. Healthcare professionals inevitably bring both 'official' values (the importance of improved health and preservation of life) and 'private' (often subconscious) values and biases when making recommendations and judgements. Assessments of decision-making capacity are no different to other assessments. Such judgements are not based solely on descriptions of the criteria but are intrinsically normative in nature and will be influenced by the values of the assessor. Hence, it is unsurprising that people may be evaluated differently depending on which assessor they encounter, and that it might be possible to 'shop around' for a hawk (paternalistic) or a dove (libertarian) assessor depending on which answer is sought in a given case.

A recent study provides empirical support for the influence of clinicians' personal values on capacity judgements. A large survey of personality traits and values in senior physicians in Switzerland found that physicians who valued relatively highly success in life and the maintenance and protection of their own prestige and public image were more likely to favour risk relativity – applying a higher standard for mental abilities required to judge someone as capacitous if a decision may have serious adverse consequences.[35] In contrast, physicians who strongly emphasised equal opportunity and equal treatment for all, and conformity to laws and rules, were less supportive of risk relativity.

Healthcare professionals may also be influenced by the normative climate of the culture in determining capacity. An expectation that 'the vulnerable' will be 'protected' is widespread and, in the event of a person's decision resulting in a poor outcome, an assessor might expect criticism that he or she didn't foresee and prevent this outcome.

Courts may sometimes be unduly deferential to the judgements of professionals. Anselm Eldergill has commented, for example, in the context of personal welfare disputes under the MCA, on the reluctance of some judges to override the recommendations of professionals or of the Official Solicitor and that such

[34] TL Beauchamp and JF Childress, *Principles of Biomedical Ethics*, 5th edn (Oxford, Oxford University Press, 2001), 138–41.

[35] H Hermann, M Trachsel and N Biller-Andorno, 'Physicians' personal values in determining medical decision-making capacity: a survey study' (2015) 41(9) *Journal of Medical Ethics* 739.

judges add '"little value" to the process from the viewpoint of the incapacitated person and their family'.[36]

Ultimately, the flexibility in interpreting the statutory criteria allows considerable latitude to assessors and courts and it is arguable that the statutory criteria for capacity determinations and the expert opinions of healthcare professionals often provide an objective veneer to what are often mainly subjective judgements. As Alec Buchanan has noted: 'where gravity is extreme, doctors and courts allow their dislike of what a patient proposes to outweigh their desire to see that person's wishes respected, whatever the patient's capacity.'[37]

IV. IMPROVING PRACTICE IN FUNCTIONAL ASSESSMENTS OF CAPACITY

These are serious and troubling problems and not easily rectified. The following are some strategies – either as points of emphasis in codes of practice and guidelines for healthcare professionals or as procedural safeguards – that I believe may be helpful.

A. Give Non-cognitive Factors Adequate Weight

A purely rationalism-based assessment of capacity based on understanding and reasoning is artificial and unrealistic and hence unreasonable. Conflicts between values, goals and emotions may often underlie differences between those seeking a capacity assessment and those being assessed. Of course, 'reasoning' about a treatment decision implies that individual emotions, values, goals and experiences should be balanced against, say, the medical pros and cons of a particular decision. However, people may often have difficulty in articulating, and having to explain, often deep-seated values. Onerous and rationalistic capacity criteria are particularly unfair on those with any cognitive difficulties:

> While it is likely that the healthy and the well-educated will be able to provide the 'correct' answers to questions based on such an assessment, irrespective of how they really make their decisions (rather like cheating on an aptitude test), this approach is also likely to disempower the poorly educated, the eccentric, the particularly honest and those with cognitive or sensory difficulties.[38]

Questions about the ability of a person to 'use or weigh' information particularly arise in the context of risky behaviour on the part of the person. In such

[36] A Eldergill 'DOLs: Courts v Tribunals' (2017): https://www.ucc.ie/academic/law/docs/mental-health/conferences/2017/12.30-A.Eldergill-08April2017.pdf, accessed 21 May 2021.

[37] A Buchanan, 'Mental capacity, legal competence and consent to treatment' (2004) 97 *Journal of the Royal Society of Medicine* 416.

[38] ST O'Keeffe, 'Clinician's perspective on issues of capacity in care' (2008) 14 *Medico-Legal Journal of Ireland* 14, 45.

cases, 'use or weigh' is inextricably linked with values, those of the person as well as those of healthcare professionals and judges. As McDonald J noted:

> a person cannot be considered to be unable to use and weigh information simply on the basis that he or she has applied his or her own values or outlook to that information in making the decision in question and chosen to attach no weight to that information in the decision making process.[39]

Hence, it is essential that anyone assessing capacity takes care to elicit the broader values and goals of the person, the person's preferred decision-making style and his or her background and experiences. In many cases, seeing the person's preferences from the person's own perspective will make them explicable and understandable. In other cases, it may appear that the person's choices are inconsistent with prior values or that values and emotions are problematic and interfere with their decision-making abilities.[40] Overall, while the statutory criteria remain at the heart of assessment, there should be a deeper, more individual and context-specific assessment than an arid and rigid 'measurement' of capacity based entirely on the criteria.

B. Challenge the Use of Non-statutory Criteria

The concepts of 'appreciation', 'insight' and 'executive brain function' can in some cases be regarded as imbedded within the concepts of understanding and of using and weighing information. In other cases, however, it is not always clear just how these abilities map onto the statutory criteria. In particular, the lack of clarity about how 'lack of insight' and 'impaired executive/frontal lobe function' are defined means they can easily be used to medicalise dissent and to widen the net of capacity assessments. These terms should be seen as 'red flags' in any assessment report, and their use without clear reference to and justification by the statutory criteria should be challenged.

C. Standardisation of Capacity Assessment

One appealing approach to reduce the arbitrariness of capacity judgements and the poor agreement among assessors is to standardise assessments and 'scoring systems'. Multiple such instruments have been developed and validated.[41]

[39] *King's College Hospital NHS Foundation Trust v C and V* [2015] EWCOP 80.

[40] H Hermann and others, 'Emotion and value in the evaluation of medical decision-making capacity: A narrative review of arguments' (2016) 7 *Frontiers in psychology* 765.

[41] SYH Kim and others, 'Current state of research on decision-making competence of cognitively impaired elderly persons' (2002) 10 *American Journal of Geriatric Psychiatry* 151. See for a review of available instruments LB Dunn and others, 'Assessing decisional capacity for clinical research or treatment: a review of instruments' (2006) 163 *American Journal of Psychiatry* 1323.

Most rely on a semi-structured interview, but they vary greatly in format, in whether they are 'generic' or adaptable to real decisions, in item content and in scoring procedures. None is intended as a stand-alone assessment of capacity; rather, they are designed as an adjunct to professional assessment. While none can be regarded as the 'gold standard', the MacArthur competence assessment tool-treatment (MacCAT-T) is the most widely used and the best validated.[42]

Overall, studies show that when clinicians use such instruments, their judgements of competence tend to achieve good inter-rater (different clinicians rating the same interview of the patient) agreement and there is greater transparency as to how they reached their judgements.[43] Importantly, it has also been found that legal assessments of mental incapacity, based on definitions used in Ireland and in other jurisdictions, agree closely with clinical assessments using the MacCAT-T.[44]

In 58 studies where the functional capacity of patients to make decisions was examined systematically, usually by psychiatrists using a standardised capacity assessment tool, the average proportion of patients with incapacity was 45 per cent; for medical settings, the average proportion of patients with incapacity was 34 per cent.[45] One of the largest such studies examined the actual decisions to be made by hospital patients (rather than the theoretical vignettes used in many other studies). It concluded that 40 per cent of hospital patients of all ages and more than 70 per cent of older patients were incompetent to make the particular decisions they faced.[46]

These startling findings suggest that use of standardised instruments runs the risk of widespread 'failure' of persons whose capacity is assessed. However, these tools consistently identified a lack of capacity in many patients that had not been noticed by their clinicians or relatives. While systematic assessment studies are interesting, and academically important, they should not be used as screening tests in actual practice. In real life, the presumption of capacity would and should have applied: 'P has to "prove" nothing'.[47] Also, one might expect that decision-making supported by one's actual clinician would have better results than assessment by an 'outside' psychiatrist. Thus, used appropriately, standardised assessments may be helpful in improving the reliability and transparency of assessments.

[42] T Grisso, PS Appelbaum and C Hill-Fotouhi 'The MacCAT-T: a clinical tool to assess patients' capacities to make treatment decisions' (1997) 48 *Psychiatric Services* 1415.

[43] RJ Gurrera and others, 'Agreement between instruments for rating treatment decisional capacity' (2007) 15 *American Journal of Geriatric Psychiatry* 268.

[44] A Curley and others, 'Concordance of mental capacity assessments based on legal and clinical criteria: A cross-sectional study of psychiatry inpatients' (2019) 276 *Psychiatry Research* 160.

[45] P Lepping, T Stanly and J Turner, 'Systematic review on the prevalence of lack of capacity in medical and psychiatric settings' (2015) 15(4) *Clinical Medicine* 337.

[46] V Raymont and others, 'Prevalence of mental incapacity in medical inpatients and associated risk factors: cross-sectional study' (2004) 364 *The Lancet* 1421.

[47] 39 Essex Chambers (AR Keene et al), 'A Brief Guide to Carrying Out Mental Capacity Assessments' (2021): www.39essex.com/mental-capacity-guidance-note-brief-guide-carrying-capacity-assessments/, last accessed 21 May 2021.

D. Setting an Attainable Threshold for Capacity and Supporting the Person to Reach it

It is arguable that the cognitive demands of capacity are surprisingly low, unless healthcare professionals make them otherwise. Research using vignettes in children suggests that the intellectual capabilities needed to provide informed consent are attained by age 14 years for full adult information and by nine years for simplified information.[48] If the amount of information provided, and how and when it is provided, are tailored to the person's needs and abilities and if the person is adequately supported, then facilitating people to make their own decisions in their own way is achievable in most circumstances.

The key to success in supporting people to make their own decisions and respecting those decisions often lies more in the attitude of healthcare professionals than in the abilities, or lack of abilities, of people. The risk for people who have difficulties making decisions is that the bar will be set higher for them, that assessors are tempted to 'dig deeper' and that the presumption of capacity is reversed, especially if the person is thought to be making an unwise choice.

It is easy for a healthcare professional assessing capacity to act like an *examiner*: setting, and marking an exam, and perhaps with one eye on maintaining standards and avoiding grade inflation. Instead, when interacting with a person who needs to make a decision, he or she needs to be like a *teacher* dealing with a student facing an exam. Good teachers seek to support their students and want them to do well. They have a responsibility to provide information effectively to their students in lessons, by encouraging questions and by providing learning materials such as notes. If a student is 'weak' or disadvantaged in some way, they will take extra time and make an extra effort to help that student. If the student does not do well, it also reflects badly on their teachers. Finally, good teachers know there is more to life than exams: they want their students to develop and thrive in the broadest sense.

E. Procedural Safeguards to Ensure Fairness during Capacity Assessments

If an assessor is to determine that somebody may lack the ability to retain, understand, use and weigh information in order to make decisions, an assessment process must occur to obtain the information necessary to make that determination. There are a number of ways in which capacity assessments may be conducted that are potentially unfair to the person by: not providing all documentation that may be used by an assessor in forming an opinion; not informing a person explicitly when capacity is being assessed; and not seeking informed

[48] LA Weithorn and SB Campbell, 'The competency of children and adolescents to make informed treatment decisions' (1982) 53 *Child Development* 1589.

consent for a capacity assessment. It is important that procedural safeguards are in place to rectify these problems, and striking how silent most codes and guidelines for healthcare professionals are on these issues.

(i) Ensuring the Person has Access to All Documentation

There should be some 'trigger' or reason suggesting the need for a capacity assessment in the first place. This may include concerns raised or observations by a variety of people in the person's life such as family and friends, healthcare professionals and others. If there are third-party letters, reports or notes suggesting decision-making incapacity – even if submitted 'confidentially' – which may influence or be used by an assessor in forming an opinion (and perhaps writing a report) regarding capacity, the person is entitled to see them, just as a defendant in a trial would be entitled to know the charges and the evidence against him or her.

(ii) Informing a Person Explicitly when Capacity is Being Assessed

For doctors, Appelbaum has suggested that 'assessment of the patient's capacity to make decisions is an intrinsic aspect of every physician-patient interaction. Usually, the assessment will be implicit …'[49] It is certainly true that the doctors interacting with patients will form a view as to whether or not they may have difficulties in understanding and processing information in order to reach a decision. They should tailor the way information is presented to the individual person according to his or her needs. Framed as an approach to support people to make their own decisions, this is a useful, even essential, approach. However, there is also the more troubling implication that doctors may conduct covert assessments of decision-making capacity and potentially reach conclusions that the person, despite all efforts of support, does not have capacity.

It may be difficult sometimes to determine where the dividing line is, particularly during what is sometimes called an 'informal' assessment, but there is an important difference between evaluation to support a person's decision-making and an evaluation that might result in the person losing the right to make certain decisions. The former has a clear therapeutic purpose; the latter, a more forensic purpose. If, during a conversation the thoughts of the clinician gradually morph from 'how can I help him or her understand?' to mentally ticking off the statutory criteria for incapacity, a change in the purpose and possible outcome of that conversation has occurred. A capacity assessment is distinct from usual care or from an 'ordinary' conversation between a clinician and patient about treatment options, and it should not be conducted by stealth.

[49] PS Appelbaum, 'Assessment of patients' competence to consent to treatment' (2007) 357(18) *New England Journal of Medicine* 1834.

(iii) Need for Informed Consent for Capacity Assessment

An assessment regarding capacity to make a particular decision is an intervention itself and one distinct from the original decision. As an intervention, informed consent is required. There is no justification for treating a capacity assessment differently from any other intervention. A capacity assessment is not a trivial matter. There are potential benefits and risks for the person, and they are entitled to know and consider these and make their own decision whether to participate. An 'implied consent' from someone who answers an assessor's questions in ignorance of the purpose of those questions and of what is at stake is, I suggest, invalid.

There are a number of reasons to believe that the need for informed consent is not recognised and that consent is not obtained. There is a vast disparity between the extensive literature examining how to assess the capacity of someone to give informed consent to an intervention and the meagre literature discussing informed consent for a capacity assessment.[50] Recommendations that consent be sought prior to capacity assessments are made primarily to 'outside' professionals such as consultation-liaison psychiatrists in North America, where, for example, Kathryn Kaye and Michael Kenny state: 'In all cases, you should have written authorization before you begin to directly examine a person for forensic purposes'.[51]

In contrast, the need for explicit consent is not mentioned in guides to capacity assessment for healthcare professionals, although there are discussions of how to proceed if someone refuses or will not agree to or will not 'cooperate' with assessment. For example, the Code of Practice for the MCA states:

> There may be circumstances in which a person whose capacity is in doubt refuses to undergo an assessment of capacity or refuses to be examined by a doctor or other professional. In these circumstances, it might help to explain to someone refusing an assessment why it is needed and what the consequences of refusal are.[52]

This is the first mention in this code of explaining to the person themselves why an assessment is needed.

The same requirements apply to consent for capacity assessments as to other interventions: the person must receive sufficient information in a comprehensible manner about the nature, purpose, benefits and risks of the intervention; he or she must not be acting under duress and must understand they have a choice whether or not to proceed; and he or she must have the capacity to make the particular decision. A person asked to cooperate in a capacity assessment

[50] J Moye, 'Clinical frameworks for capacity assessment' in SH Qualls and MA Smyer (eds), *Changes in decision-making capacity in older adults: Assessment and intervention* (Hoboken, NJ, John Wiley & Sons, 2007).

[51] K Kaye and M Kenny, 'The business of geropsychology: Billing and preparing legal reports and testimony' in SH Qualls and MA Smyer (eds), *Changes in decision-making capacity in older adults: Assessment and intervention*. (Hoboken, NJ, John Wiley & Sons, 2007).

[52] MCA Code of Practice (2007) para 4.57.

should receive a truthful explanation of the risks of cooperation, namely that they may lose the right to make some decisions for themselves. It is arguable that an outside assessor – someone not directly involved with the person's care called in specifically to assess capacity – should also seek consent to access the person's confidential information for the purpose of the assessment.

It is likely that seeking consent will, especially if it may result in the person's own preferences being disregarded, result in more refusals of assessments than acceptances. Such a person might reasonably say 'What's the benefit for me of submitting to this assessment?'. Jeffrey Spike, commenting on a patient who refused to talk to a psychiatrist, reached the (only partly tongue in cheek) conclusion that: 'A patient's defiance and refusal to talk to psychiatry may be prima facie evidence of capacity' on the grounds that if a patient had enough insight to understand what psychiatry was there for, and to understand the risk of being found to lack capacity, it was sensible to refuse to take that risk.[53] However, the possibility of refusal is never a reason for not seeking consent for an intervention. If someone refuses to consent to a capacity assessment to determine whether they have capacity to consent to a different intervention, do they need a capacity assessment to determine their capacity to give or refuse consent to the original capacity assessment? Of course, this may seem absurd at first but perhaps they do![54]

F. Importance of Independent Advocacy

I have argued that healthcare professionals should behave as good teachers do when helping a student to pass an important exam. However, sometimes, for whatever reasons, professionals do not act this way, and the safeguards proposed above are not in place. The exam dream (or nightmare) is a common one: it is the day of an important exam and you realise that you did the wrong course or had forgotten the exam or are not prepared in some way. A person facing a capacity assessment that might remove their right to make their own decision is in a novel and threatening situation. They will be judged (marked) on their responses and failure will have serious consequences. They often have not had a chance to prepare or to study the relevant information. Indeed, they may never have seen some of the relevant information (such as previous reports regarding their conduct). The 'formal' assessment interview may be the culmination of previous informal capacity assessments (continuous assessment) of which they were unaware. The examiner may be biased and predisposed to fail them.

[53] JP Spike, 'Informed consent is the essence of capacity assessment' (2017) 45(1) *The Journal of Law, Medicine & Ethics* 95.

[54] SA Hurst, 'When patients refuse assessment of decision-making capacity: how should clinicians respond?' (2004) 164(16) *Archives of Internal Medicine* 1757.

Providing the person with an independent advocate, if they agree, is an important protection in these circumstances and is particularly vital if a finding of incapacity may result in the person's own wishes and preferences being overturned. In other circumstances, of course, the person, such as a patient in hospital, can rely on family or friends, to 'fight their corner' if they are too sick to do so effectively for themselves. When it comes to issues regarding capacity, however, it is not uncommon to find that family and friends share the concerns of healthcare professionals about decision-making capacity and may even have initiated a capacity assessment. Their intentions, and those of professionals, are usually good (and their concerns may be well-founded), but the person needs someone to ensure their own voice is heard to best effect.

The roles of an advocate might include preparation for a capacity assessment, such as reading reports and helping the person to clarify their own wishes and preferences, ensuring that assessments occur at a time and in a place that suits the person, sitting in on the assessment itself and ensuring it is conducted fairly, and seeking a second opinion on behalf of the person if necessary.

G. What's it Like to Have Your Capacity Called into Question?

Much of the literature on capacity assessments is written for, and from the perspective of, the professionals and often as a 'how to do' technical manual. There is an extensive literature on the experience and perspective of people who interact with mental health services. An underlying theme of many accounts is of coercion (often extra-legal), of being a passive recipient of care, of the often illusory nature of 'choice', and of a lack of respect for personal decision-making.[55] However, there is little on the specific experience, in mental health services and elsewhere, of having one's capacity called into question and assessed. I suspect, for the reasons given earlier, that this is stressful and threatening for many, but there is a pressing need for exploration of this topic to guide better practice.

V. CONCLUSIONS

In many circumstances, a functional approach to capacity in practice is unreasonable because the emphasis on rational decision-making and on the need for patients to reason with and balance options does not reflect how people actually make decisions in real life. The reliability of assessments is often poor and influenced by the biases and values of assessors. However, a functional approach

[55] BA Pescosolido, CB Gardner and KM Lubell, 'How people get into mental health services: Stories of choice, coercion and "muddling through" from "first-timers"' (1998) 46(2) *Social Science & Medicine* 275; BG Link and JC Phelan, 'Labeling and stigma' in CS Aneshensel, JC Phelan and A Bierman (eds), *Handbook of the sociology of mental health* (Dordrecht, Springer, 2013) 525.

is not always unreasonable or lacking objectivity. There are significant problems in how capacity assessments using the functional approach are conducted and interpreted by healthcare professionals. Some problems seem to be intrinsic difficulties with this approach to capacity, while others relate to how the functional approach is applied by professionals. Procedural safeguards, such as ensuring the person has access to all documentation prior to assessment, informing a person explicitly when capacity is being assessed and seeking informed consent for assessment, and ready access to independent advocacy are likely to be particularly helpful in mitigating such problems.

6

Charting a Path to Non-coercive Mental Healthcare: The Rhizomatic Nature of Universal Legal Capacity and the Support Paradigm

SUZANNE DOYLE GUILLOUD[1]

I. INTRODUCTION

DISCOURSE SURROUNDING THE right to liberty of persons with psychosocial disabilities under the UN Convention on the Rights of Persons with Disabilities (CRPD), specifically its interpretation by the Committee on the Rights of Persons with Disabilities ('CRPD Committee' or 'Committee') as requiring States to abandon systems of coercive mental healthcare, has seen the entrenchment of normative chasms. Those opposed to the abolition of such mechanisms have raised concerns of excessive idealism or libertarianism on the part of both the Committee and disability rights advocates who call for its implementation. Whilst the interpretation of Article 12 of the CRPD and its requirement for the recognition of universal legal capacity has been much disputed, both at the State Party level and amongst commentators within the academic literature,[2] there have at least been some moves towards its

[1] My thanks to the participants at the 'Supporting Legal Capacity in Socio-Legal Context' workshop which took place at the International Institute for the Sociology of Law in Oñati, Spain in July 2019 for their helpful feedback on an earlier draft of this chapter. All errors are my own.

[2] For commentary supportive of the CRPD Committee's interpretation of Article 12, see A Arstein-Kerslake and E Flynn, 'The General Comment on Article 12 of the Convention on the Rights of Persons with Disabilities: a roadmap for equality before the law' (2016) 20(4) *The International Journal of Human Rights* 471. For examples of commentary which disagrees with either the premise and/or feasibility of the CRPD's interpretation of the requirements of Article 12, see G Szmukler, R Daw and F Callard, 'Mental health law and the UN Convention on the rights of persons with disabilities' (2014) 37 *International Journal of Law and Psychiatry* 245. For examples of States Parties' objections to the Committee's interpretation of Article 12, see UN Office of the High Commissioner for Human Rights, 'Submissions to the Draft General Comment on Article 12 of the Convention – Equal Recognition before the Law and Draft General Comment on Article 9 of the Convention – Accessibility': https://www.ohchr.org/EN/HRBodies/CRPD/Pages/DGCArticles12And9.aspx, last accessed 25 October 2020.

implementation amongst States,[3] although the compatibility of such reforms with the CRPD Committee's interpretation of the requirements of Article 12 is doubtful and has not been accepted by the Committee itself.[4] The same cannot be said for the right to liberty as contained in Article 14, which, along with what are perceived to be the more boundary-pushing elements of Article 12, has been either expressly or implicitly rejected by most signatories to the CRPD.

Within this chapter, focus will be placed on the interconnectivity of the rights contained in the CRPD – a dimension of the social model upon which the treaty is based, and which has been consistently emphasised by the CRPD Committee in its Concluding Observations – as a means by which to overcome these barriers to realisation. Such an approach is consistent with views which have been espoused by a number of commentators on the CRPD's provisions as they apply to persons with psychosocial disabilities,[5] with Anna Arstein-Kerslake suggesting that the CRPD 'pushes human rights law back to its origins in the Universal Declaration where civil and political rights and social, economic and cultural rights co-exist'.[6] She finds in the CRPD

> an acknowledgement that the protection of the individual within the colossal institutional legal and societal structures that exist can only occur if there is a living, breathing arterial network connecting the rights and evermore pumping lifeblood between the rights in order to allow them to grow simultaneously – feeding off each other and providing nutrients to each other. Within this structure, each right nourishes the other, but simultaneously struggles against the others for access to nourishment. The balance of rights is an eternal war that is both confounding and essential to the growth of each right.[7]

This chapter will argue that it is the flourishing of that 'arterial network', with supported decision-making flowing throughout, which will move States Parties towards the realisation of the right to liberty of persons with disabilities and

[3] For examples, see Ireland's Assisted Decision-Making (Capacity) Act 2015; Peru's Legislative Decree No 1384; Costa Rica's Ley para la Promoción de la Autonomía Personal de las Personas con Discapacidad (2016) and India's The Rights of Persons with Disabilities Act, 2016.

[4] For the Committee's criticisms of certain State's Parties' attempts and/or proposals for Article 12-compatible reform, see Committee on the Rights of Persons with Disabilities, 'Concluding observations on the initial report of Norway', CRPD/C/NOR/CO/1 (7 May 2019), paras 19–20; Committee on the Rights of Persons with Disabilities, 'Concluding observations on the initial report of Nepal', CRPD/C/NPL/CO/1 (16 April 2018), paras 21–22; Committee on the Rights of Persons with Disabilities, 'Concluding observations on the initial report of the Czech Republic', CRPD/C/CZE/CO/1 (15 May 2015), paras 22–23.

[5] T Minkowitz, 'Prohibition of Compulsory Mental Health Treatment and Detention Under the CRPD' (30 June 2011). Available at SSRN: https://ssrn.com/abstract=1876132; T Minkowitz, 'The United Nations Convention on the Rights of Persons with Disabilities and the right to be free from nonconsensual psychiatric interventions' (2006) 34 *Syracuse Journal of International Law & Commerce* 405, P Bartlett and M Schulze, 'Urgently awaiting implementation: The right to be free from exploitation, violence and abuse in Article 16 of the Convention on the Rights of Persons with Disabilities (CRPD)' (2017) 53 *International Journal of Law & Psychiatry* 2.

[6] A Arstein-Kerslake, *Restoring Voice to People with Cognitive Disabilities: Realising the Right to Equal Recognition Before the Law* (Cambridge, Cambridge University Press, 2017), 19.

[7] Ibid, 19–20.

the creation of systems of non-coercive mental healthcare. It will then interrogate the nature of the resistance to the full vindication of the right to liberty of persons with disabilities[8] at the State level, taking Ireland as a case study. It will propose a core explanation for the current inertia – a misunderstanding by States regarding the nature of the CRPD as a holistic human rights instrument and a consequent lack of focus on the progressive realisation of certain other key rights within the CRPD.

Consistent with Arstein-Kerslake's imagery of a 'circulatory system' of disability rights, Gilles Deleuze and Félix Guattari's use of the rhizome will be loosely drawn on as a conceptual framework for both describing the current landscape of coercive mental healthcare and illuminating the means by which States Parties could meet their CRPD obligations.[9] Deleuze and Guattari suggest that all things are 'assemblages' which are themselves part of a wider network or 'rhizome'. This is to be contrasted with a root–tree–branch approach, which, when applied to rights realisation, conceptualises certain aspects as being foundational and therefore antecedent to others. The rhizome theory, when applied to CRPD rights, is useful in illustrating the dynamic and interconnected nature of those rights and their realisation.[10] A focus on what have traditionally been viewed as 'positive' rights will be pointed to as neglected assemblages of the disability rights rhizome. Relying on Deleuze and Guattari's contention that any 'rupture' or decay in the rhizome is not definitive and is capable of regeneration, it will point to such rights as key aspects of the realisation of systems of non-coercive mental healthcare.

II. THE RIGHT TO LIBERTY WITHIN THE CRPD

Article 14(1) of the CRPD states that persons with disabilities should enjoy the right to liberty and security on an equal basis with others and that 'the existence of a disability shall in no case justify a deprivation of liberty'. In September 2015 the Committee adopted its 'Guidelines on article 14 of the Convention on the Rights of Persons with Disabilities: The right to liberty and security of persons with disabilities'.[11] Eilionóir Flynn notes that although the Guidelines do not have the status of a General Comment, which is an authoritative interpretation of the text of a treaty provision by its monitoring body (although not legally

[8] This chapter does not purport to provide a comprehensive analysis of the right to liberty, focusing as it does on the implications of Article 14 for mental health legislation as applied to adults and which is not (generally) based on 'capacity' determinations.

[9] My thanks to Dr Ezgi Taşcıoğlu for suggesting the relevance of this theory to my arguments.

[10] G Deleuze and F Guattari, *A Thousand Plateaus: Capitalism and Schizophrenia* (London, Continuum, 1987).

[11] UN Committee on the Rights of Persons with Disabilities, 'Guidelines on article 14 of the Convention on the Rights of Persons with Disabilities: The right to liberty and security of persons with disabilities' (Adopted September 2015).

binding in the same way as the treaty text), 'they nonetheless represent the most up to date interpretation of Article 14 and give context for how the Committee will address States which come before it'.[12] The CRPD Committee's Guidelines can therefore be viewed as a form of soft law which seeks to clarify and codify the pre-existing interpretations which had been made of Article 14, but which fall below the authoritative status of a General Comment.[13]

Within the Guidelines, the Committee's interpretation of Article 14 establishes its normative roots within the recognition of universal legal capacity contained in Article 12 – itself an aspect of the overarching equality and non-discrimination norm. But the Committee also emphasises a link between the right to liberty and the right to freedom from exploitation, violence and abuse (Article 16), the right to live independently and be included in the community (Article 19), and the right to health (Article 25).[14] This system can be equated with Deleuze and Guattari's idea of the rhizome as representing 'multiplicities' rather than hierarchical structures. Some of these 'linked' rights within the CRPD rhizome will now be examined in more detail in order to provide an overview of the system of inter-reliance which exists.

This chapter will demonstrate how those rights can be viewed as part of a broader philosophy of disability concretised in a human rights model, with non-discrimination as a grounding principle for the recognition of legal capacity and the right to liberty, bolstered by the recognition of the right to health and to live independently and be included in the community. This capacity of the CRPD to move beyond merely explaining disability and towards a human rights model which 'encompasses the values for disability policy that acknowledges the human dignity of disabled persons' has been discussed by Degener.[15] She concludes that '[o]nly the human rights model can explain why human rights do not require absence of impairment'[16] and that the CRPD 'goes beyond the social model of disability and codifies the human rights model of disability.'[17]

In its 2015 Guidelines, the Committee confirms that Article 14 'is, in essence, a non-discrimination provision'[18] and that, as such, it provides evidence of the

[12] E Flynn, 'Disability, Deprivation of Liberty and Human Rights Norms: Reconciling European and International Approaches' (2016) 22 *International Journal of Mental Health and Capacity Law* 75, 83.

[13] It is also instructive to examine similar documents adopted at a UN level such as the *Basic Principles and Guidelines on the Right to a Remedy and Reparation for Victims of Gross Violations of International Human Rights Law and Serious Violations of International Humanitarian Law*, UN Doc. E/CN.4/2005/L.48 (13 April 2005) which, in their Preamble, state that they do not constitute new international or domestic legal obligations but 'identify mechanisms, modalities, procedures and methods for the implementation of existing legal obligations under international human rights law and international humanitarian law which are complementary though different as to their norms'.

[14] For discussion of how reform in India has engaged with the interconnection of these articles, see Pathare & Kapoor, Chapter 8, this volume.

[15] T Degener, 'Disability in a Human Rights Context' (2016) 5(3) *Laws* 35, para 3.1.

[16] Ibid.

[17] Ibid para 2.

[18] UN CRPD (n 11), para 4.

'close interrelation with the right to equality and non-discrimination.'[19] The Guidelines state that detention on grounds of actual or perceived impairment,[20] even where there are other reasons for the detention of an individual (including dangerousness to self or others or need for care/treatment), is incompatible with Article 14 as it is discriminatory in nature and amounts to arbitrary deprivation of liberty.[21] The Committee points to the resolution of this question as early on as the Ad Hoc Committee stage of the CRPD negotiations.[22] The Committee has also taken the opportunity in its General Comment on Article 5[23] to characterise the principles of equality and non-discrimination contained in the CRPD as 'an interpretative tool for all the other principles and rights enshrined in the Convention'.[24]

III. LINKAGES WITHIN THE RHIZOME: LEGAL CAPACITY, COMMUNITY, HEALTH

A. Equal Recognition Before the Law

The provisions most frequently cited by the Committee as pillars for the realisation of the right to liberty of persons with disabilities are Articles 12 and 19. This tapestry of rights was also brought to the fore by the Committee where it recognised the link between Article 12 and 14 in its first General Comment – its interpretation of Article 12.[25] Within this analysis of the right to legal capacity, the Committee noted that the recognition of that right is 'inextricably linked to the enjoyment of many other human rights provided for in the Convention'[26] and that '[w]ithout recognition of the person as a person before the law, the ability to assert, exercise and enforce those rights, and many other rights provided for in the Convention, is significantly compromised.'[27]

The General Comment also includes a specific section which analyses the link between Article 12 and other provisions of the CRPD. Here, the Committee linked the principles of equality and non-discrimination contained in Article 5

[19] UN CRPD (n 11), para 5.

[20] This is an important inclusion in terms of ensuring that those individuals who do not self-identify as having an impairment (eg members of the 'mad' community) are still able to avail of the protections contained in Article 14 where their detention is based on a perceived impairment.

[21] UN CRPD (n 11), para 13.

[22] UN CRPD (n 11), para 7.

[23] Committee on the Rights of Persons with Disabilities, *General Comment No 6 (2018) on equality and non-discrimination*, CRPD/C/GC/6, 9 March 2018.

[24] Ibid, para 12.

[25] UN Committee on the Rights of Persons with Disabilities, *General Comment No 1 – Article 12: Equal recognition before the law* (19 May 2014), CRPD/C/GC/1: https://documents-dds-ny.un.org/doc/UNDOC/GEN/G14/031/20/PDF/G1403120.pdf?OpenElement.

[26] Ibid, para 31.

[27] Ibid, para 31.

to the recognition of legal capacity[28] and specifically noted the relationship between Article 14 and Article 12:

> Respecting the right to legal capacity of persons with disabilities on an equal basis with others includes respecting the right of persons with disabilities to liberty and security of the person. The denial of the legal capacity of persons with disabilities and their detention in institutions against their will, either without their consent or with the consent of a substitute decision-maker, is an ongoing problem. This practice constitutes arbitrary deprivation of liberty and violates articles 12 and 14 of the Convention.[29]

B. Living Independently and Being Included in the Community

Article 19 affirms the right of all persons to live in the community 'with choices equal to others'. It requires States Parties to 'take effective and appropriate measures' to facilitate full enjoyment of this right by persons with disabilities, including by ensuring that persons with disabilities can: choose their place of residence and where and with whom they live; have access to support services 'to support living and inclusion in the community, and to prevent isolation or segregation from the community'; and have access to 'community services and facilities' on an equal basis with the general population.

Article 19 has been the subject of a General Comment which developed the links between that provision and the right to liberty.[30] It supports the Committee's previous interpretation of Article 19,[31] noting that the historic focus on investing in institutions has 'led to abandonment, dependence on family, institutionalization, isolation and segregation'.[32] The Committee highlighted the link between Article 19 and the right to liberty[33] and that a 'core element' of Article 19 was the legal capacity to decide 'where, with whom and how to live for all persons with disabilities, irrespective of impairment'.[34] In its clearest delineation of the interdependence of Articles 14 and 19, the Committee pointed out that:

> Involuntary institutionalization on the grounds of impairment or associated circumstances such as presumed 'dangerousness' or other factors as elaborated by the Committee in its guidelines on article 14 is often caused or increased by a lack of disability-specific support services. Implementing article 19 thus will ultimately prevent violation of article 14.[35]

[28] Ibid, section IV (paras 31–49).

[29] Ibid, para 40.

[30] Committee on the Rights of Persons with Disabilities, *General Comment No 5 (2017) on living independently and being included in the community*, CRPD/C/GC/5 (October 2017).

[31] See, for example, the Committee's interpretation of Article 19 in its Concluding observations on the initial report of China (15 October 2012), CRPD/C/CHN/CO/1, para 31, Concluding observations on the initial report of Austria (30 September 2013), CRPD/C/AUT/CO/1, paras 30 and 37 and Concluding observations on the initial report of the Cook Islands (15 May 2015), CRPD/C/COK/CO/1, para 40.

[32] CRPD, General Comment No 5 (n 30), para 1.

[33] Ibid, para 27.

[34] Ibid, para 38(a).

[35] Ibid, para 82.

The exact requirements for full implementation of Article 19 which were set out by the Committee in this General Comment will be examined in the section on progressive realisation below.

C. Health

The Committee's 2014 General Comment No 1, on Article 12, also links Article 14 with Article 25 and states that '[t]he right to enjoyment of the highest attainable standard of health (art. 25) includes the right to health care on the basis of free and informed consent'.[36] Article 25, when read in conjunction with the supported decision-making requirements of Article 12, challenges legal frameworks which provide for the imposition of coercive treatment which is carried out against the expressed will of the person based on a finding a lack of mental capacity.

The above interpretations by the Committee sketch the rhizome which signposts the system of healthcare provision which should exist for persons with psychosocial disabilities – recognition of legal capacity based on the provision of chosen support and the outcroppings of that in the form of processes of deinstitutionalisation which are based on choice of place and manner of living, as well as the provision of mental healthcare to the same standard as for others.

IV. NEW 'MULTIPLICITIES'

Recent human rights reports, scholarship and activism have continued to sketch the parameters of the 'arterial network' and how non-coercive mental healthcare might be achieved. A golden vein running through all of these elements are certain core principles: the need to combat stigma and ensure that persons with disabilities themselves are at the core of informing proposals for reform; that systems of supported decision-making which vindicate the right to liberty should be grounded in the social, environmental and cultural norms of the jurisdiction in which it operates; and that recognition should be afforded to non-legal/informal forms of support decision-making in this area, with appropriate safeguards where necessary. To be clear, recognition of jurisdictional variance and informality in the implementation of systems of supported decision-making should not be taken as endorsement of unbridled relativism which acts as a cloak for impunity in the implementation of Article 12 in a manner inconsistent with the CRPD Committee's interpretation. It is instead an acknowledgement of the need for a process of 'decolonisation' regarding structures supportive of legal capacity and the multifarious forms that they might take, as well as the fact that these may be dependent on their time, location, user-group and available resources.

[36] CRPD, General Comment No 1 (n 25), para 41.

Within her report on disability-specific forms of deprivation of liberty,[37] the UN Special Rapporteur on the Rights of Persons with Disabilities called for the repeal of all legislation which allows for deprivation of liberty on the basis of disability and that this be replaced with 'rights-based support services'. These support arrangements should be 'available, accessible, adequate and affordable; [and] provided on a voluntary basis'. Drawing on Article 19 of the CRPD, she also called for a process of deinstitutionalisation which would have at its core the adoption of

> a plan of action with clear timelines and concrete benchmarks, a moratorium on new admissions, the redistribution of public funds from institutions to community services and the development of adequate community support, such as housing assistance, home support, peer support and respite services.

She especially highlighted the role of advance planning in exercising legal capacity and ensuring respect for the will and preferences of the individual in crisis situations. Consistent with her call for a reimagining of expenditure in this area, she took an expansive view of 'community support', including within its scope the need for disability-inclusive social protection systems which could contribute to reducing deprivation of liberty of persons with disabilities by ensuring income security and access to social services.[38]

A literature review commissioned by the UN Special Rapporteur on the Rights of Persons with Disabilities highlighted a number of themes which emerged on reducing, ending and preventing coercion.[39] Firstly, that 'both top-down and local-level leadership are important in order to create and maintain culture change toward reducing, ending and preventing coercion' as well as strong indications that 'leadership should include peer involvement for ultimate effectiveness'.[40] While hospital-based support should be maintained, the need for community-based crisis services, hospital diversion and step-down supports also came to the fore in this review. This would include crisis respite houses, intensive home-based support, and residential programmes as well as independent advocacy, housing support and personal assistance. Quoting the UK's National Survivor User Network it concluded that 'getting the right support, at the right time, in the right place, from the right person is likely to have the one of the greatest impacts in reducing all forms of coercion in the context of mental health care.'[41]

[37] Special Rapporteur on the rights of persons with disabilities, 'Report of the Special Rapporteur on the rights of persons with disabilities to the 40th session of the Human Rights Council, 11 January 2019, A/HRC/40/54.

[38] Ibid, p 16.

[39] P Gooding and others, 'Alternatives to Coercion in Mental Health Settings: A Literature Review' (Melbourne Social Equity Institute, 2018).

[40] Ibid, p 116.

[41] Ibid, p 116.

A number of findings and conclusions were made in an analysis of disability-specific forms of deprivation of liberty that was also requested by the UN Special Rapporteur to inform her aforementioned report.[42] Crucially, a key narrative within the data collected from individuals, families and healthcare professionals was the absence of alternative forms of support for individuals seeking mental healthcare or who were experiencing a period of crisis, making institutional placement or involuntary hospitalisation the default response. Deprivation of liberty became a gateway to access not only healthcare but housing, education and support for families.[43] In identifying the path towards alternatives to deprivations of liberty, the report pointed to support for individuals and families based on strong family and community networks. Access to justice, particularly restorative justice and diversion programmes also formed part of the pathway, as did peer support. The report concluded that 'a key factor in the continued existence of disability-specific deprivation of liberty is the lack of alternatives and support in the community and lack of inclusion in mainstream education, employment and community'.[44]

All the above recommendations speak to the practical realities of implementing CRPD-compliant, non-coercive models of mental healthcare at the domestic level, recognising the progressive nature of certain rights linked to the right to liberty and to supported decision-making, while also emphasising the need for sustained progress towards the full achievement and availability of those rights – the nourishment of assemblages of the rhizome.

V. A FAILURE TO FLOURISH – THE EXAMPLE OF IRELAND

Having examined the CRPD Committee's interpretation of the requirements of rights related to non-coercive mental healthcare, as well as the growing body of literature on what non-coercive systems of mental healthcare might look like, Ireland will now be taken as a case study in order to demonstrate the nature of some of the political blockages which currently exist in the area of coercion and mental healthcare.

A. Limited Reform of Mental Health Legislation

The Mental Health Act 2001 governs the system of involuntary psychiatric detention in Ireland. It provides for detention based on the existence of a mental disorder in conjunction with either a perceived need for 'care and treatment'

[42] E Flynn, M Pinilla-Rocancio and M Gómez-Carrillo de Castro, *Disability-specific forms of deprivation of liberty* (Centre for Disability Law and Policy, Institute for Lifecourse and Society, National University of Ireland, Galway, 2019).

[43] Ibid, p 86.

[44] Ibid, p 112.

or dangerousness to self or others. As such, it mirrors the primary elements of mental health laws globally. While the 2001 Act has been subject to a number of pieces of amending legislation,[45] the only ones which could be said to substantively impact on the right to liberty of persons with psychosocial disabilities are the Mental Health (Renewal Orders) Act 2018 – which limited the duration of renewed admission orders to six months – and the Mental Health (Amendment) Act 2018 – which has not yet been commenced and will be set out in more detail below. While certainly improving both procedural and substantive aspects of the 2001 Act, neither of these pieces of legislation fundamentally alters the legal paradigm which provides for involuntary detention.

Ireland signed the CRPD in March 2007 and in October 2015 the Department of Justice published its 'Roadmap to Ratification of the United Nations Convention on the Rights of Persons with Disabilities (UN CRPD)'.[46] This document proffered the dualist nature of Ireland's constitutional order as justification for ensuring that Ireland's legislative framework was in compliance with the CRPD before ratification took place.[47] It listed a number of areas where the State believed that either legislative amendment or innovation was required in order for Ireland to comply with (and therefore ratify) the CRPD.[48] These included equality provisions, the criminal law on sexual offences[49] as well as the key issue of equal recognition before the law.[50] Within the Roadmap the government stated its intention to amend the 2001 Act and to lodge a 'declaration with regard to involuntary detention, along lines of Australia and Norway'.[51]

The intention to lodge a declaration with regard to involuntary detention was repeated by the Minister of State for Disability Issues when the Disability (Miscellaneous Provisions) Bill 2016 was debated at Second Stage in the Dáil. Addressing queries by a number of Deputies regarding the proposed declarations in respect of Articles 12 and 14, the Minister stated that '[t]he problem arises due to the misinterpretation of said articles, in an extremist way, by the UN Committee.'[52]

[45] These include the Mental Health (Amendment) Act 2015, which removed the statutory power to administer either electro-convulsive therapy or medicine (after 3 months) to a refusing individual who is deemed to have decision-making capacity, as well as amendments contained in Ireland's legislative response to the Covid-19 pandemic – Emergency Measures in the Public Interest (Covid-19) Act 2020.

[46] Department of Justice, 'Roadmap to Ratification of the UN Convention on the Rights of Persons with Disabilities (UN CRPD)' (October 2015).

[47] Ibid, p 1.

[48] For a more detailed examination of the process of ratification, see S Doyle and E Flynn, 'Ireland's ratification of the UN convention on the rights of persons with disabilities: challenges and opportunities' (2013) 41 *British Journal of Learning Disabilities* 171 and E Flynn, 'Ireland' in Lisa Waddington and Anna Lawson (eds), *The UN Convention on the Rights of Persons with Disabilities in Practice: a comparative analysis of the role of courts* (Oxford, Oxford University Press, 2018).

[49] Now addressed by the Criminal Law (Sexual Offences) Act 2017.

[50] Now addressed by the Assisted Decision-Making (Capacity) Act 2015.

[51] Department of Justice, 'Roadmap to Ratification of the UN Convention on the Rights of Persons with Disabilities (UN CRPD)', October 2015, p 7.

[52] Dáil Éireann, Vol 940 No 2, p 39, 23 February 2017: https://data.oireachtas.ie/ie/oireachtas/debateRecord/dail/2017-02-23/debate/mul@/main.pdf.

Ireland eventually ratified the CRPD in March 2018. The ratification was accompanied by a reservation and a number of declarations, with the declarations and reservation in relation to Articles 12 and 14 stating Ireland's rejection of any obligation to eliminate 'substitute decision-making arrangements', as well as asserting the lawfulness of substitute decision-making 'where such arrangements are necessary, in accordance with the law, and subject to appropriate and effective safeguards'. It also declared its understanding that the CRPD did not prohibit 'compulsory care or treatment of persons, including measures to treat mental disorders, when circumstances render treatment of this kind necessary as a last resort, and the treatment is subject to legal safeguards'.[53]

The first declaration and reservation are based on similar statements made upon ratification by both Australia and Canada. The Committee has already found Canada's declaration and reservation in respect of Article 12 to be incompatible with the 'object and purpose' of the CRPD. Ireland's declaration and reservation in respect of Article 12 is similarly likely to be found to be incompatible with the CRPD Committee's jurisprudence on the requirements of that provision, in particular its General Comment No 1 on equal recognition before the law.

Ireland's declaration in respect of the right to liberty is identical to that of Norway apart from the fact that Ireland titled its declaration as being in respect of Articles 12 and 14, whereas Norway entitled its statement 'Articles 14 and 25'. It seems likely that in framing the declaration in terms of Articles 12 and 14, Ireland was primarily concerned with legislative reform measures which it is currently undertaking in respect of 'deprivation of liberty safeguards'. Such a declaration is likely to be treated as a de facto reservation and be deemed inconsistent with both the negotiation history of the CRPD and the jurisprudence of the Committee, particularly its 2015 Guidelines on Article 14 and the understood object and purpose of the CRPD – to provide equal rights to persons with disabilities without discrimination. Further, Ireland has acceded to the Vienna Convention on the Law of Treaties (VCLT),[54] Article 19(c) of which expressly states that it does not permit reservations which are incompatible with the 'object and purpose' of a treaty. In addition, a declaration, unlike a reservation, cannot 'exclude or alter' the legal effect of the CRPD. As such, the Committee would be justified in finding such provisos to be incompatible with the CRPD and therefore invalid, while at the same time finding that a State was still a party to the CRPD (ie, its ratification of the treaty was unaffected by such a finding of invalidity) and therefore bound by its provisions in full.

Such an approach would also be consistent with Article 31(1) of the VCLT which sets out the general rule of treaty interpretation 'in good faith in accordance with the ordinary meaning to be given to the terms of the treaty in their context and in the light of its object and purpose.' Article 31(2) states that

[53] Convention on the Rights of Persons with Disabilities: Declarations and Reservations (Ireland), opened for signature 30 March 2007, 999 UNTS 3 (entered into force 3 May 2008).

[54] Accession took place on 7 August 2006.

the 'context' of terms of the treaty includes not only the text (including the preamble and annexes) but also any agreements or instruments made by the parties regarding the treaty.[55] Anna Arstein-Kerslake suggests that Article 31(1) 'mandates against a solely textually objective approach and disallows a narrow reading of treaty provisions'.[56]

Consistent with a concept of CRPD rights realisation as part of a rhizomatic constellation, it is notable that some of the norms within Ireland's Assisted Decision-Making (Capacity) Act 2015, Ireland's primary reforming legislation on legal capacity which purports to meet its obligations under the CRPD, have been transposed into reforms of the Mental Health Act 2001 by way of the Mental Health (Amendment) Act 2018. When the 2018 Act is commenced it will replace the principle of 'best interests' (the current 'principal consideration' for decisions made under the 2001 Act) with those contained in the 2015 Act. The 2001 Act will therefore have as its guiding principles respect for the will and preferences of the individual and that decisions made in respect of that individual will be made in a manner that minimises the restriction of the person's rights, and their freedom of action, have due regard to the need to respect the right of the person to dignity, bodily integrity, privacy, autonomy, be proportionate, and have due regard to the need to have access to health services that have as the aim of those services the delivery of the highest attainable standard of mental

[55] However, not all States which have ratified the CRPD have ratified the VCLT. Such States are therefore not bound by its terms but would still be bound by Article 46(1) of the CRPD which states that reservations 'incompatible with the object and purpose' of the CRPD shall not be permitted. They are therefore constrained in their ability to lodge reservations or interpretative declarations in similar terms to States Parties which have ratified the VCLT.

For those States to whom the VCLT does apply, the question of incompatibility has been a fraught one, with two strands of thought emerging amongst international law commentators. One school takes the 'permissibility' approach and posits that any incompatible reservation is void *ab initio* while there is an alternative argument that Article 19(c) vests 'non-reserving' States Parties with the ultimate power to decide on compatibility with the relevant treaty (known as the 'opposability' approach). For a more detailed analysis of these two schools of thought on the compatibility of reservations, see ET Swaine, 'Reserving' (2006) 31 *Yale Journal of International Law* 307, 314–17.

Related to this latter view of the permissibility of reservations is Article 20(5) of the VCLT which provides that 'a reservation is considered to have been accepted by a State if it shall have raised no objection to the reservation by the end of a period of twelve months after it was notified of the reservation or by the date on which it expressed its consent to be bound by the treaty, whichever is later'. There is therefore a scheme of tacit approval which operates between States Parties to any treaty regarding the permissibility or validity of a particular reservation and there must generally be a stated objection by another State Party to the particular treaty. Article 21(1) of the VCLT provides that such an objection will serve only to affect the legal relationship between those two States. This approach has been criticised by the UN Human Rights Committee in a General Comment adopted in 1994 (UN Human Rights Committee (HRC), CCPR General Comment No 24: *Issues Relating to Reservations Made upon Ratification or Accession to the Covenant or the Optional Protocols thereto, or in Relation to Declarations under Article 41 of the Covenant*, 4 November 1994, CCPR/C/21/Rev.1/Add.6.) and is indicative of the different relationships which are created by general international law treaties between States as opposed to human rights-specific treaties which create a relationship between the State and the individual.

[56] A Arstein-Kerslake, *Restoring Voice to People with Cognitive Disabilities: Realising the Right to Equal Recognition Before the Law* (Cambridge, Cambridge University Press 2017), 17.

health, as well as the person's right to his or her own understanding of his or her mental health.[57]

B. A Failure to Vindicate the Right to Live Independently and Be Included in the Community

In 2003, an Expert Group was appointed by the Irish Minister of State of the Department of Health and Children with special responsibility for mental health to propose a model of mental health service provision in Ireland. Their report, *A Vision for Change* (AVFC),[58] was published in 2006 and made several recommendations, including the provision of a community-based service with a particular emphasis on multidisciplinary CMHTs (Community Mental Health Teams), individualised care plans, the enhancement and formalisation of links between specialist mental health services, primary care services and voluntary groups that are supportive of mental health. It also called for the creation of a plan for the closure of all mental hospitals and the ring-fencing of the proceeds of their sale for reinvestment in the mental health service as well as substantial extra funding for the implementation of these new policies.

However, implementation of AVFC has been piecemeal, with staff shortages and a lack of a clear implementation plan being pointed to as causative factors.[59] An evidence review published by the Department of Health to inform the parameters of a planned refresh of mental health policy in Ireland 10 years after the publication of AVFC also contained no reference to the requirements of the CRPD.[60] In terms of recommendations for policy reform from the legislature, the Oireachtas Joint Committee on the Future of Mental Health Care began its work in July 2017 'with the aim to achieve cross-party agreement on the implementation of a single, long-term vision for mental health care and the direction of mental health policy in Ireland.'[61] Again, no reference was made to Ireland's obligations under the CRPD in its final report.[62]

[57] Mental Health (Amendment) Act 2018, s 3.

[58] Department of Health and Children, *A Vision for Change – Report of the expert group on mental health policy* (2006).

[59] For analysis of the implementation of AVFC see: H Johnston, *All Vision but No Change? Determinants of Implementation: The Case of Ireland and Mental Health Policy* (Institute of Public Administration 2014) and Mental Health Reform, *A Vision For Change Nine Years On: A coalition analysis of progress* (June 2015).

[60] Department of Health, *Evidence Review to Inform the Parameters for a Refresh of A Vision for Change (AVFC): A wide-angle international review of evidence and developments in mental health policy and practice* (February 2017 – Published July 2017).

[61] Houses of the Oireachtas, *Joint Committee on the Future of Mental Health Care Final Report* (October 2018), p 5.

[62] Houses of the Oireachtas, *Joint Committee on the Future of Mental Health Care Final Report* (October 2018).

The successor to AVFC, *Sharing the Vision: A Mental Health Policy for Everyone*,[63] was finally published in June 2020, with scant mention being made of Ireland's CRPD obligations. However, one of the principles which it emphasises is that of respect for human rights, particularly the right of everyone to the highest attainable standard of physical and mental health, with service users leading 'in the planning and delivery of their care'.[64] Like AVFC before it, central to *Sharing the Vision* is the provision of advocacy supports, with the primary role of advocates being described as 'to support an individual around decision-making or having their voice heard'.[65] However, its approach to the CRPD is concerning, referring to it as part of an 'evolving understanding' of human rights and suggesting that involuntary detention could still be reserved for 'a life-saving emergency' within any reforming mental health legislation.[66]

C. Discriminatory Standards on Informed Consent

Ireland's National Consent Policy,[67] despite having been revised after the adoption of the Assisted Decision-Making (Capacity) Act 2015, relies on a functional approach to decision-making capacity. It contains a presumption of capacity and acknowledges that '[b]est practice and international human rights standards favour "supported decision-making" where possible',[68] as well as a corresponding duty on clinicians to 'maximise' decision-making capacity. However, it also makes provision for assessment of capacity 'if, having been given all appropriate help and support' and individual 'is unable to communicate a clear and consistent choice' or 'is obviously unable to understand and use the information and choices provided'.[69] Where the individual is found to lack capacity based on this assessment, healthcare decisions are to be made in their 'best interests'.

Viewed through the lens of its obligations under the CRPD, Ireland's current framework for the provision of mental healthcare demonstrates multi-assemblage failure and the refusal to engage in CRPD-compatible reform, with the apparent rationale for such resistance being a narrative of the 'helpless' or 'dangerous' individual who may either need to be saved from themselves or for their threat to others to be managed. As such, it is hardly surprising that advocacy efforts for the abolition of detention on the basis of disability have been received by legislators and policy-makers as both unrealistic and unrealisable.

[63] Department of Health, *Sharing the Vision: A Mental Health Policy for Everyone* (June 2020).
[64] Ibid, p 17.
[65] Ibid, p 58.
[66] Ibid, p 110.
[67] National Consent Policy, V.1.3: June 2019: www.hse.ie/eng/about/who/qid/other-quality-improvement-programmes/consent/national-consent-policy-hse-v1-3-june-2019.pdf, last accessed 4 June 2021.
[68] Ibid, para 5.2.
[69] Ibid, para 5.4.

VI. UNDERSTANDING PROGRESSIVE REALISATION AS THE FACILITATOR OF RHIZOMIC CONNECTION

The interconnection between Article 14 and a number of other rights in the CRPD, as well as the apparent rejection of the requirements of Article 14 by States Parties such as Ireland as a result of State failure to engage with those linked rights has been established above. It will now be suggested that an (at least partial) explanation for the current vista for the right to liberty of persons with psychosocial disabilities and systemic shifts towards non-coercive systems of mental healthcare is the failure on the part of some actors to engage with the requirements of law reform when the CRPD is viewed holistically.

In general, the demands of Article 14 have been viewed in isolation by States Parties. As such, much of the 'pushback' from States is based on a false understanding of what a human rights model of disability requires, particularly in the context of the right to liberty. For example, while the implementation of the right to equal recognition before the law has been well-established in the literature and, as has been mentioned above, has begun to be realised to a certain extent in a number of jurisdictions, the role of supported decision-making in the realisation of the right to liberty and the creation of systems of non-coercive mental healthcare has been, at least until recently, under-explored, as has the linked question of the progressive realisation of other connected rights.

Article 4(2) of the CRPD addresses the question of progressive realisation where it states:

> With regard to economic, social and cultural rights, each State Party undertakes to take measures to the maximum of its available resources and, where needed, within the framework of international cooperation, with a view to achieving progressively the full realization of these rights, without prejudice to those obligations contained in the present Convention that are immediately applicable according to international law.[70]

While the right to liberty on an equal basis with others is itself a 'negative', immediately realisable right, its practical realisation relies on the vindication of a number of other CRPD rights which are themselves subject to progressive realisation ie, the right to live independently and to be included in the community and the right to health.

The Committee has provided some insight into the operation of progressive realisation in the context of the CRPD in its General Comment No 5 on Article 19.[71] While it is to be emphasised that the right to liberty itself is not subject to

[70] Much of the jurisprudence on progressive realisation has emerged from the Committee on Economic, Social and Cultural Rights (CESCR) in its interpretation of Article 2(1) of the International Covenant on Economic, Social and Cultural Rights (ICESCR). General Comment No 3 of the Committee, adopted in 1990, detailed the nature of States Parties' obligations under Article 2(1). Thus the concept of 'a minimum core obligation to ensure the satisfaction of, at the very least, minimum essential levels of each of the rights' was born.

[71] CRPD, General Comment No 5 (n 30).

progressive realisation, this General Comment is particularly relevant given the aforementioned link between Articles 14 and 19 of the CRPD. Article 19 is also informative in that it has elements which are subject to both immediate and progressive realisation – Article 19(a) is immediately realisable whereas Articles 19(b) and (c) are subject to progressive realisation. In its General Comment, the Committee gives a concise synopsis of its perspective on progressive realisation by stating that it 'entails the immediate obligation to design and adopt concrete strategies, plans of action and resources to develop support services as well as making existing, as well as new, general services inclusive for persons with disabilities.'[72] The Committee continues by stating that States Parties must take steps which are 'deliberate, concrete, targeted and use all appropriate means'.[73] Also drawing on the Committee on Economic, Social and Cultural Rights' (CESCR) jurisprudence, the Committee addresses the issue of retrogressive measures, stating that States Parties are prohibited from taking retrogressive measures with respect to minimum core obligations of the right to live independently with the community[74] and where such measures are introduced more generally, the State must demonstrate that they are 'temporary, necessary and non-discriminatory and that they respect its core obligations'.[75]

The Committee adopted the same approach as that of the CESCR by using what Urfan Khaliq and Robin Churchill call 'a three-fold typology of obligations: respect, protect and fulfil'.[76] Of particular relevance to Article 14 and its realisation, General Comment No 5 requires States Parties, in fulfilling their obligations, to adopt a strategy and a concrete plan of action for deinstitutionalisation which should include the duty to implement structural reforms, to improve accessibility for persons with disabilities within the community and to raise awareness among all persons in society about inclusion of persons with disabilities within the community.[77] This process of deinstitutionalisation also requires what the Committee describes as 'a systemic transformation', which not only means the closure of institutions but also the establishment of a range of individualised support services.[78]

In terms of the right to health, the Committee has constantly emphasised the need to eliminate barriers to the progressive realisation of this right,[79] with particular focus on the right to free and informed consent in relation to medical

[72] Ibid, para 39.

[73] Ibid, para 41.

[74] Ibid, para 45.

[75] Ibid, para 43.

[76] U Khalil and R Churchill, 'The protection of economic and social rights: a particular challenge?' in H Keller and G Ulfstein (eds), *UN Human Rights Treaty Bodies: Law and Legitimacy* (Cambridge, Cambridge University Press, 2012).

[77] General Comment No 5 (n 30), para 57.

[78] Ibid, para 58.

[79] See, for example, Committee on the Rights of Persons with Disabilities, 'Concluding observations on the initial report of Morocco', 25 September 2017, CRPD/C/MAR/CO/1 and 'Concluding observations on the initial report of Italy', 6 October 2016, CRPD/C/ITA/CO/1.

treatment. Of some guidance in terms of the nature of state obligations is the CESCR's General Comment No 14.[80] Of particular assistance in the context of the right to health for persons with disabilities, within this General Comment the CESCR established that while the right to the highest attainable standard of health is subject to progressive realisation:

> [I]t also imposes on States parties various obligations which are of immediate effect. States parties have immediate obligations in relation to the right to health, such as the guarantee that the right will be exercised without discrimination of any kind (art. 2.2) and the obligation to take steps (art. 2.1) towards the full realization of article 12 [the right to health]. Such steps must be deliberate, concrete and targeted towards the full realization of the right to health.[81]

The CESCR also emphasised that there was a strong presumption against the permissibility of retrogressive measures. In such circumstances States Parties would have to prove that

> they have been introduced after the most careful consideration of all alternatives and that they are duly justified by reference to the totality of the rights provided for in the Covenant in the context of the full use of the State party's maximum available resources.[82]

The 'respect, protect and fulfil' triad was also endorsed and the Committee identified four essential elements of the right to health: availability, accessibility (being of particular relevance containing as it does the requirements of non-discrimination, physical accessibility, economic accessibility (affordability) and information accessibility), acceptability and quality.[83]

The above requirements represent a clear path for State Parties that fully implement the Committee's interpretation of Article 14 and reform their laws accordingly. Given that Article 14 is subject to immediate effect, legislation which provides for detention on the basis of the existence of a disability/impairment must be repealed. But given State reluctance to take such a normative step (as seen in the case of Ireland), support for that element of the CRPD arterial network must be built. As such, more focus should be placed on the requirements for States to ensure that certain minimum core obligations are met in terms of the right to live independently and be included in the community and the right to health by legislators and policy-makers. These rights must be progressively realised to their fullest extent, with the reasonableness of State action being the core standard of evaluation. As Broderick suggests, 'the interaction of the equality norm and socio-economic rights in the Convention may provide the key to

[80] Committee on Economic, Social and Cultural Rights, *General Comment No 14: The right to the highest attainable standard of health (article 12 of the International Covenant on Economic, Social and Cultural Rights)*, 11 August 2000, E/C.12/2000/4.

[81] Ibid, para 30.

[82] Ibid, para 32.

[83] Ibid, para 12.

unlocking the structural inequalities faced by disabled people, in order to bring them fully into the mainstream.'[84]

VII. CONCLUSION

Article 14 of the CRPD and its obligation to create systems of non-coercive mental healthcare must not be viewed simply as a limited, 'negative' right to liberty. Both the jurisprudence of the CRPD Committee as well as a growing body of scholarship has established the links between it and the 'positive' rights to live independently and be included in the community and to health.

As Deleuze and Guattari explain within their rhizome analogy, 'the rhizome pertains to a map that must be produced, constructed, a map that is always detachable, connectable, reversable, modifiable, and has multiple entranceways and exits and its own lines of flight.'[85] The requirement to repeal laws which justify the involuntary detention of individuals on the basis of the existence of a disability should be viewed as part of a systemic overhaul of domestic law and policy. This would require the recognition of universal legal capacity, the implementation of appropriate supports for the realisation of legal personhood in order to give effect to an individual's will and preferences, the diversion of resources away from institutions towards the development of systems which support the right of persons with disabilities to live independently and be included in the community, as well as the provision of a mental healthcare system which allows persons with disabilities to freely access consent-based services. Fundamentally, this rhizomic system of rights calls for a redrawing of the balance between paternalism and autonomy and a fundamental reconstruction of public expenditure by States Parties in order to achieve the implementation of a human rights model of disability.

[84] A Broderick, *The long and winding road to equality and inclusion for persons with disabilities: the United Nations convention on the rights of persons with disabilities* (Cambridge, Intersentia, 2015), 400.

[85] Deleuze and Guattari, *A Thousand Plateaus* (n 10), p 21.

Part II

Reforming Capacity Law: Making, Shaping and Interpreting Legal Frameworks

7

The (Contested) Role of the Academy in Activist Movements for Legal Capacity Reform: A Personal Reflection

EILIONÓIR FLYNN[1]

ACADEMICS ARE OFTEN trained to maintain a critical distance between their research and the efforts of grassroots activists to achieve political, legal and social change. When I began my work in the field of disability rights, I felt that as an academic, my role would be to inform and equip activists who could use research evidence to ground arguments for change – but that I would not, and should not, play a central role in the (often messy and fraught) politics of change myself. In part, my view on this was shaped by my awareness of the tensions between the disabled people's movement and non-disabled academic researchers.[2] However, as my work evolved, I found myself more and more directly engaged with policy-makers and legislators. This work was usually collaborative – both with other researchers, and with civil society organisations, including, although to a lesser extent than would be desirable, disabled people's organisations.

In this chapter I will reflect on my experiences with the development of the Assisted Decision-Making (Capacity) Act 2015 in Ireland, through my engagement with a coalition of civil society organisations co-chaired by the Centre

[1] This chapter could not have been completed without the invaluable support and guidance of many colleagues and helpful feedback received from participants in a workshop on legal capacity and supported decision-making organised by Mary Donnelly and Rosie Harding. I want to acknowledge in particular the helpful insights offered during the writing process by my past and present colleagues at the Centre for Disability Law and Policy, especially Anna Arstein-Kerslake, Suzanne Doyle-Guilloud, Maria Ní Fhlatharta and Clíona de Bhailís.

[2] See Emma Stone and Mark Priestley, 'Parasites, Pawns and Partners: Disability Research and the Role of Non-Disabled Researchers' (1996) 47 *British Journal of Sociology* 699; Tom Shakespeare, 'Rules of Engagement: Doing Disability Research' (1996) 11 *Disability & Society* 115; Jenny Morris, 'Personal and Political: A Feminist Perspective on Researching Physical Disability' (1992) 7 *Disability, Handicap & Society* 157.

for Disability Law and Policy at National University of Ireland, Galway and Amnesty Ireland's Mental Health Campaign.[3] I will consider the challenges presented, the experiences of collaboration and efforts at consensus-building, and how these processes have shaped my own thinking and the further development of my academic work in this field.

I. BACKGROUND TO THE LEGISLATIVE REFORM

My involvement in this process of reform began in 2011 when I was working as a Senior Research Fellow in the Centre for Disability Law and Policy at NUI Galway. Ireland's legislative framework on legal capacity was at the time (and is still) governed by the Regulation of Lunacy (Ireland) Act 1871, which established the ward of court system. A ward of court is defined as 'a person who has been declared to be of unsound mind and incapable of managing his person or property.'[4]

This legislative framework has long been recognised as outdated and in need of reform. The first major development in the reform process was the publication of the Law Reform Commission's Report on Vulnerable Adults and the Law in 2006.[5] This report recommended the introduction of an adult guardianship system based on a functional test of mental capacity. It further recommended that a multi-disciplinary guardianship board would assess mental capacity and appoint guardians accordingly.[6] Ireland was one of the first countries to sign the CRPD in 2007, but at this point there did not seem to be much awareness at domestic level of what some of the more innovative articles of the Convention, such as Article 12, required in practice. The Government published the General Scheme of the Mental Capacity Bill in 2008, to establish a system of adult guardianship. Shortly after this publication, Ireland became impacted by the global economic crisis, and this legislation became much less of a political priority.

From about 2009 onwards, in response to parliamentary questions about Ireland's progress towards ratification of CRPD, successive ministers noted that Ireland would not be in a position to ratify the Convention until it reformed its laws on capacity.[7] The Programme for Government 2011 also included a

[3] This account is a personal reflection based on my own memory and perception of events – which may be different from others including those who were also involved. I have pieced together this account using my own notes and minutes from meetings, memos, briefing documents and email exchanges, and from video recordings of various events where these were available – but any errors are mine alone.

[4] Order 67 of the Rules of the Superior Courts. See also the Lunacy Regulation (Ireland) Act 1871.

[5] Law Reform Commission, *Vulnerable Adults and the Law* (LRC 83-2006).

[6] However the Report makes no mention of the Representation Agreement Act of 1996 in British Columbia (despite discussing guardianship law in British Columbia), which has long been recognised as a mechanism for supported decision-making. See Robert M Gordon, 'The emergence of assisted (supported) decision-making in the Canadian law of adult guardianship and substitute decision-making' (2000) 23(1) *International Journal of Law and Psychiatry* 61.

[7] Dáil Deb 1 December 2009, Vol 696, No 3; Dáil Deb 22 May 2012, Vol 766 No 1.

commitment to introduce a 'Capacity Bill that is in line with the UN Convention on the Rights of Persons with Disabilities'.[8] Subsequently, the parliamentary joint committee on Justice, Defence and Equality called for submissions in August 2011 from interested parties on the content of what was being referred to at the time as the Mental Capacity Bill.[9] From this call for submissions, a coalition was formed of interested organisations and individuals in the fields of intellectual disability, mental health, and older people, co-chaired by the Centre for Disability Law and Policy and Amnesty Ireland. Our purpose was to discuss whether a joint approach to legal capacity reform could be developed across these interest groups.

The Coalition took some important decisions at the outset of its work. First, we decided that we would develop a set of principles for the forthcoming legislation. Another key decision made by the coalition was to organise a series of conferences and workshops on supported decision-making, to bring public attention to the possibilities for legal recognition of these mechanisms in Ireland.[10] Our final key decision was to use all means possible to influence the legislative process in the drafting of the Bill and to emphasise the need for compliance with the CRPD. In the following sections I will reflect on each of these decisions; how they shaped what eventually became the Assisted Decision-Making (Capacity) Act 2015,[11] and how the role I played in the process shifted over time from a purely academic one to a much more involved and ultimately activist position. Following this discussion, I will attempt to draw out the possibilities and limitations of this activist-academic role in legal capacity reform which may be of interest to those engaged in similar debates and campaigns in other jurisdictions.

II. THE DEVELOPMENT AND EVOLUTION OF THE COALITION

Amnesty convened the first meeting of the group that became the coalition in September 2011. Representatives were invited predominantly from mental health groups, suggested by Amnesty based on its existing Mental Health Campaign, and disability organisations, suggested by the Centre for Disability Law and Policy (CDLP). A number of individual academics working on disability and mental health were included in the invitation, along with some statutory agencies

[8] Department of An Taoiseach, *Programme for Government 2011* (Government Publications, 2011), p 8: http://www.taoiseach.gov.ie/eng/Publications/Publications_Archive/Publications_2011/Programme_for_Government_2011.pdf, accessed 21 April 2020.

[9] Oireachtas Joint Committee on Justice, Defence and Equality, 'Mental Capacity Legislation – Invitation for Submissions' (*Oireachtas*, 2 August 2011), http://www.oireachtas.ie/parliament/mcl/, accessed 23 April 2020.

[10] For more information on each event see Amnesty Ireland, *Mental Health Campaign Archive* (Amnesty 2013): www.amnesty.ie/tag/mental-health-campaign/, accessed 21 April 2020.

[11] At the time of writing (January 2021), the Act has not yet been commenced. Various estimates have been given since enactment for the full commencement of the Act, the most recent being that the Act will not be operational until at least mid-2022. See Dáil Deb 26 November 2020, Vol 1001 No 5.

and human rights bodies such as the Law Reform Commission and Irish Human Rights Commission. The membership of the group evolved through time to include more older people's organisations.[12]

However, there were some important limitations in the membership of the group which should be acknowledged at the outset. In the initial membership, the only group which could be described as a Disabled People's Organisation (DPO)[13] was the Irish Advocacy Network, made up of peer advocates with lived experience of the mental health system. This group was relatively sceptical from the outset about the potential of the capacity legislation to impact positively on their community and felt that it was only worth being involved to the extent that this legislation might directly impact on reform of the Mental Health Act. At the time we began this work there was no national DPO representing people with intellectual disabilities,[14] and indeed no cross-disability DPO at the national level.[15] Therefore, the groups in the room represented a mix of disability and mental health service providers, families and carers, as well as those working with and for disabled people, older people and people with lived experience of the mental health services. This configuration meant both that the overwhelming majority of the membership was made up of those who had no direct personal experience of a denial of legal capacity, and the impact that this could have on a person's dignity and human rights, and that concerns about adult protection and safeguarding were often to the forefront of discussions.

CDLP and Amnesty agreed from the outset that it was important to have the Law Reform Commission (LRC) and the Irish Human Rights and Equality Commission at the table for these discussions. However, given their roles as

[12] The membership of the coalition changed throughout the four years in which we worked consistently on this legislation, and many meetings included individuals and organisations who did not officially endorse documents produced by the group. However, key organisations involved in meetings included Amnesty (and later its Mental Health Experts by Experience panel), the Irish Advocacy Network, Mental Health Reform, Mad Pride Ireland, St Patrick's Mental Health Services, Bri (the Acquired Brain Injury Advocacy Association), the Disability Federation of Ireland, Inclusion Ireland, the National Federation of Voluntary Bodies, the Irish Human Rights Commission, the Free Legal Advice Centres, the Public Interest Law Alliance, the Law Reform Commission, Justice for Wards, Alzheimers' Society of Ireland and Age Action.

[13] UN Committee on the Rights of Persons with Disabilities, 'General comment No 7 (2018) on the participation of persons with disabilities, including children with disabilities, through their representative organizations, in the implementation and monitoring of the Convention' UN Doc CRPD/C/GC/7 at para 11.

[14] The National Platform of Self Advocates officially launched as a national DPO of people with intellectual disabilities in 2014, see: thenationalplatform.ie/who-we-are/. Inclusion Ireland was a member of the coalition and had made efforts to involve self advocates more in the structure of the organisation, but did not bring self advocates to the coalition meetings. The National Platform announced its closure due to lack of a sustainable source of funding on 3 December 2019. See National Platform of Self Advocates, 'Closure of the National Platform of Self Advocates' (3 December 2019): https://thenationalplatform.ie/closure-national-platform-self-advocates/, accessed 22 April 2020.

[15] For more on the history of the disabled people's movement in Ireland and the dissolution of the Forum of People with Disabilities and its replacement People with Disabilities in Ireland, see Eilionóir Flynn, *From Rhetoric to Action: Implementing the UN Convention on the Rights of Persons with Disabilities* (Cambridge University Press, 2011), 324–53.

statutory bodies it was unlikely that either body would be able to formally sign up to the Principles developed by the coalition. This work was often challenging, as the LRC had recommended a system of adult guardianship to replace the ward of court system in its 2006 report, and remained steadfast in its support of this position.[16] This was so despite the growing awareness at international level of the concept of supported decision-making and explicit calls from the UN Committee on the Rights of Persons with Disabilities for States to reject substituted decision-making regimes such as adult guardianship.[17] While the membership of the coalition changed somewhat throughout the course of the Bill's development, the groups representing only those with direct lived experience of legal capacity denial were always outnumbered by those representing families, service providers or other interest groups, and this is important to acknowledge when considering the stances the coalition took on various issues related to the legislation.

III. AGREEING THE PRINCIPLES – 'DON'T MISTAKE SILENCE FOR CONSENSUS!'

Following the advice of Canadian colleagues, the coalition began by looking at the principles adopted by a similar coalition in British Columbia[18] as a starting point for our own discussions. A general format was agreed upon whereby the Centre for Disability Law and Policy would enumerate headline issues, which would become the principles, in consultation with Amnesty, and then clarify their application with a small number of sub-points. My colleague Anna Arstein-Kerslake and I developed some of the initial headline issues based on the Concluding Observations of the CRPD Committee and the writings of those who had been involved in the negotiations of CRPD, primarily, Amita Dhanda,[19] Michael Bach[20]

[16] See for example, the statements of Ms Patricia Rickard-Clarke and Mr Ray Byrne of the Law Reform Commission during the pre-legislative scrunity hearings on mental capacity legislation of the Joint Oireachtas Committee on Justice, Defence and Equality (Dublin, 29 February 2012): www.oireachtas.ie/en/debates/debate/joint_committee_on_justice_defence_and_equality/2012-02-29/3/, accessed 23 April 2020.

[17] See for example *Consideration of reports submitted by States parties under article 35 of the Convention: Concluding observations of the Committee on the Rights of Persons with Disabilities*, Committee on the Rights of Persons with Disabilities: Fifth session, 4 (April 11–15, 2011): tbinternet.ohchr.org/_layouts/15/treatybodyexternal/Download.aspx?symbolno=CRPD%2fC%2f5%2f5&Lang=en, accessed 29 April 2020.

[18] Christine Gordon, 'The Representation Agreement Act British Columbia: The Right to Supported Decision Making in Canada' presented at International Conference on Good Policies for Persons with Disabilities (22–23 January 2012, Vienna, Austria): www.nidus.ca/PDFs/Nidus_Presentation_Intl_Accessibility_Summit_2012.pdf, accessed 27 April 2020.

[19] A Dhanda, 'Legal Capacity in the Disability Rights Convention: Stranglehold of the Past or Lodestar for the Future?' (2006–2007) 34 *Syracuse Journal of International Law & Commerce* 429.

[20] M Bach and L Kerzner, *A New Paradigm for Protecting Autonomy and the Right to Legal Capacity*, prepared for the Law Commission of Ontario, 58 (October 2010): www.lco-cdo.org/en/our-current-projects/the-law-and-persons-with-disabilities/disabilities-call-for-papers-january-2010/commissioned-papers-the-law-and-persons-with-disabilities/a-new-paradigm-for-protecting-autonomy-and-the-right-to-legal-capacity/, accessed 5 May 2020.

and Tina Minkowitz.[21] As the meetings developed, I read out these headline issues and sub-points at each session and discussed them with the group, making changes throughout the meetings, and checking in with Amnesty before each subsequent meeting to incorporate their changes too.

This format had the advantage that it allowed for a wide-ranging discussion and gave those present plenty of opportunities to raise concerns. However, as time went on, and the membership of the group continued to evolve, it often happened that those who had joined the discussion at a later point would reopen challenges that had previously been addressed. This would sometimes encourage others within the group who were more sceptical about the potential of supported decision-making to further air their concerns. I found this incredibly frustrating as I increasingly chaired these discussions, feeling that I was losing ground and the groups that I thought I had brought a step forward were just as likely to take two steps back, depending on who else was in the room that day.

At one such meeting, as I read out each of the principles, one member, who had missed some of the previous meetings, was challenging almost every key point in the draft principles, and gaining support from some of the others in the group who had previously agreed to these same points. Eventually I came to a section which she didn't immediately challenge, and as no one else made a comment on this point, I suggested that there seemed to be agreement and that we should move on. She made a comment which I couldn't catch, and when I asked her if she wanted to add something to this part of the draft, she said 'Don't mistake silence for consensus!' At the end of the process, her organisation were among those who did not sign up to the principles, but they certainly had an impact throughout our discussions – particularly on those members who were not convinced that supported decision-making would work for all, or that it could fully replace substituted decision-making.

When I reflect on the work of the Coalition in developing the principles and my own role in this process, a number of thoughts come to mind. A desire to ensure the human rights compliance of the legislation was a shared aim of all in the Coalition, so the emerging guidance from the UN Committee on the Rights of Persons with Disabilities was clearly relevant to our discussions. However, at that time, in late 2011 and early 2012, there was not much to rely on apart from the repeated recommendation in Concluding Observations that States replace substituted decision-making with supported decision-making.[22] There was significant confusion about what these two terms meant, and little academic literature or other resources to clarify how these could be interpreted.

[21] T Minkowitz, 'The United Nations Convention on the Rights of Persons with Disabilities and the Right to be Free from Nonconsensual Psychiatric Interventions' (2006–2007) 34 *Syracuse Journal of International Law & Commerce* 405.

[22] See for example, Committee on the Rights of Persons with Disabilities, *Consideration of reports submitted by States parties under article 35 of the Convention: Concluding observations of the Committee on the Rights of Persons with Disabilities*, CRPD Fifth session (April 11–15, 2011), 4.

Reliance on Bach and Kerzner's framework was critical at that point,[23] as the only concrete expression for how this right could be realised in legislation to replace adult guardianship.

However, despite a shared commitment to human rights among the coalition members, it would not have been enough for me to argue that supported decision-making was necessary simply because human rights law demanded it. Instead, I needed to persuasively build the case for change with coalition members, and it needed to be located within an Irish-specific context. The fact that Canada, or Sweden,[24] had implemented forms of supported decision-making was all very well, members of the group would argue, but that didn't mean it would work here. Even if people didn't call what they were doing 'supported-decision-making' – the reality was that on the ground in Ireland, people were trying to support their loved ones and others to ensure their wishes were respected in key decisions regarding medical treatment, the choice of where and with whom to live, and many others. As I discuss in the following section, this is where the conferences and workshops organised by the coalition were particularly important, in building public confidence that this change was both necessary and feasible.

At a more personal level, I had to work hard to gain the trust of the members of the coalition as I increasingly took the lead in drafting the principles document. This was not what I anticipated when the work began – Gerard Quinn, as the more senior academic, should have been the chair, but competing commitments meant he often missed the meetings. While the meetings were co-chaired between Amnesty and CDLP, Amnesty would often start with an overview of political developments or possibilities for the legislative process, and then I would take on the role of talking the group through the draft Principles, explaining our positions, and negotiating changes. Given my position as a researcher, others in the room often challenged my perspective on legal capacity by suggesting that I was too idealistic and didn't understand the lived realities that they and their members – especially service providers and families – were facing.

I had in fact faced real life legal capacity dilemmas within my own family – including the involuntary detention of one family member under the Mental Health Act and a process of end-of-life decision-making for another family member following a brain haemorrhage. On reflection now, I don't think I ever used these examples in the room to combat the perception of me as an ivory tower academic – or perhaps – a naïve young woman, both of which may have been in fact operating simultaneously to undermine my potential to lead these discussions.

[23] M Bach and L Kerzner, *A New Paradigm for Protecting Autonomy and the Right to Legal Capacity*, prepared for the Law Commission of Ontario, 58 (October 2010): www.lco-cdo.org/en/our-current-projects/the-law-and-persons-with-disabilities/disabilities-call-for-papers-january-2010/commissioned-papers-the-law-and-persons-with-disabilities/a-new-paradigm-for-protecting-autonomy-and-the-right-to-legal-capacity/, accessed 5 May 2020.

[24] PO Skåne, 'Swedish User-Run Service with Personal Ombud (PO) for Psychiatric Patients' (*PO Skåne*, 22 June 2000): www.po-skåne.org, accessed 24 April 2020.

I'm not quite sure why I didn't use these – perhaps I didn't feel they were my stories to tell (and I'm still not sure if I should be sharing them), or perhaps I just felt that we needed to be arguing from first principles based on human rights standards, not based on emotion and personal experience. I now see the fallacy of efforts to neatly separate these concepts, particularly given everything I have learned about the emotional debates from which the CRPD itself emerged,[25] but I nonetheless find it interesting to reflect on how I instead chose to respond to challenges to my legitimacy within the group.

As I reflect on the evolution of my positioning as an activist-academic through working with this coalition, I recognise the body of scholarship which demonstrates the value of experiential knowledge in socio-legal research generally,[26] and specifically within disability[27] and mad studies.[28] There is also a growing body of literature within disability studies within which scholars who are also family members describe the tightrope they walk between theory and practice[29] – but I also do not think that my reflections here fit within that canon. I am more comfortable positioning my reflections within the broader literature on the experiences of activist academics, especially those from feminist legal perspectives.[30]

In general, I think I leaned in to quite a gendered role in how I approached the chairing of these discussions.[31] Rather than taking a hard-line approach and vigorously opposing proponents of substituted decision-making in the room, I focused very much on validating those who raised concerns about whether supported decision-making could really work. As in most discussions on legal

[25] A Dhanda, 'Legal Capacity in the Disability Rights Convention: Stranglehold of the Past or Lodestar of the Future?' (2006–2007) 34 *Syracuse Journal of International Law and Commerce* 429.

[26] See for example C Menkel-Meadow, 'Uses and abuses of socio-legal studies' in N Creutzfeldt, M Mason and K MacConnachie (eds), *Routledge Handbook of Socio-Legal Theory and Methods* (Abingdon, Routledge, 2019), pp 35–57.

[27] See, for example, L Barton, 'Emancipatory research and disabled people: Some observations and questions' (2005) 57(3) *Educational Review* 317–27; and C Barnes and G Mercer (eds), *Doing Disability Research* (Leeds, Disability Press, 2000) 4; E Stone and M Priestley, 'Parasites, Pawns and Partners: Disability Research and the Role of Non-Disabled Researchers' (1996) 47(4) *British Journal of Sociology* 699.

[28] See A Faulkner, 'Survivor research and Mad Studies: the role and value of experiential knowledge in mental health research' (2017) 32(4) *Disability & Society* 500–520; A Sweeney, 'Why mad studies needs survivor research and survivor research needs mad studies' (2016) 5(3) *Intersectionalities: A Global Journal of Social Work Analysis, Research, Polity, and Practice* 36–61; P Beresford and J Russo, 'Supporting the sustainability of Mad Studies and preventing its co-option' (2016) 31(2) *Disability & Society* 270–74.

[29] See for example, E Feder Kittay, *Love's Labor: Essays on Women, Equality and Dependency* (New York, Routledge, 1999); *Learning from My Daughter: The Value and Care of Disabled Minds* (Oxford University Press, 2019); M Bérubé, 'Equality, freedom, and/or justice for all: A response to Martha Nussbaum' (2009) 40(3–4) *Metaphilosophy* 352–65; K Runswick-Cole and S Ryan, 'Liminal still? Unmothering disabled children' (2019) 34(7–8) *Disability & Society* 1125–39.

[30] C Cann and E DeMeulenaere, *The activist academic: Engaged scholarship for resistance, hope, and social change* (Gorham ME, Meyers Education Press, 2020).

[31] S Acker, 'Chairing and Caring: Gendered Dimensions of Leadership in Academe' (2012) 24(4) *Gender in Education* 411; L Mullany, 'Gender, politeness and institutional power roles: Humour as a tactic to gain compliance in workplace business meetings' (2004) *Multilingua* 13.

capacity reform, the coalition spent a long time discussing the 'hard cases'[32] – including those with whom we couldn't communicate, like a coma patient, and people taking decisions that might endanger their own life, wellbeing or safety, or that of others. I was conscious that most people in the room were hearing these ideas for the first time, and for many of them, their first point of reference was to think about how families and frontline staff would handle a situation, rather than the experience of the disabled person facing a deprivation of their legal capacity. In doing this, I learned so much from my colleague Anna Arstein-Kerslake, and her skills in validating the concerns of those opposed to supported decision-making, and turning them on their head to argue that this was precisely why we needed a different approach.

The result was that once the coalition completed the gruelling process of negotiating the Principles, I gained a level of trust among the coalition members and found it easier to build on our shared understanding, as articulated in the Principles, when the coalition took the next steps in the reform process. In the following section, I now turn to discuss the process of developing public confidence in the approach advocated in the Principles, particularly through the organisation of conferences and workshops, before considering how we attempted to influence the development of the legislative framework itself.

IV. GETTING THE MESSAGE OUT ON SUPPORTED DECISION-MAKING

With funding supplied by Amnesty's campaign, we set about organising a series of public conferences and workshops which would be free to attend, to raise awareness of the value of supported decision-making in an Irish context.[33] Unlike the traditional approach to knowledge exchange more often employed in academic conferences, these events were very clearly aimed at sending a specific political message – that supported decision-making was both necessary and feasible, and could be recognised in the Irish legislative context. Speakers who we believed would be most persuasive in changing the perspectives of key political decision-makers were those invited. Various strategies were employed to ensure that the Minister and relevant civil servants and ministerial advisors not only attended but actually engaged with the substance of each event. One such strategy used was to give the Minister for Disability a speaking slot at the end of

[32] A Arstein-Kerslake and E Flynn, 'The General Comment on Article 12 of the Convention on the Rights of Persons with Disabilities: A roadmap for equality before the law' (2016) 20(4) *The International Journal of Human Rights* 471.

[33] Amnesty Ireland and Centre for Disability Law and Policy Seminar, *Getting it right: capacity legislation and the Convention on the Rights of Persons with Disabilities* (Dublin, 29 November 2011); Amnesty Ireland and Centre for Disability Law and Policy, *Looking globally, legislating locally: the Irish Legal Capacity Bill* (Dublin, April 2012); Amnesty Ireland and Centre for Disability Law and Policy, *Supported Decision-Making in Theory and Practice: Ireland's Capacity Bill* (Dublin, April 2013).

an event rather than the beginning to ensure she stayed until the end rather than leaving after opening remarks.[34]

As I reflect on what was so important about these events, I find myself returning to the contributions of those with lived experience of the existing system, including people with intellectual disabilities and users and survivors of psychiatry, who so clearly and powerfully articulated what was wrong with our law and why it needed to change. One particular exchange at a conference in April 2012, between Nuala Coughlan and Mary Kealy, stands out as one of the most persuasive arguments for change.[35] Nuala, who was at that time living independently with the support of the Brothers of Charity services, and Mary, who was the CEO of the Brothers of Charity Clare, reflected in conversation about what they had been doing at various stages of their lives. The distinction between Nuala and Mary's experiences was stark – when Mary was starting out her career as a social worker, Nuala was living in an institution. Nuala spoke softly and gently and described how all the women living in the institution had their hair cut in the same way, were not allowed to choose or buy their own clothes, and how they worked in the institution, cooking, cleaning and doing other kinds of domestic labour, without pay. As I looked around the room during her talk, I could see tears welling up in the eyes of more than one audience member. This really reinforced for me the power of personal experience to create political change, and how our emotional connections to each other as humans were much more influential on our desire for legal change than any abstract human rights instrument.[36]

V. PUBLICATION OF THE BILL AND EMERGING LEGISLATIVE CLARITY

Amnesty's mental health campaign ended in May 2013, and two months later, on the last day of parliament sitting before the summer break, the Assisted Decision-Making (Capacity) Bill was published. This presented new challenges – as the Centre for Disability Law and Policy was now taking on the lead role in chairing the coalition, with Amnesty keeping a 'watching brief' on legislative developments, but without the resources of a full-time campaign to devote to the process. The Bill as published represented a significant departure from its predecessor, the Scheme of Mental Capacity Bill 2008.

One of the most significant changes, and one which had been strongly advocated for by the coalition, was the removal of 'best interests' – the key guiding

[34] Amnesty Ireland and Centre for Disability Law and Policy, *Looking globally, legislating locally: the Irish Legal Capacity Bill* (Dublin, April 2012).

[35] M Kealy and N Coughlan, 'Experts by Experience' presented at Amnesty Ireland and Centre for Disability Law and Policy, *Looking globally, legislating locally: the Irish Legal Capacity Bill* (Dublin, April 2012).

[36] L Barton, 'Disability, Struggle and the Politics of Hope' in L Barton (ed), *Disability, Politics and the Struggle for Change* (London, Routledge, 2013) 1.

principle of the 2008 Bill, and its replacement with 'will and preferences' in the guiding principles of the 2013 Bill.[37] The Bill also, in contrast with the 2008 Bill, did not propose to introduce a system of adult guardianship. Instead, it proposed the introduction of a tiered system of support and intervention – including decision-making assistance agreements, co-decision-making agreements and decision-making representatives. However, the functional test of mental capacity remained at the core of the Bill, as the key which would determine whether someone could access a particular support, or have a decision-making representative imposed on them.[38]

Once the Bill was published, I worked with the members of the Coalition to quickly develop a response document, which set out eight key concerns with the Bill and sought amendments to the legislation on these issues.[39] Of these eight issues, six were addressed to some extent as the Bill progressed through parliament. The two which were not addressed related to strengthening assisted decision-making and the deprivation of liberty of those deemed to lack capacity. In the following section I will reflect on the main amendments to the Bill which were agreed during the parliamentary debates and the approaches the coalition used to influence those debates.

VI. PARLIAMENTARY ENGAGEMENT AND POLITICAL NEGOTIATION

In order to become law, a Bill must progress through the Dáil (lower house) and the Seanad (upper house) before being signed into law by the President. Before entering the parliament, Bills undergo pre-legislative scrutiny by the relevant parliamentary Committee, in this case, the Committee for Justice, Defence and Equality.[40] The Bill's passage through parliament is led by the responsible Minister; in this case, it was led by Kathleen Lynch, as Minister of State for Disability, Equality and Mental Health. There are four stages of debate in each house, and two of these (Committee and Report Stage) allow for amendments to be introduced by government and opposition politicians.

A number of very significant amendments were made during the legislative process, many of which related to key points raised in the coalition's response document. In this section I reflect on the twin-track approach of the coalition in influencing these amendments by working with civil servants on the one hand, and with parliamentarians, on the other. Throughout this work, my goal was to

[37] Assisted Decision-Making (Capacity) Bill 2013 (Ireland), s 8(7)(b).

[38] Section 3(2).

[39] Centre for Disability Law and Policy, *Equality, Dignity and Human Rights: Does the Assisted Decision-Making (Capacity) Bill 2013 fulfil Ireland's human rights obligations under the Convention on the Rights of Persons with Disabilities?* (Galway, September 2013).

[40] However, the pre-legislative scrutiny had been conducted on the General Scheme of the Mental Capacity Bill 2008, which differed significantly from the 2013 Bill. See Joint Oireachtas Committee on Justice, Defence and Equality (Dublin, 29 February 2012): www.oireachtas.ie/en/debates/debate/joint_committee_on_justice_defence_and_equality/2012-02-29/3/, accessed 23 April 2020.

present decision-makers with solutions to the problems with the Bill identified in the coalition's response document. While some of these ideas made it into the text of the final Act, many were disregarded. Nevertheless, I offer an explanation of these ideas here as they may be useful to others engaged in similar reform efforts.

A. Engaging with the Minister and Her Officials

In the initial period following the publication of the Bill, I had focused the coalition's efforts solely on engaging with the Minister of State for Disability, and the civil servants in the Department of Justice who were responsible for drafting Ministerial amendments to the legislation. I wrote a memo for the Department of Justice with my colleague Piers Gooding, outlining a way to bring the Bill into compliance with General Comment No 1. The memo explained how the Bill could change the criteria for different decision-making arrangements (eg assisted decision making, co-decision-making etc) so individuals did not have to pass a functional test of mental capacity to access support. Instead, we suggested adults could choose their preferred arrangement (with support, where required) as long the individual's will and preferences were known. The last resort appointment of a decision-making representative could be reserved for situations in which the person's will and preferences are unknown, after significant efforts have been made to support the person and to discover her will and preferences. In such situations, we argued that decisions made by these representatives would be guided by the principle of 'best interpretation of will and preferences' as set out in General Comment No 1.[41] The memo included our suggested wording of amendments to the Bill which would achieve our recommended changes, and was supported with reference to existing proposals for legal capacity reform, especially those developed by the Canadian Association for Community Living.[42] However, these proposals did not ultimately bear fruit in the amendments drafted by officials and put forward by the Minister.

Following an opposition politician's request during the parliamentary debates for the Minister to engage more deeply with NGOs,[43] officials from the Department of Justice invited members of the coalition to a meeting in early November to discuss our ongoing concerns about the Bill. A separate follow-up meeting was organised a few weeks later with officials from the Department of

[41] Committee on the Rights of Persons with Disabilities, *General Comment No 1 – Article 12: Equal Recognition Before the Law*, paragraphs 12–15, UN Doc CRPD/C/GC/1, adopted at the 11th Session (April 2014).

[42] Canadian Association for Community Living, *A Draft Statutory Framework for the Right to Legal Capacity and Supported Decision Making: For Application in Provincial/Territorial Jurisdictions in Canada* (Toronto, February 2014): cacl.ca/wp-content/uploads/2018/05/Draft-Statutory-Fmwk-Legal-Capacity-June-9.pdf, accessed 6 May 2020.

[43] Dáil Éireann, Debates, Wednesday, 21 October 2015, Vol 893 No 3, p 24.

Health who were responsible for drafting the Bill's provisions on advance healthcare directives. In a departure from how Amnesty and CDLP had originally conducted such meetings, I decided to have an open invitation to all members of the coalition and not to limit the numbers who could attend. This was a potentially risky strategy, as meetings with large numbers can be unwieldy and the need to keep the group focused and 'on message' regarding our core concerns was a challenge. However, as I had engaged in more and more activist work as an academic, I felt that it was not my place to decide which groups or individuals 'deserved' to be part of this audience – and felt a more open approach was more fitting to the discussion of personal autonomy which I expected to occur. There was a clear political mandate for the meeting given the request to the Minister, but no clear sense of what exactly we could accomplish at this stage, given that the Minister had also given a firm commitment that the Bill would be enacted by the end of the calendar year.

In advance of each meeting we had agreed a strategy among those who would attend about the key points we wished to raise and who from the group would lead on each issue. This did not exactly play out as planned during each meeting. Emotions were running high within the group, particularly for members who had lived experience of legal capacity denials or close family members with these experiences. My overriding impression of our meeting with the Justice officials was that we were politely listened to, but most of our suggestions made no impact on future amendments put forward by the Minister. There was one notable exception to this. A mother of a ward of court in this meeting objected that her son would have to choose between her and her husband in deciding who to appoint as his decision-making assistant, when he wanted to have both of them supporting him equally in key decisions. The same point had been made by Michael Bach in a meeting a year earlier with the same officials and was then dismissed – but following this meeting an amendment was introduced by the Minister to allow appointers to choose as many assistants as they wished and instruct them to act jointly in supporting their decision-making.[44]

The meeting with the officials from the Department of Health was in many ways more fraught with conflict. Several of those who attended this meeting had direct experience of involuntary treatment and coercion in mental health services and as a group we were determined to impress upon the officials the injustice of making advance healthcare directives non-binding for mental health decisions upon involuntary admission. At the outset of this meeting, the lead official informed the group that she agreed with us that this should change, but explained that such change was impossible in the current Bill as she believed the Mental Health Act would first need to be amended to enable such directives to have full legal force. Fiona Morrissey and I disputed this position and argued

[44] Seanad Éireann, Assisted Decision-Making (Capacity) Bill 2013, Committee Stage Amendments, 9 December 2015, Amendment No 31.

that the Mental Health Act could be amended by inserting the relevant provision in the Capacity Bill,[45] but this idea was immediately dismissed.

After some back and forth on the technicalities of legislative amendment, an official from the Department stated that she wanted to hear from those with lived experience, not from the lawyers, as we had reached an impasse about the options available in the legislative process. This seemed to me grossly unfair – to ask people with lived experience to relive their trauma – when it had already been made clear that regardless of these experiences, there would be no legal change forthcoming in the Capacity Bill. Many of those individuals personally affected were clearly upset during and after the meeting, and I felt responsible for having brought them into a space where they were expected to lay bare their personal experiences without any possibility of return in the law-making process.

B. Engaging with Parliamentarians

I was aware that the best chance of getting amendments accepted was to ensure that they were put forward by the Minister and so focused most of my time and energy on convincing the officials of the need for a different approach. However, the process of tabling legislative amendments is such that all amendments – from both the Minister and other parliamentarians, need to be submitted at the same time. I did not have advance notice of whether our proposed amendments would be put forward by the Minister and had to decide whether to simultaneously approach other politicians who were members of the Parliamentary Committee on Justice and Equality. There were concerns among the coalition that doing so might jeopardise our relationship with the Minister and her officials, if we were seen to be 'going behind their backs' and offering amendments to opposition politicians in particular. In the end, the coalition agreed that I would approach government members of the Committee first, as amendments might be viewed more favourably if they came from the Minister's government colleagues.

As a result, two government politicians tabled important amendments about the abolition of informal decision-making[46] and the need to provide legal aid for individuals whose capacity was being determined by the court.[47] Neither of these amendments were accepted initially by the Minister. In fact, the legal aid amendments were ruled out of order by the Committee clerk, as their acceptance could have resulted in a charge on the Exchequer, despite the fact that this was proposed by a government, rather than an opposition, politician. However, amendments achieving almost identical results were later introduced

[45] F Morrissey, 'Assisted decision making bill: Some decisions are less equal than others', *Irish Examiner* (Cork, 21 November 2015) 6.

[46] Dáil Éireann, Assisted Decision-Making (Capacity) Bill 2013, Committee Stage Amendments, 16 June 2015, Amendment No 17.

[47] Ibid, Amendment No 112.

by the Minister herself.[48] In later debates, opposition politicians introduced amendments to change the definition of 'capacity' in the Bill and the criteria for entry into decision-making assistance, co-decision-making and the appointment of decision-making representatives (based on the original memo I wrote with Piers Gooding to the Department of Justice). These were not accepted by the Minister, and she did not introduce similar amendments herself. It would be futile to speculate on the extent to which the offering of amendments from government colleagues of the Minister was more influential than these opposition amendments; nevertheless, it is an interesting factor to consider for others engaged in similar law reform efforts.

C. Reflections on the Parliamentary Process

Throughout the entire legislative process, with colleagues in the CDLP and other groups in the coalition we livetweeted the parliamentary debates, issued press releases, wrote opinion pieces and did radio interviews on the Bill, and continued to write and speak directly to the politicians who were sympathetic on the issue to have our points raised during the debates. When the final debate concluded on 15 December 2015,[49] I felt a sense of crushing disappointment that despite years of work, and coming so close to what could have been such a progressive piece of legislation, we had failed to accomplish what we sought to do. Many other colleagues in the coalition and beyond were at pains to reassure me in the weeks and months to follow that we had improved the Bill greatly beyond what it would have looked like without our intervention, and that there would be opportunities for further reform when the Bill came up for review within five years of its commencement. Nevertheless, I remained deflated, thinking of what we could have achieved, if only the officials had been open to our ideas. Part of my disappointment was that I never got clarity on their reasons for not pursuing the approach offered. I assume they did not pursue our suggested strategy for reframing the Bill away from assessing mental capacity to discovering will and preferences because no other jurisdiction had done this before, or perhaps because they felt that the assessment of mental capacity had an element of scientific certainty, which interpretations of will and preference would lack – but we had presented so much evidence on the subjective and value-laden nature of capacity assessments that I found it difficult to believe they still held such a view.

When I reflect now about the lessons learned from this legislative process, I think about what I might do differently. One early, hard-earned lesson was not to wait for the Minister to reject possible amendments we had offered her

[48] Dáil Éireann, Assisted Decision-Making (Capacity) Bill 2013, Report Stage Amendments, 19 October 2015, Amendment No 81.

[49] Dáil Debates, Thursday 17 December 2015, Vol 901 No 3, pp 26–47.

before giving these amendments to the opposition. I was enticed by the opportunity to work with government parliamentarians; but this process meant that we lost valuable time and ultimately that some important arguments were not put forward, or were not sufficiently pressed. Government parliamentarians did help to communicate our concerns to the Minister but the challenge was that they would be assured the Minister was drafting a similar amendment and would then not put theirs forward on this basis, and it would turn out that the Minister's amendment was either non-existent or nowhere near as progressive as we had hoped.

I learned that an amendment can fail because the parliamentarian is not actually present in the room at the precise moment an amendment is due to be discussed and that this can result in the loss of a hard fought opportunity – without the Minister having to provide any reasons for not accepting the amendment. One crucial amendment to change the functional assessment of mental capacity to a process of discovering the individual's will and preferences was not moved at Report Stage of the Bill because a senator left the room briefly, as the debate was progressing slowly and late into the evening, to grab something to eat.[50] In her brief absence, the debate moved quickly and she lost the opportunity to enter the amendment. This meant that all the work we had done, not only to draft the amendment and brief the senator, but to write the senator's speech on the amendment, with rebuttal arguments anticipating the Minister's objections to the amendment, went unused.

In an academic debate, the holders of the different positions can engage directly with each other, and ideological differences are (usually) tackled head-on, albeit often in highly performative ways through responses to journal articles or in question and answer sessions at academic conferences.[51] In this parliamentary debate, the different positions held by civil society and civil servants were being advanced through intermediaries – parliamentarians and the Minister. Despite opportunities to engage directly with these interlocutors prior to and following on from each stage of the parliamentary debates, I could not tackle the claims they made head on when it mattered most – during the parliamentary debates themselves. Handing over the power of making the argument to others and not being able to participate – except while livetweeting the parliamentary debates – felt like sitting on my hands. This is of course exactly what we are trained to do as academics, to wait and see the outcome of the legislative process, and then to write about it and to critique it,[52] but I was so much more

[50] Seanad Éireann, Assisted Decision-Making (Capacity) Bill 2013, Report Stage Amendments, 15 December 2015, Amendment No 17.

[51] One way in which this debate is 'performed' is by academics publishing replies or responses to those whose views they disagree with – sometimes in the same publication (usually a peer reviewed journal) where the author's original argument appeared. See for example, M Oliver, 'Book Review: Disability Rights and Wrongs' (2007) 27(2) *Disability and Society* 230.

[52] C Thomas, 'Feminism and Disability: The Theoretical and Personal Significance of the Personal and Experiential' in L Barton (ed), *Disability, Politics and the Struggle for Change* (London, Routledge, 2013) 48.

deeply invested in this specific topic, that I rejected the idea of holding that critical distance. The notion of simply holding back to see the outcome and criticising the result felt empty when I knew the cost of the changes the coalition had worked so hard on, but ultimately could not achieve. In the final section, I reflect on what I have taken away from the process as a whole – from the formation of the coalition and development of the principles, through the legislative debates, to the present day, and consider some ways forward for future activist-academic work of this nature.

VII. CONCLUSION

Looking back, I am faced with the conclusion that my options for approaching similar work in the future would take me in one of two very clearly diverging directions. I can either fully embrace the activist role, and be prepared to make my position clear from the outset, working with government, opposition and anyone else who might listen, with less concern than I had a decade ago for the need to preserve relationships with those perceived to be key political decision-makers. Alternatively, I can accept the likely futility of this kind of academic intervention in these debates, and remain outside them, with a critical eye to what emerges, without becoming personally invested in the process. Neither option seems immediately appealing, although if there is a stark choice to be made, my experience tends to tempt me towards a more activist role in future, but only for something that I cared about as passionately as this legislation, and I am not sure at this moment what that might be (apart from an amendment to this very Act).

This leads me to question why exactly I was so invested in this specific piece of legislation. Many of those who are passionate about the subject of legal capacity have had direct personal experience of legal capacity denial – but this is not something that I have experienced. As described above, there have been what I now call 'legal capacity dilemmas' in my own immediate family, but at the time these situations occurred I was blissfully unaware of Article 12 or its potential application to these kinds of experiences. It may simply be explained by the fact that I find the topic endlessly fascinating – and have become more and more interested in the difficult questions it raises the more I research the subject. When I first learned about Article 12, I was initially highly sceptical about whether such a 'radical' notion was possible to achieve. However, my conversion, since it occurred, has been complete, proving that there really is no zealot like a convert when it comes to Article 12.[53]

In thinking about what I have learned from this work and my journey from more traditional academic practice into a more activist role, it comes clear that

[53] See K Booth Glen, 'Changing Paradigms: Mental Capacity, Legal Capacity Guardianship, and Beyond' (2012) 44 *Columbia Human Rights Law Review* 93.

the real players are not actually those 'performing' legislative debates, or even those of us who attempt to influence them. The 2015 Act, as with all capacity laws, has the potential for such a deep and wide-ranging impact on the lives of disabled people – and yet they, and their concerns, were mostly invisible in the debate. Sometimes a few disabled people made it to the public gallery; others watched online; others still had no idea it was happening and no one bothered to explain to them what it would mean or create a space for them to try to influence it.

As I continue my work in this field, I am trying to focus less on my own disappointment at not being able to create change, and more on how I can make space at the decision-making table for those who live under these regimes, and can so powerfully articulate what is wrong with them and what needs to change. In some of my subsequent work on this issue, such as the VOICES project,[54] it has become clear to me that even well-intentioned, so-called 'progressive' legislative reform, is unlikely to bring about the kinds of change that people really need to see a difference in their daily lives. The solutions are much more likely to lie with people, but also in challenging the power structures – which the law often bolsters and upholds – that govern our lives.

[54] E Flynn, A Arstein-Kerslake, C de Bhailís and ML Serra (eds), *Global Perspectives on Legal Capacity Reform: Our Voices, Our Stories* (London, Routledge, 2018).

8

Enabling Supported Decision-making in India's Mental Healthcare Act, 2017: Learnings from a Low-Resource Country Setting

SOUMITRA PATHARE AND ARJUN KAPOOR[1]

I. INTRODUCTION

INDIA'S MENTAL HEALTHCARE Act, 2017 (MHCA) provides for mental healthcare and services for persons with mental illness, and aims to protect, promote and fulfil the rights of persons with mental illness while receiving mental healthcare and treatment. The MHCA came into force on 29 May 2018 following an eight-year legislative process that involved several consultations with government stakeholders and civil society representatives of persons with mental illness, caregivers, families, disability rights activists, mental health advocates and civil society organisations working on mental health.

The MHCA is a radical law since it is one of the first examples of mental health legislation in the world to mandate compliance with the United Nations Convention on the Rights of Persons with Disabilities[2] (CRPD) to the extent possible in India's existing socio-economic and cultural realities. The MHCA has received widespread attention for its potential to revolutionise the landscape of mental healthcare and treatment in India. An editorial in the *British Journal of Psychiatry* noted 'India will have done the world a profound service by stepping forward and making the right to mental healthcare a reality for so many people' and urging the rest of the world to 'watch, listen and learn'.[3] The Report of the

[1] One of the authors of this article, (SP) was appointed as a technical consultant to the Ministry of Health and Family Welfare, Government of India in February 2010 to assist the Ministry in reforming mental health legislation.

[2] A/RES/61/106 Annex 1.

[3] RM Duffy and BD Kelly, 'The right to mental healthcare: India moves forward' (2019) 214 *British Journal of Psychiatry* 59, 60.

Independent Review of the Mental Health Act 1983 in the United Kingdom has recognised the MHCA for its radical approach to ensuring treatment for persons with mental illness.[4] Within domestic quarters the Supreme Court of India's reliance on the provisions of the MHCA in some of its landmark judgments legalising passive euthanasia[5] and decriminalising homosexuality[6] bear testimony to the importance of the MHCA as anti-discrimination and health legislation.

Given its rights-based approach to mental healthcare and treatment, the MHCA heralds the possibility of a revolution in the mental healthcare system and can be a possible game-changer for the rights of persons with mental illness. In this chapter we will demonstrate how the MHCA recognises that rights do not exist in isolation and how it weaves together requirements for the provision of support under Article 12 of the CRPD with other rights such as those recognised under Article 14 (right to liberty and security of person), Article 19 (right to live independently and being included in the community), Article 25 (right to health) and Article 26 (right to habilitation and rehabilitation) of the CRPD.[7] We start with a brief account of the history of mental health laws in pre-independence India and a critique of the Mental Health Act, 1987 (MHA), the predecessor to the MHCA, followed by a discussion on the right to health as recognised under the Constitution of India by judicial pronouncements of the Supreme Court of India. The discussion on the right to health in India is an important prelude to understanding the significance of a legally-binding right to mental healthcare and treatment that the MHCA ensures. This is followed by a section highlighting the MHCA's provisions on supported decision-making. The subsequent discussion addresses the critiques of the law by different stakeholders and the UN Committee on Rights of Persons with Disabilities and ends with some concluding observations.

II. RIGHT TO HEALTH UNDER THE INDIAN CONSTITUTION

Although the Constitution of India does not explicitly recognise the right to health as a fundamental right, the Supreme Court of India has, in several judgments, recognised the right to health as a constitutional right. The Court based its judgments on the Directive Principles of State Policy (DPSP) in the Constitution which are non-binding policy prescriptions that the State is expected

[4] Department of Health and Social Care, *Modernising the Mental Health Act: Increasing choice, reducing compulsion: Final report of the Independent Review of the Mental Health Act 1983* (London, 2018).

[5] *Common Cause (A Registered Society) v Union of India & Another* (2018) 5 SCC 1.

[6] A Kapoor and S Pathare, 'Section 377 and The Mental Healthcare Act, 2017: Breaking barriers' (2019) 4(2) *Indian Journal of Medical Ethics* 111; *Navtej Johar & Others v Union of India* AIR 2018 SC 4321.

[7] For more on the interconnected nature of rights in the CRPD, see Doyle Guilloud, Chapter 6, this volume.

to incorporate in the governance of the country and while making laws. With respect to health, the DPSP recognises the duty of the State to ensure that the health and strength of workers, men and women, is not abused (Article 39(e)); to make effective provisions for public assistance in the case of unemployment, old age, sickness and disablement (Article 40); to provide for early childhood care for children below the age of six years (Article 45); and the primary duty of the State to improve public health (Article 47). The Court has also relied on international laws and conventions such as the Universal Declaration of Human Rights (UDHR) and the International Covenant on Economic, Social and Cultural Rights (ICESCR) which provide for the right to enjoyment of the highest attainable standard of physical health and mental health.

The Supreme Court has, in a series of cases, developed the jurisprudence on the right to health by reading it as an integral aspect of the right to life and personal liberty under Article 21 of the Constitution. In the landmark case of *Bandhua Mukti Morcha v Union of India*,[8] the Supreme Court first recognised the link between the right to life and personal liberty, and the protection of health. The Court held that since the right to live with human dignity under Article 21 draws its scope from the DPSP, it includes protection of health. The Court further went on to develop the right to health in subsequent cases pertaining to different contexts. While upholding the right to health of workers working in asbestos industries, the Court held that 'the right to health and medical care is a fundamental right under Article 21' and further that 'the right to life includes protection of the health and strength of the worker and is a minimum requirement to enable a person to live with dignity.'[9] In another case pertaining to workers, the Court observed that 'the maintenance of health is the most imperative constitutional goal whose realisation requires interaction of many social and economic factors.'[10]

Significantly, the Court has extended the scope of the right to health to cover public health within its ambit as a high priority, while emphasising the obligation of a welfare state to 'ensure the creation and the sustaining of conditions congenial to good health'.[11] While recognising the right to health, the Court has observed that the government also has a constitutional obligation to provide health facilities.[12] The Court has also said that it is a government hospital's duty to provide timely medical treatment to a person in need of such a treatment, and failure to do results in a violation of the right to life under Article 21.[13] While recognising that health is the pith and substance of life and that it is the primary duty of the government to improve public health, the Court has acknowledged

[8] *Bandhua Mukti Morcha v Union of India* (1997) 10 SCC 549.
[9] *Consumer Education & Research Centre v Union of India* 1995, SCC (3) 42.
[10] *Kirloskar Brothers Ltd. v Employees' State Insurance Corporation* 1996, SCC (2) 682.
[11] *Vincent Panikurlangara v Union of India and Others* 1987, SCC (2) 165.
[12] *State of Punjab & Others v Mohinder Singh Chawla* 1997, SCC (2) 83.
[13] *Paschim Banga Khet Mazdoorsamity v State of West Bengal & Another* 1996, SCC (4) 37.

that the right to health is not an absolute right and is subject to 'constraint on the health budget on account of financial stringencies'.[14]

The above discussion is significant, as even though the Right to Health has been recognised as a fundamental right by the Supreme Court of India, it has never been recognised as a statutory right by imposing specific obligations on the government to ensure access to the same. However, with the enforcement of the MHCA, for the first time, the right to access mental healthcare and treatment *has* been made a statutory right. This is a remarkable achievement for the right to health movement in India. The irony is that the mental health sector has paved the way for the right to health despite its neglect on the governance agenda. As discussed subsequently, the MHCA 2017 places numerous obligations on the government to provide infrastructure and resources to ensure a whole range of entitlements for people to access mental healthcare and treatment.

III. THE MENTAL HEALTHCARE ACT, 2017 (MHCA)

A. Background to the Enactment of the MHCA 2017

The first laws pertaining to mental health in pre-independence India were based on England's colonial mental health legislation which established mental asylums and procedures with the objective of protecting society from persons with mental illness who were seen as 'dangerous' and were segregated from society by being admitted to asylums. Subsequently, with the adoption of the UDHR and the enforcement of India's Constitution which recognised the fundamental rights of citizens, the Parliament enacted the Mental Health Act in 1987 (MHA). The MHA has been critiqued for its 'large number of complicated procedures, defects and absurdities', which have resulted in poor implementation, and difficulty in understanding the Act.[15] In particular, the Act has been criticised for its administrative and legalistic approach devolving extensive powers upon the judiciary to take decisions regarding admissions, treatment and discharge of persons with mental illness thus giving mental health a 'criminal flavour'. This was further exacerbated by the fact that decisions of the magistrate or the medical professional under the MHA were not subject to judicial review even though these decisions involved the possibility of depriving a person of their personal liberty.[16]

[14] *State of Punjab v Ram Lubhaya Bagga* 1998, SCC (4) 117.

[15] CL Narayan and D Shikha, 'Indian legal system and mental health' (2013) 55(Suppl 2) *Indian Journal of Psychiatry* S177.

[16] A Dhanda and R Raturi (eds), *Harmonizing Laws with the UNCRPD* (Human Rights Law Network, 2010).

'Mental illness' was not defined under the law, which went against prevailing medical standards for determining whether a person had mental illness.[17] This provided unbridled power to psychiatrists to make a determination of mental illness often against the interests of persons who might be labelled as having a mental illness merely on grounds that they were exhibiting non-conforming behaviour.[18] The constitutionality of the MHA was also questioned because it provided for life-time institutionalisation without a procedure for judicial review or any obligations to look for less restrictive alternatives.[19] India ratified the CRPD[20] in October 2007 and this provided the impetus for reform of mental health legislation, resulting in the drafting and enactment of the MHCA in 2017.[21]

B. Provisions of the Mental Healthcare Act, 2017

The MHCA adopts a rights-based approach to mental healthcare and treatment of persons with mental illness (PwMI) while addressing the defects and gaps that plagued the erstwhile MHA. In this section, we describe the MHCA's key provisions on supported decision-making which enable PwMI to make their own treatment and care decisions with varying levels of support.

(i) Capacity to Make Decisions

The MHCA draws a distinction between mental illness and decisional capacity as two separate concepts. Section 3 of the MHCA ensures that the determination of a 'mental illness' must be in accordance with such nationally or internationally accepted medical standards as may be notified by the Central Government of India. On the other hand, 'capacity' or 'decisional capacity' refers to the ability of a person to make decisions in respect of their personal matters and legal relationships. The MHCA recognises the capacity of a person only with respect to taking decisions regarding one's mental healthcare and treatment.

[17] SB Math, P Murthy and CR Chandrashekar, 'Mental Health Act (1987): need for a paradigm shift from custodial to community care' (2011) 133(3) *Indian Journal of Medical Research* 246; AB Dutt, 'The Long March of Mental Health Legislation in Independent India: Dr L.P. Shah Oration' delivered at IPS-WZ Conference at Goa, 2001 (Goa Psychiatric Society, 2001).

[18] A Dhanda and R Raturi, *Harmonizing Laws with the UNCRPD* (n 16); A Dhanda and T Narayan, 'Mental health and human rights' (2007) 370 *The Lancet* (9594) 1197.

[19] A Dhanda and R Raturi, *Harmonizing Laws with the UNCRPD* (n 16).

[20] A/RES/61/106 Annex 1.

[21] SP was appointed as a technical consultant to the Ministry of Health and Family Welfare, Government of India in February 2010 to assist the Ministry in reforming mental health legislation. During 2011 and 2012, SP worked on multiple drafts of the new mental health legislation after 5 regional consultations and 1 national consultation where the draft of the law was discussed with a mixed group of stakeholders and their representative organisations, including mental health professionals, care-givers, service users and human rights advocates.

Section 4(1) of the MHCA creates a presumption of capacity: every person is deemed to have capacity to make decisions regarding their mental healthcare and treatment if the person is able to (i) understand the information that is relevant to take a decision on the treatment or admission or personal assistance; (ii) appreciate any reasonably foreseeable consequence of a decision or lack of decision on the treatment, admission or personal assistance; and (iii) communicate the decision by means of speech, expression, gesture or any other means. Furthermore, the MHCA stipulates that a person cannot be denied capacity merely on the basis that a decision made by them in respect of mental healthcare and treatment is perceived as 'inappropriate' or 'wrong' by others. Section 4 is crucial since it forms the basis of the MHCA's supported decision-making (SDM) provisions which recognise the right of PwMI to make their own mental healthcare and treatment decisions with varying levels of support. The MHCA does not define 'support' but provides for certain support measures, such as advance directives and nominated representatives, which facilitate the exercise of decisional capacity for PwMI.

(ii) Advance Directives

Section 5 of the MHCA recognises the right of all persons (except minors) to make an advance directive (in writing) to specify all or any of the following: (i) the way the person wishes to be cared for and treated for a mental illness, (ii) the way the person wishes not to be cared for and treated for a mental illness, and (iii) the individual or individuals (in order of precedence) the person wants to appoint as their nominated representative. Advance directives are invoked only when the person loses capacity to make decisions regarding their mental healthcare and treatment, and are effective until the person regains capacity. Advance directives have to be registered with the relevant Mental Health Review Board (MHRB), a quasi-judicial review body, and made available on an online register.

Advance directives can also be reviewed, altered, modified or cancelled based on an application to the relevant MHRB submitted by a mental health professional, or relative, or care-giver who does not wish to follow the person's advance directive. It is the responsibility of the person writing the advance directive and their nominated representative to ensure that the health professional treating the person has access to the advance directive when required. Any health professional treating the person has a duty to propose or provide treatment in accordance with the valid advance directive, if they have been made aware of it.

(iii) Nominated Representatives

Section 14 of the MHCA states that any person, including a PwMI can appoint a nominated representative in writing, approved with the person's signature or thumb impression. The nominated representative is required to be an adult and competent to discharge duties and perform functions under the MHCA. The duties of nominated representatives include providing support to the PwMI to assist them to take decisions.

The MHCA also provides for default alternatives in a situation where a PwMI has not appointed a nominated representative. The list of default options (in order of precedence) includes (i) the individual appointed as a nominated representative in the advance directive, and if not available (ii) a relative, and if not available or willing (iii) a care-giver, and if not available or willing (iv) a suitable person appointed by the MHRB, or (v) if there is no such person then the MHRB can appoint the Director, Department of Social Welfare or the designated representative. The MHCA also ensures that representatives of civil society organisations working for PwMI can make an application to the medical officer or psychiatrist in charge of a person's treatment to be a temporary nominated representative until the MHRB appoints one.

Section 17 of the MHCA lays down the duties of nominated representatives, which include (i) providing support to the PwMI in making treatment decisions, (ii) applying to the mental health establishment for supported admission of the PwMI, (iii) applying to the MHRB against a violation of rights of the PwMI or for discharge from a mental health establishment. According to the provision, nominated representatives are required to consider the current and past wishes, life history, values, cultural background **and** best interests of the PwMI. Section 17 therefore deviates from the CRPD Committee's emphasis solely on 'will and preferences' to the exclusion of 'best interests'. The Indian law thus recognises that the two concepts of 'will and preferences' and 'best interests' are not antithetical to each other and most decisions in life are usually a combination of both these principles. The nominated representative is obligated to give particular credence to the views of the PwMI to the extent that the person understands the nature of decisions taken by them.

(iv) Admissions, Treatment and Discharge

The MHCA provides for two types of admissions to mental health establishments: (i) independent or voluntary admissions whereby a PwMI can make an application to admit themselves if they have decisional capacity and require minimal support; and (ii) supported admissions or involuntary admissions whereby the nominated representative of a PwMI can make an application if the person does not have decisional capacity and requires very high support. Supported admissions can only be initiated by a nominated representative applying for admission to the psychiatrist in charge. They are limited to a period of 30 days; and on expiry, the nominated representative can apply for continued supported admission based on whether the PwMI requires further admission. Supported admissions are made based on fulfilment of the applicable conditions during assessment by psychiatrists and medical practitioners. These conditions include situations wherein a person has a mental illness and is either (i) harming the self, or (ii) causing harm to another person, or (iii) unable to take care of the self (the law requires actual evidence of harm/lack of self-care, rather than a risk of harm/lack of self-care).

Any individual who is admitted as a supported admission has the right to challenge the admission before the MHRB, and such hearings have to be completed within seven days. During supported admissions, the nominated representative is obligated to provide varying levels of support to the PwMI in the latter's treatment and care. If the PwMI lacks decisional capacity, the nominated representative can provide temporary informed consent until such time that the PwMI regains their decisional capacity. Additionally, the MHCA makes provision for emergency treatment by any medical practitioner in any place for a period of 72 hours (consent of the PwMI is not required); bans the use of electro-convulsive therapy without muscle relaxants and anaesthesia and provides for safeguards during the use of physical restraints.

C. Rights of Persons with Mental Illness

(i) Right to Access Mental Healthcare

Section 18 of the MHCA guarantees *every* person the right to access mental healthcare and treatment from mental health services that are *run* or *funded* by the Central or State Governments. The right to access mental healthcare and treatment means that mental health services provided must be: of affordable cost; geographically accessible; available in sufficient quantity; and of good quality. Further, such services must be provided to all persons without discrimination based on gender, sex, sexual orientation, religion, culture, caste, social or political beliefs, class, disability or *any other basis.* Lastly, mental health services provided must be acceptable to PwMI and their families and caregivers. The MHCA mandates the Central and State Governments to provide for a range of basic mental health services at the primary, secondary and tertiary levels of the public health system, which must meet the minimum quality standards of mental health services specified by the State Mental Health Authorities (SMHAs). Governments are also mandated to reimburse PwMI costs for treatment from private establishments where public mental health services are not available in the district where the PwMI resides. Mental health treatment and services must be provided free of any charge to PwMI living below the poverty line, destitute or homeless. Additionally, all medicines on the Essential Drug List should be made available free of cost to all PwMI at all health establishments run or funded by the Government, starting from the community health centres and upwards in the public health system.

(ii) Rights of PwMI During Mental Healthcare and Treatment

The MHCA lays down a charter of rights for all PwMI who are provided mental healthcare and treatment. These rights include the right to equality and non-discrimination; right to medical insurance; right to protection from cruel, inhuman and degrading treatment; right to make complaints against deficiencies in services and the right to confidentiality. Additionally, the MHCA recognises rights which facilitate supported decision-making such as the right to information (regarding the person's mental healthcare and treatment); right to access medical records; right to legal aid (in case of rights violations); and the right to personal contacts and communication (receiving or refusing visitors and receiving or making telephone calls or emails). Most significantly, the MHCA recognises the right to community living which implies that every PwMI has the right to live, receive treatment and recover in their community with adequate support.

IV. SUPPORTED DECISION-MAKING UNDER THE MHCA: ADDRESSING CRITIQUES

India is one of the first countries to reform its mental health legislation after ratification of the Convention on the Rights of Persons with Disabilities. During the drafting of the legislation (from 2011 to 2016) as well as after it was passed by Parliament in 2017, the law has been criticised both in respect of its broad philosophy and its specific contents. Not surprisingly, the criticism has come from diametrically opposite perspectives. Mental health professionals, especially psychiatrists, have criticised the law as going too far towards CRPD compliance and not taking the socio-cultural realities of mental healthcare into account, as exemplified by provisions for advance directives and nominated representatives in the law.[22] On the other hand, activists and human rights advocates have criticised the law for not being compliant with the CRPD because there is no absolute ban on substituted decision-making and the law allows PwMI to be admitted to hospital with the consent of proxy decision-makers.[23]

In the following paragraphs, only sections related to supported decision-making are discussed in detail. The provisions of the law relating to the right to access mental healthcare are also discussed in the context of the provisions for supported decision-making.

[22] A Kala, 'Time to face new realities: Mental Health Care Bill' (2013) 55(3) *Indian Journal of Psychiatry* 216.

[23] B Davar, 'Legal Frameworks for and against People with Psychosocial Disabilities' (2015) 47(52) *Economic and Political Weekly* 7.

A. Advance Directives

Clinicians have argued that a legal provision for advance directives 'assumes that patients including paranoid psychotics have the wisdom to make the right treatment decisions for themselves!'.[24] Others have pointed out that India is not ready for advance directives due to the lack of medical and judicial human resources and economic constraints and argue this will result in unnecessary litigation.[25] Referring to the one Cochrane review on advance directives, critics have also suggested that there is not sufficient evidence to recommend advance directives.[26] Richard Duffy and Brendan Kelly highlighted some other concerns expressed by psychiatrists, including the criminalisation of PwMI who decline treatment (through an advance directive) but come in contact with the criminal justice system by committing an offence, and advance directives limiting psychiatrists' ability to treat patients with mental illness.[27] Activists have also been critical of advance directives because the choices expressed by a person through the advance directive are not absolute (the law allows advance directives to be over-ruled under certain circumstances) and also do not apply in situations where a person is being given emergency treatment.[28]

General Comment No 1 of the Committee on Rights of Persons with Disabilities specifically identifies advance planning statements such as advance directives as a form of supported decision making.[29] The Indian law provides everyone with the option of writing an advance directive but does not compel anyone to do so. While the law makes provision for over-ruling advance directives, they cannot be over-ruled by the treating clinician, and the grounds for challenging an advance directive are limited to certain circumstances. They may be over-ruled by a MHRB after hearing all parties and specifically taking into consideration whether: (i) the advance directive was made of the person's own free will; (ii) the person wished these directives to apply to the specific condition; (iii) the person was sufficiently well informed when making the advance directive; (iv) the person had capacity when the advance directive was made; and (v) the contents of the advance directive are not contrary to other laws or the Constitution. Emergency treatment is a limited provision in the law when there is *imminent* danger of death or irreversible harm to the person or to others and is limited to 72 hours. Advance directives do not apply to emergency treatment

[24] JT Antony. 'Mental health legislation: A journey back to "madhouses era?"' (2016) 58(2) *Indian Journal of Psychiatry* 114.

[25] GP Rao, SB Math, MSVK Raju, G Saha, M Jagiwala, R Sagar et al, 'Mental Health Care Bill 2016: A boon or bane?' (2016) 58(3) *Indian Journal of Psychiatry* 244.

[26] Ibid; A Sarin, 'On psychiatric wills and the Ulysses clause: The advance directive in psychiatry' (2012) 54(3) *Indian Journal of Psychiatry* 206.

[27] RM Duffy and BD Kelly, 'Concordance of the Indian Mental Healthcare Act 2017 with the World Health Organization's Checklist on Mental Health Legislation' (2017) 11(1) *International Journal of Mental Health Systems* 48.

[28] Davar, 'Legal Frameworks' (n 23).

[29] Committee on the Rights of Persons with Disabilities, *General Comment No. 1: Article 12: Equal Recognition before the Law*, UN Doc CRPD/C/GC/1 (New York, 2014).

as it is felt to be unreasonable to expect medical practitioners to be worried about an advance directive in such circumstances.

The inclusion of advance directives in the draft mental health legislation has seen the publication of a number of studies on this topic from India in recent years.[30] Across these studies, anywhere from 75–100 per cent of subjects wanted to write an advance directive. In one study, 15 per cent refused future hospitalisations, 47 per cent refused future electroconvulsive therapies (ECTs), and 62 per cent refused physical restraints.[31] In another study, a large majority (>90 per cent) refused ECTs in an advance,[32] while 80 per cent followed their doctors' advice in their PAD in a study from Mysore in South India.[33] A review of barriers to using advance directives in psychiatric practice identified system-level barriers (legal liability, legal provisions to over-ride an advance directive and resource concerns); clinician-level barriers including fears such as legal liability, difficulty communicating about advance directives, fears of complete treatment refusals, concerns about users' capacity to write advance directives and a fear that advance directives will interfere with clinical care; and service-user barriers such as lack of trust in health professionals, lack of knowledge about advance directives, lack of support to write one and fear of a negative attitude from health professionals.[34]

The advance directive provision in the mental health legislation has led to legal provisions for passive euthanasia in India. In March 2018, the Supreme Court of India allowed a public interest litigation (PIL) petition and made provision for advance directives for passive euthanasia.[35] This judgment refers extensively to the provision of advance directives in the MHCA, including protections in the Act against misuse and the provisions for over-ruling the advance directive. The Court noted that, 'in the context of mental illness, Parliament has now expressly recognised the validity of advance directives and delineated the role of nominated representatives in being associated with healthcare and treatment decisions'

[30] TR Kumar, S John, S Gopal, G Mohan, J Joseph, T Rangaswamy et al, 'Psychiatric advance statements: An Indian experience' (2013) 59(6) *International Journal of Social Psychiatry* 53; LS Shields, S Pathare, SD van Zelst, S Dijkkamp, L Narasimhan and J Bunders, 'Unpacking the psychiatric advance directive in low-resource settings: an exploratory qualitative study in Tamil Nadu, India' (2013) 7 *International Journal of Mental Health Systems* 29; GS Gowda, EO Noorthoorn, P Lepping, CN Kumar, RB Nanjegowda and SB Math, 'Factors influencing advance directives among psychiatric inpatients in India' (2018) 56 *International Journal of Law and Psychiatry* 17; S Pathare, L Shields, R Nardodkar, L Narasimhan and J Bunders, 'What do service users want? A content analysis of what users may write in psychiatric advance directives in India' (2015) 14 *Asian Journal of Psychiatry* 52–56; B Tekkalaki, V Patil, S Patil, S Chate, R Dhabale and N Patil, 'How do our patients respond to the concept of psychiatric advance directives? An exploratory study from India' (2018) 40(4) *Indian Journal of Psychological Medicine* 305.

[31] Tekkalaki et al, 'How do our patients respond' (n 30).

[32] Kumar et al, 'Psychiatric advance statements' (n 30).

[33] Gowda et al, 'Factors influencing advance directives (n 30).

[34] LS Shields, S Pathare, AJ van der Ham, J Bunders, 'A Review of Barriers to Using Psychiatric Advance Directives in Clinical Practice' (2014) 41(6) *Administration and Policy in Mental Health & Mental Health Services Research* 753.

[35] *Common Cause (A Registered Society) v Union of India & another* (2018) 5 SCC 1.

and concluded that this was a precedent for the Court to follow. The provisions for advance directives for passive euthanasia made by the Supreme Court draw upon and are similar to the provisions and protections available in the MHCA.

B. Nominated Representative

The provision in India's mental health legislation of an option to name a person of one's choice to act as nominated representative (someone who provides support to the person in making decisions and, in a situation of decisional incapacity, also acts as substitute decision-maker) has been critiqued by clinicians as well as activists. Clinicians worry that family members in the Indian context provide community care to PwMI and a Nominated Representative breaks the very backbone and fabric of our society "the family".[36] They worry that families may disown and abandon the 'patient' which will thus result in increased homelessness amongst PwMI. Activists complain that the nominated representative is akin to a guardian and therefore promotes substituted decision-making which is contrary to the CRPD.[37]

Critics often over-look the fact that the nominated representative has substituted decision-making powers only when the PwMI lacks decisional capacity (limited to decisions relating to mental healthcare and treatment) and cannot make proxy decisions when the person has decision-making capacity. It may be argued that this meets the CRPD Committee's standard of 'best interpretation of a person's will and preferences' when such will and preference cannot be determined despite best efforts. Further, the nominated representative is to be appointed by the person themselves and the person has the right to change the nominated representative if they wish. In case a person does not name a nominated representative, a family member or caregiver is appointed as the default nominated representative.

The Supreme Court of India in the judgment on passive euthanasia referred to above has recognised the important role of a nominated representative and quoted extensively from the nominated representative provisions in the MHCA. The guidelines framed by the Court for executing an advance directive for passive euthanasia give the person the right to also appoint a family member or relative of their choice, similar to a nominated representative in the mental health legislation. This appointed family member or close relative can make proxy decisions on behalf of the person to execute the advance directive for passive euthanasia, in the event of the person 'becoming incapable of taking decisions at the relevant time.' Thus, the Supreme Court of India has also accorded judicial recognition to the concept of nominated representative appointed by a person, as a substitute decision-maker when the person lacks decisional capacity.

[36] Rao et al, 'Mental Health Care Bill 2016' (n 25) 246.
[37] Davar, 'Legal Frameworks' (n 23).

During the consultations on the MHCA, women's rights groups and representatives of the LGBTQI community wanted the right to name their own nominated representative. This has to be understood in the context of a patriarchal, paternalistic and caste-ist society where traditionally women and sexual minorities have felt powerless and marginalised in the existing family structures. It is worth noting that during consultations on the law, family caregivers groups were also supportive of the right to name a nominated representative, which is contrary to the fears expressed by clinicians that such a provision will be detrimental to family caregiving for PwMI. Recently, the Mental Health Act Review in the UK also recommended replacing the provision on 'nearest relative' in UK mental health law and providing PwMI the option to nominate a person of their choice (nominated person).[38]

V. THE CRPD AND SUPPORTED DECISION-MAKING

A. The CRPD Committee's Position

It has been argued that the MHCA does not comply with the provisions of the CRPD because it allows substituted decision-making by proxy decision-makers (nominated representatives), based on a finding of decisional incapacity.[39] Critics of India's mental health law from this perspective also refer to General Comment No 1 (2014) of the Committee on Rights of Persons with Disabilities (the Committee) as explicitly rejecting the use of 'mental capacity' in any form to determine what supports might be needed for the exercise of legal capacity, arguing that 'mental capacity is not, as is commonly presented, an objective, scientific and naturally occurring phenomenon'.[40] The Committee also calls for a complete ban on involuntary or non-consensual treatment directly or indirectly based on a person's impairments. The Special Rapporteur on the Rights of Persons with Disabilities, in her report submitted to the 37th Session of the Human Rights Council (2017), has supported the Committee's position while further advocating for the repeal of mental health legislation, since it 'creates a separate legal regime for persons with psychosocial disabilities, contrary to the obligations of the States under the CRPD.'[41] Further, in her report to the 40th session of the Human Rights Council (2019) she stated that all States must immediately 'repeal all legislation that allows for deprivation of liberty on the basis of actual or perceived impairment, whether in public or private settings' and has called for the abolition of all disability-related legislation since it has

[38] Department of Health and Social Care, *Modernising the Mental Health Act* (n 4).

[39] Davar, 'Legal Frameworks' (n 23).

[40] UN CRPD, *General Comment No. 1: Article 12: Equal Recognition before the Law* (n 29). See BD Kelly, 'Mental health, mental illness, and human rights in India and elsewhere: What are we aiming for?' (2016) 58 (Suppl 2) *Indian Journal of Psychiatry* S168.

[41] A/HRC/37/56.

a 'disproportionate and adverse impact on the right to liberty of persons with disabilities.'[42] The Committee's position on repealing laws on involuntary or non-consensual treatment has also been endorsed by the UN High Commissioner for Human Rights in his report submitted to the 34th Session of the Human Rights Council (2017).[43]

B. Critique of the CRPD Committee's Position

However, the CRPD Committee's position on supported decision-making is beset by its own internal contradictions and inconsistencies which lead to opposing conclusions. For example, the Committee implicitly accepts (contrary to its assertions on removing substituted decision regimes) that there will be situations when substituted decisions will be required as persons will not have decisional capacity and are unable to express their will and preferences. It says '[w]here, after significant efforts have been made, it is not practicable to determine the will and preferences of an individual, the "best interpretation of will and preferences" must replace the "best interests" determinations.'[44] The phrase 'best interpretation of will and preferences' implies a substitute decision-maker arriving at this interpretation.

There are two specific issues with this position: (i) the Committee fails to account for situations where it will not be possible to ascertain the best interpretation of will and preferences; and (ii) the Committee unfortunately, in our opinion, sees 'will and preferences' and 'best interests' as being mutually exclusive, whereas in reality there will be a significant overlap between these two principles in many situations. For example, if A finds P lying unconscious on the road, A is likely to find it in the best interests of P to shift them to a hospital immediately for emergency treatment. It is highly probable that conveying P to a hospital in such a state would be P's will and preference as well (if they had been aware of such a possibility). Now consider another situation: P is lying unconscious on the road and has a written advance directive on them which states that under no circumstances should P ever be put on a ventilator. Now, A comes across this advance directive on P, but finds it in the best interests of P to take them to a hospital for treatment but also informs the doctors of P's will and preference to not be put on a ventilator. In such a situation, taking P to a hospital for treatment is in their best interests and likely to be P's will and preference so long as they are not put on a ventilator. However, we would like to emphasise that in every situation where it is not possible to ascertain a person's will and preferences, it is imperative that all reasonable efforts are taken to identify the

[42] A/HRC/40/54.
[43] A/HRC/34/32.
[44] General Comment No 1 (n 29), para 21.

person's life history, current and past wishes, values, cultural context and any other aspects which can help arrive at an interpretation of their will and preferences. In such situations, the best interpretation of will and preferences should prevail over a best interests determination.

Furthermore, in General Comment No 1, the Committee identifies three characteristics of substitute decision-making, which include 'a substitute decision-maker can be appointed by someone other than the person concerned, and this can be done against his or her will.'[45] This implies that the Committee does not object to a substitute decision-maker per se, as long as this substitute decision-maker is chosen by the individual, which is appropriate given the Committee's insistence on respecting a person's will and preferences.

As outlined above, India's mental health legislation follows these principles: the individual has the right to appoint their own nominated representative; the nominated representative can make substituted decisions only when it is not practical to determine the individual's will and preference due to lack of decisional capacity; and the nominated representative makes the substituted decision based on 'the current and past wishes, life history, values, cultural background **and** best interests of the person with mental illness' (emphasis added).[46] The nominated representative is also obligated to give particular credence to the views of the PwMI to the extent that the person understands the nature of decisions taken by them.[47] However, since the nominated representative is to be appointed by the person themselves, this would not be regarded as a substitute decision-making by the Committee. The law requires that the person's capacity to make decisions be reviewed every seven days (supported admission up to 30 days) and every 14 days (supported admission beyond 30 days). These provisions of India's mental health law are similar to Bach and Kerzner's model for supported decision-making for PwMI[48] with minor changes made to take into account the human resources situation and role of families in India's sociocultural context.

It is also pertinent to point out that not all authorities agree with the Committee's interpretation of Article 12 of the CRPD as a ban on all involuntary admission (forced treatment). Many countries which have ratified the CRPD gave their responses on the Draft General Comment No 1 to the Committee on

[45] General Comment No 1 (n 29), para 27. The Committee issued a Corrigendum to the General Comment in January 2018 (after MHCA was passed by Indian Parliament).The text of para 27 now reads: '(a) legal capacity is removed from a person, even if this is in respect of a single decision; (b) a substitute decision maker can be appointed by someone other than the person concerned, and this can be done against his or her will; **or** (c) any decision made by a substitute decision maker is based on what is believed to be in the objective "best interests" of the person concerned, as opposed to being based on the person's own will and preferences.'

[46] MHCA s 17(a).

[47] MHCA s 17(b).

[48] M Bach and L Kerzner, *A new paradigm for protecting autonomy and the right to legal capacity* (Law Commission of Ontario, 2010). See also Donnelly, Chapter 2, this volume.

Rights of Persons with Disabilities, almost all uniformly disagreeing with the Committee on this issue.

In its response to the draft General Comment 1, the Government of the Federal Republic of Germany stated that it did not share the Committee's basic assumption that Article 12 of the Convention affords all persons with disabilities unlimited capacity to exercise legal rights and duties.[49] Germany also stated that 'the Committee's interpretation is not shared by the State Parties in general; not even by a substantial minority.' The Finnish Human Rights Centre conveyed its disagreement by stating '[t]he Convention cannot, and by the pure text and the general understanding of it, does not totally ban the possibility of substituted decision-making in some, be it limited and clearly specified, cases.'[50] The Danish Institute for Human Rights, disagreeing with the Committee's interpretation of Article 12 of the Convention asked the Committee to:

> acknowledge that the interpretation of the Committee is different from that of other human rights bodies (and practically all national legislation) and explain why it has been necessary for the Committee to come to these conclusions. If the Committee can in any way recognize that the right to legal capacity may not be absolute, it would be helpful to receive guidance on this issue.[51]

Similarly, the Government of Denmark, the Australian Human Rights Commission, the Equality and Human Rights Commission, the Equality Commission for Northern Ireland, the Northern Ireland Human Rights Commission and the Scottish Human Rights Commission also disagreed with the Committee's interpretation of Article 12 as an absolute ban on non-consensual treatment.[52]

A recent judgment of the German Federal Constitutional Court took a similar view.[53] A person who had been admitted to a closed psychiatric hospital and subjected to physical restraint had challenged the local court order authorising the use of physical restraints. The Constitutional Court held that the use of physical restraints may be justified to avert imminent and serious damage to the health of the persons concerned themselves or other persons such as care staff or doctors. Equally importantly, the Court ruled that Article 12 of the CRPD does not give rise to a general prohibition of measures carried out against the 'natural will of the persons concerned and tied to their limited capacity for self-determination resulting from their illness'. The Court further rejected the Committee's right to issue binding interpretations of the CRPD or to further develop international conventions beyond what has been agreed by State Parties.

[49] Federal Republic of Germany. German Statement on the Draft General Comment on Article 12 CRPD (2014).

[50] Finnish Human Rights Centre. Response to draft General Comments Article 9 and Article 12 of CRPD (2014).

[51] Danish Insitute for Human Rights, *Draft General Comments on Article 9 and 12* (2014).

[52] See: www.ohchr.org/en/hrbodies/crpd/pages/dgcarticles12and9.aspx.

[53] BVerfG, Judgment of the Second Senate of 24 July 2018, 2 BvR 309/15, para 90.

The Court ruled that while the Committee's Statements have significant weight, they are not binding on international tribunals or domestic courts.[54]

The Committee takes a position against mental capacity because of the subjectivity of capacity assessment by mental health professionals, stating that

> mental capacity is not, as is commonly presented, an objective, scientific and naturally occurring phenomenon. Mental capacity is contingent on social and political contexts, as are the disciplines, professions and practices which play a dominant role in assessing mental capacity.[55]

However, the Committee also favours the 'best interpretation of will and preferences',[56] which is necessarily a subjective judgement likely to be made by the same professionals. Thus, while the Committee is against mental capacity assessment because of its subjective nature, it inexplicably does not find any problem with a subjective interpretation of a person's will and preferences, which are likely to be equally contingent on social and political context. The Committee fails to offer any explanation or resolution for these inconsistencies, which raises concerns on the overall coherency of its position on supported decision-making.

The Committee states that mental capacity 'refers to decision making skills of a person',[57] thus equating mental capacity with decision-making skills. It continues that the concept of mental capacity is 'highly controversial, in and of itself' and mental capacity is 'not a naturally occurring phenomenon'.[58] The Committee's reductive position with respect to decision-making skills does not provide a nuanced model of decisional capacity which addresses important theoretical considerations as well as practical concerns in real-world settings. Unfortunately, neither does the Committee provide any evidence to support its claims regarding mental capacity and decision-making skills. It is generally accepted that all individuals may have periods in their lives when their decision-making skills may be impaired and, in some situations, where they lack complete mental capacity, for example, alcohol intoxication or losing consciousness. The Committee's opposition to any kind of assessment of decision-making skills implies that the Committee believes no person can *ever* be assessed as lacking mental capacity necessitating some substitute decision-making, albeit little or temporary, which in our opinion is an untenable position. The Committee's position has been critiqued by various scholars on some of the grounds mentioned above. John Dawson, in particular argues for a 'conservative' interpretation of the CRPD for a more 'realistic and workable' application of its provisions.[59] This position critiques the Committee's understanding of 'discrimination' and

[54] Ibid, para 91.

[55] General Comment No 1 (n 29), para 14.

[56] General Comment No 1 (n 29), para 21.

[57] General Comment No 1 (n 29), para 13.

[58] General Comment No 1 (n 29), para 14.

[59] J Dawson, 'A realistic approach to assessing mental health laws' compliance with the UNCRPD' (2015) 40 *International Journal of Law and Psychiatry* 70.

'capacity' as inadequate, since it doesn't provide satisfactory solutions for situations wherein a person due to impaired capacity (albeit arising due to a mental illness) is at risk of harming the self or others, or is unable to make decisions despite being provided adequate support. Instead, he argues for a limited application of substitute decision-making or involuntary treatment in exceptional situations (wherein a person is unable to make decisions with support) with adequate safeguards and an independent judicial review of the same.

VI. CONCLUDING OBSERVATIONS OF THE CRPD COMMITTEE

In October 2019, the Committee published its Concluding Observations on India's compliance with the CRPD.[60] In its recommendations in respect of Article 12 of the CRPD, the Committee calls upon India to:

> Eliminate all types of guardianship from its national and state legislation and practices, including in the Rights of Persons with Disabilities Act (sect. 14), the Mental Health Care Act (sect. 4) and the National Trust for the Welfare of Persons with Autism, Cerebral Palsy, Mental Retardation and Multiple Disabilities Act.[61]

Section 4 of the MHCA, as discussed above, provides a statutory protection to a presumption of capacity for PwMI and it is truly inexplicable why the Committee finds this provision of the Act protecting decisional capacity, to be a form of guardianship.

Further, with respect to Article 14 (Liberty and Security) of the CRPD, the Committee recommends that India should:

> Repeal provisions of the Mental Health Care Act and the Bombay Prevention of Begging Act that allow for institutionalization on the basis of impairment, and adopt strategies to end all forms of institutionalization, involuntary commitment and segregation on the basis of impairment, and the seclusion of persons with intellectual or psychosocial disabilities in all types of institutions.[62]

The Committee does not identify which particular sections of the MHCA it finds problematic in this respect. There is no definition of institutionalisation provided in this document – does the Committee mean that PwMI should never be admitted to any mental health facility? Furthermore, the Committee calls upon India to repeal provisions for seclusion of persons with intellectual and psychosocial disabilities but fails to recognise that India has banned seclusion in mental health facilities in the MHCA.[63]

[60] Committee on the Rights of Persons with Disabilities, *Concluding Observations on the Initial Report of Indiai*, UN Doc CRPD/C/IND/CO/1.

[61] Ibid, para 27.

[62] Ibid, para 31.

[63] MHCA s 97.

Under CRPD Article 25 (Health) and Article 26 (Rehabilitation) the Committee, while calling upon India to '[a]dhere to article 25 of the Convention in its efforts to achieve targets 3.7 and 3.8 of the Sustainable Development Goals'[64] and calling upon India to '[e]nsure universal health-care coverage and access for all persons with disabilities in rural and urban areas',[65] fails to recognise and acknowledge the steps taken under the MHCA to provide universal free access to mental healthcare and the provisions for parity of health insurance for mental illness with physical illness.

A. Right to Access Mental Healthcare

A right to supported decision-making and autonomy without the right to access appropriate mental healthcare is an empty promise. The rights protected by Article 26 of the CRPD are as important as Article 12 rights, and should be seen together. The provisions of the MHCA need to be seen in the context of the provision of (or lack of) mental healthcare in India currently. Unfortunately, commentators on India's mental health legislation have paid little attention to what in our view, is the most important provision of the legislation, namely, the right to mental healthcare being made a statutory right in the legislation. This right is spelt out in detail in section 18 of the MHCA and lays down a minimum level of mental health services that must be provided in every district in the country.[66] In the absence of such public provision of mental health services, the law gives individuals the right to access mental healthcare from any private provider and puts a responsibility on the Government to reimburse the costs of such treatment. The right to mental healthcare also includes the right to get free psychotropic medicines for all from the Essential Drug List and puts a duty on the Government to make adequate budgetary provisions for fulfilling this right.

The National Mental Health Survey in 2016[67] showed a treatment gap ranging from 70–92 per cent for different psychiatric disorders. Research also shows that India devotes hardly 1 per cent of the public health budget to mental healthcare,[68] and the public health budget itself is approximately 1.25 per cent of GDP.[69] In the absence of formal services, families in India provide most of the continuing care for their family members with mental illness. There is also evidence to show that high out-of-pocket expenses for healthcare contribute to

[64] *Concluding Observations* (n 60), para 53.

[65] Ibid.

[66] India has 739 districts.

[67] National Mental Health Survey of India, 2015–16: Mental Health Systems (Bengaluru, 2016).

[68] S Pathare, 'Beyond ECT: priorities in mental health care in India' (2003) 11(1) *Issues in Medical Ethics* 11.

[69] Comparable figures in most countries are anywhere from 5–7 per cent and 2–4 per cent respectively.

a significant number of people (8 per cent) sliding into poverty every year.[70] This provision in the law therefore holds the promise of reducing the chances of poverty (one of the important Sustainable Development Goals) and reducing the treatment gap for mental illness in the country by increasing public expenditure on mental health services and the development of public mental health services in the under-served parts of the country. It is also worth noting that India does not have a statutory right to healthcare and this is the first health legislation in the country to make healthcare (even if it is only limited to mental healthcare) a statutory right. It therefore sets an important precedent for eventually legislating for a right to healthcare in India.

It is an accepted truism that rights are indivisible and there is no hierarchy of rights. The right to receive care and to be cared for in periods of ill-health is as important as the right to autonomy and personal choice. The right to autonomy also means the right to exercise one's own will and preferences, free of any undue influence, including the influence of illness which may affect a person's decision-making capacity. In our opinion, restoration of decisional capacity has to be seen as an integral part of exercising one's own will and preferences. India's mental health law addresses both these issues, balancing the right to healthcare with the right to autonomy and choice, providing sufficient safeguards and protections against abuse without privileging either of these rights.

B. Other Rights

For the first time in India, a mental health law has explicitly protected a number of rights recognised in the CRPD, which are also linked to the provision of support and the exercise of other important rights protected in the CRPD.

Many people in India are stuck in a mental hospital because their families are unwilling to take them back home or they have no families or caretakers.[71] In both these situations, these persons cannot be discharged because there is a dearth of community living facilities with mental healthcare appropriate to their needs. The abandonment of persons with serious mental illness also leads to a risk of homelessness, with India's National Mental Health Policy also recognising the need for services for this vulnerable population.[72] The MHCA recognises the right to community living and says that the mere absence of community facilities cannot be grounds for continued stay in a mental hospital. The law

[70] K Kumar, A Singh, S Kumar, F Ram, A Singh, U Ram et al, 'Socio-Economic Differentials in Impoverishment Effects of Out-of-Pocket Health Expenditure in China and India: Evidence from WHO SAGE' (2015) 10(8) *PLOS One* e0135051.

[71] H Nair, 'Hundreds of patients cured of mental illness have nowhere to go, SC expresses concern', *India Today*, 2016.

[72] Ministry of Health and Family Welfare, *New Pathways, New Hope: National Mental Health Policy of India* (New Delhi, 2014).

thus puts a responsibility on the government to make provision for community facilities according to need. Thus, the MHCA supports the objectives of the National Mental Health Policy and has the potential to accelerate the development of supported community living options for PwMI.

The MHCA also provides detailed provisions for protection from cruel, inhuman and degrading treatment, the right to information about one's own mental healthcare and treatment, the right to confidentiality, the right to access medical records, the right to legal aid and the right to make complaints about deficiencies in services. While many of these rights seem obvious from a medical perspective, this is the first instance that India has provided statutory protection for these rights in the mental health context. All these rights protections are coherent with the rights protected in the CRPD. The MHCA bans seclusion, but not physical restraint, which is permitted with significant restrictions, thus recognising the harmful effects of these practices. The MHCA also bans un-modified Electro-convulsive therapy (ECT) and only permits ECT in children with the approval of the MHRB, based on international recommendations from the WHO[73] as well as the World Psychiatric Association.[74] Surprisingly, however, the Indian Psychiatric Society has objected to these restrictions and published a position statement of its own with detailed guidelines on the use of un-modified ECT.[75]

VII. CONCLUSION

While the MHCA has been hailed as being progressive and likely to 'revolutionise' mental healthcare in India,[76] there are concerns about its implementation.[77] These concerns are justified due to India's past experience of poorly implementing well-designed legislation and already noticed delays in implementing certain provisions of this legislation;[78] the significant financial and human resources challenges;[79]

[73] World Health Organization, *WHO Resource Book on Mental Health, Human Rights, and Legislation* (Geneva, Switzerland, World Health Organization, 2005).

[74] World Psychiatric Association (MT Abou-Saleh and G Christodoulou), *The WPA position statement on the ethics of the use of unmodified electroconvulsive therapy* (2009) 20(1) *Arab Journal of Psychiatry* 57.

[75] C Andrade, N Shah, P Tharya, M Reddy, M Thirunavukarasu, R Kallivayalil et al, 'Position statement and guidelines on unmodified electroconvulsive therapy' (2012) 54(2) *Indian Journal of Psychiatry* 119.

[76] V Patel, 'New law is the most progressive globally', *Hindustan Times*, 14 September 2018; R Duffy, C Narayan, N Goyal and B Kelly, 'New legislation, new frontiers: Indian psychiatrists' perspective of the mental healthcare act 2017 prior to implementation' (2018) 60(3) *Indian Journal of Psychiatry* 351.

[77] Duffy et al (n 76).

[78] N Ashraf, 'Indian law says mentally ill should get health insurance, but do companies offer them?', *The News Minute*, 4 April 2018.

[79] P Chatterjee, 'Economic crisis highlights mental health issues in India' (2009) 373 (9670) *The Lancet* 1160; R Kakuma, H Minas, N Van Ginneken, MR Dal Poz, K Desiraju, JE Morris et al, 'Human resources for mental health care: Current situation and strategies for action' (2011)

and psychiatrists' opposition to certain aspects of the legislation.[80] The legislation with its emphasis on autonomy, choice and rights of the individual has already changed the power dynamic in the clinician-patient-family triad,[81] which will require adjustments and changes for all stakeholders, including mental health professionals.

There are reasons for cautious optimism for effective implementation of the MHCA. These include a nascent, but increasingly vocal, user community who are aware of their rights; heightened interest in the new law in popular press with numerous articles in recent months; an activist judiciary which accords importance to the protection of rights of vulnerable groups; and policy-makers in Federal and State governments increasingly cognisant of the need for policy and financial priority to health issues. Duffy et al capture this optimism: 'whatever its outcomes, however, the new legislation has commanded international attention and may well become the mould for the next generation of rights-based mental health legislation.'[82]

378(9803) *The Lancet* 1654; SK Khandelwal, HP Jhingan, S Ramesh, RK Gupta, VK Srivastava, 'India mental health country profile' (2004) 16(1–2) *International Review of Psychiatry* 126.

[80] Duffy et al (n 76).

[81] Duffy et al (n 76).

[82] Duffy et al (n 76).

9

Reflections on the Reform of Spanish Civil Legislation on Legal Capacity of Persons with Disabilities

PATRICIA CUENCA GÓMEZ[1]

I. INTRODUCTION

UNDER THE HEADING 'Equal recognition before the law' Article 12 of the Convention on the Rights of Persons with Disabilities (CRPD) lays down a set of provisions that constitute a true revolution, challenging the common approach to legal capacity of persons with disabilities in domestic legal systems. This chapter reflects the human rights approach – that embeds the shift from understanding persons with disabilities as 'objects' of charity, medical treatment and social protection, to thinking of them 'as subjects' with full and equal human rights[2] – and the social model of disability – that emphasises the impact of social barriers on the difficulties experienced by persons with disabilities regarding the exercise of those rights.[3] In accordance with these assumptions, Article 12 recognises that all persons with disabilities should enjoy full legal capacity and have the right to exercise it on an equal basis with others in all aspects of life. Consequently, it advocates moving from a model of substituted decision-making to a model of supported decision-making by a thorough revision of traditional legal institutions.

[1] This chapter has been developed in the context of the following projects: 1) Access to Justice and Vulnerability, PID2019-108918GB-I00 R+D+I, funded by the Spanish Ministry of Science and Innovation, and 2) New Challenges of Law project, Action Agreement, Carlos III University of Madrid – Community of Madrid. I would like to thank Alessandro Di Rosa for his help with the language and the editors of this book for all their suggestions.

[2] G Quinn, 'Personhood and Legal Capacity: Perspectives on the Paradigm Shift of Article 12 CRPD' (Conference on Disability and Legal Capacity under the CRPD, Harvard Law School, 2010).

[3] A Palacios, *El modelo social de discapacidad: orígenes, caracterización y plasmación en la Convención Internacional sobre los derechos de las personas con discapacidad* (Colección CERMI Madrid, Ediciones Cinca, 2008).

After years of delays and unfulfilled commitments, the Spanish Parliament approved Law 8/2021 of 2 June to reform the civil and procedural legislation to support persons with disabilities in the exercise of legal capacity.[4] This chapter analyses the conformity of this reform with the obligations arising under Article 12, as it has been interpreted in General Comment No 1 by the Committee on the Rights of Persons with Disabilities (CRPD Committee).[5] First, the chapter introduces the basic features of the pre-reform legal position. Secondly, it exposes the backdrop and the key aspects of the reform and, finally, it assesses the new regulation on legal capacity in the light of the CRPD. The reform represents a major advance since it does not allow any formal restriction of legal capacity on the basis of disability and establishes support measures in decision-making. However, the new regulation perpetuates some elements of substituted decision-making including some controversial limits to the principle of respect of the will and preferences of persons with disabilities.

II. THE PRE-REFORM SUBSTITUTED DECISION-MAKING FRAMEWORK IN SPAIN

Before the reform, Spanish Law strongly reflected the medical model of disability and the perspective of assistentialism.[6] From this point of view, this regulation met the common characteristics of substituted decision-making regimes, as these have been defined by the CRPD Committee.[7]

The Spanish Civil Code recognised legal personality (the ability to be considered as a person before the law) and legal capacity[8] (which included only – departing from the concept of legal capacity in the CRPD – the ability to be holder of rights and duties) as universal traits attributed to all persons without restrictions. However, capacity to act (the ability to exercise those rights and duties) could be denied or diminished for persons with cognitive disabilities.[9] According to Articles 199 and 200 of the Civil Code, persons with 'persistent

[4] This Law entred into force on 2 September 2021.

[5] See A Arnstein-Kerslake and E Flynn, 'The General Comment on Article 12 of the Convention on the Rights of Persons with Disabilities: a Roadmap for Equality before the Law' (2015) 20 *The International Journal of Human Rights* 471.

[6] See P Cuenca Gómez, 'El sistema de apoyo en la toma de decisiones desde la Convención Internacional sobre los Derechos de las Personas con Discapacidad: principios generales, aspectos centrales e implementación en la legislación española' (2012) 10 *Revista electrónica del Departamento de Derecho de la Universidad de La Rioja (REDUR)* 61.

[7] CRPD Committee, *General Comment No 1. Article 12: Equal recognition before the Law* (adopted 19 May 2014), CRPD/C/GC/1, para 27.

[8] See regarding these concepts inspired by the Latin tradition, F De Castro, *Derecho civil de España*, (Madrid, Civitas, 1984) and L Díez Picazo, *Sistema de derecho civil. Volumen I* (Madrid, Tecnos, 2003).

[9] The term 'cognitive disability' is chosen to encompass all disabilities that affect cognitive functioning. See A Arnstein-Kerslake, *Restoring Voice to People with Cognitive Disabilities: Realizing the Right to Equal Recognition before the Law* (Cambridge, Cambridge University Press, 2017).

physical or mental illnesses which prevent governing' themselves could be 'incapacitated' via a judicial process.[10]

In theory, since the legal reform of Law 13/1983, the Spanish incapacitation system was gradual and flexible, requiring the accommodation of the restriction of capacity to act to the level of self-government of each person, and including different forms of protection. On a textual analysis of these provisions, Spanish legislation could be considered close to the functional approach to legal capacity, which relies on individual assessment of a person's mental capacity – of 'the level of self-government' in the terms used by Spanish Law – and denied legal capacity accordingly.

Nevertheless, in its judicial application the approach generally ended up conforming with the status approach, since deprivation of legal capacity was decided simply on the basis of the diagnosis of an impairment. In practice, the expert medical opinions required in the judicial procedure failed to assess the different aspects of personal decision-making ability, and the mere diagnosis of a cognitive impairment was the only criteria taken into account in the declaration of legal incapacity, without analysing its impact on self-government.[11] As a result, incapacitation judgments did not include an exhaustive determination of the extent and limits of the declaration of incapacity[12] and relied on generic and stereotyped assumptions.

This judicial practice – without explicit legal support – established two rigid levels of legal incapacitation. In cases of full incapacitation, judgments simply declared that the person was deprived of the capacity to manage their personal and financial affairs and a plenary guardian (a tutor) with the power to exercise all legal rights and duties on their behalf was appointed.[13] In cases of partial incapacitation, judgments stated that a guardian (a curator) must assist the person in carrying out certain acts.[14] Although legislation allowed more tailored approaches and less restrictive options, full incapacitation and plenary guardianship were systematically overused, reflecting the hyper-paternalistic tendency underlying legal incapacitation.[15]

[10] On disability and legal capacity in Spain see eg, JJ Soto Ruiz, 'El estatus jurídico de las personas con discapacidad en las leyes de cabecera del ordenamiento jurídico privado' in R De Lorenzo García and LC Pérez Bueno (eds), *Tratado sobre Discapacidad* (Pamplona, Thomson-Arandazi, 2007) and F Bariffi, 'Capacidad jurídica y capacidad de obrar de las personas con discapacidad a la luz de la Convención de la ONU' in LC Pérez Bueno (ed), *Hacia un Derecho de la Discapacidad, Estudios en Homenaje a Rafael de Lorenzo* (Pamplona, Thomson Reuters Aranzadi, 2009).

[11] For example, regarding the case of a person with dementia, the judgment of the Provincial Court in Barcelona, 22 April 2003, stated that this cognitive impairment 'determines and entails, in short and without the need for further consideration, his impossibility of self-government and the need for assistance by third parties, both in financial affairs, as well as in the personal, for which reason we should declare him totally incapable for all legal purposes'.

[12] Despite this requirement was included in the Art 760 of Law 1/2000 on Civil Procedure.

[13] Art 267, Spanish Civil Code.

[14] Art 287, Spanish Civil Code.

[15] G Quinn, 'From Object to Subject. Reflections on Personhood & Disability in the 21st Century' (AJUPID, Final Conference, Sofia, 2016). See also JA Seoane Rodríguez and N Álvarez Lata, 'El proceso de toma de decisiones de la persona con discapacidad: una revisión de los modelos de

Guardianship could also take the form of 'extended parental authority' in cases of children with cognitive disabilities to whom incapacitation was applicable upon their coming of legal age. Extended parental authority was subject to the provisions of the incapacitation judgment and, on a residual basis, to the general rules that govern parental authority, leading to the infantilisation of adults with disabilities. Finally, Article 303 of the Civil Code referred to the 'de facto custody' as a provisional form of custody until legal incapacitation was adopted, which revealed a lack of trust in informal support mechanisms and promoted judicial intervention in the lives of persons with disabilities.

Judicial proceedings for legal incapacitation were a civil and adversarial process, conceived as a dispute between opposing parties where the incapacitated person was the defendant, and an 'expert medical opinion agreed upon by the court' was the only compulsory evidence.[16] Furthermore, the safeguards required in Article 12(4) CRPD were not included properly in Spanish legislation. The will and preferences of the person did not have to be respected or even taken into account during the incapacitation procedure.[17] The Civil Code did not oblige the guardian to consider the person's wishes, only to act 'for the benefit' of the incapacitated person – that is, for the protection of their 'best interests' – a principle that is not considered by the CRPD Committee to comply with Article 12.[18] A judicial defender could be appointed in a case of conflict of interest, but effective measures in order to ensure the identification of such conflicts were not available. The Spanish legal system also failed to adequately prevent abuse and undue influence. In addition, guardianship measures were in principle instituted for an unlimited period of time and judgments of incapacitation were not subject to periodic review.[19]

As in other countries, deprivation of legal capacity led to 'civil death',[20] since, by having their legal capacity denied, people with cognitive disabilities were deprived of engagement in legal transactions and from exercising their rights, including human rights (such as the right to access to justice or the right to consent for medical treatment[21] etc). Despite the fact that incapacitation also

representación y guarda a la luz de la Convención sobre los derechos de las personas con discapacidad' (2010) 4 *Derecho privado y Constitución* 11, 29.

[16] See Articles 757 and ff of the Spanish Civil Procedural Law.

[17] The person's opinion on the appointment of the guardian was heard only if they were of sound mind.

[18] CRPD/C/GC/1, para 21.

[19] A specific procedure was available aimed at fostering recovery of the person's capacity to act or at amending the scope of the declaration of incapacity, but this is an exceptional proceeding applicable only where new 'circumstances come about'. Of further concern, deprivation of capacity to act led to the loss of the person's right to appear before the court; therefore fully incapacitated persons could not act in these proceedings on their own behalf unless they 'obtain the court's express authorisation' (Art 761).

[20] Quinn, 'From Object to Subject' (n 15) and E Flynn and A Arnstein-Kerslake, 'Legislating Personhood: Realising the Right to Support in Exercising Legal Capacity' (2014) 10 *International Journal of Law in Context* 81.

[21] In December 2018, the legislation on political participation, that allowed the deprivation of the right to vote of persons legally incapacitated, underwent reform.

impacted on personal affairs, the Spanish Civil Code focused on the regulation of financial matters.

Although the contradiction between Spanish legislation and Article 12 CRPD and the need of reform were already noticed by the CRPD Committee in its Concluding Observations on the initial Report of Spain in 2011,[22] the only legal change has been a purely terminological one: since 2015, incapacitation proceedings were named 'proceedings for the modification of the capacity to act'.[23] Regarding judicial developments, in 2009 the Spanish Supreme Court initiated a new line of jurisprudence, considering incapacitation as a 'tailored suit' and requiring the determination of its exact scope and the assessment of the capacity of the person for self-government in different areas. The Supreme Court also promoted curatorship, interpreted as a form of support,[24] as a general rule. However, this position, which is closer to the functional approach,[25] was not followed by many judgments of first instance.[26] In March 2019 the CRPD Committee again advised Spain to review its laws allowing for guardianship and trusteeship, and develop laws and policies to replace regimes of substitute decision-making by supported decision-making.[27]

III. THE REFORM OF LEGAL CAPACITY LAW

In April 2018, the Ministry of Justice opened an online public consultation in order to collect opinions from interested parties about the necessity for reform of the civil and procedural law on legal capacity. In September 2018, a preliminary draft adopted by the Ministry of Justice's General Commission of Codification, was published to enable experts, stakeholders and the wider public to comment on the proposals. As a result of this process of pre-legislative scrutiny and of several meetings with disability organisations, this Draft incorporated significant improvements. The reform was interrupted by political instability, with the calls for general elections in April 2019 and November 2019, and in 2020 the pandemic also altered the legislative agenda. Finally, in July 2020 the Council of Ministers sent to Parliament the Bill to reform the civil and procedural legislation

[22] See CRPD/C/ESP/CO/1, paras 33 and 34.

[23] See Law 15/2015, 2 July on Voluntary Jurisdiction.

[24] Current curatorship's significant gaps as a form of support in the light of the CRPD should be noted, since it involves the restriction of legal capacity and the curator's role consists of providing a substitute or complementary consent in certain legal acts, not of providing assistance during the decision-making process.

[25] It is important to note that functional approach is also discriminatory according to the CRPD Committee, CRPD/C/GC/1, para 15.

[26] Spain does not publish official data in this field in violation of Article 33 of the CRPD. According to a report by the Guardianship Foundations Association, between 2010 and 2015, 87% of persons with intellectual disabilities whose legal protection was assumed by the association were subject to full guardianships compared to 12% under curatorship.

[27] CRPD/C/ESP/CO/2-3, paras 22 and 23.

to support people with disabilities in the exercise of their legal capacity. In the following months, disability organisations made proposals to the parliamentary groups for amendments to the Bill, and some of their representatives and other experts appeared in the Congress. The debate on the text and the amendments started on 4 February 2021[28] and finally the Bill was approved on 21 May and published on 2 June. This section examines the main aspects of this reform.

A. General Backdrop to the Legal Reforms

The Explanatory Introduction of Law 8/2021 of 2 June describes the reform as a 'decisive step' and a 'fundamental milestone' in the adaptation of Spanish legislation to the CRPD, which expresses, more than a 'merely terminological' change, 'a new and more accurate approach to reality' and an awareness of 'something that has gone unnoticed for a long time: that persons with disabilities are holders of the right to make their own decisions, a right that must be respected'.

Likewise, the Explanatory Introduction assumes the approach to disability and legal capacity adopted by the CRPD and General Comment No 1. According to this perspective, the right of a person with disabilities to make her own decisions is explicitly considered as a 'human rights issue'. Consequently, human dignity, the protection of fundamental rights and respect for the autonomy and free will of persons with disabilities are mentioned as the major principles inspiring the new regulation. The Explanatory Introduction maintains that legal capacity includes both being a holder of rights and having the power to exercise them, citing General Comment No 1. It also considers that legal capacity 'is inherent to the condition of a human person and therefore cannot be modified.' In addition, it categorically rules out that the measures regarding the exercise of legal capacity may imply the deprivation of rights 'whether personal, patrimonial or political'.

In line with the social model, the Explanatory Introduction emphasises that many of the limitations traditionally faced by persons with disabilities in the exercise of their legal capacity are not a result of their personal conditions, but of the social 'environment', that is, of 'physical, communicational, cognitive, attitudinal and legal barriers that have curtailed their rights and the possibility of their exercise'. The relevance of attitudinal barriers is highlighted when the Explanatory Introduction states that the legal reform must be linked to 'a transformation of the social mentality' and 'especially' of the mentality of the justice system professionals who should act according to the new principles and leaving aside 'paternalistic attitudes'.[29]

[28] Firstly, discussions took place behind closed doors, secondly in the Justice Commission and, finally, the text was debated in plenary sessions of the Congress and later in the Senate.

[29] A Pau, 'De la incapacitación al apoyo. El nuevo régimen de la discapacidad intelectual en el Código civil' (2018) 5(3) *Revista de Derecho Civil* 5, 8 ff.

Within this framework, the Explanatory Introduction affirms the necessity of a shift from the previous system, which was based on the incapacitation of persons who are considered 'not capable enough' and where substituted measures 'predominate', to 'another system' whose 'main idea' is support – understood in a broad sense identified by the CRPD Committee[30] – based on the respect of the will and preferences of persons with disabilities. However, this shift is not reflected in some of the concrete provisions included in the Spanish reform.

B. Key Aspects of the Reform of Substantive Law

As regards substantive law, the new Title XI of the Civil Code entitled 'On support measures for persons with disabilities to exercise their legal capacity', replacing the Title IX called 'On incapacitation', contains the major innovations of the reform.

The first and most important aspect of the reform is that there is no restriction of capacity on the basis of disability. Accordingly, the traditional substitution mechanisms in decision-making, such as guardianship (tutorship) and extended parental authority, are removed from the field of disability. The new Title XI replaces these institutions with 'support measures' aimed at ensuring the effective exercise of legal capacity for persons with disabilities.

The new Article 249 of the Civil Code sets out the general principles guiding the support model adopted in the reform. It stipulates that support measures shall be inspired by the protection of the dignity of the person and their rights, shall respect their will, wishes and preferences and shall comply with the principles of necessity and proportionality. This article also indicates that the essential purpose of support measures is helping individuals to 'develop their own decision-making process, informing them, helping them in their understanding and reasoning and facilitating them to express their preferences' This provision reflects the most relevant feature of the support model, in which the intervention of the supporter does not take place by replacing the person in the adoption of decisions with legal effect, but rather by assisting the person in their decision-making process.[31]

Support institutions may have representative functions only in exceptional situations, when despite a 'considerable effort, it is not possible to determine the will, wishes and preferences of the person'. In these cases, the supporter can make decisions on behalf of the person receiving support, taking into account

[30] See, for example P Gooding, 'Navigating the "Flashing Amber Lights" of the Right to Legal Capacity in the United Nations Convention on the Rights of Persons with Disabilities: Responding to Major Concerns' (2015) 15(1) *Human Rights Law Review* 45, 50.

[31] In this sense the reform is focused on supporting decision-making arrangements 'where one or more people assist another to make a decision and communicate it to others', L Series, 'Relationships, Autonomy and Legal Capacity: Mental Capacity and Support Paradigms' (2015) 40 *International Journal of Law and Psychiatry* 80, 85.

'the life history of the person with disability, their beliefs and values, as well as the factors that they would have taken into consideration in order to make her decisions if they did not require representation'.

The new Article 250 of the Civil Code purports to give priority to 'voluntary' support measures designed by the person, establishing who should provide support and to what extent. According to the Article 255 persons of legal age or emancipated minors can arrange support measures (personal or financial) in a public document before a notary in anticipation of future circumstances or in appreciation of current circumstances that may hinder the exercise of their legal capacity on equal terms with others.[32]

Measures of 'legal or judicial origin' should only be adopted 'in the absence of the will of the person'. As subsidiary measures of support, Article 250 mentions de facto guardianship, curatorship and the judicial defender. Therefore, the new support model relies on old figures whose new role shall be 'to assist the person with disability in the exercise of their legal capacity in the areas where it is necessary, respecting their will, wishes and preferences'. The new regulation reinforces 'de facto guardianship'[33] as an informal or natural support institution, shifting it from a provisional measure to a mechanism of permanent assistance.[34] The judicial defender is defined as an occasional support for certain types of situations: to meet support needs that are not guaranteed by another measure, in situations of conflicts of interest, or in the event of the temporary inability of the supporter to provide it.

The reform pays special attention to the regulation of the curatorship[35] conceived as a permanent support judicially established and applicable when no other measure is available or sufficient.[36] According to the new Article 268 of the Civil Code, the curator should always respect the maximum autonomy of the person who needs assistance in the exercise of their legal capacity and must favour their will, wishes and preferences. Curatorship is designed as a formal and tailored support with varying degrees of intensity, and the new Article 269 states that the judicial authority shall determine the acts in which the person requires the intervention of the curator according to their specific support needs. The judicial authority shall also specify the acts in which, in exceptional cases, the curator will have representative functions. The judicial resolution will never include the 'mere' deprivation of rights.

[32] In the previous version of the Law, the right to choose and arrange support before a notary was expressly regulated only as a way of planning for the future. See P García Rubio, 'Las medidas de apoyo de carácter voluntario, preventivo o anticipatorio' (2018) 5(3) *Revista de Derecho civil* 29.

[33] See M Pereña Vicente 'La transformación de la guarda de hecho en el Anteproyecto' (2018) 5(3) *Revista de Derecho Civil* 60.

[34] The new Art 263 states that if the de facto guardian needs to accredit representation of the person, a judicial authorisation that may include diverse acts of ordinary administration shall be requested through a voluntary jurisdiction proceeding in which the person concerned must be heard.

[35] New Chapter IV of the Title XI of the Civil Code, Articles 268 and ff.

[36] See PA Murnar Bernat, 'La curatela: principal medida de apoyo para las personas con discapacidad' (2018) 5(3) *Revista de Derecho Civil* 121.

The new Article 271 governs the 'self-curatorship' that allows the designation of a curator by means of an advanced directive before a notary.[37] In application of this provision, any person of legal age or any emancipated minor, in anticipation of future needs of support to exercise their legal capacity, may appoint or exclude from appointment as curator one or more persons and may establish provisions on the scope, functioning and content of the curatorship, including control measures.

In any case, the curator is always formally appointed by a judicial decision. Persons of legal age 'who, in the opinion of the judicial authority' are suitable to exercise support functions, and foundations and other non-profit public or private legal entities that work in the promotion of autonomy and assistance for persons with disabilities, may be designated as curators. The supporter proposed by the person in need according to Article 271 (self-curatorship) shall be appointed by the judge as curator. In the absence of such a proposal, Article 276 establishes an order giving priority to the closest relatives, which can be modified by the judicial authority once the person who needs support has been heard. If the will of the person is not clear, the judicial authority may also alter the legal order by appointing as curator the person who is most suitable 'to understand and interpret the will, wishes and preferences of the person who needs support'. The removal of the curator can be ordered by the judicial authority, ex officio or at the request of the Public Prosecutor or of the supported person, when there are circumstances that compromise the correct functioning of the curatorship.

Finally, concerning the safeguards, according to Article 249 the judicial authority may establish safeguards in order to ensure that the exercise of support measures complies with the general principles, and, in particular, that these measures respect the will, wishes and preferences of the person. In addition, Article 250 mentions that, when determining support measures, efforts to avoid conflicts of interest or undue influence should be made.

Judicial supervision of support measures and judicial control is also included in the concrete regulation of the institutions of support.[38] Furthermore, the new Article 250 stipulates that support must not be exercised by persons who, by means of a contractual relationship, provide welfare, residential or similar services to the person, and Article 275 establishes that persons who have a conflict of interest with the person cannot be appointed as curators. In cases of support with representative functions, the requirement of judicial authorisation for certain legal acts can also serve as an effective safeguard. New Article 268

[37] See JA Escartín Ipiéns, 'La autocuratela en el Anteproyecto de Ley sobre la modificación Código civil y otras leyes complementarias en materia de discapacidad' (2018) 5(3) *Revista de Derecho Civil* 85.

[38] See Art 270 that states that the judicial authority 'shall establish in the resolution that constitutes the curatorship, or in a later one, the control measures' deemed 'appropriate to guarantee the respect of the rights, will and preferences of the person that needs support, as well as to avoid abuses, conflicts of interest and undue influence'. The curator can be required at any time by the judge to report on the personal or patrimonial situation of the person concerned. The Public Prosecutor may also at any time request information.

orders a periodic review of the support measures established by the judicial authority within a maximum period of three years.[39]

C. Key Aspects of the Reform of Procedural Law

As the Introductory Explanation of Law 8/2021 of 2 June states, the legal reform must include a new procedure that may no longer have as a result a declaration of incapacity or a restriction of rights, but instead the provision of support. However, in the preliminary version of the draft, this proceeding still responded to the medical model and the assistentialist perspective. This traditional approach is shown by the terminology used in some articles, the explicit mention of the criterion of the 'best interest', the absence of accessibility measures and procedural accommodations, the disregarding of the will and preferences of the person and the possibility to decide about the support measures with the guidance only of a medical opinion. Thus, this procedure focused on the diagnosis of impairments and not on the assessment of support needs. The evident shortcomings of this approach, strongly criticised during the public discussion process, were resolved in the final version of the bill.

The final text of the reform provides that the procedure for providing support shall take place by means of voluntary or non-contentious jurisdiction, where the intervention of a court is necessary for the protection of rights and interests but there are no matters opposed or in contention.[40] The contentious jurisdiction should only be used to deal with cases in controversy.

In the Civil Procedural Law and in the Law on Voluntary Jurisdiction, a new Article 7bis on 'Accommodations for persons with disabilities' has been incorporated, stipulating that, in all proceedings in which persons with disabilities participate, 'all the necessary adaptations and flexibilities shall be adopted', including communication supports such as simple and accessible language, easy read documents, interpretation in sign languages and the assistance of professional facilitators (intermediaries), etc.[41]

According to the Law on Voluntary Jurisdiction, voluntary proceedings can be initiated by the Prosecutor's Office, the person with disability, their spouse from whom they are not legally or de facto separated or those who are in a similar situation, and their descendants, ascendants or siblings, provided that they live with the person who needs support. The application must be accompanied by documents that prove the need for support measures, as well as an expert

[39] However, the judicial authority may establish, exceptionally and giving specific arguments, a longer review period that may not exceed six years. Support measures adopted will be reviewed, in any case, in the event of any change in the person's situation that may require a modification of these measures.

[40] This option is also adopted in Colombian reform in Law 1996/2019.

[41] The regulation of these adjustments was significantly improved in the parliamentary discussion on the text.

opinion from social and health care professionals, who advise about the suitability of the support measures in each case. In addition, the person concerned must have legal assistance, the judge must hold a personal interview with them, and other persons can also be heard. The judicial authority may also ask for a report from the public entity that, in the respective territory, has the function of promoting autonomy and assistance to people with disabilities, or from a third-sector social action entity authorised as a collaborator of the Administration of Justice, on support alternatives and on the possibility of providing support without requiring the adoption of any judicial measure. In the judicial interview, the person may be informed about these alternatives to obtain support either through their social or community environment, or through the design of voluntary measures before a notary. If the person chooses alternative support measures, the judicial proceedings will end.

The opposition of the person with disability or of any of the interested parties to the adoption of the support measures will end the voluntary proceedings, and contentious proceedings will be opened. According to the new regulation, controversy over the designation of a specific person as curator is not considered an opposition that makes the contentious proceedings necessary.

The regulation of contentious proceedings for the provision of support measures also contains significant innovations. With particular respect to the procedure for the provision of support measures, the new Article 758.2 of the Civil Procedural Law establishes that a Lawyer of the Administration of Justice shall ensure that the person with disability can understand the object, purpose and procedures in conformity with Article 7 bis mentioned above.

Moreover, the final version of the reform of the Civil Procedural Law eliminates stigmatising terminology and incorporates notable improvements: 1) the interview with the person who needs support is now a mandatory requirement; and 2) support needs should be assessed by an interdisciplinary team.[42]

Regarding the appointment of the curator, the new regulation establishes that if the person who needs support has not proposed the designation by means of advance directives, the judge 'shall hear the person with disability' as well as closer relatives and other persons as deemed necessary by the judicial authority. As explained in the previous section, the judge shall appoint the curator according to the order of priority established in the Civil Code (which can be altered after hearing the person who needs support).

A valuable safeguard, mentioned also in the reform of substantive law, is the periodic review of the support measures judicially adopted by means of a procedure under voluntary jurisdiction. Furthermore, the person with disability and other parties can request the modification of support measures under

[42] This interdisciplinary evaluation, included also in the Argentine 2015 reform of the Civil Code, means that the assessment of the person should not be just medical, but also requires the evaluation by other specialised professionals, such as social workers: AE Martínez Pujalte, 'Legal Capacity and Supported Decision-Making: Lessons from Some Recent Legal Reforms' (2019) 8(4) *Laws* 1, 9.

voluntary or contentious jurisdiction, depending on the nature of the first judicial resolution.

IV. ASSESSMENT OF THE LEGAL REFORM IN LIGHT OF THE CRPD

The reform of civil and procedural legislation by Law 8/2021 of 2 June represents a substantial advance in the regulation of legal capacity, in that the general approach and its main milestones are fully consistent with the CRPD. Nevertheless, some crucial aspects of the regulation seem not completely satisfactory.

A. The General Approach and Principles of the Reform

Undoubtedly, the most laudable feature of the Spanish reform is that it does not allow any formal restriction of legal capacity on grounds of disability. In other words, according to the new legislation, incapacitation will be not a civil status anymore. Recognising universal legal capacity, Spanish reform is in line with Peruvian[43] and Colombian[44] reforms, and departs from the regulation of Argentina whose Civil and Commercial Code continue to speak of restrictions on capacity.[45] Thus, the Spanish option reflects the paradigm pointed to by the CRPD that leads us to avoid the rigid schematism of traditional legal regimes based on a binary model of capacity or incapacity. In this way, the Spanish reform does not create a separate category of people who are legally incapacitated with regard to some or all decisions, which can be 'profoundly disempowering'[46] and stigmatising and has been argued to justify multiple restrictions of rights.[47]

However, this great advance should have been completed with the inclusion of a provision explicitly declaring that all persons with disabilities have full legal capacity to act on an equal basis with others in all aspects of life.[48]

[43] Decree N° 1384/2018.

[44] Law 1996/2019.

[45] Indeed, the 2015 Argentine reform links the need of support in decision-making with restrictions of legal capacity and also maintains instances of traditional full incapacitation. Specifically, the last paragraph of Art 32 of the Civil Code provides that 'when the person is absolutely unable to interact with the environment and express his or her will in any appropriate way or format and the support system is ineffective, the judge may declare incapacity'. The effect of this declaration of incapacity is the provision of a figure, which the Argentine Civil Code calls 'curator', who has the same functions as the guardian of minors (Art 138, first paragraph). See on this reform, Martínez Pujalte, 'Legal Capacity and Supported Decision-Making' (n 42), 12.

[46] See E Flynn and A Arstein-Kerlake, 'The Support Model of Legal Capacity: Fact, Fiction, or Fantasy' (2014) 32 *Berkeley Journal of International Law* 124, 130–31.

[47] Report of the Special Rapporteur on the Rights of Persons with Disabilities on Legal Capacity Reform and Supported Decision-Making (2017), A/HRC/37/56, para 82.

[48] In this sense the new Art 42 of the Peruvian Civil Code expressly states that all persons with disabilities have full capacity to exercise their rights on an equal basis with others and in all aspects of life.

Moreover, in coherence with the Explanatory Introduction, it would have been desirable to mention accessibility requirements and the right to reasonable accommodations[49] in performing legal acts, with special emphasis on cognitive disabilities.

Regarding the beneficiaries of support measures, the new regulation sometimes refers to persons with disabilities and other times to any person needing support in exercising their legal capacity. In my view, leaving aside the idea of 'special' measures only for persons with disabilities, which stem from the medical model, support measures must be available to all persons who face difficulties in the exercise of their legal capacity, thus covering other situations, for example the needs of older persons, and using the potential of the inclusive approach of the support paradigm to benefit society as a whole.[50]

In any case, the general principles on which the model of support adopted in the reform is based and identified in new Article 249 of the Civil Code align with the CRPD's philosophy. All support measures aim to assist in decision-making and should respect the will and preferences of the person. This view seems to advance the more realistic understanding of autonomy that inspires the supported decision-making approach, which challenges the traditional conception of autonomy as isolated and 'purely' independent, emphasising its relational nature.[51] The support paradigm acknowledges that individuals have the right to exercise their autonomy, but that autonomy may be exercised through the help and assistance of others. Within this framework, the final aim of the process of support is not to impose an external decision taken by a third person based on an objective view of what is in the best interests of a person with disability, but to arrive at a decision with the individual as informed as possible by their will and preferences.[52]

This approach clearly inspires the way in which Article 249 deals with the (hard) cases where is not possible to discern a person's will and preferences.[53]

[49] This is one of the most remarkable strengths of the Colombian reform that includes accessibility as a general principle and recognises the right to reasonable accommodations in the exercise of legal capacity (Art 5 of Law 1996/2019).

[50] See for example Flynn and Arstein-Kerslake, 'Legislating Personhood' (n 20), 82–83.

[51] See generally Arstein-Kerlake, *Restoring Voice to People with Cognitive Disabilities* (n 9); Series, 'Relationships, Autonomy and Legal Capacity' (n 31), 81 and P Gooding, 'Supported Decision-Making: A Rights-Based Disability Concept and its Implications for Mental Health Law' (2013) 20(3) *Psychiatry, Psychology and Law* 431, 435.

[52] C De Bhailis and E Flynn, 'Recognising Legal Capacity: Commentary and Analysis of Article 12 CRPD' (2017) 13(1) *International Journal of Law in Context* 6, 17; Donnelly, Chapter 2, this volume; Keeling, Chapter 3, this volume.

[53] Most of the critiques regarding Art 12 are focused on these cases, where will and preferences remain unknown, and also on situations, that will be considered below, where respecting the individual's autonomy would result in serious harm, suggesting that, in such circumstances, legal capacity cannot be absolute, and that some form of substituted decision-making must be allowed: see M Browning, C Bigby and J Douglas, 'Supported Decision Making: Understanding How its Conceptual Link to Legal Capacity is Influencing the Development of Practice' (2014) 1(1) *Research and Practice in Intellectual and Developmental Disabilities* 34; MC Freeman and others, 'Reversing Hard Won Victories in the Name of Human Rights: A Critique of the General Comment on

With respect to these situations, exceptionally, this Article allows support with representative functions and rightly includes the only valid standard formulated by the CRPD Committee to take such decisions: the best interpretation of the will and preferences of the individual, determined by considering 'the life history of the person with disability, their beliefs and values, as well as the factors that they would have taken into consideration in order to make their decision if they did not require representation.'[54] This criterion reflects the narrative approach to human agency,[55] invites us to rethink how decisions are 'made for' people in exceptional circumstances[56] and rests on the presumption that it is almost always possible to come to some level of understanding of a person's values, beliefs and views which ultimately underpin their will and preferences.[57]

In my opinion, in these challenging cases, operating on the basis that the person, and not the supporter, should be regarded as the agent making the decision is a legal fiction. In reality, it should be recognised that the decisions are made on behalf of the person by a third party.[58] However, according to the approach adopted by the CRPD and assumed by Article 249, such representative function would not fall within the substituted decision-making model but would conform with the support paradigm. It is crucial to clarify that understanding representative actions as 'intensive forms of support' instead of 'substituted decisions' is not trivial and neither is it merely a semantic issue. This is not only because this option means that the persons retain their legal capacity,[59] but also, above all, because it shifts the guiding principle for taking the decisions from the 'best interests' to the 'best interpretation of will and preferences', involving a critical difference that may alter substantially the nature and results of such decisions.

Article 12 of the UN Convention on the Rights of Persons with Disabilities' (2015) 2(9) *The Lancet Psychiatry* 844; J Dawson, 'A Realistic Approach to Assessing Mental Health Law Compliance with the UNCRPD' (2015) 40 *International Journal of Law and Psychiatry* 70; A Ward, 'Abolition of Guardianship? "Best Interests" versus "Best Interpretation"' (2015) 32 *Scots Law Times* 150. In Spain, M Alemany, 'Igualdad y diferencia en relación con las personas con discapacidad. (Una crítica a la Observación General n.1 (2014) del Comité (UN) de los derechos de las personas con discapacidad' (2018) 52 *Anales de la Cátedra Francisco Suárez* 201; M Pereña Vicente, 'La Convención de Nueva York y su incidencia en el ejercicio de la medida de protección' in *Código de buenas prácticas en el ejercicio de las medidas de protección jurídica* (Fundación Manantial, 2016) Annex 3, p 141.

[54] Similar standards have been included in Peruvian and Colombian reforms.

[55] M Bach and L Kerzner, *A New Paradigm for Protecting Autonomy and the Right to Legal Capacity* (Law Commission of Ontario, October 2010), http://www.lco-cdo.org/disabilities/bach-kerzner.pdf (accessed 10 January 2021) and B Jennings, 'Agency and moral relationship in dementia' in EF Kittay and L Carlson (eds), *Cognitive Disability and its Challenge to Moral Philosophy* (Wiley-Blackwell, 2010) 171.

[56] Gooding, 'Navigating the "Flashing Amber Lights"' (n 30), 52.

[57] De Bhailis and Flynn, 'Recognising Legal Capacity' (n 52), 17.

[58] Series, 'Relationships, Autonomy and Legal Capacity' (n 31), 86 and 87. In recognition of this approach, the Spanish reform includes more stringent safeguards for support with representative functions, requiring judicial authorisation regarding certain acts.

[59] The opposite option is adopted by the Argentine reform, which treats these exceptional instances as cases of traditional incapacitation as it has been explained above.

B. Other Reform Provisions

Unfortunately, as advanced above, the development of the general principles proclaimed in the new Article 249 by other provisions of the reformed law reveals significant deficiencies. A first relevant drawback of the Spanish reform is that its model of support for the exercise of legal capacity is not sufficiently innovative and flexible, since it relies upon traditional institutions such as curatorship and de facto guardianship – terms that reflect the assistentialist perspective (the function of caretaking and protection) and not the promotion of autonomy. Although keeping traditional institutions already known by families and professionals may generate legal security and confidence, the creation of new support figures could have laid out more clearly the profound break with the previous model. Perhaps, correctly interpreted, the promotion of the de facto guardian as a natural support, only requiring formalisation for certain acts, may respect the way of life of the person and avoid overregulation. Nevertheless, the design of such a figure needs to be improved in order to function as a real support, and the right to choose and arrange other informal supports should have been explicitly recognised.

The priority that the reform affirms should be given to the will of the person in the design of support measures was manifestly inadequate until the latest version of Law 8/2021, where relevant improvements were included in order to promote 'voluntary' measures. According to the final text of the reform, the person concerned can choose and arrange their system of support before a public notary not only ahead of time, as in the previous versions, but also for contemporaneous support needs.[60] Even during judicial proceedings to establish the curatorship, the person, after being informed about these options, can choose other alternative forms of community support or decide to arrange support measures before a public notary, avoiding judicial measures by adopting voluntary measures.

In addition, despite the general principle mentioned in Article 249, representative functions are not really conceived as exceptional in the regulation of support institutions. For example, Article 269 does not explicitly limit curatorship with representative functions to situations where it is not possible to determine the person's will and preferences, but rather extends such functions to cases where representation is considered 'indispensable', taking into account 'the situation of the person'. These instances may not be interpreted as exceptional, especially if the circumstances are assessed under the criterion of best interests. Of special concern is the explicit reference to a 'representative curator' in the new Article 289 of the Civil Code.

[60] This possibility is also included in Peruvian and Colombian reforms. For example, as an important innovation compared with the previous regulation, the Colombian reform – following the model of British Columbia – establishes 'support agreements' by means of which a person, of legal age, formalises before a public notary the appointment of the person or persons, natural or legal, who will assist them in making decisions regarding one or more specific legal acts.

Therefore, the new legislation seems to establish a formal difference between the 'supporter curator' who assists the person in decision-making and the 'representative curator' who has a power of representation of 'general scope'; that is to say, a general authorisation to decide on behalf of the person in a plurality of situations. This latter role is not limited to decisions that need to be taken or to situations where will and preferences remain unknown, making it very difficult to distinguish the 'representative curator' from the substituted institution of full guardianship (tutor). Regarding this issue, it is worth remembering that support with representative functions also entails substituted decision-making, if it is not strictly limited to the cases in which it is not possible to verify will and preferences by any means.[61]

These provisions establish that the support system in decision-making is interpreted as 'the general rule', as literally defined in the Explanatory Introduction of the Law 8/2021 of 2 June, whereas an improved substitution system remains in force as an exception. This is a serious weakness of the Spanish reform since, as the CRPD Committee has pointed out in General Comment No 1, 'the development of supported decision-making systems in parallel with the maintenance of substitute decision-making regimes is not sufficient to comply with Article 12 of the Convention.'[62] Moreover, there is strong evidence to think that the appointment of a 'representative curator' will in the future become the generally accepted response, especially taking into account the judicial practice in the application of incapacitation that systematically promoted the most restrictive options.

Some unequivocal evidence of the influence of the substituted model can also be identified in the regulation of the judicial constitution of the curatorship. In the design of the system of support and in the appointment of the curator, the judicial authority must hear the person who needs support, but there is not any explicit and clear reference to the obligation to respect their will and preferences. In fact, the judge is not bound to do so, except in cases of self-curatorship.[63] This is another serious limitation of the reform, that the judge can impose support (curatorship) not only without considering the will of the person, but even against it. Thus, as long as a supporter can be appointed by a third party against the will of the person and the right to choose and to refuse the support measures are not recognised,[64] the model proposed in the Spanish reform does not comply with Article 12 as interpreted by General Comment No 1.[65]

[61] Martínez Pujalte, 'Legal Capacity and Supported Decision-Making' (n 42), 10.

[62] CRPD/C/GC/1, para 28.

[63] It is true that the Law on Voluntary Jurisdiction includes the respect of the will and preferences of the person with disability, but in a very confusing way (see new Art 45).

[64] It should be noted that these rights – the right to choose and to refuse support as all the rights of persons with and without disabilities – are not absolute rights, pointing out limitations in some situations. However, they must be explicitly recognised and respected in general terms and their restrictions should be treated as borderline cases.

[65] See specially AL Martínez Pujalte, 'A propósito de la reforma de la legislación española en materia de capacidad: la voluntariedad como nota esencial del apoyo' (2020) 42 *Cuadernos electrónicos de Filosofía del Derecho* 240.

From this point of view, in the voluntary proceedings for provision of support, although the appointment is made before the judge, the judge should be bound by the decision of the individual who needs support. When the will and preferences of the person cannot be determined, in spite of efforts through accessibility measures and reasonable accommodation, and when the designation of the curator is necessary for the protection of rights, the judge should appoint the supporter by taking into account the relationships of friendship, trust or kinship of the person who needs assistance in decision-making, and determine the extent and effects of such support. In doing so, the judge should always try to obtain the best possible interpretation of the will and preferences of the person according to their life story.[66] This would mean that, in exceptional situations, support can be provided without the will of the person who needs it. The legal reform should have also included a general provision declaring that the curatorship will not be constituted if the person concerned expressly refuses this measure. Finally, if it is admitted as an exception that the supporter may be appointed against the will of the person in extreme cases, which is very controversial from the point of view of the CRPD, the procedure should certainly become an adversarial one, in order to prove the existence of those exceptional circumstances.[67]

It could be said that the major shortcomings of the Spanish legal reform on legal capacity reveal that the best interests model, although not explicitly mentioned, is still considered a valid argument for the limitation of the principle of respect for the will and preferences of persons with disabilities. In my opinion, this core principle can only be restricted in exceptional cases on the basis of the safeguards mentioned in Article 12.4 of the CRPD; that is, in order to avoid serious risks of abuse, conflict of interest or undue influence, and in instances of real risk of harm to person's human rights. Obviously, if situations of manipulation, abuse or undue influence occur in the support relationship, the decision is not an *authentic* expression of a person's will and preferences.[68] Thus, if one of these situations exists, it may be justified on an exceptional basis to override the wishes of the person concerning a specific decision, such as, for example, the appointment of the supporter, in order to protect their real will.

Hard cases of a risk of harm raise a question of how potentially conflicting rights should be balanced, calling for the application of the principle of proportionality. In my view, a correct application of the proportionality test – taking into account the central role of the right to legal capacity and the need to rebalance protection and autonomy in the context of disability – would allow divergence from the will and preferences of the person only in situations in which

[66] This proposal is inspired by the Peruvian legal reform on legal capacity.

[67] Peruvian and Colombian reforms do not allow this possibility.

[68] L Series and A Nilsson, 'Article 12 CRPD: Equal Recognition before the Law' in I Bantekas, MA Stein and D Anastasiou (eds), *The UN Convention on the Rights of Persons with Disabilities: A Commentary* (Oxford, Oxford University Press, 2018).

respect for will and preferences would give rise to a grave and imminent risk to other equally relevant human rights.[69] This would also entail demonstrating that less restrictive alternatives are insufficient and ensuring that the benefits of the intervention outweigh the harms. This parameter has the potential to be applied in a truly disability-neutral manner justifying paternalistic interventions in the sphere of freedom of people with and without disabilities.[70]

In sum, Spanish legal reform on legal capacity does not abandon the influence of the principle of best interests, does not rely decidedly on a framework based on will and preferences, and does not take seriously the right of persons with disabilities to take risks and make their own mistakes.[71] In this sense, the new regulation hides some dilemmas and legitimises certain practices of substituted decision-making, which will inevitably be subject to extensive interpretation. Spanish legal reform should have considered expressly and carefully the interventions in these hard cases and should have incorporated clear legal principles and reinforced appropriate safeguards[72] for dealing with them based on the support paradigm of legal capacity.[73]

Legal capacity reform will have a knock-on effect on many areas of law and, as the CRPD Committee has remarked in General Comment No 1,[74] requires other additional legal and policy shifts in order to ensure that persons with disabilities have real opportunities to make meaningful choices in their lives. Moreover, as in other countries, a practical and cultural change is needed in Spain, involving persons with disabilities, key professionals, families and society as a whole, as the only effective way to combat not only formal, but also informal substituted decision-making.

V. CONCLUSION

It should be concluded that the Spanish legal reform on legal capacity does not fully respect the requirements of Article 12 CRPD and perpetuates some elements of substituted decision-making, as the UN Special Rapporteur of Disabilities has highlighted in regard to the reforms of other domestic legal systems.[75]

[69] E Flynn and A Arstein-Kerslake, 'State Intervention in the Lives of People with Disabilities: The Case for a Disability-Neutral Framework' (2017) 13 *International Journal of Law in Context* 39.

[70] In any case, this is a very controversial issue. See other proposals to deal with these hard cases in Series, 'Relationships, Autonomy and Legal Capacity' (n 31), 87 and 88.

[71] Risk is viewed 'as an often crucial component of decision-making that people with disabilities, particularly cognitive disabilities, can historically be seen to have been denied, ostensibly for reasons of protection', P Gooding, 'Supported Decision-Making' (n 51), 436 and 437. This right is explicitly mentioned in Colombian reform.

[72] Series, 'Relationships, Autonomy and Legal Capacity' (n 31), 87.

[73] It is worth highlighting that hard cases remain as issues of significant difficulty under substituted decision-making. Arstein-Kerslake and Flynn, 'The General Comment on Article 12' (n 5), and Gooding, 'Navigating the "Flashing Amber Lights"' (n 30), 58.

[74] CRPD/C/GC/1, para 52.

[75] A/HRC/37/56 (n 47), para 42.

Despite such limitations, the reform impacts on a fundamental issue at the core of our legal frameworks[76] and includes relevant innovations in Civil Law, a traditional area particularly resistant to major changes. Indeed, it can be considered a courageous and positive step forward that has taken place after overcoming strong resistance. Indeed, it is being questioned by some experts and stakeholders for being too radical in challenging the old substituted decision-making regime.

In order to convince experts, including legal professionals, stakeholders, families and the public in general about the necessity of the legal reform, it is essential to highlight that the paradigm shift proposed by Article 12 does not mean a lesser obligation to 'protect' people with disabilities, but it reappraises protection and its shape in the context of disability. Article 12 provides the tools to challenge a model where 'protection' must come in the form of denial of legal agency and taking the voice of the person away, and move to a system that encourages 'protection' of all human rights, promoting autonomy and empowerment, supporting decision-making and ensuring the respect of will and preferences of persons with disabilities.[77]

[76] Flynn and Arstein-Kerslake, 'The Support Model of Legal Capacity' (n 46), 137.

[77] Gooding, 'Supported Decision-Making' (n 51), 436; Flynn and Arstein-Kerslake, 'The General Comment on Article 12' (n 5), 3; and Quinn, 'From Object to Subject' (n 15).

10

Adapting or Discarding the Status Quo? Supporting the Exercise of Legal Capacity in Scottish Law and Practice

JILL STAVERT[1]

I. INTRODUCTION

ARTICLE 12(2) OF THE Convention on the Rights of Persons with Disabilities (CRPD) requires that states recognise that persons with mental disabilities enjoy the exercise of legal capacity on an equal basis with others in all aspects of life. This means that one's will and preferences – integral to freedom of control over one's life – must be given effect to the same extent as is the case for those without mental disabilities.[2] It also means that support for the exercise of legal capacity must be available to overcome any difficulties with decision-making that might impact on one's ability to do this.[3]

This chapter will consider the challenges faced in using and adapting existing legal frameworks to drive forward these CRPD requirements. In doing so, I will focus on Scotland where mental health and capacity legislation is currently under review and the considerations that face those conducting such review if they are to ensure Article 12 CRPD compliance going forward. I will discuss the CRPD equality and non-discrimination message and how Article 12 CRPD seeks to give effect to this. This will include looking at the existing support framework for expressing and giving effect to the views of persons with mental disabilities that is recognised in such legislation and the extent to which it does, or can be made to, achieve Article 12 CRPD compatibility. I will then suggest

[1] I would like to express my thanks to Professors Rosie Harding and Mary Donnelly and Dr Ezgi Taşcıoğlu, the editors of this book, for their helpful comments on earlier versions on this chapter. My thanks also go to Dr Simon Webster whose paper and insights into the Capabilities Approach in the context of the Scottish Mental Health Law Review have been very useful although this should not be taken to be the adopted position of the review.

[2] Article 12(4) CRPD.

[3] Article 12(3) CRPD.

that the most effective way to give effect to Article 12 is to adopt the 'capabilities approach', espoused by Amartya Sen and Martha Nussbaum and further articulated by Sridhar Venkatapuram in the context of health, closely aligned to a framework which seeks to realise the highest attainable standard of mental health. I will argue that concentrating on the multi-faceted nature of achieving the right to the highest attainable standard of mental health, together with ensuring the capabilities to attain this, will direct the attention of legislation and related practice away from simply limiting non-consensual interventions and towards a more effective meeting of all the needs, including respect for individual choice, of persons with mental disabilities.

II. THE CRPD PARADIGM SHIFT: IT IS ALL ABOUT EQUALITY!

The CRPD paradigm shift reconceptualises approaches to the enjoyment of human rights by persons with mental disabilities.[4] Giving effect to this reconceptualised approach requires full stakeholder engagement with what is actually meant by the equal and non-discriminatory enjoyment of rights, including how this translates in terms of support for the exercise of legal capacity and thus equal recognition before the law.[5] This full engagement further necessitates an appreciation that traditional human rights approaches may be discriminatory when applied to persons with mental disabilities. Such traditional approaches have tended to view the rights of persons with mental disabilities in terms of preventing unwarranted intervention and protection[6] rather than proactive empowerment.[7] In this it has adhered to the long-established precept that different treatment of individuals with certain characteristics is permitted, with commensurate limitation of rights, where objective and reasonable justification exists.[8]

[4] T Minkowitz, 'CRPD and transformative equality' (2017) 13(1) *International Journal of Law in Context* 77; BA Clough, 'New Legal Landscapes: (Re) Constructing the Boundaries of Mental Capacity Law' (2018) 26(2) *Medical Law Review* 246; J Stavert, 'Paradigm Shift or Paradigm Paralysis? National Mental Health and Capacity Law and Implementing the CRPD in Scotland' (2018) 7 *Laws* 26.

[5] Stavert, 'Paradigm Shift' (n 4).

[6] OM Arnardóttir 'A Future of Multidimensional Disadvantage Equality' in OM Arnardóttir and G Quinn (eds), *The UN Convention on the Rights of Persons with Disabilities: European and Scandinavian Perspectives* (Leiden and Boston, Martinus Nijhoff, 2009), 41–66; P Bartlett, 'Implementing a Paradigm Shift: Implementing the Convention on the Rights of Persons with Disabilities in the Context of Mental Disability Law' in *Torture in Healthcare Settings: Reflections on the Special Rapporteur on Torture's 2013 Thematic Report* (Washington DC, Centre for Human Rights and Humanitarian Law, American University Washington College of Law, 2014) 169.

[7] LO Gostin and L Gable, 'The Human Rights of Persons with Mental Disabilities: A Global Perspective on the Application of Human Rights Principles to Mental Health' (2004) 63 *Medical Law Review* 20; R Kayess and P French, 'Out of Darkness into Light? Introducing the Convention on the Rights of Persons with Disabilities' (2008) 8(1) *Human Rights Law Review* 1.

[8] A Nilsson, 'Objective and Reasonable? Scrutinising Compulsory Mental Health Interventions from Non-discrimination Perspective' (2014) 14 *Human Rights Law Review* 459; Human Rights

However, by reinforcing equality and non-discrimination and in integrating civil, political, social and economic rights the CRPD disallows different levels of enjoyment of all rights based on disability.[9] The CRPD's focus is on breaking down impediments to equal rights enjoyment for persons with mental and physical disabilities. This removal of obstacles is achieved through creating conducive environments and access to appropriate support (for example, supported decision-making, universal design and reasonable accommodation)[10] so that there is an equal opportunity to participate in society on the same basis as others.

The CRPD stance on equal rights enjoyment is evidenced in, amongst other things, the CRPD requirements concerning the exercise of legal capacity in Article 12 (equal recognition before the law), particularly as interpreted by the Committee on the Rights of Persons with Disabilities (CRPD Committee).[11] Article 12 CRPD identifies the universal right to exercise legal capacity and, in interpreting this, the CRPD Committee has made it clear that supported decision-making must replace substitute decision-making if persons with mental disabilities are to enjoy the right to exercise legal capacity on an equal basis with others.[12] This is on the basis that substitute decision-making restricts legal capacity and is invariably triggered by mental capacity and best interests assessments which are fraught with misconceptions and biases about the ability of persons with mental disabilities to make valid decisions. The Committee has condemned this viewpoint as discriminatory and highlighted the fact that mental capacity, a cognitive function, is not the same as legal capacity which is the legally enforceable recognition of a person's will and preferences.[13] Legal capacity is something which is held by all regardless of impairment and mental capacity issues, manifesting in decision-making challenges, can be overcome with appropriate support thus enabling those who experience such challenges to exercise legal capacity in the same way as others. This support is even interpreted

Committee, *Gillot and others v France* (932/2000), A/57/40 at 270, 15 July 2002; 10 IHRR 22 (2003) paras 13.2 and 13.17; Human Rights Committee, *Guido Jacobs v Belgium* (943/2000), CCPR/C/81/D/943/2000, 17 August 2004, para 9.5; Committee on Economic, Social and Cultural Rights, *General Comment No 20: Non-discrimination in economic, social and cultural rights (Art. 2(2))*, E/C.12/GC/20, 2 July 2009; 16 IHRR 925 (2009) para 13.

[9] Committee on the Rights of Persons with Disabilities, *General Comment No 6 (2018) on equality and non-discrimination*, CRPD/C/GC/6. 9 March 2018; JE Goldsmidt, 'New Perspectives on Equality: Towards Transformative Justice through the Disability Convention?' (2017) 35(1) *Nordic Journal of Human Rights* 1–14; J Stavert and R McGregor, 'Domestic legislation and international human rights standards: the case of mental health and incapacity' (2018) 22(1) *International Journal of Human Rights* 70–84.

[10] Articles 2, 4, 5, 12, 14, 19, 24 and 27 CRPD.

[11] Committee on the Rights of Persons with Disabilities, *General Comment No 1 (2014) Article 12: Equal recognition before the law* (CRPD/C/GC/1., 11 May 2014) (General Comment No 1).

[12] CRPD General Comment No 1, paras 7, 9, 25, 26. 28 and 42.

[13] General Comment No 1, para 13.

as extending to making a 'best interpretation' of an individual's will and preferences where it is impossible to ascertain these.[14]

Article 12 CRPD supported decision-making regimes would therefore appear to transcend capacity assessments and are there to assist the decision-making capability of an individual who struggles to exercise individual autonomy alone[15] and, where necessary, to put in place practical arrangements to ensure that such decisions are given legal effect. What is important is that the end result reflects a person's will and preferences as an expression of their autonomy.[16] Such an approach recognises that all persons have legal capacity but do not necessarily possess the requisite capabilities to exercise this and thus require support to do so.[17] This is based on the notion – mirroring the 'capabilities approach' which I discuss further in section V below – that simply because a person experiences challenges does not mean that they cannot be assisted and developed, and states must therefore recognise this and support them to do this.[18] The purpose of such support is to provide the means of ascertaining a person's wishes which are autonomously arrived at as the result of one's own values, beliefs and chosen influences and without 'best interests' decisions, conflict of interest or undue influence adulterating this – which strongly suggests that the CRPD regards individual autonomy as relational.[19] As Eilionoir Flynn and Anna Arstein-Kerslake have written,

> social justice theorists from Kant onwards have asserted the need for the state to refrain from interference with an individual's autonomy – but in recent decades, the need for a more flexible approach has emerged – one which protects from unwanted interference but simultaneously recognises the interdependence of human decision-making and includes proactive measures to support individuals to exercise their legal capacity to make decisions.[20]

Once the level playing-field has been established for persons with mental disabilities it does not mean that there can be no involuntary interventions but that

[14] General Comment No 1, para 21; E Flynn and A Arstein-Kerslake, 'The Support Model of Legal Capacity: Fact, Fiction, or Fantasy?' (2014) 32 *Berkeley Journal of International Law* 134–53, 141–42.

[15] This might also include support to make meaningful use of support for decision-making.

[16] Article 12(4) CRPD.

[17] A Dhanda, 'Legal Capacity in the Disability Rights Convention: Stranglehold of the Past or Lodestar for the Future?' (2006–2007) 34 *Syracuse Journal of International Law & Commerce* 429; M Bach and L Kerzner, 'A New Paradigm for Protecting Autonomy and the Right to Legal Capacity', prepared for the Law Commission of Ontario (October 2010), available at: www.lco-cdo.org/wp-content/uploads/2010/11/disabilities-commissioned-paper-bach-kerzner.pdf (accessed 5 February 2021); E Flynn and A Arstein-Kerslake, 'Legislating personhood: realising the right to support in exercising legal capacity' (2014) 10(1) *International Journal of Law in Context* 81, 90.

[18] Flynn and Arstein-Kerslake, 'Legislating personhood' (n 17), 90.

[19] R Harding, 'Care and relationality: Supported decision making under the UN CRPD' in R Harding, R Fletcher and C Beasley, *Revaluing Care in Theory, Law and Policy: Cycles and Connections* (Abingdon, Routledge, 2017).

[20] Flynn and Arstein-Kerslake, 'Legislating personhood' (n 17), 93.

these must take place on the same basis for all. Equal rights enjoyment also means equal rights limitation. Where non-consensual action is taken that overrides an individual's will and preferences – for example, to protect that person or the public – then this is permissible provided that the same action would be taken whether or not the person has a disability or impaired decision-making. However, whilst this general concept might be clear, how it is to be applied to different situations in practice is much less so. Operationalising the Article 12 support model is not without its challenges.

Firstly, there is an issue of terminological clarity in the literature and generally about the meaning of 'supported decision-making', which has arguably not been helped by the CRPD Committee referring to both 'support for the exercise of legal capacity' and 'supported decision-making' interchangeably in its General Comment No 1.[21] That being said, it is clear that Article 12(3) CRPD refers to support for the exercise of legal capacity, which includes not only supporting a person with mental disabilities to express their will and preferences but also ensuring that such will and preferences are given legal recognition and effect on the same basis as others.[22] Support *with* or *for* decision-making of itself would therefore appear to fall short of support for the exercise of legal capacity.[23] As Piers Gooding states, the supported decision-making regime envisaged by Article 12 CRPD 'includes supported decision-making, support with decision-making and broader support to exercise legal capacity, across a range of law, policy and practice.'[24] The purpose of supported decision-making has also not always been clear. On the one hand, it has been given a broad interpretation which includes helping someone to be involved in decisions that are important to them both within and outside substitute decision-making situations.[25] On the other hand, it has been interpreted in terms of being a viable replacement for substitute decision-making,[26] which is how it has been interpreted by the CRPD Committee in its General Comment No 1.

Secondly, affording equality in the exercise of legal capacity in this way has been highly controversial. Some commentators have, for example, expressed

[21] RD Dinerstein, 'Implementing Legal Capacity under Article 12 of the UN Convention on the Rights of Persons with Disabilities: The Difficult Road from Guardianship to Supported Decision-Making' (2012) 19 *Human Rights Brief* 8–12; M Browning et al, 'Supported Decision-Making: Understanding How its Conceptual Link to Legal Capacity is Influencing the Development of Practice' (2014) *Research and Practice in Intellectual and Developmental Disabilities* 34, 36–37; P Gooding, 'Navigating the "Flashing Amber Lights" of the Right to Legal Capacity in the United Nations Convention on the Rights of Persons with Disabilities: Responding to Major Concerns' (2015) 15 *Human Rights Law Review* 45, 50–52.

[22] Martin et al, *The Essex Autonomy Project* (n 28 below), 23–26.

[23] Browning et al, 'Supported Decision-Making' (n 21) 41.

[24] Gooding, 'Navigating the "Flashing Amber Lights"' (n 21), 52; P Gooding, 'Supported Decision-Making – A Rights Based Disability Concept and It's Implications for Mental Health Law' (2013) 20(3) *Psychiatry, Psychology and Law* 437, 445.

[25] ACT Disability, Aged and Carer Advocacy Service, *Submission to Austrialian Human Rights Commission Access to Justice Inquiry* (July 2013).

[26] Browning et al, 'Supported Decision-Making' (n 21) 37.

concern that allowing persons with mental disabilities to exercise autonomy on the same basis as others may result in vital support not being provided or leave others at actual or potential risk.[27] Others have attempted to adopt a pragmatic approach, arguing that Article 12 CRPD can be interpreted to encompass co-existence between supported and substitute decision-making and that this can be given effect within an appropriately adapted legal and practice framework.[28] The reality, however, is that most (if not all) states, have not fully abandoned substitute decision-making models. At best they have either adopted or proposed frameworks which provide for enhanced respect for an individual's will and preferences and the least restrictive and invasive actions to be taken in the circumstances, whilst still ultimately allowing for substitute decision-making where a person's decision-making ability is considered to be impaired and where a perceived risk of harm is present.[29] It is questionable, however, whether simply adapting existing legislative models which authorise non-consensual psychiatric treatment and other interventions will ultimately result in equal and non-discriminatory rights enjoyment by persons with mental disabilities.[30]

III. THE ROLE OF NATIONAL LEGISLATION AND SUPPORTED DECISION-MAKING

Legislation plays an important role as the vehicle of policy and driver of practice.[31] To be Article 12 CRPD compliant, the primary objective of such legislation must be to ensure support for the exercise of legal capacity, or 'supported decision-making', so as to secure equal and non-discriminatory rights enjoyment by persons with mental disabilities.[32] That being said, the full realisation of equal and non-discriminatory rights enjoyment can only be achieved if it is also accompanied by significant cultural changes in policy, practice, resourcing

[27] MC Freeman et al, 'Reversing hard won victories in the name of human rights: a critique of the General Comment on Article 12 of the UN Convention on the Rights of Persons with Disabilities' (2015) 2 *Lancet Psychiatry* 844–50; P Appelbaum, 'Saving the UN Convention on the Rights of Persons with Disabilities – from itself' (2019) 18(1) *World Psychiatry* 1–2.

[28] W Martin et al, *The Essex Autonomy Project Three Jurisdictions Report: towards compliance with CRPD Art. 12 in capacity/incapacity legislation across the UK* (Report, University of Essex, 6 June 2016): https://autonomy.essex.ac.uk/wp-content/uploads/2017/01/EAP-3J-Final-Report-2016.pdf (accessed 12 June 2019); Pathare and Kapoor, Chapter 8, this volume.

[29] For example, UK Government (Department of Health and Social Care), *Modernising the Mental Health Act – final report from the independent review* (Gov UK, December 2018). See also the other chapters in this book.

[30] Stavert, 'Paradigm Shift' (n 4).

[31] CRPD General Comment No 1, paras 7 and 9; J Stavert, 'Scottish Mental Health and Capacity Law: Replacing the Old with the New or the Old in Policy, Law and Practice?' in C Spivakovsky, L Steel and P Weller (eds), *The Legacies of Institutionalisation: Disability, Law and Policy in the 'Deinstitutionalised' Community* (Oxford, Hart Publishing, 2020).

[32] Article 12(4) CRPD; CRPD General Comment No 1, paras 7, 9, 25 and 42.

and judicial approaches.[33] The challenges that this presents can be illustrated in attempts to encourage and guide the use of supported decision-making within the current and future legal frameworks in Scotland.

A. Scotland and Support for the Exercise of Legal Capacity

Over the last decade certain legislative reviews have had to consider, or are considering, the implications of, and how to operationalise, the requirements of Article 12 CRPD, including giving effect to its supported decision-making paradigm. These have included the Scottish Government's review of the Adults with Incapacity (Scotland) Act 2000 (AWIA) which authorises and regulates the making of health, welfare, financial and property decisions for adults[34] who are deemed to lack capacity by reason of 'mental disorder'[35] or physical disability.[36] It also strongly influenced the *Independent Review of Learning Disability and Autism in the Mental Health Act* which reported in December 2019,[37] which considered whether learning disability and autism should continue to fall under the remit of the Mental Health (Care and Treatment) (Scotland) Act 2003 (MHA). Moreover, the *Independent Scottish Mental Health Law Review* (Scott Review)[38] commenced in 2019. This latest review is undertaking a comprehensive review of the MHA as well as consideration of its convergence with the AWIA and the Adult Support and Protection (Scotland) Act 2007 (ASPA).[39] The influence of the CRPD in terms of prioritising individual autonomy and meeting not only needs for medical care and treatment but also wider needs with its in human rights terms can be identified in the Scott Review's terms of reference, which state that one of its objectives includes:

> making recommendations that gives effect to the rights, will and preferences of the individual by ensuring that mental health, incapacity and adult support and protection legislation reflects people's social, economic and cultural rights including [CRPD] and ECHR requirements.[40]

[33] CRPD General Comment No 1, paras 25 and 42.

[34] Persons aged 16 years of age and older (s 1(6) AWIA).

[35] The AWIA adopts the same definition of 'mental disorder' as the current mental health legislation (s 87(1) AWIA as amended by the Mental Health (Care and Treatment) (Scotland) Act 2003, Sch 4, para 9(5)(c)), which includes 'mental illness, personality disorder, or learning disability' (s 328(1) Mental Health (Care and Treatment) (Scotland) Act 2003).

[36] s 1(6) AWIA.

[37] *Independent Review of Learning Disability and Autism in the Mental Health Act: Final Report*, December 2019. Available at: https://webarchive.nrscotland.gov.uk/20200313213229/https://www.irmha.scot/wp-content/uploads/2020/01/IRMHA-Final-report-18-12-19-2.pdf (accessed 1 February 2021).

[38] Chaired by John Scott QC.

[39] Scottish Government, *Review of the Mental Health Act*, 19 March 2019: www.news.gov.scot/news/review-of-the-mental-health-act/ (accessed 12 June 2019). See also review website: www.mentalhealthlawreview.scot/.

[40] *Scottish Mental Health Law Review, Terms of Reference (updated)*, 15 January 2020. Available at: https://cms.mentalhealthlawreview.scot/wp-content/uploads/2020/01/Terms-of-Reference-1.pdf.

B. Existing Supported Decision-Making Mechanisms in Scotland

A number of encouraging ingredients are already present in Scottish mental health, capacity and adult support and protection legislation, although, as will be discussed later, there remain several CRPD challenges.

An underlying principle in each of the AWIA, MHA and ASPA is that those considering and implementing interventions must have regard to the individual's present and past ascertainable wishes and feelings (arguably the equivalent of Article 12(4) CRPD 'will and preferences', although less strong in terms of intention, in the Scottish legislation).[41] Moreover, implicit in the consideration of interventions under any of the Acts is that capacity is presumed, that any lack of capacity must be decision-specific and that any substituted decision is a last resort. Each Act requires interventions to be the least restrictive alternative and only to be utilised where they provide a benefit not otherwise attainable.[42] 'Best interests' tests have no formal place in the Scottish legislation. This test was not included in the AWIA on the recommendation of the Scottish Law Commission, which considered that it does not give due weight to the adult's views and was developed in the context of child law where a child's level of understanding is progressive which tends not to be the case with adults, thus rendering a 'best interests' assessment inappropriate for adults.[43] Again, the Millan Report[44] which led to the enactment of the MHA did not advocate a 'best interests' approach, but put forward other principles regarded as more conducive to ensuring that the patient's voice is heard when compulsory psychiatric measures are being considered. However, Adrian Ward and Alex Ruck Keene have stated that the extent to which this is witnessed in judicial practice is debateable:

> despite the explicit rejection of a best interests test for the purposes of the AWI[A] … sheriffs have [frequently] at least in part chosen to base their decisions on what they considered to be in the relevant adult's best interests.[45]

Additionally, a number of supports – which can arguably be described as amounting to supported decision-making – exist to facilitate this and are either recognised in legislation or operate alongside it.[46] The support identified in legislation includes advance planning in the form of financial and welfare powers of attorney which are recognised and regulated by the AWIA,[47] and psychiatric

[41] s 1(4)(a) AWIA; s 1(3)(a) MHA; s 2(b) ASPA.

[42] ss 1(2) and (3) AWIA; s 1(3)(f) and (4)(c) MHA; s 1 ASPA.

[43] Scottish Law Commission, *Report on Incapable Adults* (Scot Law Com No 151, 1995) para 2.50.

[44] Scottish Executive, *New Directions: Report on the Review of the Mental Health (Scotland) Act 1984*, 2001 SE/2001/56: www.mhtscotland.gov.uk/mhts/files/Millan_Report_New_Directions.pdf.

[45] A Ward and A Ruck Keene, 'With or Without Best Interests: the Mental Capacity Act 2005, the Adults with Incapacity (Scotland) Act 2000 and Constructing Decisions' (2016) 22 *International Journal of Mental Health and Capacity Law* 17, 32.

[46] Mental Welfare Commission for Scotland, *Good Practice Guide: Supported Decision-Making* (Edinburgh, 2016).

[47] ss 15–16 AWIA.

advance statements which are recognised by the MHA.[48] The role of independent advocacy as a vehicle for communicating an individual's wishes and feelings is recognised when determining interventions in the AWIA.[49] Local authorities 'must have regard to the importance of the provision of appropriate services (including, in particular, independent advocacy services) to the adult concerned' under the ASPA.[50] Moreover, the MHA imposes a statutory duty on health boards and local authorities to provide independent advocacy to persons with a mental disorder, whether or not they are subject to compulsion under the Act.[51]

Less specific, but acknowledging that the wishes and feelings of the individual are integral to the process and must be supported, the MHA and ASPA both explicitly require that individuals are encouraged to participate in decisions made under their auspices and are provided with the necessary information and support to do this.[52] The AWIA[53] requires that those authorised to exercise functions under the Act encourage the adult to exercise and develop their skills to manage their own affairs.

Non-statutory support for decision-making is summarised in the Mental Welfare Commission for Scotland's supported decision-making guidance,[54] which mentions the support that trusted persons (professional and otherwise), peers and communities can provide for the exercise of legal capacity. It also mentions the role for clear and tailored appropriate forms of communication, technological support and advocacy in a wider context than that envisaged under the legislation.

C. Identifying Article 12 CRPD Challenges in Scottish Law and Practice

The support mechanisms that are currently recognised in Scotland have the potential to enable an individual's wishes and feelings to be reflected in all decisions, voluntary or involuntary, that concern them insofar as this is possible. However, they are arguably some way from the requirements of CRPD supported decision-making.

The fact that existing support for ascertaining an individual's wishes and feelings in Scotland largely operates within substitute decision-making regimes is unlikely on the face of it to find favour with the CRPD Committee. However, it is worth considering whether the system might actually be interpreted as

[48] ss 275–276 MHA.

[49] s 3(5A) AWIA.

[50] s 6(2) ASPA.

[51] s 259 MHA.

[52] s 1(3)(c) and (d) MHA; s 2(d) ASPA.

[53] s 1(5) AWIA.

[54] Mental Welfare Commission for Scotland, *Good Practice Guide: Supported Decision-Making* (n 46).

containing at least some elements of the Article 12 CRPD requirements for supporting the exercise of legal capacity where non-consensual interventions are in effect 'best interpretation' situations envisaged by General Comment No 1. Naturally, of primary concern here is the weight given to an individual's rights, will and preferences.

At present, 'capacity assessments'[55] linked to diagnosis are essential ingredients in non-consensual interventions under the AWIA and MHA. Where mental incapacity is determined, statutory principles require that regard must be had to an individual's wishes and feelings and that the least restrictive intervention be adopted when deciding and implementing such interventions. However, these principles are not afforded any particular priority. These two principles are simply listed as two considerations alongside a number of others.

Sections 1 and 2 of the MHA detail the principles that must guide decisions about psychiatric compulsion. There is a duty to 'have regard' to 'the present and past wishes and feelings of the patient that are relevant to the discharge of the function [under the Act]',[56] the importance of patient participation[57] and a requirement to discharge such functions 'in the manner that appears to the person to be the manner that involves the minimum restriction on the freedom of the patient that is necessary in the circumstances'[58] and range of options available.[59] Section 1 of the AWIA details the principles that govern interventions authorised, or regulated, by that Act. There are requirements to take account of

> the present and past wishes and feelings of the adult so far as they can be ascertained by any means of communication, whether human or by mechanical aid (whether or an interpretative nature or otherwise) appropriate to the adult[60]

and that any 'intervention shall be the least restrictive option in relation to the freedom of the adult, consistent with the purpose of the intervention.'[61] As previously mentioned, the AWIA also requires anyone carrying out functions under the Act to encourage the adult to exercise and develop their skills concerning property, finances and personal welfare,[62] and the MHA requires that regard is had to providing such information and support as is necessary to enable the patient to participate in decisions on their care and treatment.[63] However, both Acts do not state how or where this information and support should be provided

[55] An 'incapable adult' is defined in s 1(6) AWIA. The MHA applies a 'capacity test' of 'significantly impaired decision-making' as a result of the mental disorder (ss 36(4)(b), 44(4)(b) and 64(5)(d)). The MHA does not define this term but the Act's Code of Practice suggests a test not dissimilar to the 'capacity test' in the AWIA but one that is specific to psychiatric treatment. This test is thus wider and narrower than the test for an 'incapable adult' under the AWIA.

[56] s 1(3)(a) MHA.

[57] s 1(3)(c) MHA.

[58] s 1(4) MHA.

[59] s 1(3)(c) MHA.

[60] s 1(4)(a) AWIA.

[61] s 1(3) AWIA.

[62] s 1(5) AWIA.

[63] s 1(3)(d) MHA.

and, again, these principles are amongst those which must be afforded equal weight when determining non-consensual interventions.

In terms of overcoming challenges with decision-making, with the exception of independent advocacy, the provision or recognition of support for the expression of the will and preferences of individuals is triggered by mental capacity assessments. This is contrary to the continuum of supported decision-making allowing for the individual's voice to be heard at all times, irrespective of mental capacity assessments, envisaged by the CRPD, and therefore potentially makes it much more difficult to consider advance planning mechanisms that do not respect inevitable changes in an individual's wishes over time. Moreover, it is evident that capacity and risk assessments leave a great deal to be desired in terms of avoiding paternalistic and discriminatory restrictions of the rights of persons with mental disabilities.[64]

The current focus in the legislation and related codes of practice on assistance with communication only – rather than supported decision-making in its wider sense – is problematic. This does not take into account the support required to be in a position to make a decision, making a decision itself and putting into effect that decision. Further, it is unclear – owing to the absence of specific direction in current legislation or legislative codes of practice – when the identified support should be provided and who should actually provide this support. At present, it is very much regarded as something to be provided at the time, as opposed to before, interventions are to be considered, although in practice there are some instances of the courts now requiring evidence that support is provided before they will consider, for example, guardianship applications.[65]

A fundamental challenge further exists in addressing competing European Convention on Human Rights (ECHR) and CRPD approaches to rights enjoyment in the context of persons with mental disabilities. The Scottish Government is not averse to incorporating international human rights treaties into Scots law[66] and proposed devolved legislation and policy in Scotland can be prevented by the UK Government if it is likely to place the UK in breach of its international obligations,[67] including those under the CRPD. However, the CRPD is not currently incorporated into Scottish law and its rights are not therefore enforceable through Scottish courts and tribunals. The ECHR, on the other hand, carries greater legal weight by virtue of the Human Rights Act 1998 and Scotland Act 1998.[68] However, the approach adopted in ECHR jurisprudence concerning the autonomy of persons with mental disabilities tends to accept that, subject to safeguards, limitation of the enjoyment of legal capacity

[64] McKay and Stavert, *Scotland's Mental Health and Capacity Law* (n 76 below).

[65] For example, Sheriffdom of Lothian and Borders, *Practice Note No 1 of 2016, Applications under the Adults with Incapacity (Scotland) Act 2000* (11 March 2016).

[66] See, for example, the United Nations Convention on the Rights of the Child (Incorporation) (Scotland) Bill 2020.

[67] s 35(a)(i) Scotland Act 1998.

[68] ss 2, 3 and 6 Human Rights Act 1998; ss 35 and 29(2)(d) and 57(2) Scotland Act 1998.

is sometimes justified on the basis of the existence of diagnosis of mental disability or related impairment.[69]

The existing legislative framework in Scotland may thus be more conducive to shared decision-making but not necessarily supported decision-making, as envisaged by the CRPD, that ensures that an individual's will and preferences take precedence in all decisions made concerning them. Scotland therefore faces a number of difficulties if its proposed legislative reform is to result in a CRPD-compatible supported decision-making approach. Moreover, for the Article 12 CRPD paradigm shift to be made real supported decision-making also needs to be adequately resourced. Enthusiasm for aspects of the CRPD exhibited in legislative reviews in Scotland is one thing but when accompanied by, for example, Legal Aid cuts, reduced resourcing for the already over-burdened independent advocacy provision in Scotland,[70] and, more recently, the economic impact of the coronavirus pandemic, one has to wonder how effective this will be.

IV. EQUAL AND NON-DISCRIMINATORY RIGHTS ENJOYMENT FOR PERSONS WITH MENTAL DISABILITIES

As I previously indicated, there have been suggestions about how to address the CRPD Committee's Article 12 CRPD requirements. For example, the *Three Jurisdictions Report*[71] recommended, and such recommendations were taken on board by the Scottish Government's previous AWIA review,[72] that CRPD compliance can be achieved provided that: (1) there is a statutory presumption in favour of respect for the individual's will and preferences; (2) there is a statutory requirement that evidence that appropriate supported decision-making has been made available before interventions are considered; and (3) interventions may occur but as a last resort and taking into account the individual's will and preferences, but such will and preferences may be overridden where a high level of risk exists and the individual, disabled or non-disabled, would benefit from protection/care and treatment.

It is certainly arguable that this might work to some extent. However, this approach does not fully address the fact that CRPD compliance prohibits persons with mental disabilities being singled out for intervention on the basis of their disability. The suggested 'solution' only works if one fully understands,

[69] See, for example, *A-MV v Finland* (App no 53251/13), decision of 23 March 2017.

[70] Scottish Independent Advocacy Alliance, *Map of Advocacy across Scotland 2015–2016 edition* (2017): www.siaa.org.uk/wp-content/uploads/2021/02/SIAA_Advocacy_Map_2015-16-1.pdf; Mental Welfare Commission for Scotland, *The Right to Advocacy – A Review of Advocacy Planning Across Scotland* (March 2018).

[71] Martin et al, *The Essex Autonomy Project* (n 28).

[72] Scottish Government, *Responses to the Scottish Government's Consultation on the Scottish Law Commission's Review of Adults with Incapacity*, Report (Edinburgh, June 2016); Scottish Government, *Adults with Incapacity (Scotland) Act 2000 Proposals for Reform*, Consultation Paper (Edinburgh, January 2018).

and lives, the equal and non-discrimination message of the CRPD. Failure to understand this – and the role that supported decision-making plays here – will only bring about partial CRPD compliance.[73] As stated in section II above, the CRPD requires that support is available to overcome practical and institutional difficulties that persons with disabilities may face in exercising their rights, thus providing the opportunity to enjoy rights on the same as others. This includes ensuring access to support for the exercise of legal capacity, in order to overcome any decision-making challenges resulting from mental disability and to give effect to the individual's will and preferences.[74]

For CRPD compliance to be achieved in Scotland the challenge is therefore the extent to which a system can be created that moves beyond a shared decision-making regime that does not give priority to an individual's will and preferences. There will need to be a framework where such priority is given and where individuals are supported to ensure that this actually happens. The extent to which the Scott Review will ultimately be able to achieve this obviously remains to be seen although such considerations fall within its remit.[75] The report *Scotland's Mental Health and Capacity Law: the Case for Reform*,[76] which features in the review's terms of reference, whilst acknowledging the potential value of the *Three Jurisdictions Report* approach, went further than this in urging the Scottish Government to seriously consider what equal and non-discriminatory rights enjoyment for persons with mental disabilities looks like. However, the issue of tackling the necessary reconceptualising of the approach to care, support, treatment and protection of persons with mental disabilities remains.

V. ARTICLE 12 IMPLEMENTATION USING THE CAPABILITIES APPROACH

In terms of addressing the reconfigured approach to the care, support, treatment and protection of persons with mental disabilities, I propose that this might be achieved through realising a widely interpreted right to the attainable standard of physical and mental health. The Capabilities Approach, as espoused by Sen and Nussbaum, and further developed in the context of health by authors such as Venkatapuram, might significantly assist in bringing about such change.

A widely interpreted right to mental health follows the World Health Organization interpretation of mental health as 'a state of well-being in which

[73] Stavert, 'Paradigm Shift' (n 4).

[74] J Stavert, 'Supported Decision-Making and Paradigm Shifts: Word Play or Real Change? (2021) *Frontiers in Psychiatry*, 11 January 2021: https://doi.org/10.3389/fpsyt.2020.571005.

[75] Scottish Mental Health Law Review, *Terms of Reference (updated)*, 15 January 2020. Available at: https://cms.mentalhealthlawreview.scot/wp-content/uploads/2020/01/Terms-of-Reference-1.pdf (accessed 4 February 2021).

[76] C McKay and J Stavert, *Scotland's Mental Health and Capacity Law: the Case for Reform* (Centre for Mental Health and Capacity Law/Mental Welfare Commission for Scotland, May 2017), 73.

every individual realises his or her own potential, can cope with the normal stresses of life, can work productively and fruitfully, and is able to make a contribution to his or her community.'[77] Similarly, the Committee on Economic, Social and Cultural Rights in its General Comment No 14 interprets the right to physical and mental health not merely in terms of the right to be healthy but as the sum of the realisation of many different rights and as constituting both freedoms and entitlements.[78] Such freedoms include the right to autonomy, to control one's health and body, and to be free from interference, whilst the entitlements are connected with the underlying determinates of health which are defined as 'a wide range of socio-economic factors that promote conditions in which one can lead a healthy life',[79] although it is important to look beyond this in terms of the provision of services.[80]

Arising from the use of economic theory and philosophy to develop an alternative approach to measuring progress – one that is concerned with social justice – the focus of the capabilities approach is on ensuring equality and developing human potential. Its basic precept is that human well-being is best seen in terms of what individuals can actually be and do in their daily context. Nussbaum's development of the capabilities approach seeks to explain human rights. Although her focus is a feminist critique of human rights approaches, it can arguably also be applied more widely including in the context of mental disability and related inequalities and across all categories of rights, as her approach encompasses civil, political, social, economic and cultural rights. Countering the traditional understanding of equality that assumed that human beings are free, equal and independent, the capabilities approach recognises every person's inherent value as a human being but also that individuals have unequal abilities and needs. If an individual is to be truly equal then it is important that appropriate opportunities exist to develop each person's potential and allow an individual to determine the sort of life they wish to live. 'Capabilities' are those outcomes that an individual is actually able to do and to be if they are given the appropriate opportunities to achieve this and, Nussbaum suggests, a measure of equality.[81]

[77] World Health Organization, *Mental Health: Strengthening our Response* (30 March 2018): www.who.int/news-room/fact-sheets/detail/mental-health-strengthening-our-response (accessed 15 November 2021).

[78] Committee on Economic, Social and Cultural Rights, *General Comment No 14: The Right to the Highest Attainable Standard of Health (Art 12 of the International Covenant on Economic, Social and Cultural Rights)*, 11 August 2000, UN Doc. E/C.12/2000/4, para 8.

[79] Ibid, para 4.

[80] JP Ruger, 'Toward a Theory of a Right to Health: Capability and Incompletely Theorized Agreements' (2006) 18(3) *Yale Journal of Law and the Humanities* 280; J Stavert and R McGregor, 'Domestic legislation and international human rights standards' (n 9) 70–89, 72–84.

[81] MC Nussbaum, *Women and human development: The capabilities approach*, 1st edn (Cambridge, Cambridge University Press, 2000), 5.

Unlike Sen, who considers that capabilities must be a matter of public agreement and not predetermined,[82] Nussbaum identifies 10 central capabilities – life, bodily health, bodily integrity, senses, imagination and thought, emotions, practical reason, affiliation (towards others and self-respect), other species (meaning cooperative and mutually supportive relations between all species), play, and control over one's political and material environment – which are important human entitlements that are inherent to social justice.[83] These can be closely aligned to, and complement, human rights, and encompass actions and choices and creating the circumstances that make it possible to exercise the particular function required to achieve the capability.[84] Whilst Nussbaum's identification of specific capabilities – rather than, as Sen advocates, allowing these to be realised through agreement – could be regarded as limited, many of the 10 central capabilities she identifies do align with disability and autonomy in the sphere of physical and mental health. The different approaches to identifying capabilities in Sen's and Nussbaum's theories, including the argument that Nussbaum's 10 central capabilities allow for certain rights to have priority over others (along with the issue of the potential pecking order between these 10 central capabilities themselves), does admittedly appear to fly in the face of the maxim that all human rights are interrelated and indivisible, and that therefore one right does not 'trump' another. However, Nussbaum's approach has already been considered by various authors seeking to align her capabilities approach to human rights more generally and to persons with disabilities and the CRPD in particular.[85] In relation to health, for example, Venkatapuram writes that such an approach allows rights related to health to be morally grounded in terms of the appropriate support and legal and other environments for persons with disabilities that are conducive to achieving a healthy life.[86]

[82] A Sen, 'Human Rights and Capabilities' (2005) 6(2) *Journal of Human Development and Capabilities* 151, 158.

[83] MC Nussbaum, 'Capabilities, Entitlements, Rights: Supplementation and Critique' (2011) 12(1) *Journal of Human Development and Capabilities* 23.

[84] Nussbaum (n 83).

[85] See, for example, A Arstein-Kerslake, Working Paper: *Cognitive Disability and the Capabilities Approach: Exploring a Human Right to Individual Development* (HDCA Conference, 2012); M Bach and L Kerzner, *A new paradigm for protecting autonomy and the right to legal capacity* (Toronto ONT, Law Commission of Ontario, 2014); J Craigie et al, 'Legal capacity, mental capacity and supported decision-making: report from a panel event' (2019) 62 *International Journal of Law and Psychiatry* 160; EW Bannister and S Venkatapuram, 'Grounding the right to live in the community (CRPD Article 19) in the capabilities approach to social justice' (2020) 69 *International Journal of Law and Psychiatry* 101551; S Fukuda-Parr, 'The metrics of human rights: complementarities of the human development and capabilities approach' (2011) 12(1) *Journal of Human Development and Capabilities* 73.

[86] S Venkatapuram, *Health Justice – An Argument from the Capabilities Approach* (Cambridge, Polity Press, 2011). See also W Bannister and S Venkatapuram, 'Grounding the right to live in the community (CRPD Article 19) in the capabilities approach to social justice' (2020) 69 *International Journal of Law and Psychiatry* 1015518 and S Venkatapuram, 'Mental disability, human rights and the capabilities approach: Searching for the foundations' (2014) 26(4) *International Review of Psychiatry* 408.

A person's capability to have the highest attainable standard of physical and mental health is made up of a combination of interacting internal and external factors, such as the person's biology, knowledge and skills and their external environment including social, material and environmental factors. However, this capability cannot be realised where the components necessary to achieve a healthy life exist without the individual being physically or financially able to access them. Thus, it is necessary to provide the goods, the support and right environment to achieve this and the freedom of an individual to conceive, plan and pursue their own idea of a good life.[87]

The CRPD, in turn, offers a good vehicle by which to give effect to the right to mental health through the capabilities approach. In adopting a social model of disability, the CRPD views the state and society's attitudes to disability as the disabling factors (rather than individual impairments) and requires states to proactively remove obstacles to, and to support, equal rights enjoyment by persons with disabilities.[88] It reinforces equality and non-discrimination in the enjoyment of all categories of rights, which may require access to support for the exercise of legal capacity (supported decision-making), reasonable accommodations and universal design in order to be achieved, as the CRPD disallows different levels of rights enjoyment based on disability.[89] The social nature of capabilities also arguably correlates with, and reinforces, the relational nature of individual autonomy arguably envisaged by the CRPD that I mentioned earlier.[90] Whilst it has been suggested that Nussbaum's capabilities approach correlates with the CRPD approach, it has been noted that it includes persons with significant mental disabilities but excludes persons with cognitive disabilities (which tend to predominantly be confined to challenges in communication, taking care of oneself and perceived social skills).[91] This appears to be at odds with the message of Article 12 CRPD in terms of equality in the exercise of legal capacity and the role of supported decision-making in this context. However, that is not to say that the capabilities approach cannot be extended to persons with cognitive disabilities[92] or used as the basis for assisting the realisation of all or at least some CRPD rights.

Realising the right to health through the CRPD and a capabilities approach lens, for example, has several advantages. It strongly encourages sufficiency and efficacy of services and support, and addresses emergency, crisis and

[87] Venkatapuram (2011) and (2014) (n 86); Bannister and Venkatapuram (n 86).

[88] Stavert, 'Paradigm Shift' (n 4).

[89] CRPD, *General Comment No 6* (n 9); Goldsmidt, 'New Perspectives on Equality' (n 9); Stavert and McGregor, 'Domestic legislation and international human rights standards' (n 9).

[90] Harding, 'Care and relationality' (n 19); M Longshore Smith and C Seward, 'The relational autonomy of Amartya Sen's capability approach' (2009) 10(2) *Journal of Human Development and Capabilities* 213–35.

[91] Nussbaum, 'Capabilities, Entitlements, Rights' (n 83). C Harnacke, 'Disability and capability: Exploring the usefulness of Martha Nussbaum's capabilities approach for the UN disability rights convention' (2013) 41(4) *The Journal of Law, Medicine and Ethics* 768.

[92] Arstein-Kerslake, 'Cognitive Disability and the Capabilities Approach' (n 85).

public safety situations. It also removes the primary focus away from – but still addresses – the highly contentious issue of non-consensual interventions and provides a framework for the revisiting of thresholds for non-consensual interventions such as mental capacity and risk assessments, which are currently widely considered, by patients, families and many clinicians, as problematic.[93] Finally, such an approach helps to address the often referred to challenge of the aforementioned differing approaches of the CRPD and CRPD Committee and the ECHR jurisprudence relating to limitations of the autonomy of persons with mental disabilities. Whilst the focus of the ECHR is on setting the limits for interventions, a combined CRPD-right to health-Capabilities Approach model, properly enshrined in legislation and embraced in practice, will ensure that instances where it is necessary to consider non-consensual interventions impacting on individual autonomy are reduced.

VI. CONCLUSION

Article 12(3) of the CRPD requires that access to appropriately tailored support for the exercise of legal capacity is provided. The purpose of this is to ensure that the rights, will and preferences of persons with mental disabilities are respected on an equal basis with others.[94] This might require not only assisting someone to make a decision but also taking steps to ensure that this is given actual effect. It also requires that where it is deemed necessary to override a person's rights, will and preferences then this must be done on an equal basis for all, with disability or related impairment not being used to justify such action.

Notwithstanding the current legislative and other constraints already mentioned, in Scotland there is certainly scope for the different types of support for the communication of individuals' wishes and feelings to be used in a way that does amount to supported decision-making as envisaged the CRPD. However, the danger is that what they actually amount to in practice are merely enhancements to shared decision-making which may simply be informed by, but not driven by, an individual's will and preferences.

Fundamental cross-sectorial changes are required if Scotland is to truly live the CRPD support for the exercise of legal capacity requirements. Appropriately framed legislation, accompanied by adequate and specifically targeted resourcing and the necessary culture change in practice and society to fully understand and embrace the CRPD paradigm concerning the equal and non-discriminatory enjoyment of rights by persons with mental disabilities, are required to achieve this. Adopting the capabilities approach in implementing CRPD realisation will arguably help to achieve such culture change.

[93] McKay and Stavert, *Scotland's Mental Health and Capacity Law* (n 76).

[94] Article 12(4) CRPD.

11

Performing Disability Rights: State Reporting and Turkey's (Non)Engagement with the CRPD

EZGİ TAŞCIOĞLU[1]

I. INTRODUCTION

IN OCTOBER 2019, the United Nations Committee on the Rights of People with Disabilities (the Committee) issued its concluding observations on the initial report of Turkey.[2] The general concerns of the Committee focused on 'the prevalence, in practice, of the medical, charitable and paternalistic approaches to disability'[3] and the lack of transparent information and recorded progress on the rights of persons with disabilities in the country. Regarding Article 12 of the United Nations Convention on the Rights of People with Disabilities (CRPD) on equal recognition before the law, the Committee documented its concerns on:

(a) The guardianship regime in the Civil Code that limits the capacity to act of persons with disabilities on the basis of psychosocial, intellectual or hearing impairments, and that at least 13,934 persons with disabilities are reported to remain under guardianship and institutionalized in public and private institutions;

(b) The reported ongoing practice of having two witnesses for notarial acts for persons with visual, hearing or speech impairments, despite amendments in 2005 to the notary proceedings prohibiting it;

[1] I would like to express my gratitude to the Oñati International Institute for the Sociology of Law for hosting our 'Supporting Legal Capacity in Socio-Legal Context' workshop in July 2019, to all workshop participants for their contributions, and to Mary Donnelly and Rosie Harding for being such great collaborators and for their comments on this chapter.

[2] UN Committee on the Rights of People with Disabilities, *Concluding observations on the initial report of Turkey*, 1 October 2019, CRPD/C/TUR/CO/1, available at: https://tbinternet.ohchr.org/_layouts/15/treatybodyexternal/Download.aspx?symbolno=CRPD%2fC%2fTUR%2fCO%2f1&Lang=en (last accessed 16 June 2020).

[3] Ibid, 1.

(c) The lack of transparent and effective data on safeguards and remedies, as well as access to information in cases of violations of the right to legal capacity of persons with disabilities, in particular with regard to the rights to marry and to vote;
(d) The lack of information on the planned transition from substitute decision-making to supported decision-making.[4]

The recommendation of the Committee noted the need to revise legislative measures that deprive disabled people of their legal capacity and to ensure that equal recognition before the law is reflected in institutional and legal practice, including through capacity-building and raising awareness about supported decision-making in consultation with national, regional and local disability rights organisations.

Echoed in these recommendations is the CRPD's call to States Parties to ensure the enjoyment of legal capacity by disabled people on an equal basis with others in all aspects of life. By detaching legal capacity (the formal ability to hold and to exercise rights and duties) from mental capacity (decision-making skills of a person), Article 12 of the CRPD has called into question systems that deny disabled people legal capacity on the basis of disability or impairment. It has also provided an important push into thinking about decision-making by intellectually disabled people beyond persistent medical approaches to intellectual disability. The CRPD foregrounds a support paradigm to protect disabled people's right to legal capacity and introduces an obligation on States Parties to 'take appropriate measures to provide access by persons with disabilities to the support they may require in exercising their legal capacity.'[5] The Committee has been clear that States Parties must replace regimes of substituted decision-making with systems of supported decision-making.[6]

The tensions between the global aspirations of the CRPD and restrictions of intellectually disabled people's legal capacity by domestic capacity laws have been acknowledged in a burgeoning body of legal and socio-legal scholarship.[7] Over the last decade, these studies have shown the myriad ways in which intellectually

[4] Ibid, 6.

[5] UN Convention on the Rights of Persons with Disabilities (UN CRPD) Article 12(3).

[6] UN Committee on the Rights of Persons with Disabilities, *General Comment No 1 (2014) Article 12: Equal Recognition before the Law*, CRPD/C/GC/1, adopted 11 April 2014: www.ohchr.org/EN/HRBodies/CRPD/Pages/GC.aspx (last accessed 16 June 2021).

[7] A Dhanda, 'Legal Capacity in the Disability Rights Convention: Stranglehold of the Past or Lodestar for the Future' (2007) 34 *Syracuse Journal of International Law & Commerce* 429; M Donnelly, 'Capacity assessment under the Mental Capacity Act 2005: delivering on the functional approach?' (2009) 29(3) *Legal Studies* 464; E Flynn and A Arstein-Kerslake, 'Legislating personhood: realising the right to support in exercising legal capacity' (2014) 10 *International Journal of Law in Context* 81; A Arstein-Kerslake and E Flynn, 'The General Comment on Article 12 of the Convention on the Rights of Persons with Disabilities: a roadmap for equality before the law' (2016) 20(4) *The International Journal of Human Rights* 471; C de Bhailís and E Flynn, 'Recognising legal capacity: commentary and analysis of Article 12 CRPD' (2017) 13(1) *International Journal of Law in Context* 6; R Harding and E Taşcıoğlu, 'Supported Decision-Making from Theory to Practice: Implementing the right to enjoy legal capacity' (2018) 8(25) *Societies* 1.

disabled people have been stigmatised and excluded from decision-making in their own lives, and dealt with the question of how supported decision-making can be achieved as an alternative to the existing substituted decision-making models that have curtailed intellectually disabled people's legal capacity in law and practice. Another line of inquiry has focused on the ratification process of the CRPD by States Parties and the tensions that arise in the relationship between the CRPD and its interpretation by the Committee on the one hand and domestic laws and treaty reservations of national governments on the other.[8]

As part of their treaty obligations, states that have signed and ratified the CRPD are required to submit to the Committee regular state reports on the steps that they have taken on the implementation of their obligations under the CRPD.[9] The Committee seeks comprehensive review of all the measures the States Parties have taken to harmonise national law and policy and the progress made in that regard in relation to each CRPD article.[10] In recent years, as the monitoring and reporting of States Parties expands, scholars have sought to gain a deeper understanding of the reporting process and dynamics involved therein.[11] In this chapter, I aim to add to this developing body of work by focusing on Turkey's State Party report to the Committee on its progress on disability rights. By examining the State Party report alongside Turkish laws on disability rights and legal capacity, I demonstrate the deep chasm between the CRPD's paradigm for the realisation of disability rights and the paradigm within which Turkish legal framework and self-reporting practice operate.

More specifically, I trace Turkey's 'ritualistic' acquiescence to the formal expectations of the CRPD's human rights regime, while discarding its aspirations to comprehensively address violations and its obligations as a State Party with regard to disability rights. In making this statement, I am engaging the concept of 'regulatory ritualism'[12] that refers to the formal forms of

[8] S Doyle and E Flynn, 'Ireland's ratification of the UN convention on the rights of persons with disabilities: challenges and opportunities' (2013) 41(3) *British Journal of Learning Disabilities* 171; E Flynn, 'The Long Road to Ratification: Ireland and the CRPD' (p 133), EJ Kakoullis 'A Consultative Culture? The Ratification Process for the CRPD in Cyprus' (p 157), and AS Kanter, 'The failure of the United States to Ratify the CRPD' (p 97), all in EJ Kakoullis and K Johnson (eds), *Recognising human rights in different cultural contexts: The United Nations convention on rights of persons with disabilities* (Switzerland, Springer Nature, 2020).

[9] UN CRPD Article 35.

[10] UN CRPD Article 36. For some recent studies that look at monitoring and reporting process under the CRPD.

[11] A Dhanda, 'The Process of State Party Reporting to the CRPD Committee: The Indian Experience' (p 353); and D Afrianty, 'The Role of Disabled People's Organisations in Promoting the CRPD in Indonesia' (p 333) in EJ Kakoullis and K Johnson (eds), *Recognising human rights in different cultural contexts: The United Nations convention on rights of persons with disabilities* (Switzerland, Springer Nature, 2020).

[12] H Charlesworth and E Larking (eds), *Human Rights and the Universal Periodic Review: Rituals and Ritualism* (Cambridge, Cambridge University Press, 2014); H Charlesworth and others, 'Strengthening the International Human Rights System: Rights, Regulation and Ritualism' Australian Research Council Project (Acton ACT, Centre for International Governance and Justice, Australian National University) (2010–2015) available at: www.regnet.anu.edu.au\\research\\research-projects\\details\\535\\strengthening-internationalhuman-rights-system-rights (last accessed 16 June 2021).

participation in a human rights mechanism (domestic or international) by States Parties, but while ignoring its substantive, transformative goals to achieve legal and societal change. I argue that Turkey's ritualistic (non)engagement with the CRPD in its report prioritises the satisfaction of formal criteria over reflection and focus 'on substance and practical realities, and problems encountered.'[13] As such, the reporting process in Turkey's practice turns into a mere performance of disability rights for an international audience, that fails to facilitate a meaningful engagement with the CRPD and accountability for a rights-based policy implementation of disability rights. In what follows, the chapter first provides an overview of the Turkish legal framework on disability in general and on the regulation of intellectually disabled people's decision-making in particular, before moving to discuss Turkey's submission to the Committee about its work and progress on the rights of disabled people and its international legal commitments under the CRPD against this background.

II. DISABILITY LEGISLATION AND POLICY IN TURKEY

Since the decline of the Ottoman Empire, modern law has been an integral part of Turkey's political, economic and social history and its aspirations to belong to the European order. The abolition of the Sultanate, the constitution of the Turkish Republic in 1923, the abrogation of the Caliphate[14] in 1924 and the outlawing of the religious orders in 1925, followed by the adoption of Swiss Civil and Italian Criminal Codes in 1926, aimed to mark a decisive break with the Ottoman past and shape the country into a modern and secular 'European' nation state. Turkey's European Union (EU) candidacy since 1999 has stimulated further political and legal reforms for the promotion and incorporation of EU norms into the domestic legal order. In one of the most dramatic amendments made to the Turkish Constitution in 2004, international treaties were given supremacy over domestic law in case of a conflict between domestic law and international agreements in the area of fundamental rights and freedoms.[15]

[13] CH Heyns and FJ Viljoen, 'The Impact of the United Nations Human Rights Treaties on the Domestic Level' (2001) 23 *Human Rights Quarterly* 483, 485.

[14] The spiritual leadership of the Muslim world that had resided with the Ottoman Empire since 1571.

[15] Until 2004, Article 90 of the Turkish Constitution on ratification of international treaties accorded international agreements the force of law once duly put into effect, but without clearly defining their role in national legislation or rank within the hierarchy of laws. The amendment of Article 90 in 2004 granted international human rights treaties 'in the area of fundamental rights and freedoms' preferential treatment over domestic law 'in the case of a conflict between international agreements duly put into effect and the domestic laws.' On the status of international laws and transnational legal arrangements in Turkish law, particularly in the context of Turkey's international commitments deriving from the ECHR, see E Örücü, 'The Turkish Experience with Judicial Comparativism in Human Rights Cases' in E Örücü (ed), *Judicial Comparativism in Human Rights Cases* (London, British Institute of International & Comparative Law 2003);

Although disability rights and legislation did not form part of Turkey's EU accession negotiations, significant improvements in the field of disability rights took place in the 2000s alongside extensive nationwide legal and judicial reforms, mainly those pertaining to human rights, intensified by the EU harmonisation process. In 2007, Turkey became one of the first signatories of the CRPD, which it ratified alongside the Optional Protocol in 2009. In accordance with the specific status accorded to international treaties by the Constitution, the ratification of the CRPD made it legally binding on domestic legislation and courts and gave rise to obligations on the Turkish state to realise disability rights in line with the CRPD.

Following the ratification of the CRPD, one of the most dramatic steps taken by the Turkish government about disability rights was the amendments made to the Turkish Disability Act no 5378 (TDA) in 2014. The TDA, which originally came into force in 2004, was heavily reliant on a derogatory term for disabled people (*özürlü*)[16] and a medicalised understanding of disability as a deficit that 'limits a person's inclusion into social life and ability to fulfil their daily needs.' The 2014 amendments replaced this term with 'person with disability' (*engelli*) to refer to 'a person who is impacted by attitudes and environmental conditions that limit their full and effective participation in society on an equal basis with others due to their various levels of physical, intellectual, physiological or sensory impairments.'[17] The TDA prohibits all forms of discrimination based on disability,[18] and mandates public entities to offer accessible services.[19] In developing a framework for the protection of rights of disabled people, the TDA's key aims are grounded in fostering and providing fundamental rights and freedoms for disabled people and 'strengthening the respect to their dignity acquired by birth' in order to ensure their inclusion in social life on an equal basis with others.[20] Importantly, the TDA also recognises the inviolability of disabled people's pride and dignity and foregrounds respect for freedom and independence of disabled people, including intellectually disabled people, to make their decisions on their own lives.[21]

Despite its marking an important milestone towards a rights-based approach to disability, the extent to which the TDA contributes meaningfully

K Başlar, 'Uluslararası Antlaşmaların Onaylanması, Üstünlüğü ve Anayasal Denetimi Üzerine' (2004) 24(1–2) *Milletlerarası Hukuk ve Milletlerarası Özel Hukuku Bülteni: Prof. Dr. Sevin Tolner'e Armağan* 285; L Gönenç and S Esen, 'The Problem of the Application of Less Protective International Agreements in Domestic Legal Systems: Article 90 of the Turkish Constitution' (2006) 8 *European Journal of Law Reform* 485.

[16] 'Handicapped'. Özürlü literally means 'with excuse' or 'with defect'.

[17] Turkish Disability Act no 5378 (TDA), Article 3.

[18] TDA, Articles 14 and 15.

[19] TDA, Provisional Articles 2 and 3.

[20] TDA, Article 1.

[21] TDA, Article 4.

to the promotion and protection of rights of disabled people is questionable. A lack of statistical and research data about disabled people is a foundational problem in Turkey, as pointed out by the Committee in their concluding observations.[22] Turkey does not collect systematic data on the number of disabled people, their living conditions or barriers to accessing their rights with a human rights approach supported by disaggregation of data by gender, age, region and ethnic identification etc. The '2002 Turkey Disability Survey' of the Statistical Institute of Turkey (TÜİK), the primary source of country-level data on disability to this date, states that disabled people constituted 12.29 per cent of the total population.[23] The survey defined disabled person as a 'person unable to ensure by himself or herself, wholly or partly, the necessities of a normal individual and/or social life, as a result of deficiency, either congenital or not, in his or her physical capabilities.'[24] Nine years later, in 2011, a second TÜİK survey found out that 6.9 per cent of the Turkish population is disabled.[25] This survey defined a disabled person as 'a person over 3 years old with a minimum of one impairment (in seeing, hearing, speaking, walking, climbing up the stairs, carrying and gripping things, learning and memory).' As such, the two nationwide disability surveys conducted by TÜİK used different (and problematic) criteria to define and measure disability, and include inconsistent and non-comparable information. Without good quality, consistent and accessible data on disability, the number of disabled people in the country is unknown, and the prospects of identifying problems experienced by disabled people, devising and implementing policies to address those problems and monitoring progress in disability rights remain poor.

The implementation and enforcement of the positive aspects of the TDA have been very limited as well. Perhaps the most visible shortcoming of the TDA can be seen in its failure to ensure compliance with one of its main targets: to ensure accessibility in public spaces and transport. The TDA, in its initiation in 2004, had stipulated a legal requirement for all public entities to meet certain accessibility criteria within seven years.[26] Failure to meet these criteria by this deadline would be met with administrative fines. Yet not only did the lengthy period offered to institutions initially mean a significant

[22] UN CRPD, *Concluding observations on the initial report of Turkey* (n 2), para 62.

[23] Statistical Institute of Turkey (TÜİK), *2002 Turkey Disability Survey* (2002), available at: https://kutuphane.tuik.gov.tr/pdf/0014899.pdf (last accessed 16 June 2021). According to this survey, 78.3 per cent of the adult disabled population did not participate in the labour force; 36.3 per cent were illiterate; and 34.4 per cent of them had never been married.

[24] Ibid, p X.

[25] TÜİK, 2011 Population and Housing Census (2011) available at: https://data.tuik.gov.tr/Bulten/Index?p=Nufus-ve-Konut-Arastirmasi-2011-15843 (last accessed 4 November 2021).

[26] TDA, Provisional Articles 2 and 3. The accessibility standards are set by the Turkish Standards Institution (TSE).

delay for the provision of the accessibility, but the deadline to comply with this requirement had been extended six times by 2020. As this chapter goes to press, the most recent extension has postponed the deadline to 2023.[27] The accessibility requirement is in this way put off periodically and shelved until the next deadline, diminishing the TDA's effectiveness to encourage compliance and ensure accountability, while inaccessibility remains a major problem in disabled people's everyday lives.[28]

The limitations of the TDA are evident in the absence of enforcement mechanisms and of a set of processes with the ability to influence the broader legal framework and institutional behaviour. Historically, the country's welfare regime has offered little social support for disabled citizens, assigning them to the sphere of familial care and charity.[29] The provision of social care continues to be family centred and to depend on a highly medicalised approach to disability, based on 'assessments of loss of organ or functional ability' in percentages.[30] Disability-related allowances are largely intended for family members of disabled people who are paid as care providers, based on a means test of the household income of the person with 'severe' disability, and do not facilitate independent living.[31] Despite the TDA's anti-discrimination clauses, discrimination against disabled people remains embedded in many laws. To this day, for example, disabled people cannot serve as judges or prosecutors according to the Law of Judges and Prosecutors 1983. This law mandates that judges and prosecutors shall not have any 'physical and mental illness, or disability that would prevent them from fulfilling their duties on a permanent basis around the country', including 'disability in speaking in an unusual way that can be considered odd by the community and problems in controlling limbs.'[32] A similar language of deficiency dominates legal regulations around intellectual disability[33] and is used to withhold from intellectually disabled people the right to exercise legal capacity, which this chapter now turns its focus to.

[27] Omnibus Bill (no 31119) 28 July 2020, Article 7.

[28] For an account of everyday experiences of inaccessibility of disabled people in Istanbul, Turkey, see: S Yardımcı and D Bezmez, 'Disabled Istanbulites' everyday life experiences as "urban citizens": accessibility and participation in decision-making' (2018) 22(5) *Citizenship Studies* 475.

[29] V Yılmaz, *The Political Economy of Disability in Turkey* (Saarbrücken, LAP Lambert, 2011).

[30] The Regulation on Disability Assessment for Adults (no 30692) 2019.

[31] Omnibus Bill (no 31119) (n 27).

[32] Law of Judges and Prosecutors [*Hakimler ve Savcılar Kanunu*] (no 2802), Article 8.

[33] The Turkish system does not distinguish between intellectual disability, neurodegenerative conditions like dementia and mental health conditions, which are instead subsumed in law under categories of 'mental illness', 'mental infirmity' or 'mental condition'. As such, the regulations that I discuss in this chapter also apply to people with dementia and mental health conditions, although my focus here is on the legal conceptualisations of and responses to intellectually disabled people and their decision-making.

III. LEGAL CAPACITY IN TURKISH LAWS

The Turkish Constitution declares 'equality before the law'[34] and every citizen's 'inherent fundamental rights and freedoms, which are inviolable and inalienable.'[35] However, the Turkish Civil Code delineates the strictly demarcated limits of access to legal capacity. As in many other civil law jurisdictions,[36] the Turkish legal system relies on a two-tiered approach to legal capacity, setting up two forms of capacity: capacity to be the holder of rights[37] and capacity to act.[38] Article 8 of the Civil Code declares that capacity to be a rights-holder applies to each and every citizen. And yet, Articles 9 and 14 of the Civil Code directly remove the capacity to act from people who do not have 'power of discernment' and from those who are 'restricted'. By decoupling the capacity to act from the capacity to be a holder of rights, the Civil Code removes from the holder of rights the right to exercise those rights.[39] This poses a material conflict between the CRPD and Turkish laws. The Committee has made clear that legal capacity means that all people, including disabled people, 'have legal standing and legal agency simply by virtue of being human'.[40] In contrast to this understanding of legal capacity by the CRPD, the Turkish state continues to insist on removing legal agency from the definition and understanding of 'legal capacity' and denying legal agency on a number of grounds linked to disability.

The first ground for the denial of 'capacity to act' for a person under Turkish law is 'lack of power of discernment'. 'Power of discernment' – a similar concept to the one of 'mental capacity' often used in common law jurisdictions – is presumed to be held by every citizen unless one lacks 'the ability to act reasonably [...] due to reasons like mental illness, mental infirmity and intoxication.'[41] From this legal formulation two conditions emerge for a person to be found not to have the 'power of discernment'. The first is that the person should be unable to act 'reasonably'. The Court of Cassation has clarified to some extent what 'acting reasonably' means in law: one's capacity to understand, weight up and discern the reasons and consequences of one's actions.[42] The second condition

[34] The Constitution of the Republic of Turkey, Article 10.

[35] Ibid, Article 12.

[36] For a discussion on the Spanish law's historical approach to 'capacity' and its recent law reform on the legal capacity of intellectually disabled people, see P Cuenca Gómez, Chapter 9, this volume.

[37] Turkish Civil Code [*Türk Medeni Kanunu*] (no 4721) 2001, Article 8.

[38] Ibid, Article 9.

[39] The official translation of the CRPD into Turkish reflects this bifurcated understanding of legal capacity. Legal capacity (*hukuk ehliyeti*) is translated as 'capacity to be the holder of rights' (*hak ehliyeti*), excluding 'right to act' (*fiil ehliyeti*) and undermining legal capacity to hold rights. In this way, the translation of the concept of legal capacity into Turkish law differs from the definition of 'legal capacity' used by the CRPD.

[40] UN Committee on the Rights of Persons with Disabilities, *General Comment No 1* (n 6), para 14.

[41] Turkish Civil Code, Article 13.

[42] The Court of Cassation 14.HD. 2007/2003 E.-2007/3315 (27.3.2007).

is that there should be a causal connection between the person's failure to act reasonably and their 'mental condition'.[43] 'Mental infirmity' is not defined in the Civil Code but has been understood by the courts as 'developmental deficit or regression in mental functions.'[44] A person who cannot act reasonably due to their condition is thus deemed to be without 'power of discernment' and stripped of their capacity to act by the courts.[45]

The lack of power of discernment is not the only way through which one's legal capacity can be restricted under Turkish laws. The Turkish Civil Code has one further category for the removal of legal capacity from persons who retain power of discernment, either *ex officio* or upon the request of the person.[46] According to Article 405, 'every person who, due to mental illness or mental infirmity', is in a condition where they (i) are not able to fulfil their tasks, (ii) require permanent support for their protection and care, or (iii) put other people's safety at risk, must be 'restricted'. The demeaning implications of the language aside, this resonates with a common juxtaposition of disability with need for care and protection and/or dangerousness.[47] The danger a person poses to others purportedly due to their intellectual disability is seen as a legitimate reason to restrict them and curtail their legal capacity. Furthermore, the care and support that a person may need in their daily life are also posited as a ground to remove their legal capacity and subject them to guardianship. In contrast to the support requirement in the CRPD, receiving support in daily tasks or permanent care become the very reason that an intellectually disabled person could be deemed incapable of exercising their right to act. 'Restricted' people with power of discernment are called in law 'persons with limited incapacity'. As a rule, they do not hold, but exceptionally are given, the right to act. While people who are deemed to lack power of discernment cannot make any legally-binding decision, persons with limited incapacity are able to exercise their rights in relation to 'gratuitous acquisitions and exercising strictly bonded personal rights.'[48]

In sum, under the current legal regime a guardian can be appointed for an intellectually disabled person (i) if the person is deemed to lack the power of discernment, or (ii) the person retains the power of discernment but is deemed 'restricted'. In both cases the Civil Court of Peace, as the guardianship authority, adjudicates the matter based on an official medical board report and appoints the guardian. The guardian should be the spouse or close relative of the person, unless there are good reasons not to follow this rule, and a person appointed by

[43] The Court of Cassation HGK. 12.11.1969 T. 3-1185/799.

[44] Ibid.

[45] Turkish Civil Code, Article 14.

[46] Turkish Civil Code, Article 408.

[47] R Sandland, 'Sex and Capacity: The Management of Monsters?' (2013) 76(6) *Modern Law Review* 981.

[48] Turkish Civil Code, Article 16.

the courts as guardian is required to accept the role if they live at the same address with the person.[49] As such, the Turkish guardianship regime assumes both the presence and suitability of families for guardianship and organises decision-making on behalf of intellectually disabled people accordingly. Families, around which the welfare system is structured, are expected not only to provide care to their disabled family members but also to assume the guardian role and make decisions on their behalf.

There are certain limitations and requirements on who can be a guardian. Persons who themselves are 'restricted', who have an obvious conflict of interest with the person placed under guardianship, and judges of the guardianship authority cannot be appointed as guardians.[50] Added to this list are persons who lead 'a dishonourable life' and those banned from public service. These two conditions point to the moralistic evaluations on who can be given the power to act on someone else's behalf by the courts. The gendered implications of leading 'a dishonourable life' are clear in light of the legal normalisation of the culture of honour in Turkey and the social and legal marginalisation of those who do not comply with the accepted codes of honour.[51] The exclusion of those who are dismissed from public service also indicates the selective delegation of decision-making power by the law to certain type of citizens. Given that mass dismissals from the public sector are a historically used punishment mechanism by the Turkish state against its political opponents,[52] only those who align with the political codes of the Turkish state are trusted to be guardians and make decisions on behalf of their incapacitated family members. Notwithstanding the problems with the guardianship regime, being cut from their close networks of support on these grounds poses additional limitations on intellectually disabled people's access to support to enjoy legal capacity.

Guardians are responsible for the protection of the personal and property interests of the person who has been put under guardianship and for representing them in legal affairs.[53] The provisions of the Civil Code regarding the

[49] Ibid, Article 414. According to Article 417, persons who are over the age of 60, who have physical disability or permanent disease, who parent more than four children, or who are already a guardian, may decline to accept the guardianship role. The President of Turkey, members of the Turkish Grand National Assembly and the Cabinet, and judges and prosecutors can also be exempted from the role.

[50] Turkish Civil Code, Article 418.

[51] D Koğacıoğlu, 'The Tradition Effect: Framing Honor Crimes in Turkey' (2004) 15(2) *differences: A Journal of Feminist Cultural Studies* 119; A Zengin, *İktidarın Mahremiyeti: İstanbul'da Hayat Kadınları, Seks İşçiliği ve Şiddet* (Istanbul, Metis Publishing, 2011); A Parla, 'Revisiting "honor" through migrant vulnerabilities in Turkey' (2020) 31(1) *History and Anthropology* 84.

[52] In the most recent wave of purges from public service in Turkey, more than 100,000 public sector workers, including police officers, teachers, soldiers, doctors, judges, prosecutors and academics, were dismissed under the powers of the state of emergency following the coup d'état attempt in July 2016 against the AKP (Justice and Development Party) Government. See Amnesty International, *No End in Sight: Purged Public Sector Workers Denied a Future in Turkey* (May 2017): www.amnesty.org/download/Documents/EUR4462722017TURKISH.PDF (accessed 17 November 2020).

[53] Turkish Civil Code, Article 403.

administration of guardianship primarily deal with financial matters.[54] There are certain financial transactions that cannot be made solely by guardians on behalf of the person and must be authorised by courts of law, or otherwise are deemed invalid. These are decisions considered to have significant financial or personal consequences – such as buying or selling property, moving to an education, care or health institution, or changing residence – which require the additional permission of the guardianship authority, the local Civil Court of Peace.[55] Some other personal and financial decisions need, in addition, permission of the supervisory authority; that is, the local Court of General Jurisdiction. These include decisions relating to adoption, certain inheritance issues, as well as contracts between the 'restricted' person and their guardian.[56] Being a guarantor, establishing a foundation and making significant donations on behalf of the 'restricted' person are banned.[57] Decisions on personal matters, like marriage, cannot be made on behalf of people without power of discernment, as these are considered to be executable only by the rights-holder and cannot be transferred to someone else to be exercised on their behalf.[58] Those whose legal capacity has been restricted on grounds other than lack of power of discernment may marry with the permission of their guardians.[59] One other fundamental right that Turkish citizens under guardianship cannot exercise is voting. The right to vote that is given to every citizen over 18 years old by the Constitution[60] is withdrawn from people under guardianship by the Act on Essential Principles of Elections and Registries of Electors 1961[61] in direct contradiction of Article 29 of CRPD on participation in political and public life.

In the face of such drastic measures that deprive a person of their capacity to make decisions in their own life, this web of regulations around legal capacity of intellectually disabled people lacks the necessary safeguards. Most of the safeguards in the law focus on the management of financial affairs. Before making any 'restriction' decision, the judge *may*, but is not required to, hear the person to be subject to restriction.[62] The guardians are required to ask the restricted person for their opinion only if they have 'ability to form and express an opinion'.[63] Guardianship orders can be removed when an official medical board reports that the reason for the restriction no longer exists, or if the guardian abuses their position.[64] There is not a clear pathway for objections either

[54] Turkish Civil Code, Articles 438–445.
[55] Turkish Civil Code, Article 462.
[56] Turkish Civil Code, Article 463.
[57] Turkish Civil Code, Article 449.
[58] Turkish Civil Code, Article 125.
[59] Turkish Civil Code, Article 136; Regulation on Marriage (no 85/9747) [*Evlendirme Yönetmeliği*] 1985, Article 14(2).
[60] The Constitution of the Republic of Turkey, Article 67.
[61] Law no 298 [*Seçimlerin Temel Hükümleri ve Seçmen Kütükleri Hakkında Kanun*] 1961, Article 8.
[62] Turkish Civil Code Article 409/2; The Court of Cassation E. 2004/6402, K. 2004/7656, 10.6.2004.
[63] Turkish Civil Code Article 450.
[64] Turkish Civil Code Article 474.

to guardianship orders or to a decision-maker making substituted decisions, however. Nor is there a nominated supporter scheme or a mechanism for independent advocacy.

From this account, the dissonance between Turkish disability laws and the CRPD is clear. Despite some positive developments through the amendments to the Turkish Disability Act, in legal discourse, disability – and intellectual disability in particular – remains associated with deficiency and is reduced to a state of being in need of protection and care. The Turkish legal framework also does not comply with the CRPD requirement under Article 12 that States Parties need to provide disabled people with access to the support necessary to enable them to make decisions that have legal effect. It retains a strict substituted decision-making regime where 'power of discernment' and additional 'restriction' conditions are used as the basis for withholding intellectually disabled people's legal capacity. Moreover, the support needs of an individual are framed in law as a reason why they must be restricted, in contrast to the CRPD's call for provision of support for the enjoyment of legal capacity. Guardians are designated by the courts to protect the 'interests' of people put under guardianship, rather than to support them to make decisions in line with their will and preferences. The next section looks at Turkey's state report to the Committee in this legal landscape on its progress regarding disability rights and on the measures that it has taken to realise its obligations under the CRPD, especially Article 12 mandates.

IV. TURKEY'S STATE REPORT: PERFORMING DISABILITY RIGHTS

Having ratified the CRPD in 2009, the Turkish government submitted its initial report, due in 2011, in August 2015. A response to the list of issues in relation to the initial report raised by the Committee was additionally submitted in January 2019. This section, focusing on Turkey's submissions on its progress on disability rights, examines the Turkish state's (self-)representation of the state of disability rights in the country and the extent to which it engages with the CRPD mandates, particularly of Article 12.

For this chapter, Turkey's submission is of interest in three respects: First, States Parties submissions to the Committee offer an opportunity for states to review and provide a comprehensive account of the work that a state has done in the field of disability rights. The reviews can serve to identify the country's achievements as well as failures, problems and shortcomings in ensuring CRPD compliance. In this sense, States Parties' submissions produce and share information on the current social, legal and political landscape for disabled people in the country and point to areas and issues that require development of relevant policies and practices. Secondly, the submissions are also a venue for investigating States Parties' practice of self-reporting, giving insights into their understandings and approach to disability rights. Finally, given the huge gap between CRPD principles and the disability and legal capacity laws in Turkey that the previous section demonstrated, Turkey's state report also raises questions on the benefits and limitations of the state reporting practice under the CRPD.

Turkey's disinclination in monitoring and reporting of the implementation of the CRPD was highlighted by the four-year delay in the submission of its initial report to the Committee. Eventually, Turkey's state report was produced by governmental institutions, the General Directorate of Services for Persons with Disabilities and the Elderly, of the Ministry of Family, Labour and Social Services of Turkey. In other words, despite the CRPD's requirement that states should set up independent monitoring mechanisms to monitor their implementation of the Convention, the monitoring was not carried out by an independent body or by the active involvement of disability rights organisations of the country. There was not a clear mechanism set up to ensure the participation of civil society organisations (CSOs) working on disability rights in a meaningful way in the monitoring process; some CSOs were given only 12 days to submit their comments on the draft report and without any guidance or support from the government.[65] The draft state report, the list of issues submitted to Turkey by the Committee and the replies of Turkey to the list of issues had not been shared with the public in Turkish or in an accessible format by the State Party. As a result of these barriers, some disability rights organisations could not deliver their opinions on the draft report, or their contributions were severely limited. They have largely been left to their own means with limited time and resources to contribute to Turkey's monitoring by the CRPD.

In terms of the substance of Turkey's submission to the Committee, it far from provided a substantive review of the measures that it had taken towards CRPD compliance, or their shortcomings. The 52-page document merely lists legal regulations and provisions, action plans, initiation of projects, and numerous conferences and seminars organised by governmental or non-governmental organisations, eg '2011–2013 Strategy and Plan of Action on Care Services', '1st Strategy Paper and Plan of Action on the Rights of Children (2013–2017)' or 'Year of Action for Accessibility for All'. Expressions of intent such as 'planned' and 'envisaged' dominate the submission. There is no indication of the tangible outcomes of these activities or endeavours in terms of the real impact they have

[65] Association for Monitoring Equal Rights (2018) 'An Alternative Report from the Association for Monitoring Equal Rights in relation to the State Report of the Republic of Turkey for the 21st Session of the Committee on the Rights of Persons with Disabilities', available at: https://tbinternet.ohchr.org/_layouts/15/treatybodyexternal/Download.aspx?symbolno=INT%2fCRPD%2fICO%2fTUR%2f32174&Lang=en (last accessed 16 June 2021); Disability Rights Monitoring Group (September 2018), 'Report and List of Questions on the Current Situation of Disabled Persons in Turkey: Submission to the United Nations Committee on the Rights of Persons with Disabilities', available at: https://tbinternet.ohchr.org/_layouts/15/treatybodyexternal/Download.aspx?symbolno=INT%2fCRPD%2fICO%2fTUR%2f32006&Lang=en (last accessed 16 June 2021).

had on disabled people and their living conditions. This emphasis on form without substance, action without impact, is reflected in the report's presentation of the mere passing of laws or signing of international conventions as achievements in ensuring disability rights without any detail on their implementation and/or transformations they brought about. Consider the statement in relation to the ratification of the CRPD which, according to Turkey's state report,

> brought forth significant opportunities for protection, promotion and enhancement of rights of PwDs [people with disabilities] in Turkey. Besides, it has attributed to enhancement of rights of PwDs, carrying national implementations to the level of internationally accepted standards, promotion of monitoring the implementation processes, activation of disability laws and policies in Turkey and elimination of possible shortcomings in the implementation of such policies.[66]

In a similar way, the signing of the European Convention on Human Rights is put forward as a key measure in securing of the Article 22 right to respect for privacy.[67]

Turkey's submission on Article 12 follows a similar approach. It almost exclusively recites the legislation around decision-making by intellectually disabled people and 'the conditions of incapacity'[68] in Turkish laws that were detailed in the previous section. As discussed above, the Turkish Civil Code restricts legal capacity of individuals on the basis of 'mental infirmity' and 'mental illness' and does not explicitly refer to disability as a basis of restriction of legal capacity. It is in Turkey's state report that disability emerges as a condition of legal incapacity and disabled people as the targets of such restrictions. The report names 'persons who are in a state of disability or lack distinguishing power'[69] as persons 'regarded as *non sui juris*' whose acts 'may not lead to legal consequences'.[70] This formulation of the reasons for incapacitation that uses disability and 'lack of distinguishing power' almost interchangeably is followed by the report's merging of disabled people with persons who are 'restricted' and 'have limited incapacity'. The report states that 'disabled persons with distinguishing power may not undertake any obligation by their own will unless they receive the consent of their legal representatives.'[71] The submission, in this way, not only indirectly admits that legal capacity includes the exercise of rights which is bound to specific conditions in Turkish law, but also that disabled people are legally incapacitated because of their disability. This dissonance between Turkish capacity law and Article 12 is left unproblematised, rather than confronted, addressed, or even acknowledged.

[66] Government of Turkey, 'Initial report submitted by Turkey under article 35 of the Convention', 3 August 2015, UN Doc CRPD/C/TUR/1, para 3.

[67] Ibid, para 164.

[68] Ibid, para 88.

[69] Turkey's state report uses the phrase 'distinguishing power' for power of discernment.

[70] Ibid, para 89.

[71] Ibid, para 90. This is a reference to Article 405 of the Civil Code.

Instead, the discourse of protection is promoted in the report to announce the rationale for the guardianship regime to the Committee, alongside pathologised, deficient views of intellectual disability:

> Guardianship mechanism was regulated in Turkish Law with the purpose of protecting the rights of persons. Guardians are liable for protecting the interest of persons with mental disabilities or infirmities (including interests on assets) and representing them in legal actions.[72]

The discourse of protection which undermines intellectually disabled people as objects of protection flattens the distinction between being a subject of rights and of best interests decisions made on one's behalf.

The Committee's request for further information in the 'List of issues in relation to the initial report of Turkey' did not lead to a deeper engagement with Article 12 on Turkey's side. Turkey's response ignores the Committee's queries on the steps taken to repeal provisions of the Turkish Civil Code that deprive disabled people of their legal capacity and on measures to establish a supported decision-making system.[73] An EU funded study in 2016 that aimed 'to identify and provide solutions for the problems faced in placing under guardianship the PwDs who stay in institutions affiliated with [the Ministry of Family, Labour and Social Services]' is cited without any further detail about the project than the preparation of 'a draft guidebook covering frequently asked questions and a report on examples of good practice.'[74] However, it is telling that this study, quoted as a response to the Committee's query on the move from guardianship to supported decision-making, did not problematise guardianship, but focused on problems in placing disabled people under guardianship. Turkey's response to the question on the

> number of persons with disabilities who are still under tutorship and guardianship (plus the percentage of the total number of persons with disabilities that they represent) and of those who are still subject to processes to re-establish their full legal capacity,[75]

on the other hand, demonstrates the extent of the lack of information and a monitoring system in the country: 'By October 2018, the numbers of PwDs under guardianship are 612 persons in care centers affiliated with the Ministry

[72] Ibid, para 92.

[73] UN Committee on the Rights of People with Disabilities (UNCRPD), *List of issues in relation to the initial report of Turkey*, 9 November 2018, UN Doc CRPD/C/TUR/Q/1, available at: https://tbinternet.ohchr.org/_layouts/15/treatybodyexternal/Download.aspx?symbolno=CRPD%2fC%2fTUR%2fQ%2f1&Lang=en (last accessed 16 November 2020), para 13(a) and (b).

[74] Government of Turkey, *Replies of Turkey to the list of issues*, 21 January 2019, UN Doc CRPD/C/TUR/Q/1/Add.1, available at: https://tbinternet.ohchr.org/_layouts/15/treatybodyexternal/Download.aspx?symbolno=CRPD%2fC%2fTUR%2fQ%2f1%2fAdd.1&Lang=en (last accessed 16 November 2020), para 29.

[75] UNCRPD, *List of issues in relation to the initial report of Turkey* (n 73), para 13(c).

and 13,872 persons with mental/psychological disabilities in private care centers supervised by the Ministry.' The source of this data, and how it compares to the total number of disabled people and to the number of those under guardianship but not living in public or private institutions are not shared. If we take into account that a relatively smaller number of disabled people stay in institutions in Turkey,[76] we can only assume that these numbers represent a small proportion of people under guardianship.

The collating and listing of laws, action plans, meetings and figures in Turkey's report is not insignificant. These techniques of regulatory ritualism produce a largely self-descriptive and self-serving document, turning the satisfaction of the formal standards into the purpose of self-reporting.[77] Whereas the CRPD places disability within the broader context of relations in society and proposes a comprehensive programme for change of social and legal approaches to disability, Turkey's state report translates human rights norms embedded in the CRPD into quantifiable performances of disability rights devoid of context and meaning. What is more, the self-reporting process reconstructs the institutional and discursive limits of the Turkish state by reproducing a conception of intellectually disabled people as objects of protection and care rather than challenging its existing values and conventions to catalyse change. Undermining in these ways the means by which disability rights need to be understood and can be substantially accomplished, the reporting process fails to instigate a shift to produce responsibility, accountability and transparency and to reshape state action and language.

V. CONCLUSION

This chapter provides an account of the Turkish state's approach to intellectual disability in its written laws and documents and demonstrates the deep chasm between the CRPD and Turkish legal framework and self-reporting practice. Intellectually disabled people receive very little recognition and protection under Turkish laws, which are marked by a deficit view of intellectual disability and a rigid substituted decision-making regime. In contrast to the support paradigm embedded in Article 12 of the CRPD, the framing of intellectually

[76] According to the latest report of Ministry of Family, Labour and Social Services, 29,530 persons were staying in public or private care centres (8,075 and 21,455 respectively) in September 2020. Ministry of Family, Labour and Social Services of Turkey, *Engelli ve Yaşlı İstatistik Bülteni*, October 2020, available at https://ailevecalisma.gov.tr/media/60415/istatistik_bulteni_ekim20.pdf (last accessed 16 June 2021).

[77] G Oberleitner, 'Countering Ritualism: What Does it Mean to Follow-Up Human Rights Recommendations?', Paper delivered at 'The Rituals of Human Rights' Workshop, Centre for International Governance and Justice, RegNet, Australian National University, Canberra, Australia, 25–27 June 2014, available at: http://regnet.anu.edu.au/sites/default/files/publications/attachments/2015-08/11%20Oberleitner%2C%20Countering%20Ritualism.pdf (last accessed 16 June 2021).

disabled people as recipients of support and care becomes the way in which they are excluded from full ownership of legal capacity. These shortcomings have remained intact in the CRPD reporting process. Turkey's submission mirrors the startling failure to engage with the issues raised by the CRPD and further consolidates the construction of disabled people as objects of care and the state's (and their families') role as protector of their 'interests'.

Sally Engle Merry argued that the reformulation of soft law norms of human rights into quantitative indicators to specify and measure compliance comes 'at the cost of a simplification and decontextualization that runs counter to human rights legal thinking'.[78] In Turkey's report we can see a similar, ritualistic over-reliance on quantification with a similar simplifying and de-contextualising effect. The report presents a collation of laws, action plans, meetings and figures, devoid of any acknowledgement of disabled people's real-life conditions, intellectually disabled people's right to legal capacity, or of the state's obligation to provide support for the enjoyment of legal capacity by disabled and non-disabled persons on an equal basis. These repetitive and formalistic patterns of 'rituals of verification'[79] turn the state report into a mere performance of disability rights for an international audience, without any substantive or meaningful engagement with the conditions of disabled people in Turkey or Turkey's international human rights obligations under the CRPD. In this way, Turkey's (non)engagement with the CRPD undermines the potential impact of the CRPD's state reporting and monitoring process as well as the broad vision of legal and societal transformation that the CRPD aims to effect.

Alternative and shadow reports by disability rights organisations shed light on some of the silences and absences in Turkish laws and state report to some extent. For instance, it is through the Shadow Report of the Confederation of the Disabled of Turkey that we (and the Committee) learn that people with visual, hearing or speech impairments are also subject to varying degrees of legal incapacitation in the practice of notaries and banks, which require them to have two witnesses to carry out procedures despite the requirement being abolished in the amendments made to the Notary Law in 2005.[80] However, as discussed above, in a context such as Turkey where CSOs operate with extremely limited resources and with limited support from the state, their participation in the monitoring of law and policy development processes remain constrained.

[78] S Engle Merry, 'Firming Up Soft Law: The Impact of Indicators on Transnational Human Rights Legal Orders' in T Halliday and G Shaffer (eds), *Transnational Legal Orders and Human Rights Law* (Cambridge, Cambridge University Press 2015), 375.

[79] M Power, *The Audit Society: Rituals of Verification* (Oxford, Oxford University Press, 1997).

[80] The Confederation of the Disabled of Turkey, 'Shadow Report Turkey' (2018) available at: https://tbinternet.ohchr.org/_layouts/15/treatybodyexternal/Download.aspx?symbolno=INT%2fCRPD%2fCSS%2fTUR%2f33877&Lang=en (last accessed 16 June 2021).

These tensions raise questions about the benefits and limitations of 'soft law' regulatory processes in Turkey and similar contexts out of step with the kinds of human rights ideals and ideas that are embodied by the CRPD. This is not to trivialise the potential of the CRPD and its monitoring of the States Parties, which can serve as leverage for the promotion and advocacy of disabled people's rights at national and local levels. My aim is rather to point out the complex interfaces of top-down and bottom-up impetuses for legal change. Following the constitutive socio-legal scholarship,[81] I would argue that as the CRPD norms and the idea of universal legal capacity continues to spread around the world, there is an ongoing need for more bottom-up inquiries. From disability rights advocates who translate the globalised aims of the CRPD for domestic advocacy, to intellectually disabled people and their support networks who navigate the substituted decision-making regimes on a daily basis, a focus on the actors and processes on the ground opens up a rich avenue for critically engaging with how people understand concepts and principles of the CRPD, and how they engage with those understandings for social and legal change. The everyday lives of the CRPD at the intersections of the global and the local can be where much of its yet to be realised potential and promise lie, and where we can trace and understand signs for deepening of such transformation in law and society.

[81] P Ewick and S Silbey, *Commonplace of Law: Stories from Everyday Life* (Chicago IL, University of Chicago Press, 1998); SE Merry, *Human Rights and Gender Violence: Translating International Law into Local Justice* (Chicago IL, University of Chicago Press, 2006); M Goodale and SE Merry, *The Practice of Human Rights: Tracking Law Between the Global and the Local* (Cambridge, Cambridge University Press, 2007).

Part III

Supporting Legal Capacity in Everyday Life: Balancing Empowerment and Safeguards

12

Autonomy of a Person under Guardianship: Self-determination in the Theory and Practice of Guardianship Law in Finland

ANNA MÄKI-PETÄJÄ-LEINONEN

I. INTRODUCTION

AT THE END of 2018, there were 74,652 persons under guardianship in Finland,[1] of whom 12,723 were aged 0 to 17 years, 25,523 were aged 18 to 64, and 36,406 were over 65.[2] The reason for the appointment of a guardian for an adult is usually dementia, mental illness, intellectual disability or disability due to substance abuse. The Finnish Guardianship Act (442/1999) is based on the principle that no one's right to decide on one's own affairs should be limited more than is necessary to protect them. The majority of adults under guardianship retain their formal, *de jure*, legal capacity alongside their guardians. The right of a person under guardianship to take independent decisions has been much discussed not merely in jurisprudence, but also in relation to practical guardianship matters.

This chapter deals with the autonomy of a person under guardianship by reference to three subdivisions of self-determination: the right of a legally competent person to make independent decisions; the right to be heard as part of self-determination; and respect for the previously expressed or presumed wishes of an incapacitated person.[3] I argue that, following the ratification of the United

[1] Finland's official total population at the end of 2018 was 5,517,919. See Official Statistics of Finland (OSF): Population Projection. [e-publication]: https://www.stat.fi/til/vrm_en.html.

[2] Digital and Population Data Services Agency: About the Agency/Open data/Open data from local register offices: www.dvv.fi/mare/.

[3] On the three sub-divisions of autonomy, see eg A Mäki-Petäjä-Leinonen, 'Protecting a Person with Dementia through Restrictions of Freedom? Notions of Autonomy in the Theory and Practice of Elder Care' in A Griffiths, S Mustasaari and A Mäki-Petäjä-Leinonen (eds), *Subjectivity, Citizenship and Belonging in Law: Identities and Intersections* (London, Routledge 2016) 146–70.

Nations Convention on the Rights of Persons with Disabilities (CRPD) in June 2016, it is important to evaluate Finland's Guardianship Act and its application in the light of the CRPD. The application of the Guardianship Act should take more account of clients' autonomy, and guardians should seek to support their clients in decision-making more than is the case at present. In practice, guardians play a significant role in the realisation of their client's autonomy.

This chapter addresses internal inconsistencies in the Guardianship Act regarding the client's legal capacity and the tension between the weight placed on the client's views and those of their guardian. This is done by analysing guardianship through the lens of supported decision-making, utilising doctrinal legal analysis, reported ombudsman cases and interviews with public guardians.

The interview data consists of four interviews with the public guardians and two guardians' secretaries, working in the same guardianship office in Southern Finland, about their experiences in supporting their clients' autonomy and the potential challenges involved. I interviewed guardians in order to map out how they interpret the law and apply it in their work. I chose to interview public guardians and their secretaries (instead of private persons appointed to be a guardian to their close relative) as they are professionals and therefore have extensive expertise in different guardianship matters.[4] While it is also important to map out the experiences of people who are under guardianship, I regard that as an issue to be addressed in future research. These data are derived from six thematic interviews ranging between 30 and 92 minutes in duration, which produced 103 pages of transcript, and are used here to describe these employees' views on whether guardianship practice supports the theory of autonomy of a person under guardianship. Due to the smallness of the sample,[5] the data is used only to give some examples of guardianship practices: I do not seek to generalise the findings to cover all guardianship practices in Finland.

II. THE RIGHT TO SELF-DETERMINATION OF A PERSON UNDER GUARDIANSHIP

A. Self-determination De Jure and De Facto

This section assesses the extent to which the Finnish Guardianship Act (442/1999) facilitates an appropriate balance between protection and autonomy and what this means for the self-determination of people under guardianship. The Act

[4] A guardian is appointed by a local register office (for a person who is in need of a guardian and who applies themselves and understands the significance of the matter) or a court. The public guardian is usually a public official employed by a public guardianship office. In 2018, 34,193 clients had a public guardian, 43,541 clients had a private person as a guardian, and 4085 clients had guardians that were private service providers acting in that capacity. See www.dvv.fi/mare/.

[5] In Finland there are 23 guardianship offices, some 195 public guardians and 350 guardian secretaries.

Figure 12.1 The guardianship system under the Finnish Guardianship Act

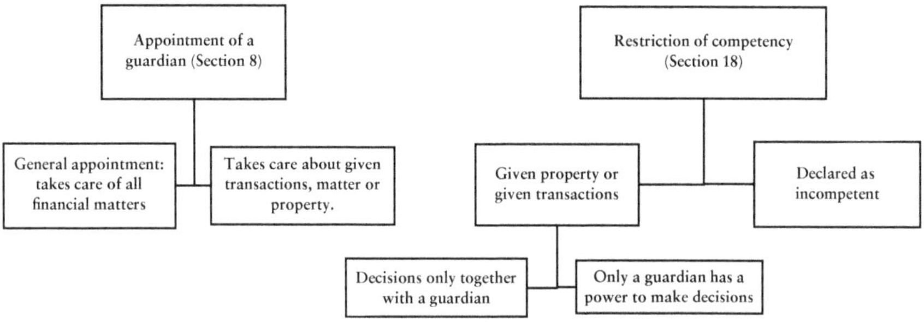

provides that a court may appoint a guardian for an adult who is incapable of looking after their own interests or dealing with personal or financial affairs that require care and are not being properly handled in any other way (section 8.1). Usually, a guardian is tasked with dealing with all the client's financial affairs. In some cases the guardian's task may be restricted to covering only certain transactions, matters or property. If the court has so ordered, the guardian may also have competence to represent the client in matters pertaining to their person (such as medical treatment issues), if the client cannot understand the significance of the matter (section 29.2).

The Guardianship Act provides that the mere appointment of a guardian does not affect the client's legal capacity per se. The client may continue to decide on the use and management of their property and, as regards property that the client can decide on, such property shall not be taken into administration (by the guardian) against the client's wishes (section 37.2). However, a client's competency may be restricted in circumstances where they are clearly not fully legally capable. Section 18 provides that if an adult is unable to take care of their financial affairs and their important interests are thereby *endangered* a court may restrict their competency by ordering that: (1) a client may enter into given transactions or administer given property only in conjunction with the guardian; (2) a client is not competent to enter into given transactions or to administer given property; (3) a client is declared incompetent. The table shows the entire guardianship system under the Guardianship Act.

A decision that limits the client's ability to act under section 18 clearly restricts their legal capacity. In practice, however, the restriction of a client's competency is rare. In 2018, 0.9 per cent of those under guardianship were declared incompetent and a further 0.8 per cent had their competency restricted in another way.[6] It is therefore interesting to consider, how in a de facto if not de jure sense, the mere appointment of a guardian under section 8 may also affect the client's practical decision-making ability.

[6] Digital and Population Data Services Agency: About the Agency/Open data/Open data from local register offices: www.dvv.fi/mare.

The points raised above give the impression that if a client's legal capacity is not restricted under section 18 of the Guardianship Act, the guardian has only a supporting role in relation to the client's actions. This is also emphasised in the preparatory works for the Guardianship Act. The government proposal states that the appointment of a guardian *does not affect* a person's legal capacity or ability to deal with their assets.[7] However, the reality of how a client is able to act in practice may be different. This is due to the caveat contained in section 14 of the Act to the effect that the appointment of a guardian does not restrict the client's freedom to act, *unless otherwise provided elsewhere in the law*. In this respect, the Guardianship Act contains one very significant exception.

Section 31.2 of the Guardianship Act provides for the use of client bank accounts by stating that if the client has an account with a credit institution, the guardian shall notify the institution as to who has the right to withdraw funds from the account. The government proposal for the Act indicated that the rule applies irrespective of whether the client is fully legally capable or whether their capacity is restricted under the law.[8] In practice, the appointment of a guardian may therefore mean that the client loses their actual right to hold a substantial portion of their assets; the right to use their own bank account will be lost even though such economic sovereignty is viewed as a fundamental right by the majority of people.

However, the legislator has emphasised the guardian's discretion regarding access to the client's bank account. The preparatory works for the Act state that in many cases it is appropriate for part of the client's funds to be kept in an account from which the client is free to withdraw money for personal use.[9] In addition, the assets deemed reasonable by reference to the client's needs must always be left to their administration.

Loss of access to a bank account may cause a problem if the client is still able to understand the meaning of the matter. For instance, many people with memory disorders find it important to withdraw money from an ATM independently, and this may form part of their day-to-day routine. In such a situation, suddenly losing the right to withdraw money can reasonably be assumed to be against the client's interests: it may cause distress and even behavioural problems. If, on the other hand, a fairly small amount of money is kept in the account, the economic loss that could be caused by the loss of the money or as a result of economic exploitation of the client is quite small. Thus, the client retains a sufficient degree of independence and at the same time their financial interests are protected.[10] The Finnish Parliamentary

[7] HE 146/1998. Government proposal to Parliament to reform Guardianship legislation, pp 19 and 34. See eg p 19: 'the primary means … is the appointment of a guardian … *It therefore does not affect the person's competency to decide for themselves*.' (emphasis added).

[8] HE 146/1998, p 44.

[9] Ibid.

[10] A Mäki-Petäjä-Leinonen, 'Päämies rationaalisena toimijana – teoriaa ja käytäntöä edunvalvonnassa olevan ihmisen itsemääräämisoikeudesta' 2018/1 *Lakimies* 3–28, at 16.

Ombudsman (PO)[11] emphasised the importance of cooperation between the client and the guardian in matters relating to the client's accounts in the decision outlined below.

PO Dnro 3943/4/11, 4.5.2012.

The complaint stated that it was very important for the client to decide on his own funeral, which is why he had opened a 'funeral account' with the help of his daughter. However, the guardian had both closed this account and opened new accounts without asking the client first. In his decision, the PO stated that the bank account is an important issue for a person on the basis of general life experience, and some individual accounts may also include a specific case-by-case dimension. Especially for older people, it may be a matter of personal dignity to prepare yourself for your own funeral by opening a separate account. The PO took the view that in this case it was a matter of weighing what is in the interests of the client on a case-by-case basis. The PO did not consider the procedure that had been followed, in which the client was routinely ignored in relation to his own affairs, to be indicative of case-by-case consideration.

The Act on Guardianship can therefore be criticised on the basis that it does not contain a clear formulation of guardians' apparently broad powers to make decisions regarding clients' financial issues. In addition, section 31.2 contradicts the principle underlying guardianship law that the client's right to self-determination should be compromised only to the extent necessary to protect their interests. It is obviously unnecessary to limit the client's access to cash resources whenever a guardian is appointed.[12]

The provision restricting rights in respect of clients' bank accounts represents a traditional, paternalistic approach whereby protection of the client is given priority over their autonomy. This way of thinking undeniably has some justification. As Pertti Välimäki has pointed out, practical issues of everyday life favour prioritising a guardian's views in certain situations. Furthermore, the relationship between the client and a third party sometimes requires 'paternal' clarity. However, it is essential that the guardian exercises decision-making powers in accordance with the principles laid down in the Guardianship Act, which require that the client's views are heard and respected.[13] On the other hand, Markku Helin has pointed out that a guardian is often appointed in the

[11] In Finland the Parliamentary Ombudsman has the task of ensuring that all government departments and officials follow the law. If the Ombudsman determines that a government official has not acted in accordance with the law, they can advise on the proper application of the law, reprimand the official or, in extreme cases, order a criminal prosecution. In their work, the Ombudsman also concentrates on promoting fundamental and human rights. See L Nieminen, 'Finnish Parliamentary Ombudsman as Guardian of Human Rights and Constitutional Rights: View from the University of Lapland' in I Rautio (ed), *Parliamentary Ombudsman of Finland 80 years* (Helsinki, Parliamentary Ombudsman of Finland, 2000), 79–84.

[12] A Mäki-Petäjä-Leinonen, *Dementoituvan henkilön oikeudellinen asema* (Helsinki, Suomalainen lakimiesyhdistys [Finnish Bar Association], 2003), 302–3.

[13] P Välimäki, *Edunvalvontaoikeus* (Helsinki, Sanoma Pro, 2013), 38.

first place because the client has lost the ability to control their income. Helin also opines that the guardian needs certainty about the amount of funds that will be available in the future to cover the client's necessary expenses.[14]

However, in my view, reasons relating to everyday life do not justify the restrictions under section 31.2 of the Guardianship Act. It would have been more reasonable to adopt a legal solution in which the right of access to a bank account was not affected per se by the guardianship order, but could have been done only by limiting the client's legal capacity under section 18. While adopting this legislative stance would have greatly increased the number of clients with limited capacity, it would have avoided the misleading nature of the law on guardianship today, which appears to indicate that the mere appointment of a guardian does not affect the client's legal capacity when in reality it does.

It should be noted, however, that if the legal solution mentioned above had been adopted, it would have been contrary to the principle under Article 12(2) of the CRPD concerning equal recognition before the law, which provides that persons with disabilities enjoy legal capacity on an equal basis with others in all aspects of life. Another option would have been to adopt a practice whereby the current situation, in which appointment of a guardian de facto restricts the legal capacity of a client, were translated into the de jure principle. That is, it would have been directly stated that the appointment of a guardian always limits the individual's legal capacity to some extent. It would not have increased the number of individuals with limited legal capacity but would have merely confirmed the current situation. Such an approach would also have been, in my opinion, fully compatible with the CRPD. Article 12 does not preclude restrictions on legal capacity, but Article 12(4) makes it clear that there should be safeguards to protect the enjoyment of legal capacity and such safeguards are to be proportional to the degree to which such measures affect a person's rights and interests.

In addition to the legislation currently in force, there is an unfortunate Supreme Court judgment (KKO 2005:2), which concerns the need to restrict a client's competency. In what was otherwise a high quality ruling the Court stated that it was unnecessary to restrict the competency of a client – who was not willing to cooperate with his guardian – because the mere appointment of a guardian bestows the necessary powers to act upon them. In practice, taking this sentence from the judgment out of context has led to a situation where a person's right to competence almost never needs to be restricted because guardians can rely on the fact that they can decide on behalf of their client, even when this goes against the client's will.[15] In practice, this may therefore lead

[14] M Helin, 'Yleisteos edunvalvontaoikeudesta Tornberg, Johanna – Kuuliala, Matti', 6/2016 *Lakimies* 1016–18, 1017.

[15] T Leilas, 'Yleisen edunvalvojan havaintoja päämiehen itsemääräämisoikeudesta' 2019/1 *Defensor Legis* 69–76.

to a situation where the guardian de facto restricts the client's capacity, so that there is no need to restrict it de jure. However, such an interpretation of the law was not, in my view, the original intention of the legislature and is also clearly contrary to the objectives of the CRPD.

To conclude, the main problem with the current law is the fact that the scope of the client's freedom of action remains at the guardian's discretion. In addition to decision-making power concerning bank accounts, the guardian also has discretion as to the amount of funds to be made available to the client. Section 38.1 of the Guardianship Act stipulates that the client must be provided with an amount of funds deemed reasonable in relation to their needs and other circumstances. Indeed, in practice, the client's autonomy is not always realised sufficiently. This can be seen, for example, in the matters dealt with by the Finnish Parliamentary Ombudsman in which guardians have been considered to have prevented their clients from using their assets or to have otherwise restricted the financial capacity of clients whose legal capacity is not restricted by law.[16] This kind of activity goes beyond the safeguards permitted under Article 12(4) of the CRPD.

Given the current state of the legislation, consideration should be given to how best to promote the autonomy of a client that has de jure legal capacity. In practice, the issue can be resolved by the guardian taking active steps to support the client's autonomy. For example, as to access to bank accounts, Helin reasons that where it is unnecessary for the guardian to decide on the use of the funds in an account, that account can – and should – be excluded from the scope of the property administered by the guardian. In this case, the client's rights in relation to the account remain unchanged.[17] Such a procedure would also be in line with the CRPD's stipulation that persons with disabilities shall have equal right to own property and to control their own financial affairs (Article 12(5)). Furthermore, appropriate measures are to be taken to provide access to the support they may require in exercising their legal capacity (Article 12(3)).

In my interviews with public guardians I asked about their clients' ability to make decisions in practice. Their responses made it clear that they do not follow any set guidelines even within the same guardianship office. In practice, much depends on the individual guardian and on the nature of the principles they follow in their work: some appear to be quite liberal, while others take a more paternalistic approach. The quotes below illustrate this point:

> I'm pretty liberal in the sense that I respect the client's autonomy maybe more than many others here … If you happen to have the kind of guardian and guardian secretary that think that guardianship appointment gives them a sufficient mandate to arrange a client's affairs in the way they think is a good way to live, then yes, it can be a big prison for the client. (Guardian 3)

[16] See eg *PO Dnro 1993/4/06*, 21.12.2007 (Provision of assets to the client as goods).
[17] Helin (n 14), 1017.

> Many guardians think that money should not be given; that is to say, it must be saved for the sake of certainty. Then, of course, it causes problems, because the client does not see the reason why. (Guardian 4)

These two guardians present a liberal point of view that seeks to respect the client's right to autonomy as fully as possible. They cited as a negative example guardians who determine a client's right to autonomy through their own set of values, whereby the client should live a life defined as good by the guardian, or whereby the client and their property is protected for the sake of certainty. This is also interesting from a CRPD perspective, as the Convention seeks to ensure that restrictions are tailored to reflect the client's rights, wishes and preferences, not those of the guardian. On the other hand, the example below shows how a slightly more protective guardian viewed unquestioning respect for the client's autonomy as problematic and perhaps even amounting to negligence in relation to the client.

> I want to emphasize that we do not necessarily, in our office, have a clear, common position regarding the right to self-determination and money. I'm a person who negotiates with their clients but, of course, it would be easy just to follow the client's wishes: 'Well, the client said no on the phone, so it's no.' Then they do what a client says. (Guardian 2).

This sub-section has assessed the content of the law on the autonomy of a person under guardianship and how it can be realised in practice. The next sub-section examines the right to be heard as part of the client's autonomy.

B. The Right to be Heard as an Aspect of Support for Autonomy

The realisation of the right to self-determination of a person under guardianship is largely dependent on the way in which their guardian seeks to respect that right. In the relationship between the guardian and the client, it is essential that the guardian exercises their decision-making power in accordance with the basic principles of the Guardianship Act. Välimäki opines that this will happen if the guardian acts in cooperation with their client, negotiates with them in relation to key decisions, and listens to, respects and takes the opinions of the client into account. The sole objective in these situations must be the realisation of the client's interests.[18] Thus, a client's right to participate in decisions affecting their lives can be seen as part of their autonomy.[19]

[18] Välimäki (n 13), p 38.

[19] R Harding, 'Legal constructions of dementia: discourses of autonomy at the margins of capacity' (2012) 34(4) *Journal of Social Welfare & Family Law* 425–42, 439; Mäki-Petäjä-Leinonen (n 3), 153–56. See also A McGee, 'Best Interest Determinations and Substituted Judgement: Personhood and Precedent Autonomy' in C Foster, J Herring and I Doron (eds), *The Law and Ethics of Dementia* (Oxford, Hart Publishing, 2014) 135–47, for discussion of attenuated autonomy, which takes into account a person's wishes, values and beliefs.

The significance of the client's autonomy as a guiding principle of the Guardianship Act is reflected in the provisions governing the client's right to be heard on matters that the client deems important (section 43). The importance of hearing the client is also addressed within section 42, which concerns care, treatment and rehabilitation of the client; these provisions emphasise the importance of cooperation between the guardian and the client. The preparatory works for the law indicate that the need for cooperation is greatest when the client is de jure legally competent.[20] The guardian's duty to work with the client and ask their opinion is highlighted in the decision involving the Finnish Parliamentary Ombudsman (PO) set out below.

PO Dnro 58/4/11, 10.2.2012.

> The complaint stated that a guardian who had the right to decide on matters concerning his client's person (i.e. give consent to treatment etc. if the client cannot understand the significance of the matter; section 29.2) did not inquire about his client's position on matters such as home leave. The guardian's perception of the capability of his client was based on medical judgement and the views of the medical staff. The PO's view was that there is no reason to set a threshold for cooperation with the client even though some medical or other material available to the guardian calls the client's understanding into question in some respects. The PO expressed concern about giving the client an external role in relation to their matters, particularly those concerning the protection of private life. The PO agreed with the magistrate's view that a public guardian should have sought his client's own opinion before deciding on home leave.

Consulting the client is also important when making decisions about the fate of their home furnishings when they are moving, for instance to an institutional care facility. This question has also been raised many times in matters dealt with by the PO. The solutions produced by the PO have emphasised that the delivery of the client's home furnishings is, due to the highly personal nature of this property, a measure that requires a high degree of sensitivity and in-depth consultation with the client on the part of the guardian. Consideration is also given to the fact that the sale of this property does not require the permission of the register office.[21] Furthermore, the fact that the client has expressed a wish to take particular property with them to their new apartment does not justify the conclusion that the other property may be destroyed without consulting the client. The guardian cannot act without obtaining the client's opinion on matters of such importance.[22]

One may also consider whether the client's opinion binds the guardian to any extent as to the solution adopted. Differing opinions have been put forward in the relevant legal literature. Ahti Saarenpää takes the view that the

[20] HE 146/1998 (n 7), 51.

[21] There are certain transactions in respect of which a guardian needs permission from the local register office (section 34).

[22] See *APO Dnro 168/4/06*, 3.8.2007 (Donation of a client's property) and *PO Dnro 3026/4/08*, 18.6.2010 (Guardian's procedure when clearing a client's home).

client's wishes should, as a rule, be of significance if their de jure legal capacity is not limited.[23] Markku Helin, on the other hand, starts from the premise that statements made by the client are only 'information in the light of which one is to judge how to proceed in accordance with the best interests of the client'.[24] This approach means that the client's opinion does not need to be given independent weight.

If one takes seriously the legal rule that the mere appointment of a guardian does not affect the client's legal capacity (section 14), Saarenpää's opinion is more persuasive. The starting point for interpretation must therefore be the guardian's duty to take into account the wishes of a client who has sufficient capacity to understand. It should also be noted that the rule concerning the management of the client's bank accounts laid down in section 31.2 appears to be an exception to the general rule contained in section 14. Section 14 is itself confirmed by section 43, which lays down the general rule as to the guardian's duty to consult the client and even restricts the guardian's ability to act. However, it is clear from the preparatory documents in respect of the Guardianship Act that failure to comply with the obligation to consult a client does not invalidate the legal action taken by the guardian, but may result in other penalties. Indeed, failure to listen to the client or groundlessly disregarding their opinion shows shortcomings not only in the ability to cooperate but also in terms of respect for the client's personal autonomy, and can thus lead to a complaint from the supervisory authority or even to a change of guardian.[25]

Failure to comply with the obligation to consult a client may also lead to a result where the action taken by the guardian is not ideal in terms of content. A guardian may not receive the necessary information, which is why their work may not be in the best interests of the client, even from a purely economic point of view. It should also be noted that the client's right to participate, indicated by the provisions concerning consulting a client, can play a key role in supporting their autonomy. Properly carried out, hearing a client can also strengthen that client's experienced wellbeing.[26]

In my interviews with public guardians I asked about their client's right to be heard as an aspect of support for autonomy. The guardians gave different

[23] A Saarenpää, 'Holhouksesta edunvalvontaan' 1–2/2000 *Pohjois-Suomen tuomarikoulun julkaisuja* 141–96, 165.

[24] M Helin, 'Edunvalvojan päätösvallan rajoista' 6–7/2001 *Lakimies* 1070–88, 1072–73. There is no definition of 'best interests' under Finnish law, unlike eg that laid down in section 4 of the Mental Capacity Act of England and Wales. However, section 4 of the Social Welfare Act (1301/2014) specifies the matters to be taken into account when considering the client's interests. These include the client's wellbeing and independence; timely, appropriate and adequate support for needs; and the opportunity to participate in and influence their own affairs.

[25] HE 146/1998 (n 7), 51.

[26] Mäki-Petäjä-Leinonen (n 10), 21.

examples of the ways and situations in which they seek to hear their clients. The first quote concerns a client who has an apartment:

> For example, the client has an apartment and something needs to be done. The options may be to rent or sell it or keep it empty, and that is to be discussed with the client. It is a kind of support in the way that the client may have their own opinion which they can express. (Guardian 1)

Decision-making related to the client's home may become relevant where the client moves to a 24-hour care unit. In such a situation, it is important to seek the client's opinion on what needs to be done, as this supports the realisation of their autonomy. Consulting clients is also important in situations where they 'request'? access to additional funds:

> I'm trying to make it clear to the client that if, for example, you want to spend a lot of extra money all the time, you have to remember that the money is running out and then you can't call and ask for more. However, if the client says that s/he understands that the money is going to run out eventually, but s/he wants it now, then of course I put it into the account. (Secretary 2)
>
> The role of a guardian in such a situation would be to point out that now, if we do so, you will understand that this is what happens. So, in a way, it helps the client to think for themselves about the relationship between the cause and the consequences of the matter, so that they can make the decision themselves. (Guardian 4)

The above examples illustrate how guardians seek to support their client's autonomy. The guardian or guardian's secretary negotiates with their client to make clear what will happen if the assets are used up. Giving sufficient information to the client allows them to weigh different options and make decisions accordingly.

C. Respecting the Previously Expressed or Presumed Will of a Client

This sub-section assesses the weight that can be given to a client's previously expressed or presumed healthy will, and also discusses situations where the client's current wishes conflict with their previously expressed or presumed will.

(i) Previously Expressed Will

The condition of the client may become such that they can no longer be understood by a guardian. For example, a memory disease may progress to the stage where the client is no longer able to express their own wishes. However, the client may have – when they were still well enough – expressed a wish for certain things that are important for them. For example, a client may have carried out advance care planning covering how they want their care to be conducted and/or their property to be used in the event that they can no longer make independent decisions. One may thus ask whether these kinds of advance instructions will bind future guardians and, if so, to what extent.

Section 8 of the Finnish Patients' Act (785/1992) provides that a patient's previously expressed refusal of care (in an advance directive) is legally binding. Although other forms of advance care planning are, in legal terms, predominantly non-binding wishes, it is clear that the wishes a client expresses while still capable of expressing them should be followed as closely as possible under the circumstances; this is on the basis that one is to take the client's right to autonomy seriously. Thus, if the client has given instructions, for example, to use property to obtain the best possible care and treatment in a private medical institution, the guardian is obliged to act in accordance with these instructions, provided that the client has sufficient assets to cover the cost of private care. As mentioned above, the Guardianship Act already requires compliance with the client's wishes concerning care, treatment and rehabilitation (section 42).

The client's previously expressed wishes as to the management of their affairs may also be an important source of information as to their outlook when healthy, especially when the client has a public guardian. This information can be helpful to a guardian who did not know their client earlier and may possibly also offer clues as to the client's lifestyle and consumption habits to support the guardian's decision-making. This may be important, for example, in determining the level of assets to be made available to the client under section 38.1 of the Guardianship Act.

Even today, however, planning for the future by giving advance instructions is relatively rare.[27] My interviews also made it clear that previously expressed wishes or written instructions from the client are seldom available. The public guardians did mention that on meeting their clients for the first (and usually the only) time they try to map out the clients' opinions on the issues facing them, provided that the client is in a condition to be consulted. For instance, they might ask the client's opinion on whether to sell a property, which is useful in the event that this later becomes necessary.

(ii) Presumed Healthy Will

As noted above, in most cases the client has not given any advance instructions on how to handle their affairs. In these situations, a guardian who respects the client's autonomy strives to respond to the *presumed healthy will* of their client by examining their life history, attitudes and values and taking a view based on that as to what the client would have wanted had they been able to express their wishes.[28] This principle can be taken into account in the interpretation of the Guardianship Act and is also in line with the CRPD. In its April 2014 General

[27] See eg G Sinoff and N Blaja-Lisnic, 'Advance Decisions and Proxy Decision-Making in the Elderly: A Medical Perspective' in C Foster, J Herring and I Doron (eds), *The Law and Ethics of Dementia* (Oxford, Hart Publishing, 2014) 97–99.

[28] For instance, both the UK Mental Capacity Act 2005 (section 4(6)(b)) and the Finnish Act on the Status and Rights of Patients, No 785/1992 (section 6.3) highlight the importance of respecting such wishes.

Comment No 1, the Committee on the Rights of Persons with Disabilities stated that if a decision has to be made on behalf of a disabled person, it should be done by interpreting his or her wishes and preferences instead of adopting the best interests principle.[29]

The Guardianship Act requires the guardian to manage the client's property in a manner that allows for the property and the revenue to be used for the benefit of the client and for the satisfaction of their personal needs. In carrying out this task, the guardian must take care of the rights of the client and promote their interests (section 37.1). The client's personal needs can be assessed not only by reference to their wealth and previous standard of living, but also their current or previously expressed wishes and life history. For example, if the client is wealthy and accustomed to a high standard of living, the guardian should take care to maintain that lifestyle. The amount of funds to be assigned regularly to the client should also be tailored by reference to their previous standard of living. In general, the guardian should adopt a humane and empathetic approach to their task, making decisions from the client's perspective that take into account their life history, habits, attitudes and opinions.[30]

The presumed will and preferences of the client were taken into account in the following decision of the Parliamentary Deputy Ombudsman (PDO):

PDO Dnro 1969/4/98, 29.9.2000.

> In the case, the guardianship board had not consulted the client's daughters before it allowed the guardian to sell the apartment owned by the client. In her decision, the PDO stressed that the client's right to autonomy should also be respected when deciding on their financial affairs. If the client is unable to express their will, information as to their presumed will can be obtained from their legal representatives and relatives. The PDO stated that the apartment should not have been sold if it had value for the client. Information about the presumed healthy will of the client could have been obtained by consulting her family.[31]

This decision highlights the guardian's duty to respect their client's autonomy and the importance of the client's relationships and *relational autonomy* in decision-making. Relational autonomy, which rejects the liberalism of individual autonomy, considers autonomy through relationships with other people by taking into account that autonomous choice often includes reflection on what will be best for others in the person's close web of relations.[32] The PDO's

[29] Committee on the Rights of Persons with Disabilities, *General Comment No 1 (2014) Article 12: Equal recognition before the law*, UN Doc CRPD/C/GC/1.

[30] Mäki-Petäjä-Leinonen (n 12), 330.

[31] Eduskunnan oikeusasiamies, *Eduskunnan oikeusasiamiehen kertomus toiminnastaan vuonna 2000* (Helsinki, Edita Oyj, 2001), 365–66.

[32] See eg C MacKenzie and N Stoljar, *Relational Autonomy: Feminist Perspectives on Autonomy, Agency and Social Self* (Oxford, OUP, 2000); J Nedelsky, *Law's Relations: A Relational Theory of Self, Autonomy, and Law* (Oxford, OUP, 2011); J Herring, *Caring and the Law* (Oxford, Hart Publishing 2013) 72–73. On the four approaches to relationality in the contemporary academic literature, see R Harding, *Duties to Care: Dementia, Relationality and Law* (Cambridge, Cambridge University Press, 2017) 21–27.

decision discussed above reflects relational autonomy in terms of how, in the PDO's view, the guardian could have consulted family members in interpreting the client's presumed will. The client's family members and loved ones can thus play a role in mediating and interpreting their wishes, values, and beliefs.[33]

However, whenever someone other than the client him or herself is asked about the client's opinion, there is a risk that that person will either consciously or unconsciously also communicate their own wishes. Therefore, when consulting family members and loved ones, one should consider whether their ultimate purpose is to express the client's true wishes or whether their motivation lies elsewhere; for instance, in furthering the interests of others. While the involvement of the client's close kin or family should not automatically lead to an assumption of inappropriate influence, the guardian should not exclude this possibility. Ultimately, the guardian must exercise discretion in determining the extent to which the client's relationships influence the interpretation of his or her autonomy, and is responsible for protecting their client from abuse and undue influence. Furthermore, if it is obvious that the client has already been abused in this manner, the guardian can take the matter to court. This is also in line with Article 12(4) of the CRPD, which makes clear that there need to be safeguards against undue influence.[34]

A case reported in *Helsingin Sanomat* (*HS*, 5 December 2017), a leading Finnish newspaper, illustrates this issue. In that case the guardian had the opportunity to consult the relatives and follow the known values and presumed will of his client, but decided not to do so.

> The relatives of an older man with memory illness who was known to love the forest he owned, got the forest company to cancel a timber contract, when the public guardian, based on the interests of his client, had decided on the logging of this forest. According to his relatives, clearcutting would have been contrary to the client's values and wishes. Furthermore, there were no economic grounds for selling the forest because the income from the sale was not needed for the client's care costs. In this situation, the public guardian had given no weight to the relatives' insight into the wishes of the client when healthy.

In my interviews with public guardians, the interviewees emphasised that a client's relatives can give information about the client's known or presumed will and in many cases they are good 'collaborative partners'. On the other hand, the guardians appeared quite sceptical about the value of such statements, as they often seemed concerned about clients' willingness to transfer assets or give presents to family members. The question then arises as to what weight the guardian should place on statements of this kind. After all, the guardian's responsibility is to safeguard the client's assets. On the other hand, ignoring such statements tends to ignore the relational dynamics of decision-making and how people understand family assets.

[33] Mäki-Petäjä-Leinonen (n 10), 23.
[34] See further, Hall, Chapter 15, this volume.

(iii) Previous versus Current Wishes

The issue of whether to respect instructions given in advance or to follow the client's previous values (ie their presumed will) can be an easy one if they do not have present wishes and interests in relation to the matter at hand. A problem might occur, however, if client now has wishes and desires that conflict with previous directions or personal values. There has been much philosophical discussion as to the relationship between the 'then' self that existed before a person lost their legal capacity and the 'now' self that lives in the present and may have lost all connection to the past. Proponents of the *critical interest approach* underline the importance of basing post-capacity decisions on historical lifetime values and beliefs.[35] Proponents of the *experiential interest approach* take the view that contemporary preferences and values, together with the present wellbeing of the person, should be the main source of assistance for substituted decision-making.[36] The way we approach changes in capacity thus reveals our understanding of personhood, as it forces us to question whether a person remains the same or becomes different.[37]

Indeed, there may be conflict between the client's previous values/expressed wishes and their current will. For instance, in the past the client may have clearly expressed a wish to keep their property intact for their heirs or may otherwise have been known as a very prudent person. However, on becoming ill, they might start to live as if it was their last day on earth and enjoy life by spending money on themselves and others. Although this situation might indicate a person's weakened capacity, it might also be indicative of their desire, once diagnosed, to enjoy life while they still can. Thus, instead of strictly safeguarding property, the guardian should consider what weight should be placed on the client's current wishes and their experiential interests if they conflict with their previous critical interests. The question of whether the client has made a genuine choice to reject their previous critical interests may also be asked. If that is not the case, one should consider how much rationality one needs to find in the client's decision-making if they get pleasure from the actions taken.[38]

The Nuffield Council of Bioethics has considered this issue and stressed the importance of both present and past wishes in assessing an individual's autonomy. Neither can be automatically prioritised over the other: the situation requires careful weighing. The Council considered the following factors when pondering the solution from the perspective of an individual's wellbeing: How important is the issue? How much pain or pleasure does this kind of

[35] See eg R Dworkin, *Life's Dominion: An Argument about Abortion and Euthanasia* (New York, HarperCollins, 1993) 226–29.

[36] A Jaworska, 'Respecting the Margins of Agency: Alzheimer's Patients and the Capacity to Value' (1998) 28(2) *Philosophy and Public Affairs* 105–38, 109.

[37] See, for instance, R Dresser, 'Life, Death, and Incompetent Patients: Conceptual Infirmities and Hidden Values in the Law' (1986) 28(3) *Arizona Law Review* 379–81 and 393–95; and Jaworska (n 36), 108–10.

[38] See eg Mäki-Petäjä-Leinonen (n 10), 24.

activity cause to the person with impaired capacity? Have the individual's critical interests genuinely changed or can they be interpreted in a new light? Is the individual's clear change in values due to psychosocial factors (such as fear) or is it the direct result of the dementing illness (such as sexually compulsive behaviour) or does it stem from a genuine desire to do things differently than before?[39] I would argue that it is also possible to take these issues into account when considering the interests of a person under guardianship. Thus, for instance, when considering the importance of a matter, the guardian may weigh up the significance of the matter for the client's mental wellbeing and for their finances. Furthermore, it is worth considering how much rationality can be required of the client's decision-making in general, given that the decision-making of 'healthy' people is often based on emotions rather than rational judgement.[40]

D. Respecting the Client's Autonomy in Practice

This sub-section examines situations in which the client's autonomy conflicts with the guardian's responsibility to protect the client's interests. In this situation, it may be necessary to consider how much rationality should be required of decision-making and whether it is acceptable for the client's illness to affect their decision-making at some level.

As in situations of conflict between previous and current expressions of wishes, conflicts between the client's autonomy and protection require careful consideration of the facts of each particular case. Although the guiding principle of the guardianship system is the protection of the client's financial interests, the nature of the solution may vary with the circumstances and may extend to consideration of the client's physical safety. For instance, a guardian who is asked to consider giving funds to their client to buy a fur hat in the summer faces a different challenge from one who is asked to give funds to buy a tricycle moped[41] when there is uncertainty as to the client's ability to move safely in traffic.[42]

[39] Nuffield Council on Bioethics, *Dementia: Ethical Issues* (Cambridge, Cambridge Publishers, 2009) xxiii.

[40] A Mäki-Petäjä-Leinonen and K Juva, 'Of Sound Mind? Dementia and Aspects of Assessing Legal Capacity' (2015) 22 *European Journal of Health Law* 13–37, 34.

[41] Three-wheel electric mopeds can be a good vehicle for many people with reduced mobility, as they allow independent movement. Such mopeds, which do not require a driving licence to operate, are marketed as a 'shopping bag' that you can drive without a driving licence. However, special attention should be given to the sale and marketing of electric mopeds and similar vehicles to persons who have lost their driving licence following age-based health checks. See H Nikumaa and A Mäki-Petäjä-Leinonen, 'Muistisairas ihminen liikenteessä', 1/2018 *Gerontologia* 36–52.

[42] The examples presented here were presented to the author of the paper during the Public Guardians workshop held in 2016 in Rovaniemi.

In the first situation, only the protection of the client's assets need be considered. If the client has sufficient assets to buy a fur hat and its acquisition does not affect the ability to fulfil their obligations, a client should, in principle, have the right to buy it. Whether this decision may be considered rational or not is not the key point: the guardian, in my view, may not interfere with the manner in which legally competent clients use their own financial assets. It may also be assumed that buying such a hat will have a positive impact on the client's psychological wellbeing,[43] which should be the goal of every guardian, rather than seeking to protect the client's financial interests in a strict and paternalistic way.

On the other hand, buying a tricycle moped presents a different situation: besides the financial aspect and the client's interests, there is also the question of the safety both of the client and of other people. The guardian must accordingly weigh their client's autonomous wishes against the safety of the client and that of other road users. However, from an ethical point of view, ensuring safety (the right to life) is such a strong principle that the wish to buy a moped may be blocked on a case-by-case basis, even though this may provoke feelings of frustration in the client and the impression that their autonomy is not being sufficiently respected. Conversely, obtaining a moped may even be ethically dubious if the risk of damage is clearly increased (principle of avoidance of harm).[44] Thus, the guardian will have to consider the advantages and disadvantages of buying a moped, and possibly also interview the client's relatives and/or social and healthcare professionals in order to arrive at an appropriate solution. However, the goal should be a solution that not only adequately protects the safety of the client and third parties but is also satisfactory from the client's perspective.

In recent years, the media have covered various cases in which an older driver has caused dangerous situations with an electric moped.[45] One incident occurred in spring 2017 where a person was left under an electric moped in a car park. An elderly driver hit a person three times because he was unable to shut down his vehicle. The collision resulted in minor injuries. In another case, the children of a person with a memory illness, insisting on his right to autonomy, had acquired a covered electric moped for him, which he then drove into the back of a stationary car.[46]

It may also be a matter of care for the client. For example, home-based clients living alone sometimes cause problems for public guardians when they clearly need help but refuse to accept it. There are also cases in which social and healthcare professionals have respected a person's right to self-determination too much

[43] On autonomy and wellbeing, see eg E Lagerspetz, 'Hyvinvoinnin filosofia' in J Saari (ed), *Hyvinvointi. Suomalaisen yhteiskunnan perusta* (Helsinki, Gaudeamus, 2011) 79–105.

[44] T Beauchamp and J Childress, *Principles of Biomedical Ethics* (Oxford, OUP, 2001).

[45] See eg *YLE news* on 8 April 2015 and *Kaleva*, 14 August 2016.

[46] Nikumaa and Mäki-Petäjä-Leinonen (n 10), 45–46.

in order to avoid intervening in a difficult situation.[47] However, it is up to social and healthcare professionals, and ultimately to guardians, to ensure that clients obtain the help that they need. While the key principle of the Guardianship Act is to safeguard the client's financial interests, the guardian should at least ensure that the client's security is guaranteed. In this regard, it is the guardian's duty to act as a stakeholder to ensure that the client receives the health and welfare services they need and that the situation of a client in need of help is addressed. As mentioned above, this is underlined by section 42 of the Guardianship Act, which provides that the guardian must ensure that the client is provided with care, treatment and rehabilitation that is appropriate to their needs and circumstances, as well as meeting their wishes.

Furthermore, whether the issue at stake is the client's financial or personal affairs, resolving the matter may sometimes cause problems in the relationships between the client, the client's relatives and the (public) guardian. Indeed, relatives may have strong opinions about how to deal with the client's affairs or what the client's wishes might be. The importance of this relationship has been taken into account in the Public Guardians Working Group, which states that the goal should be to communicate with the client's relatives, especially where the client has expressed a wish to provide information to them. In the absence of the expression of such a wish, the guardian may need to consider the extent of their personal contact with relatives and the confidentiality of the client's information. Although the starting point is the confidentiality of the information, serving the client's interests may require effective cooperation with relatives.[48] It is thus worth emphasising that each of these potential dilemmas or conflicts raised in this section should only be decided through a careful consideration of the individual situation, rather than application of a blanket rule in which one value will always be preferred over another.

III. CONCLUSIONS

This chapter has examined three different aspects of the autonomy of a person under guardianship in Finland: the client's right to make autonomous decisions; their right to be heard; and respect for their previously expressed or presumed wishes as an aspect of autonomy. The Finnish guardianship system has been assessed in relation to internal inconsistencies in the Guardianship Act regarding the client's legal capacity and the tension between the weight given to the client's views and those of their guardian.

The Guardianship Act takes into account and seeks to safeguard the autonomy of clients in various different ways. However, following the ratification of

[47] Mäki-Petäjä-Leinonen (n 3), 161.

[48] Yleisen edunvalvonnan kehittämistyöryhmä, 'Yhteydenpito, tavoitettavuus ja tiedonsaanti', Suositus 14.4.2011, Oikeusministeriön Oikeushallinto-osasto OM 2/33/2010.

the UNCRPD, which starts from the ideal situation in which a disabled person has the right to make supported decisions, practical implementation of the Guardianship Act must do more in this respect. Practice in Britain, where decisions taken under the Mental Capacity Act 2005 have increasingly taken into account the desires and values of the disabled person when considering a solution in his or her best interests, offers a good example of how this can be done.[49] When considering the introduction of a supported decision-making system in Finland, one solution could be to encourage guardians to support their clients in decision-making more than is the case at present by consulting the client, where this is feasible, and giving them real opportunities to influence decision-making. Guardians are, after all, an important part of their client's web of relations.

In conclusion I wish to note that guardians are required by legislation to take questions concerning clients' autonomy seriously and try to support it. However, in reality various practices are followed, depending on the guardian handling the matter, even within the same guardianship office. This may be seen as problematic from an equality perspective. Some of these tensions could be resolved through law or policy reform. In my interviews, public guardians expressed a need for national guidelines concerning support for autonomy, as this would assist them in relation to carrying out their daily routines. One solution would be to issue recommendations from the Ministry of Justice's Public Guardians Working Group to harmonise guardianship practices in a direction that supports clients' autonomy.

[49] R Harding, 'Care and relationality: supported decision making under the UN CRPD' in R Harding, R Fletcher and C Beasley (eds), *ReValuing Care in Theory, Law and Policy: Cycles and Connections* (London, Routledge, 2017) 114–30, 126–27.

13

Autonomy, Capacity, and Vulnerability: Making Decisions on Social Services for Persons with Dementia in Sweden

TITTI MATTSSON[1]

I. INTRODUCTION

IN SWEDEN AND the other Nordic countries, the trend for many years has been away from institutional living and towards home-based care. This trend is in accordance with international regulations and recommendations. The UN's Principles for Older Persons, for example, state that older persons should be able to continue living at home for as long as possible.[2] This trend has many benefits. Particularly, it makes it possible for the person in need of various forms of assistance to get access to this help without having to change his or her life situation very much. The person can remain at home in a safe and well-known environment. However, there are challenges as well, assuming that home-settings are very varied and that individuals' needs and wishes are to be fulfilled in home settings which are private and very much the care-taker's own arena. The home-based care system also demands a particular sensitivity to the individual's needs and wishes.

The issue of how to fulfil people's needs and participation rights through deliberatively supported decision-making is a central issue in capacity law.[3]

[1] I am grateful for funding from the Kamprad Family Foundation and the Crafoord Foundation as well as for adminstrative assistance by Amelie Kraft, Faculty of Law, Lunds University.

[2] *United Nations Principles for Older Persons*, UNGA Res 46/91 (16 December 1991) 6.

[3] C Kong, *Mental Capacity in Relationship: Decision-Making, Dialogue, and Autonomy* (Cambridge, Cambridge University Press, 2017) 155; P Harpur, 'Embracing the New Disability Rights Paradigm: The Importance of the Convention on the Rights of Persons with Disabilities' (2012) 27 *Disability & Society* 1; S-N Then, 'Evolution and Innovation in Guardianship Laws: Assisted Decision-Making' (2013) 35 *Sydney Law Review* 133; P Gooding, 'Supported Decision-Making: A Rights-Based Disability Concept and Its Implications for Mental Health Law' (2013) 20 *Psychiatry,*

As the population in many countries around the world ages, more and more people face the prospect, due to dementia, of needing assistance with personal care and/or the organisation of daily life.[4] Dementia is a collective name for several symptoms that are due to an injury or disease in the nerve cells of the brain. There are a large number of diseases that cause dementia and dementia is also age-related. The risk of developing dementia increases with age. All dementia diseases lead to impaired cognitive abilities, for example, impaired memory and orientation ability. The disease develops at different rates but is progressive. Dementia is characterised by a progressive deterioration in one's cognitive abilities and in one's capacity to make decisions and to live independently.[5] People with dementia are a disadvantaged group throughout the world.[6] One reason for this lies in the particular challenge that societies face in seeking to fulfil the needs of this group without impinging on their fundamental rights, such as their right to participation and to acceptable living conditions. It is not always the case that persons with dementia are fully autonomous in their capacity to make daily decisions of different kinds – personal, practical, economic, and so on. Persons with dementia are thus typically in need, sooner or later, of some type of support with making daily life decisions. For these reasons, dementia in particular is worth investigating as part of a broader investigation of supported decision-making.

In this chapter, I describe and discuss the inter-relationships between autonomy, capacity, and social services for persons with dementia in long-term home-based care in Sweden. Some of the points raised may apply equally to other groups with cognitive impairments; however, persons with dementia constitute the main focus for this chapter. The role of the State in Sweden for persons with cognitive impairments is characterised by extensive public support and an obligation for the municipalities to arrange for different kinds of services, including housing and home services according to personal needs.[7] Further, access to services is generally individualised and arranged in accordance with the individual's wishes and personal circumstances.

Psychology and Law 43; S Darwall, *Welfare and Rational Care* (Princeton NJ, Princeton University Press, 2004); N Devi, J Bickenbach and G Stucki, 'Moving towards Substituted or Supported Decision-Making? Article 12 of the Convention on the Rights of Persons with Disabilities' (2011) 5(4) *Alter* 249; K Blankman, 'Guardianship Models in the Netherlands and Western Europe' (1997) 20 *International Journal of Law and Psychiatry* 47.

[4] I Doron, 'The Demographics of Dementia' in C Foster, J Herring and I Doron (eds), *The Law and Ethics of Dementia* (London, Bloomsbury Publishing, 2014).

[5] M Prince et al, 'The Global Prevalence of Dementia: A Systematic Review and Metaanalysis' (2013) 9 *Alzheimer's & Dementia* 63.

[6] R Harding, 'Legal Constructions of Dementia: Discourses of Autonomy at the Margins of Capacity' (2012) 34 *Journal of Social Welfare and Family Law* 425.

[7] Compare Act (1993:387) Concerning Support and Service for Persons with Certain Functional Impairments (LSS) and the Parental Code (1949:381) Chapter 11.

The limited guardian (*god man*) system in Sweden is often held up in capacity law as a good-practice model.[8] There is good cause for this. The system has many benefits, in line with the aims set out in the UN Convention on the Rights of Persons with Disabilities (CRPD).[9] No adult person in Sweden can lose his or her legal capacity permanently, and individual autonomy is generally prioritised in law irrespective of the person's impairment and his or her practical abilities.[10] In addition, the system of social services in Sweden allows for a high degree of autonomy for persons with dementia. For example, applicable legislation requires that persons with dementia be provided with adequate information. They must also be offered suitable ways of participating in decisions on all personal issues, including their daily care and living arrangements (Parental Code chapter 11 paragraphs 4–5; LSS paragraphs 5–6). Furthermore, only actions in accordance with the specific consent of the user may be taken. The issue raised in this chapter is, however, the challenges, at times, in ensuring an appropriate standard of living for persons with dementia within this legislative framework.

In the fall of 2017, Swedish media gave prominent coverage to the case of an old woman with dementia whose care was neglected. Her case illustrates the above-mentioned drawbacks with current legislation:[11]

> An old woman with Alzheimer's and diabetes was furnished with home-based care by the local municipality. The personnel visited her twice a day, to help with food and to make sure she took her medication. She lived at home, as do most people with dementia in Sweden. The daughter of the old woman served as limited guardian (*god man*) for her mother. She regularly helped her mother clean the home. Due to illness, however, the daughter was in hospital for a period, during which time she was unable to provide this complementary help for her mother. The daughter contacted the municipality and applied for extended home-based care (including cleaning) for her mother during this period.

[8] RD Dinerstein, 'Implementing Legal Capacity Under Article 12 of the UN Convention on the Rights of Persons with Disabilities: The Difficult Road From Guardianship to Supported Decision-Making' (2012) 9 *The Human Rights Brief* 9; A Rimmerman, *Disability and Community Living Policies* (Cambridge University Press 2017); A Silvers and LP Francis, 'Death, Dying and the Disabled' in RM Arnold and SJ Younger (eds), *The Oxford Handbook of Ethics at the End of Life* (Oxford, Oxford University Press, 2016) 276.

[9] However, there has been some international criticism of this system. See, eg, SS Herr et al, 'Self-Determination, Autonomy and Alternative for Guardianship' in SS Herr, LO Gostin and H Hongju Koh (eds), *The Human Rights of Persons with Intellectual Disabilities: Different But Equal* (Oxford, Oxford University Press, 2003) 432.

[10] See eg the preparatory works on the Parental Code (1949:381): The Swedish Government, 'Prop. 1987/88:124 om god man och förvaltare', regarding the adoption of participation through representation and annulation of incapacitation of adults.

[11] C Öhrn, 'Mammans lägenhet stank av avföring och mögel – hemtjänsten larmade inte' ['My Mother Lived in Misery – The Home Care Did Not Report or Take Action'] *Aftonbladet* (14 December 2017): www.aftonbladet.se/a/xR3JPj (accessed 2 June 2021).

> When the daughter got well and could return to her mother, she found the old woman living in great misery. Her mother's clothes were dirty. Mould was growing on uneaten food. Used diapers and other rubbish lay round the apartment. The assistant nurse had not given the old woman her eye drops, which she needed in order not to be blind. The daughter reported the situation to the Health and Social Care Inspectorate (IVO).[12]
>
> According to the investigation of the case, not much care had been provided by the municipality during the time that the daughter was away. The care manager justified this outcome with the argument that the client had refused to approve the application by her daughter/limited guardian to get the extra help she needed. She had also repeatedly refused to let the staff clean her apartment or herself.

This illustrates a very problematic situation that can easily arise in Swedish dementia care. The case reflects the fact that applicable legislation does not allow for any contact to be made by social-service employees without both the formal consent of the services and the daily consent of the client him/herself. According to the legislation, every person with dementia or other impaired capacity in Sweden has the legal right to refuse services from the municipality at any time. An individual who wants to make decisions within his or her home has the right to do so; the legislation does not allow for any kind of compulsory action in a private setting. What personnel *can* do is to contact the person's family (and/or the limited guardian) and ask for assistance with persuading the person to accept care. Alternatively, they can ask the family members to help out themselves. If the situation is acute and the person's life is possibly in danger, the police may be alerted. The police, however, have limited powers to assist in this situation and can only act to stop acute and life-threatening incidents or to help the person to get home or to a hospital.

We are faced, then, with a dilemma. How is individual autonomy to be balanced with the need for care? My aim in this chapter is to critically discuss current legal and policy measures through which national legislation can provide cognitively impaired persons with assistance in decision-making, thereby ensuring that care is provided to persons who urgently need help but who refuse it. The point of departure is, furthermore, the dilemma that this must be done without violating the autonomy of such persons. Sweden is the case study for this analysis.

In this chapter, I will apply vulnerability theory. Martha Albertson Fineman's critique of the general social-liberal discourse – with its focus on individualism, autonomy, and rights claims by 'vulnerable groups' – offers a helpful approach here.[13] A point of departure for Fineman's theory is that the prevailing legal system in Western society holds out the autonomous subject as the model for the legal subject. Such an individual is able to make free and

[12] IVO case 8.5-44842-2017.

[13] MA Fineman, *The Autonomy Myth: A Theory of Dependency* (New York, The New Press, 2004).

autonomous choices, to speak for him/herself, to assess all possible options, and to make rational decisions. However, Fineman contends, this is a flawed conception of the human subject. Such a model fails to take into account all those persons who, for a variety of reasons, are dependent on others in order to live their lives.[14] The image of all individuals as autonomous and independent is not realistic. The ability of many persons to live independently of others and of social institutions is limited by age, illness, family situation, economic condition, and other factors.

However, people who are dependent on others *do* have the right to communicate their wishes and needs. Some are able to do so themselves, wholly or in part. Others, who are completely dependent on others for daily support, need someone to speak for them on various matters. Fineman also makes the point that all group approaches ignore the universal vulnerability that we all experience throughout life, and that they create unnecessary distances and differences between individuals and groups in society.[15] The major variations in dependency and vulnerability that take place over the lifespan of every person categorised in a 'group' illustrate the complex and varied experiences that individuals undergo. We need, Fineman argues, to take a holistic approach, and to create institutions that address the vulnerabilities common to us all at different stages of life.[16] This will enable us to ensure just and fair living conditions more comprehensively than we do today.

This chapter is organised in the following manner. Following this introduction, I present an overview of the Swedish system for providing services for persons with dementia. I then briefly describe the various forms of representatives which Swedish family and social-welfare legislation makes available to persons with cognitive impairments – and the possibilities and limitations for use of these in addressing the personal ageing situation so as to enhance individual autonomy and capacity. The final section consists of an analysis of vulnerability, in which I also briefly compare the Swedish system with those in Norway, Denmark, and Finland. My object throughout is to throw light on legal and policy alternatives that may furnish cognitively impaired persons with greater assistance in decision-making, thereby ensuring social and health services for persons who need care but refuse help – without violating the autonomy of said persons.

II. SWEDISH CARE PROVISION FOR COGNITIVELY IMPAIRED PERSONS

Methods for providing care for older persons and for those with cognitive impairments differ internationally. In many European countries, long-term care

[14] MA Fineman, '"Elderly" as Vulnerable: Rethinking the Nature of Individual and Societal Responsibility' (2012) 20 *Elder Law Journal* 102.
[15] Ibid, 115.
[16] MA Fineman, *The Autonomy Myth* (n 13).

funding is to a large extent allocated to care institutions. Statistics from 2008 show there has been a shift in the use of institutional care, with an increasing reliance on nursing homes, and at the same time a de-institutionalisation of health services for disabled persons and an increased use of community-based services.[17] Home-based care includes not just long-term care, but short-term care as well. The services offered may involve aid (cleaning, meals, exercise, etcetera), personal care, technical aid, and if applicable, nursing help. Home-based care services can be preventive, acute, rehabilitative, or palliative in kind.[18]

Sweden, like many other European countries, has relied increasingly on home-based care.[19] Community living, in the form of home-based care, is by far the most commonly used system for providing services for the elderly and for persons with cognitive impairments. Among persons aged 65–79 years, fewer than two per cent live in special housing arrangements in Sweden. Of those who have passed 80 years, 13 per cent of men and about 20 per cent of women live in special housing.[20] The number of persons receiving home care has increased since 2007, while the number of those living in residential homes has fallen. The vast majority of older people continue to live in their private home.[21] One reason for this is that many persons with special needs prefer to stay in their own home as long as possible. Another reason is that the number of available arrangements in special housing for older persons has gradually fallen over a long period in Sweden. This is partly the result of improved health among older persons, and partly the result of enhanced opportunities to remain in one's home with the help of home assistance, despite having a personal impairment. However, the changes are also due to a national policy of encouraging residents to stay in their own home as long as possible, by offering opportunities for adapting their home and for receiving home-based social care and healthcare. Among those 65–79 years of age, five per cent have home-based care in Sweden. Among those over 80, 27 per cent of men and 35 per cent of women receive home-based care.[22] In total, around 16 per cent of the population aged 65 years and older are receiving long-term home-based care in Sweden.[23]

[17] European Social Network, 'Services for Older People in Europe – Facts and Figures about Long Term Care Services in Europe' (October 2008): https://ec.europa.eu/health/sites/health/files/mental_health/docs/services_older.pdf (accessed 2 June 2021), p 13.

[18] OECD, 'Long-term Care for Older People' (OECD Publishing, 2005): https://read.oecd-ilibrary.org/social-issues-migration-health/long-term-care-for-older-people_9789264015852-en#page2 (accessed 2 June 2021).

[19] PPJ Houben, 'Changing Housing for Elderly People and Co-Ordination Issues in Europe' (2001) 16 *Housing Studies* 651.

[20] Social Services, 'Statistics on Elderly and Persons with Impairments – Management Form 2017' (The National Board of Health and Welfare, 2018): www.socialstyrelsen.se/globalassets/sharepoint-dokument/artikelkatalog/statistik/2020-3-6618.pdf (accessed 30 May 2021), p 1.

[21] Boverket, 'Allt fler 80+ i befolkningen' (2020): www.boverket.se/sv/samhallsplanering/bostadsmarknad/olika-grupper/aldre/ (accessed 30 May 2021).

[22] Ibid; European Social Network, 'Services for Older People in Europe' (n 17).

[23] Social Services, Statistics on Elderly and Persons with Impairments' (n 20).

To get home-based care, a person can apply for personal assistance and service from the local municipality. According to the Social Services Act Chapter 2 paragraph 1, each municipality is responsible for social services within its geographical area, and it bears the ultimate responsibility for ensuring that individuals receive the support and help they need. The municipality may provide these services itself, or it can engage private providers to supply them.

Furthermore, the municipality must provide these services to citizens in a rights-based manner. According to the Social Services Act Chapter 4 paragraph 1, all who are unable to meet their own needs have a right to receive assistance from the municipality for their economic maintenance, and to receive such services as they may need. Moreover, people's need for care must be met irrespective of their financial circumstances. The cost for care may vary, due to the income and/or personal assets of the persons in question. The social services are charged, then, with assuring all residents of a reasonable standard of living. Furthermore, the Act states, assistance shall be designed in such a way as to strengthen the ability of recipients to live an independent life. Thus, Sweden has an ideal system in many ways, not reached in many jurisdictions, concerning the idea of a rights-based social care system.

The Act proclaims, then, a right to individually designed care from the social services. The extent of such care is to be calibrated in accordance with a repeated close assessment of the individual needs of the person in question. Persons who need healthcare can often be provided with both healthcare and other services in their own homes (at least to the extent that advanced medical treatment is not required). It is only when a person needs assistance of a sort that is intensive and which cannot be provided in his/her own home that residential care will be made available. However, it is sometimes difficult nowadays to access residential care in Sweden, because the social services are largely home-based at this point, and the number of available residential care places is steadily falling. The administrative courts are hearing many cases where an older person has brought a claim to gain access to residential care. Despite having a duty to provide it, almost half of Sweden's municipalities lack special housing for older persons and for those with dementia, and the shortage has been increasing for several years.[24]

The variation between countries in how services for older persons are arranged and financed may have historical as well as economic causes. Viewed internationally, Sweden spends a relatively large amount on elder care. The cost is defrayed mainly by municipal taxes and by grants from the central government. In 2014, the total cost of elder care in Sweden was SEK 109.2 billion (EUR 11.7 billion). Only a very small part of that cost – four per cent – is met

[24] In the annual survey of 2019 by the National Board of Housing, Building and Planning (Boverket) on the availability of special housing, 127 of 280 municipalities reported having a shortage of special housing for the elderly and for persons with dementia. That was 11 more than in 2018. See Boverket, 'Allt fler 80+ i befolkningen' (n 21).

by charges to the client.[25] The level of such charges is not fixed; however, a maximum is set by each municipality. In 2005, 90 per cent of all home-based care for older people was provided by the municipalities themselves.[26] Since then, a good number of municipalities have contracted out these services. Today, many older persons are allowed to choose whether they want their services to be furnished by public or by private operators.[27]

In addition to the Social Services Act, there is a *lex specialis* regulation covering a small number of persons with dementia. Certain persons are entitled to additional services, according to the Swedish Act concerning Support and Services for Persons with Certain Functional Impairments (1993:387). This legislation provides for special high-quality help, such as care from a personal assistant, for individuals suffering from certain types of disability. These services are designed in such a way as to ensure 'good living conditions'. The most expensive, widely used, and personalised type of help – care provided by a personal assistant – can only be granted to people before they reach the age of 65 years. This kind of extra assistance, therefore, is not addressed in this chapter.[28]

III. PARTICIPATION THROUGH REPRESENTATION

All measures relating to home-based care taken by the municipalities must be based on consent from the client. The Social Services Act puts a strong emphasis on consent, self-determination, and the right to privacy. It stresses the autonomy of individuals, and their consequent capacity to give or to withhold their consent. Thus, all measures taken on behalf of individuals by the National Board of Health and Welfare must be formed and implemented together with them. As a result, the person's consent is required in order to assess his/her needs for assistance and service at home (as well as at a care institution).

A complicating factor here is that a person with dementia may not have the practical capacity to consent even to basic care. Together with the fact that many persons with dementia or other such impairments do not have a legal or practical representative in Sweden, this can cause serious problems. Cognitively impaired persons may have a legal representative in Sweden. There

[25] Swedish Institute, 'Elderly Care in Sweden' (sweden.se 30 June 2021): https://sweden.se/society/elderly-care-in-sweden/ (accessed 30 May 2021).

[26] N Genet, W Boerma, M Kroneman, A Hutchinson and RB Saltman (eds), *Home Care across Europe: Current Structure and Future Challenges* (Geneva, World Health Organization, 2012) 274.

[27] For an analysis of this development, see M Katzin, *Taking Care of Business? A Study of the Governing of Care Choice Systems in Swedish Elder Care* (dissertation) (Lund, Lund University Press, 2020).

[28] For a discussion of this legislation, see further T Mattsson, 'Age, Vulnerability and Disability' in I Doron and N Georgantzi (eds), *Age, Ageism and the Law: European Perspectives on the Rights of Older Persons* (Cheltenham, Elgar Edward Press, 2018) 37.

are no exact numbers on how common this is. However, we can be certain there are many older persons with dementia who do not have any type of legal supported decision-making representative in Sweden. Persons with dementia make up one of the larger groups among the cognitively impaired in Sweden.[29] In fact, legal supported decision-making representatives are most often assigned to people who possess large fortunes or who have no relatives.[30] Thus many persons with dementia receive no support with decision-making from the social services in Sweden.

For persons without the practical possibility of repeatedly granting or withholding their consent, being assigned a supported decision-making representative may be crucial for realising both their right to participation and their right to care. The term 'participation' is a recurrent concept in several human-rights treaties, as well as in national legislation relating to disability. The substantive provisions from the 1966 International Covenant on Economic, Social and Cultural Rights (ICESCR) do not explicitly mention 'participation'. However, General Comment 14, from the Committee on Economic, Social and Cultural Rights (CtteeESCR), on the Right to Health, of August 2000, does pay direct attention to aspects of participation. The Comment describes participation as important in all health-related decision-making, at both local and national levels.[31] States, it declares, must ensure the opportunity to participate in all kinds of decisions on people's health. Only by this means can the effective provision of healthcare be ensured.[32] 'Participation' rights are also clearly enunciated in human-rights documents addressed to specific groups or persons. One example is the Convention on the Elimination of All forms of Discrimination against Women (CEDAW).[33] Another is the CRPD, mentioned earlier, which is also directly applicable to persons with dementia. Participation rights also figure in human-rights documents of other kinds, among them the United Nations Principles for Older Persons. Over recent decades, then, 'participation' has become a central component of the legal framework on human rights relevant to essential public services, such as healthcare and social care.

A related crucial link exists between participation and support. Participation is closely connected to some fundamental legal concepts, such as dignity, integrity,

[29] Sweden's Ministry of Justice, *SOU 2004:112: Frågor om Förmyndare och Ställföreträdare för Vuxna [Questions about Guardians and Deputies of Adults]* (Stockholm, Norstedts, 2004).

[30] There were 68,548 limited guardianships (11:4) and 12,284 full guardianships (11:7) in 2017 in Sweden, see Länsstyrelserna, 'Statistik – Överförmyndarstatistik' (lansstyrelsen.se): https://overformyndarstatistik.lansstyrelsen.se/Statistik (accessed 14 July 2020). There is no national documentation on the reasons for guardianship.

[31] CtteeESCR, *General Comment 14 on the Right to the Highest Attainable Standard of Health* (11 August 2000) UN Doc E/C.12/2000/4, para 11.

[32] Ibid, paras 17, 23 and 54.

[33] The Preamble of the Convention on the Elimination of All Forms of Discrimination against Women (adopted 18 December 1979, entered into force 3 September 1981) 1249 UNTS 13 (CEDAW).

legal certainty, and democracy.[34] Participation rights include the opportunity to express one's views, to be listened to on decisions affecting oneself (either directly or through a representative), and when applicable to be able to act as an autonomous person. They normally include the right to speak, to have one's say on a matter, to influence, to make a decision – and also to refuse. Such issues concerning the right to participation and the close connection to the right to adequate state support fits well with a vulnerability analysis. According to the vulnerability theory, each country has to take responsibility also for people who have difficulties or who are unable to put forward their concerns themselves. Therefore, the theory becomes relevant for arguing for 'participation' as a way to make the idea of autonomy and agency meaningful. Accepting the fact that there are different needs and rights depending on the individual vulnerability, each person's participation' becomes crucial in guiding the ethics and practices appropriate for the care of the person in need of assistance. Thus, the possibility for participation of each individual in need of different services or care becomes the tool for communication with institutions, such as the social services, in view of the fact that during his or her lifespan the individual has a range of different needs that have to be communicated.

For persons with dementia, participation may not exist at all without different kinds of support. The reason is that dementia is a condition that affects, in one way or another, one's ability to participate. The care needed by people with this condition varies greatly, depending among other things on their ability to participate and to claim the services they need and wish to have. According to human-rights documents, moreover, each country must take responsibility for people who find it difficult or impossible to speak on their own behalf. The overall issue and concern in this chapter, accordingly, is how any country – in this case Sweden – can ensure that persons with dementia are guaranteed adequate service and care.

Having accepted the close link between participation and adequate social services, the follow-up issue is how to offer assistance to persons in need of participating but without personal ability to fully do it themselves. For such situations, one way to realise the right to participate is through some kind of representation. In the following section, I therefore briefly describe the relevant forms of representation for persons with dementia in Sweden currently.[35]

[34] T Mattsson, '"Participation" for All? Challenges and Tools to Realise Participation for Vulnerable Persons with a Focus on Health Services' in M Hesselman, A Hallo de Wolf and B Toebes (eds), *Socio-Economic Human Rights in Essential Public Services Provision* (London, Routledge, 2017) 205.

[35] In addition to the forms of representation described in the following, it may be noted that there is another form of (limited) representation in respect of financial affairs by family members (spouse or cohabitant, child, grandchild, parent, sibling, or nephew) regulated in the Parental Code, Chapter 17.

IV. FORMS OF REPRESENTATION

A. Limited Guardian

A common type of legal guardian in many countries is the limited guardian. This form of representation may be available for adults suffering from dementia in Sweden. The role of the limited guardian – in the Swedish context referred to as *god man* – is mainly to provide help with the client's decision-making; in addition, however, he/she can act on behalf of the client in practical matters. The person with a limited guardian may still act for him/herself, irrespective of the wishes of the guardian. A limited guardian is appointed by the district court upon application by the client, by a close relative of the client, or by the chief guardian in the municipality.[36] It is quite common that a family member is appointed as a limited guardian in Sweden, but it may also be someone not familiar to the person working professionally as a legal representative for several persons. Consent by the client is usually needed for such applications to be approved. Only in cases where the person is too ill to give such consent can this requirement be waived.

Assigning a limited guardian is a voluntary measure, meaning that the person with dementia retains his or her legal and practical capacity. According to the legislation, limited guardians have a duty to safeguard the rights of those they represent, to manage their assets, and to provide for their person.[37] Safeguarding their rights can mean taking care of their finances, ensuring they receive the help and support to which they are entitled, and/or representing them vis-à-vis various authorities in applications and appeals. Limited guardians have the authority to apply for social services, but normally only after consent from their clients. In very special circumstances, they may be able to apply for support measures without such consent; but the legislation does not precisely identify the circumstances under which they may do so. It is clear, however, that limited guardians cannot act if their clients refuse to receive social services, to move to special housing, or the like. Due to this need to obtain their clients' consent for all decisions (and for all practical steps to implement them), limited guardians find it difficult to ensure a decent standard of living for their clients if the latter do not want the services or assistance involved.

A problem that has been highlighted in the media in recent years is the inadequate competence of many limited guardians in Sweden. Several reports have

[36] Parental Code, Chapter 11 para 4.

[37] Parental Code Chapter 12 para 2. The assignment varies according to the needs of the person and the decision by the court.

drawn attention to limited guardians who have failed in their duty.[38] Part of the problem lies in the recruitment system. Many municipalities have difficulty recruiting suitable guardians, in large part due to the fact that the assignment is either voluntary or poorly paid. Another problem is the increasing complexity of the work. The task is getting more and more complicated and time-consuming. Performing it requires an increasing number of skills and more and more general competence. At the same time, municipalities demand no special skills or knowledge from limited guardians. Being a normally endowed adult able to look after one's interests is deemed sufficient.[39] Limited guardians in Sweden are a very diverse group. Some hold many such assignments, leaving them little time to assist each person. Others may be related to the client, and hold the position only once in their life. They are generally paid by the person by the person in need of assistance; however the payment is quite limited. Guardians in Sweden, then, are highly varied, and so are their duties and skills. The quality of their work is thus highly variable.

B. Full Guardian

The other type of guardian – the full guardian (*förvaltare*) – acts as a substitute decision-maker in questions relating to the client's economic and personal matters.[40] Guardians of this kind are much rarer in Sweden than limited guardians. The main difference between a limited guardian and a full guardian is that the former performs tasks on behalf of his/her principal, whereas the latter assumes the principal's legal capacity to deal with certain limited matters (such as an estate or a bank account).

A full guardian has the authority to act independently of the client's wishes, and without his or her participation. Such an assignment is thus contrary to the intent behind the Swedish system, which is to keep interventions into clients' personal and economic matters without their consent to a minimum. Appointing a full guardianship of this kind is a coercive measure, and it is done only in those rare situations when the district court considers the person in question to be absolutely incapable of taking care of themselves, of their assets, or of their other personal affairs. Persons assigned a full guardian lose the right, for a certain period, to enter into contracts or to manage their own economic affairs.

[38] See, eg, B Eliasson, L Nordquist, B Westerholm and M Ängeby, '"Systemet med gode män är kapitalt misslyckat"', *Dagens Nyheter* (Stockholm, 29 August 2019): www.dn.se/debatt/systemet-med-gode-man-ar-kapitalt-misslyckat/ (accessed 14 July 2020); J Ziegerer and J Mikkelsen, 'Efter God Man-Skandalen: Ny Kritik Mot Malmö Stad – Sydsvenskan', *Sydsvenskan* (Malmö, 22 November 2019): www.sydsvenskan.se/2019-11-22/efter-god-man-skandalen-ny-kritik-mot-malmo-stad (accessed 30 May 2021).

[39] J Wallgren and L Holmgård, *God Man, Förvaltare Och Förmyndare: Domstolarnas Handläggning* (Stockholm, Norstedts Juridik, 2015).

[40] See especially Chapter 11 paras 7–11.

The district court can decide on a trustee even without consent from the person or his/her relatives.[41]

C. Continuing Power of Attorney

A different type of supported decision-making framework was introduced in Sweden in 2017, quite late compared to many other countries. This was the continuing power of attorney, or private mandate [*framtidsfullmakt*], ie a power of attorney established for preventive purposes. For several years, the need for some type of future power of attorney had been discussed. The other Nordic countries (as well as the US and many other countries in Europe) have a history of providing assistance through a private mandate. A reason why this model came to Sweden so late may have to do with the extensive public system for dealing with many issues concerning the daily life of the population, in contrast to national systems that rely more on private and family-based systems.

This legal instrument is regulated in the *Lag (2017: 310) om framtidsfullmakter* [Act on Continuing Powers of Attorney]. The main rule here is that it is the proxy-holder who assesses whether the proxy has entered into force; ie the person intended to assist in decision-making determines when they start the practice of the power of attorney. If the proxy-holder considers that the proxy [*fullmakt*] has entered into force, he or she must promptly notify the client, the client's spouse or cohabiting partner, and the client's closest relatives.[42] An application is then submitted to the district court where the proxy-holder is registered. The district court shall then, upon application by the proxy-holder, assess said application and determine – if it deems all to be in order – that the power of attorney has entered into force. Before making this decision, however, the court must obtain a medical certificate or equivalent document regarding the health status of the client, unless that is obviously unnecessary. The client must then be given the opportunity to comment on the application, should that be possible. The client's spouse or cohabitant, his/her closest relatives, and the chief public guardian in the municipality must also be given the opportunity to comment.[43] The Act sets out some general requirements for the appointment of such a proxy-holder. For one thing, the client must still possess decision-making competence at the time of the appointment. For another, the proxy only comes into force after this competence has been lost due to illness or failing health.

[41] For a more detailed description of the mandate of the full guardian and of the limited guardian, as well as an analysis of special concerns relating to persons with dementia, see E Ryrstedt, 'Dementia and Autonomy' in N-H Ann (ed), *Elder Law: Evolving European Perspectives* (Cheltenham, Edward Elgar Publishing, 2017) 358.

[42] See sections 9–10.

[43] See section 13.

A central question for this chapter is to what extent different forms of representation offer options for supporting participation as well as care. Generally speaking, a proxy-holder covers economic and personal matters.[44] However, it is unclear to what extent it really complements the existing frameworks to give more options for support for many persons. When it comes to the group discussed in this chapter – persons with dementia – a proxy-holder may cover only limited actions, such as applying for special housing accommodation, assisting the client in dealing with the social services, and the like. But there are several restrictions as well. For example, the power of attorney does not cover matters of healthcare according to either the Health and Medical Services Act or the Act on Continuing Powers of Attorney.

A related question of importance is how well the proxy-holder fulfils the right to care. The legislation restricts the use of a proxy-holder on issues of a 'distinctly personal character'. This is a major limitation for the right to participation in everyday issues. The *förarbeten* [legislative preparatory works] to the Act on Continuing Powers of Attorney do not provide a specific list of what falls under the heading of issues of a distinctly personal character. They do state, however, that 'care' and 'housing' are usually to be considered highly personal; thus they would appear to fall outside the proxy-holder's authority.[45] Thus, decision-making on home-based care does not fall within the legal framework of the power of attorney. The preparatory works state that even if assistance vis-à-vis social authorities or healthcare personnel (initiating, assisting with, and taking part in a meeting with social-service personnel) falls within the power of attorney, the person with dementia must handle all the decision-making part him/herself on many daily matters.[46] The possibility to get help from the proxy-holder is therefore quite limited on most issues concerning the daily care of the person with dementia. From a vulnerability perspective, the continuing power of attorney in its current version in Swedish legislation appears to provide insufficient ways in which situations of dependency can be overcome in daily life for persons with dementia. From a vulnerability analysis perspective, it is hardly a legislative approach that manages to emphasise our interdependency within social institutions and the need for public responsibility of various kinds of help.

D. Discussion

In recent years, the European Union has encouraged the development of care institutions for older persons around Europe through its funding practices.

[44] See section 2.

[45] Sweden's Ministry of Justice, 'Prop. 2016/17:30: Framtidsfullmakter – en ny form av ställföreträdarskap för vuxna' (Sweden's Ministry of Justice, 22 December 2016): www.regeringen.se/48df4a/contentassets/705ce48f15a64685a55d6a6035d66400/framtidsfullmakter--en-ny-form-av-stallforetradarskap-for-vuxna-prop.-20161730 (accessed 30 June 2021), 30f.

[46] Ibid.

This trend has been criticised for violating the human rights of older people, by promoting a system which deems it generally best to deal with old age and dementia in institutions.[47] Arguments against this trend cite the non-discrimination clause in CRPD Article 5 (equality and discrimination) and Article 19 (on community living). Institutionalisation, in this view, is prima facie a form of discrimination.[48]

As stated in the introduction to this chapter, Sweden and the other Nordic countries have for many years worked actively towards home-based care. This trend is in accordance with international regulations and recommendations. The UN's Principles for Older Persons, for example, state that older persons should be able to continue living at home for as long as possible.[49] The Nordic countries have been implementing such recommendations. However, a question of great concern currently is how society is to provide a good standard of home-based care, to keep economic costs under reasonable control, to defend the interests of social-welfare personnel – and to do all these things without intruding on the rights of the individual care recipient. Two further challenges are how to avoid forcing the client's family to take on a heavy burden of responsibility for their relative's care, and how to furnish decision-making assistance without intruding on the client's rights.

These challenges are often greater in the case of persons with dementia than in the case of many other groups in society. In particular, there is a need in the former case to compensate for diminishing (or at least varying) decision-making ability in a way that upholds human rights in a setting where the person lives at home, is often alone, and is heavily dependent on others. Such a setting can give rise to serious difficulties; one of them is how to offer adjustable support for decision-making.

The limited guardian system in Sweden is often held up as an ideal method for supported decision-making. However, there are some problems with this arrangement. Social-work research shows it can be difficult to ensure a decent standard of living in long-term home-based care for persons with dementia in Sweden. In situations where the user has refused care, his/her family often has to intervene – without clear legal support – to compensate for a lack of care by the social services. Thus, due to the legal requirement that explicit consent be given on all questions relating to basic living conditions, many persons with dementia risk neglect or even danger. In previous work, two social-work researchers joined

[47] G Quinn, G de Búrca, L Weddington, M Bell, A Lawson, M Stein, T Mattsson and L Clements, *Legal Memo. The Impermissibility of Using the ESIF to Invest Monies in Long Term Care Residential Institutions for Persons with Disabilities* (European Network on Independent Living, 2018): www.eva-bap.be/images/legalmemoesiffinalediten (accessed 30 June 2021).

[48] Ibid.

[49] UNGA, 'United Nations Principles for Older Persons' adopted by UNGA Res 46/91 (16 December 1991) A/RES/46/9. See also UNGA, 'The Madrid International Plan of Action on Ageing and the Political Declaration' adopted at the Second World Assembly on Ageing in April 2002 and endorsed by UNGA Res 57/167 (18 December 2002), principles 86. (c) and 105. (b).

me in reviewing these results in light of the legal requirement for consent set out in Swedish social-care legislation described in this chapter.[50] We concluded that current legislation gives rise to great uncertainty for social-care professionals, for relatives of people with dementia, and above all for people with dementia themselves. These difficulties arise from the inability of social workers to help those who refuse aid but who urgently need some sort of assistance. A major challenge Sweden faces, then, is to find legal and policy alternatives that furnish persons with dementia with suitable support with decision-making. We must ensure services for persons in urgent need of care who refuse help – without violating their dignity and integrity.

The main problem discussed in this chapter is that a limited guardian may find it very hard to ensure a decent standard of living for a person if that person refuses, in accordance with the legal limitations of the proxy, to accept the help on offer. Thus, these challenges are common to both the limited guardian system and system of the continuing power of attorney. Another problem relates to practical limitations (ie the inadequate number of assigned guardians and their limited competence).

Thus, it has not yet proved fully possible, in the applicable Swedish legislation, to deal effectively with the potential clash between, on the one hand guaranteeing the right to everyday care for persons with dementia, and on the other hand ensuring these persons' right to participate in decision-making and to give or withhold their consent. A glimpse at the other Nordic countries reveals similar problems, but some interesting divergent features as well.

Norway's legislation in this area is similar to Sweden's. The Norwegian law on continuing powers of attorney dates from 2010, and it provided an important starting point for the Swedish legislator. One interesting difference, however, is that the Norwegian law grants the proxy-holder the right to participate, together with the client, in decisions on the latter's care and living conditions. Housing too is an issue on which the guardian may at times decide, according to the preparatory works for this law. Physical coercion or obstruction, however, does not figure among the guardian's prerogatives. The Norwegian law, like the Swedish one, leaves room for interpretation on which issues qualify as 'highly personal'. Norway has also considered introducing a method for deciding in advance on one's possible future care and accommodation, through a system resembling a life testament (but regulated by law and enforceable). A discussion has also arisen in Norway in recent years on how to avoid cases of maltreatment, due to the deaths of two older persons in home-based care a couple of years ago.[51]

[50] T Mattsson and L Giertz, 'Vulnerability, Law, and Dementia: An Interdisciplinary Discussion of Legislation and Practice' (2020) 21 *Theoretical Inquiries in Law* 139–59; L Giertz, T Mattsson and A Thelin, *Nedsatt beslutsförmåga. Rätt, riktlinjer, praktik* (Lund, Studentlitteratur AB, 2021).

[51] H Sinding Aasen, 'Forsvarlig eldreomsorg? Et kritisk blikk på dom avsagt av Oslo tingrett' in B Henning Østenstad, C Adolphsen, E Naur and H Sinding-Aasen (eds), *Selvbestemmelse og tvang i helse- og omsorgstjenesten* (Bergen, Fagbokforlaget, 2018).

In Finland, the continuing power of attorney is regulated in *Lagen om intressebevakningsfullmakt*.[52] This regulatory framework is also similar to that in Sweden. The power of attorney enters into force if the client loses the ability to deal with his or her affairs due to illness, cognitive difficulties, a weakened state of health, or other equivalent cause. This gives the proxy-holder the authority to represent the client in matters concerning the latter's property and other finances. The proxy-holder may also be granted authority to represent the person in other matters, should the latter be unable to understand their significance when the private mandate is to be used.[53]

The Danish law on continuing power of attorney, which dates from 2016, is more far-reaching than its Swedish, Finnish, or Norwegian counterparts. On personal issues, the applicable Danish legislation allows the proxy-holder to represent the client vis-à-vis public authorities in general.[54] He or she can thus apply on the client's behalf for social care, social assistance, pension payments, and the like. Where the client's residence is concerned, the proxy-holder can give the go-ahead to a forced move to a particular more suitable accommodation. Due to the wider authority accruing to the proxy-holder in Denmark, the private-mandate system in that country is also subject to more rigorous regulation.

Drawing on Fineman's theory, we can now draw some preliminary conclusions on the challenges involved in seeking to realise the right of persons suffering from dementia both to participate in decision-making and to be ensured adequate care. One conclusion is that there is no reason to draw up a single regulation designed to fit all situations and persons. The needs and circumstances are too varied for any one-size-fits-all solution. We may need a *variety of regulated assisted decision-making functions*. Fineman argues that sameness of treatment – for all members of a given group, for example – ignores both specific contexts and people's varied circumstances and abilities. It also ignores inequalities of living conditions, and it proceeds on the assumption that all have the same status and opportunities irrespective of where they are in the course of their lives. Designing a single support function, therefore, should be avoided. Instead, assisted decision-making roles of many different kinds should be designed, depending on the needs of the individual client. On the other hand, there need to be a balance. In Harding's chapter for this collection she outlines the complexities that arise from having too many roles. If too many people can make decisions on behalf of the person, or act as a supporter, then there is a risk that that the person's own voice will get lost. This is an important aspect to take into consideration. However, it must be recognised that the situation in Sweden is very far from the situation in England & Wales, which currently has

[52] *Lagen om intressebevakningsfullmakt* No 648/2007 (25.5.2007).
[53] *Lag om intressebevakningsfullmakt*, Chapter 1 para 2.
[54] *Lov om fremtidsfuldmagter* No 618/2016 (08/06/2016) § 10.

16 different supported or substituted decision-making frameworks which work together.[55]

The qualitative aspect of the services entrusted to others on personal matters is always crucial to consider, if we are to respect individual rights. For each of the assisted decision-making functions, the outcome will depend both on the quality of the legislation and on the quality of the particular proxy-holder's work. Where Sweden is concerned, critical scrutiny is needed in both regards. The vagueness of the legislation concerning what the limited guardian may do is undesirable. To what extent, for example, do questions of social care and housing fall within the mandate of the proxy-holders? Then we have the reports about the poor quality of many limited guardians. A comparison with the private-mandate systems in the other Nordic countries suggests that we need to adjust the Swedish system if we are to realise the two objectives set forth in this chapter. Good living conditions, comprehensive healthcare, and far-reaching social care are all essential for human life. Legislation must therefore make it possible for clients to engage a proxy-holder to assist in decisions on their personal living conditions and access to social care. If and when such legislation is introduced, Sweden will be better equipped to ensure persons with dementia and other cognitive impairments the right both to participate in decision making and to be guaranteed access to care. However, ensuring both of these at the same time – the right to personal help and services on the one hand, and to integrity and dignity on the other – is a delicate balance.

V. FINAL WORD

In the Swedish system of social care, the personal decision-making capacity of each adult has been recognised and promoted to such an extent that the right to care for some persons in great need has been hollowed out. Applicable legislation in this area has failed to take proper account of persons who are unable to shape their lives actively (when it comes, for example, to choosing between the services of different vendors).[56] By focusing on the situation faced by persons with dementia, the aim here has been to illustrate some of the problems arising in connection with social welfare legislation that assumes full legal capacity on the part of all persons. The overall societal goals of participation and autonomy for all persons are central in the legal systems of most countries. They are also very important for all democratic societies. However, in the context of home-based care, these goals can also be problematic at times, particularly in relation to cognitively impaired persons who need support in their decision-making, such as persons with dementia.

[55] See Harding, Chapter 16, this volume.

[56] H Brodin, *Does Anybody Care? Public and Private Responsibilities in Swedish Eldercare 1940–2000* (Umeå, Print & Media, Umeå University, 2005).

In this chapter, my aim has been to draw attention to the dilemmas and challenges that the rights to participation, autonomy and well-being for adults with impaired decision-making ability may entail in a home-based social services setting. The tension that can arise between, on the one hand, each individual's right to care and attention when needed and, on the other hand, the same person's right to integrity, participation and self-determination in their everyday life, requires continuous attention and reflection. The issue of how to fulfil people's needs and participation rights through different supported decision-making is a central issue in capacity law that needs to continue to be discussed. As the vulnerability theory points out, we need to create institutions which address the vulnerabilities common to us all at different stages of life. Only then will we be able to ensure just and fair living conditions for all. People with dementia may pose the greatest challenge when it comes to carrying out this balancing act. The holistic approach held out by Fineman offers prospects for success in this area.

14

Law's Legitimacy and Social Work Support in Safeguarding Adults at Risk of Abuse in England

JAIME LINDSEY

I. INTRODUCTION

ENGLISH LAW HAS a complex legal framework regarding how public bodies should respond when abuse of 'vulnerable' adults is suspected. This includes the intersection between the Mental Capacity Act 2005 (MCA) and the Care Act 2014, as well as various other mechanisms and relevant guidance.[1] Negotiating this framework of law is not an easy task for professionals who work with adults at risk of abuse, particularly in ways that prioritise *support* for decision-making rather than coercion. In this chapter, I argue that one way of achieving supported decision-making in practice in England is to develop the safeguarding adults legal framework with the aim of enhancing the role of social workers to better support, rather than resort to legal coercion of, adults at risk of abuse. That is not to say that legal coercion always or inevitably results from an application to court, but that law *can coerce*, and when it does so, this merely reinforces its legitimacy.[2] In making this argument I contrast perceptions of law's legitimacy with understandings of the legitimacy of social work. By resorting to legal interventions, law's legitimacy is reinforced in ways that undermine social workers' support-based interventions, which impedes social workers from providing the kind of support which they are best placed to provide.

[1] For example, see Department of Health and Social Care, *Care Act Statutory Guidance* (March 2016, updated August 2021): www.gov.uk/government/publications/care-act-statutory-guidance/care-and-support-statutory-guidance (accessed 15 November 2021). For an overview, see J Herring, *Vulnerable Adults and the Law* (Oxford, Oxford University Press 2016).

[2] For further analysis of the coercive power of mental capacity law in the CoP, see J Lindsey, 'Protecting vulnerable adults from abuse: Under-protection and over-protection in adult safeguarding and mental capacity law' (2020) 32 *Child and Family Law Quarterly* 157.

The legal framework for adult safeguarding in England centres on the Care Act 2014.[3] The primary safeguarding duty is on local authorities, who are required to protect adults with care and support needs who are experiencing, or are at risk of, abuse or neglect, and as a result are unable to protect themselves.[4] The Care Act safeguarding duties are, however, limited in scope. They require enquiries to be undertaken to investigate the presence of abuse. When abuse is identified following those enquiries, the law is much less clear about how and in what ways to respond.[5] However, the Care Act operates within a wider legislative framework, most importantly in relationship with the MCA.

The MCA deals with issues that arise in relation to adults who may be unable to make a decision for themselves because of a disturbance or impairment of the functioning of their mind or brain.[6] What this means is that, where an adult subject to a safeguarding enquiry under the Care Act is also believed to lack the mental capacity to make a decision for themselves, the MCA can be used to respond to the abusive situation. This might include making a best interests decision that it is not in that person's best interests to reside or have contact with their abuser. Conversely, where, following a safeguarding enquiry, a person is believed to have the mental capacity to make a particular decision – for example to have contact with their abuser – then the MCA cannot be invoked to protect that person. This stark dividing line between the two areas of law can often leave the adult who is vulnerable to abuse unprotected, and these boundaries of mental capacity law have been subject to criticism.[7]

In this chapter, I explore the ways that social workers can support the person to make his or her own decisions without resorting to the legal coercion permitted by the MCA. In developing my arguments about the supportive potential of social work, I draw on original qualitative research carried out into the use of mental capacity law in practice in England to provide an insight into the practice of how social workers understand and operationalise their role. I carried out eight in-depth, semi-structured interviews with social workers, each of whom had experience of working with the MCA. The interviews explored key themes, and the focus of the interviews explored in this chapter is social workers' experience of the Court of Protection (CoP) and questions around supported decision-making.[8]

[3] Ibid. The legal framework for Wales is different for safeguarding, albeit the Mental Capacity Act 2005 does apply in England and Wales.

[4] Care Act 2014, s 42(1).

[5] J Lindsey, 'Developing Vulnerability: A Situational Response to the Abuse of Women with Mental Disabilities' (2016) 24 *Feminist Legal Studies* 295; Lindsey, 'Protecting vulnerable adults from abuse' (n 2).

[6] MCA, s 2.

[7] Lindsey, 'Protecting vulnerable adults from abuse' (n 2); B Clough, 'New Legal Landscapes: (Re) Constructing the Boundaries of Mental Capacity Law' (2018) 26 *Medical Law Review* 246.

[8] As part of this research, I also carried out observational research at the CoP, including observing eight cases over 11 hearings, data which are analysed in more detail elsewhere and include findings that the subject of proceedings rarely participates in CoP proceedings, that there is a hierarchy of

In the first half of this chapter I explore the role of legitimacy, contrasting the different claims to legitimacy made by social work and law, arguing that because social work interventions are perceived as less authoritative than legal interventions, social workers resort to the coercive potential of law in the most challenging, high-risk cases. Whilst social workers may benefit from the use of law, I raise concerns about law's potential for coercion and argue that social workers need greater authority to intervene through support-based interventions. In the second half I focus on how the English legal framework on adult safeguarding should be amended to enable social workers to provide support-based interventions rather than resorting to legal coercion.

II. LEGITIMACY, AUTHORITY AND COERCION: THE RESORT TO LAW IN HIGH-RISK CASES

A. The Contrasting Legitimacy of Law and Social Work

In contrasting the differing legitimacy and authority of law and social work, I highlight the very different characterisations of the two disciplines. Law as enforceable and objective, contrasted with social work as support-based and subjective. Yet these differing legitimacy claims give law and social work quite different, and potentially conflicting, bases for their authority, which are merely reinforced when social workers resort to law in high-risk adult safeguarding cases.

Legitimacy is a form of social influence or power. If an institution is seen as legitimate then it is more likely to have authority, as people feel that they 'ought to obey'.[9] In other words, it provides a 'right to rule and the recognition by the ruled of that right'.[10] That is why legitimacy is so central to law – without it, people may not obey, which would undermine the effectiveness and authority of the law and lead to civil disobedience. Law has long been theorised as a source of legitimate power,[11] with the court being a key manifestation of that power, albeit that the justification for law's power varies between positivists, those who look more to the moral content of the law, and various schools of thought

professional evidence in mental capacity law and that CoP interventions can be used to over-protect adults vulnerable to abuse, see J Lindsey, 'Testimonial Injustice and Vulnerability: A Qualitative Analysis of Participation in the Court of Protection' (2019) 28 *Social & Legal Studies* 450; J Lindsey, 'Competing Professional Knowledge Claims About Mental Capacity in the Court of Protection' (2020) 28 *Medical Law Review* 1; Lindsey, 'Protecting vulnerable adults from abuse' (n 2). The research was approved by the University of Birmingham Research Ethics Committee and any data referred to in this chapter is anonymised and does not refer to the actual names of any of those involved in the research.

[9] TR Tyler, 'Psychological Perspectives on Legitimacy and Legitimation' (2006) 57 *Annual Review of Psychology* 375, 377.

[10] J Jackson, B Bradford, M Hough, A Myhill, P Quinton and TR Tyler, 'Why do People Comply with the Law?: Legitimacy and the Influence of Legal Institutions' (2012) 52 *British Journal of Criminology* 1051, 1051.

[11] M Foucault, *Discipline and Punish: The Birth of the Prison* (London, Peregrine Books, 1979); C Smart, *Feminism and the Power of Law* (London, Routledge, 1989).

in between.[12] Irrespective of whether law *ought* to be viewed as legitimate for these reasons, so far as law is commonly depicted, its legitimacy stems from two key features – its perceived enforceability and objectivity of application. This is an analytical, rather than normative, jurisprudential claim based on an understanding of the historical development of the English common law;[13] that is, that law is perceived as having legitimacy where it is enforceable and objectively applied in like-for-like cases.[14] Whilst enforceability and objectivity are key facets underpinning law's authority to act legitimately, people do of course comply with law for other reasons. For example, many comply for normative or moral reasons, including that they perceive the law, and those who make and enforce it, to be legitimate, that it is created and applied through fair processes, and that they agree with the substantive content of the law.[15] However, when the enforceable, and therefore coercive, power of law is evident, that merely serves to reinforce, rather than undermine, its authority. Law can be enforced through the courts, being the organs of the state with the authority to punish, backed up by force. This power gives law a legitimate claim to authority, even where citizens perhaps disagree with the substantive moral content of the law.

In contrast, adult social work's legitimacy is characterised as entirely support-based and as being more subjective in nature.[16] Law is therefore set up in stark contrast to adult social work, which does not possess these same core disciplinary claims. Historically, legitimacy developed as a result of jurisdictional claims of authority and 'scientific and ethical superiority'.[17] Other professions, such as medicine, have a similarly strong claim to possessing authority and legitimacy to that of law. Medical professionals no longer have absolute power to enforce their decisions on patients (notwithstanding some residual power in respect of those who lack capacity). In contrast, support-based professions such as social work, lack that same claim to objectivity and impartiality that law and medicine have long professed they possess.[18] This can be seen in the characterisation of the social work profession, defined as:[19]

> a practice-based profession and an academic discipline that promotes social change and development, social cohesion, and the empowerment and liberation of people …

[12] See HLA Hart, *The Concept of Law* (Oxford, Clarendon Press, 1994); R Dworkin, *Taking Rights Seriously* (Cambridge MA, Harvard University Press 1978); R Dworkin, *Law's Empire* (Cambridge MA, Harvard University Press 1986). For an overview of this topic also see M Freeman, *Lloyd's Introduction to Jurisprudence*, 9th edn (London, Sweet and Maxwell, 2014).

[13] Founded upon foundational arguments made by HLA Hart, ibid.

[14] This is despite challenges from anti-positivists that it is law's moral content that confers legitimacy, for further discussion see Dworkin, *Taking Rights Seriously* (n 12).

[15] TR Tyler, *Why People Obey the Law* (Princeton NJ, Princeton University Press, 2006).

[16] See Lindsey, 'Competing Professional Knowledge Claims' (n 8) for a full justification of the argument that mental capacity law characterises social work as a subjective knowledge claim.

[17] M Thomson, 'Abortion Law and Professional Boundaries' (2013) 22 *Social & Legal Studies* 191, 194.

[18] See the comparison between medical professionals and social work, Lindsey, 'Competing Professional Knowledge Claims' (n 8).

[19] International Federation of Social Workers, *Global Definition of Social Work* (31 July 2014): www.ifsw.org/what-is-social-work/global-definition-of-social-work/ (accessed 5 November 2021).

> social work engages people and structures to address life challenges and enhance wellbeing.

The core elements of social work are that it: is 'person-centred', is 'personally and socially contexted', is 'relationship-oriented', 'follows an integrated process' and is 'values based'.[20] Being person-centred and focusing on empowerment suggests social workers do not have the power of enforcement. They cannot compel service users to act; in fact, attempts to do so would contradict the appropriate role of adult social workers. Adult social workers' actions are most legitimate when they are carried out through support and their legitimacy therefore stems from a fact in stark contrast to this – that their decisions can be challenged. By this I mean that social workers' legitimacy is based on their ability to develop a relationship of trust with their service user, to support them and to only intervene within clear statutory boundaries. Where a social worker is perceived to overstep that role, service users can challenge their decisions and this is central to the legitimacy of social work as a profession. To achieve change, then, social workers engage in an art of discursive persuasion and negotiation, as well as using material pressures to encourage the service user to act in a particular way.[21] Yet 'social work evidence is viewed in more subjective, experiential terms'[22] and social workers' interventions are not based on technical claims of expertise but instead on experiential knowledge and their ability to support a service user in multifaceted ways. It is, I suggest, precisely because social work as a discipline does not easily fit into the same parameters as law, that results in the difficulty for social workers when operating in this area. This was evident in my empirical research. One social worker I spoke to was sensitive to the difficulties that can be caused by this process of 'going to law'. For example, I asked Sarah[23] whether she thought applying to the CoP would give her decisions more authority and she said:

> I think it would help us, in a way and feel more confident that we were backed up by something that was authoritative, and definite and coming from that place. In another way I would worry that we would then have to … we're committed to it and we've got to go with it … there's no way back once we've gone down that road, that's my worry.

[20] C Whittington, 'The Promised Liberation of Adult Social Work under England's 2014 Care Act: Genuine Prospect or False Prospectus?' (2016) 46 *British Journal of Social Work* 1942, 1953.

[21] See P Trevithick, *Social Work Skills: A Practice Handbook*, 2nd edn (London, Open University Press, 2005); C Whittington, 'The Promised Liberation of Adult Social Work under England's 2014 Care Act: Genuine Prospect or False Prospectus?' (2016) 46 *British Journal of Social Work* 1942; A Keeling, '"Organising objects": Adult safeguarding practice and article 16 of the United Nations Convention on the Rights of Persons with Disabilities' (2017) 53 *International Journal of Law and Psychiatry* 77.

[22] Lindsey, 'Competing Professional Knowledge Claims' (n 8), 2.

[23] Sarah: qualified social worker. Experience in an adult safeguarding enquiry team for four years.

This finality of a court decision reinforces its authority. However, a court decision commits the social worker to a particular course of, often coercive, action. In contrast, the interventions of a social worker might be more fluid and changeable, seemingly making them less authoritative and less objective, which in turn is perceived to undermine their legitimacy. This highlights that framing law as the objective enforcer of legal rules also impacts on those professions, such as social work, which lack a similar rhetorical claim to legitimacy.

Given the possible tension between social worker and service user, and the lack of enforceability of social work interventions, it is unsurprising that social workers turn to law to legitimate their proposed interventions. Whilst this resort to law might be disempowering in certain ways, social workers do not always view it that way. In fact, resort to law can be seen as a useful tool where they believe that law can help them to achieve a particular result. This perception was clear from my interviews. For example, David[24] told me: 'There's something to be said about decisions made in court, that people will, you know, respect and maintain it …' Similarly, Robert[25] explained when asked about how he found the court process: 'I think good that the full majesty of the law would be exerted on behalf of vulnerable people …'. Even though social workers are seen to have limited legitimacy to intervene, they do not resort to law reluctantly. The social workers I spoke to were aware of the usefulness of law to legitimate their decisions, deflecting difficult matters away from social work judgement into the jurisdiction of law. For example, talking about his views on the MCA Robert told me that:

> … from a personal view it was just terribly useful to have that framework so that if you did have a discussion … with a parent of a person with a learning disability … and they were saying 'are you telling me that I don't get to make decisions for my son?', it was very nice to have a freshly minted law to say 'no actually you don't.'

Furthermore, in many cases the local authority benefits from referring a case to the CoP. For example, if an individual was making a perceived 'risky' choice to stay within an abusive relationship, the local authority would be better served by having a court authorise their decision not to intervene, because of the risk of harm. However, it means that, in doing so, social workers are reinforcing law's coercive legitimacy and potentially undermining the benefits of support-based, non-coercive interventions.

[24] David: qualified social worker since 2009 with experience of working primarily with older adults with mental health needs.

[25] Robert: qualified social worker. Manager of a learning disability team in a local authority for six years during which time the MCA came into force, and subsequently a manager for a transition social work team for a local authority for 18 months.

B. Duty of Care and Vulnerability in High-risk Cases

Given the contrast between the perceived legitimacy of law and social work, it is in cases of abuse where seeking legal approval through the CoP was most valuable to social workers. This is because they were concerned that they had a 'duty of care' towards the service user and needed to manage the high risks. Yet they felt constrained by the notion of empowerment underpinning the MCA; that is, that the MCA was passed to provide protection for those (inherently) vulnerable adults who were *unable* to make decisions, rather than to allow interventions in relation to *unwise* decisions.[26] This is despite the MCA not specifically encompassing 'vulnerable adults'. The social workers I spoke to said they found this balance challenging and this conflict is too often resolved through prioritising protection through application to the CoP.[27]

The cases where controlling and coercive interventions through the CoP were used in the welfare context[28] were those viewed as 'risky'. This means that the social workers I spoke to were either seeking authorisation for coercive practices from the CoP, or, seeking CoP approval for 'doing nothing'. For example, Sarah, an investigating worker on a safeguarding team, told me about a case she was working on that was her first experience of the CoP. I asked her what it was about this case that made her consider taking it to court, she said:

> I think it was because we just felt that the risks were so high and we were just so worried about her ... We just kinda kept coming back to thinking this is just so, risky, and that we just wouldn't be happy just leaving it, we just couldn't think of a plan that we would be happy with and thinking 'right we've put that in place, ok, we can leave this now' and just think, 'no'. It just needed to go somewhere higher that was above us ...

Not only does she reinforce the perceived legitimacy of the CoP but her comments highlight that concerns about risk were the reason for bringing the case to court. This risk discourse reinforces my finding that welfare interventions in mental capacity law are more likely to be used in cases of abuse.[29] My interviews reinforced the pervasiveness of concerns about 'duty of care' and 'risk' that have

[26] Albeit that some have rightly questioned where this 'empowering ethos' came from given what the MCA actually does is to allow courts to intervene and make decisions on a person's behalf, even against their wishes, see L Series, 'Power and the Mental Capacity Act', *The Small Places* (18 February 2015): www.thesmallplaces.wordpress.com/2015/02/18/power-and-the-mental-capacity-act (accessed 9 December 2020).

[27] E Cave, 'Determining Capacity to Make Medical Treatment Decisions: Problems Implementing the Mental Capacity Act 2005' (2015) 36 *Statute Law Review* 86.

[28] Excluding property and affairs and medical treatment decisions as different considerations apply.

[29] Lindsey, 'Protecting vulnerable adults from abuse' (n 2).

been identified elsewhere.[30] For example, Julia[31] repeatedly explained that she had a duty of care towards her service users, saying:

> We have had situations where people will come in and get the service user to try and sign something but I think the nursing staff are now alerted to the fact they should never let anyone sign anything they, that people coming in without having some – given some thought to whether that person's got capacity, we have got a duty of care …

Similarly, I asked Andrea[32] for her views on supported decision-making. As she had not come across the term I explained it to her and our dialogue is set out below:

> *Interviewer*: So supported decision-making under the MCA is just providing all practicable steps to allow the person to make the decision themselves before substituting a decision, but it can also have an interpretation as meaning only allowing that person to make the decision with support, so never substituting their decision with yours. So there's two different interpretations, so I don't know if you've come across either or neither?
>
> *Andrea*: Well, I've come across the first.
>
> *Interviewer*: Which is providing as much support as you can. How do you find that works in practice?
>
> *Andrea*: Erm, it depends on the person … what they can understand and take on really. Because sometimes it's like you can really work with somebody over an hour or repeated visits to try and get them to understand the information, absorb it, and they may not absorb it then. But if you go several times over that period of time they may be able to absorb that then, and retain it …

Andrea then went on to focus on her concerns about risk and duty of care:

> I feel really strongly about keeping, letting people have autonomy and things but I also deal with lots of risk … Maybe they'd rather die at home and fall down the stairs. It's a real, it's a real dilemma, it's something that I struggle with in certain cases at certain times when people's feelings are really strong; when they're not so strong it tends not to worry you so much … But … people worry then about being negligent don't they, I think that's what you'd worry about, not fulfilling your duty of care and being negligent.

[30] T Jingree, 'Duty of Care, Safety, Normalisation and the Mental Capacity Act: A Discourse Analysis of Staff Arguments about Facilitating Choices for People with Learning Disabilities in UK Services' (2015) 25 *Journal of Community & Applied Social Psychology* 138.

[31] Julia: qualified social worker. Experience as a local authority social worker with families where there was a child with a disability. Her role at time of interview was as a social worker at a secure unit with inpatient and outpatient adults with mental health difficulties.

[32] Andrea: Qualified social worker. Experience working with older adults and people with learning disabilities in three different local authorities. Her role at time of interview and for three years previously was working with people with dementia.

I went on to ask if supported decision-making, in the substantive Article 12 CRPD sense of removing substituted decision-making, would be a big change in mind-set, and she said:

> Yeah it would … because I think you know we've got this duty of care always underlying everything so people don't like to take risks … it's really hard … I try to take risks but there's certain pressures that can be applied at times.

As these comments highlight, it is when others make decisions to abuse or where individuals want to live in a risky environment, that social workers are most concerned about their duty of care. Therefore most concerns in the welfare context relate to the situation that the person finds themselves in rather than being concerns about mental functioning. Sarah also highlighted this when she told me about her challenging case noted earlier. The case concerned a young learning disabled woman in her twenties who was married to a man of a similar age and with similar disabilities. The concern was that, on investigation, it became clear that this woman's husband had been charged with the rape of his sister and step-sister and that he was also being investigated for raping another woman with a learning disability. Sarah was concerned about what might happen if the case went to the CoP. Sarah was concerned that a decision would be enforced that would separate the woman from her husband against her will. Whereas all Sarah wanted to show her service user was that there is 'a life kind of beyond her husband, that there is … there's a better world' and that she could have a different, better life if she had the support to leave him.

Whilst high-risk abuse cases dominate, this is predominantly where the adults in question are 'non-compliant' with social worker advice, rather than *all* high-risk cases. This included cases both where the person was non-compliant and where a family member was non-compliant because they disagreed with the decision. For example, seven of 20 CoP case files reviewed as part of the wider project from which these data are drawn concerned cases where the person at the heart of the decision was non-compliant in that she either challenged the decision or did not agree with it, in five cases the male partner of the person was non-compliant with the local authority decision, in at least two of the forced marriage cases the local authority decision to intervene was based on a concern that parents would take the person abroad for marriage against social work advice, and in two other forced marriage cases the local authority clearly disagreed with the person's own non-compliant behaviour in respect of marriage, describing her actions as 'risky'.[33] Those cases where the person did not have anyone to advocate on her behalf, or where she was compliant, were less likely to have court scrutiny. This is problematic because, in cases of abuse, the motives

[33] For further detail on the cases see J Lindsey, *Protecting and Empowering Vulnerable Adults: Mental Capacity Law in Practice* (PhD Thesis 2018): https://etheses.bham.ac.uk/id/eprint/8527/ (accessed 9 December 2020).

of those who challenge the local authority should be questioned, particularly if they are the abusive party. Therefore if a challenge by the abuser is the primary reason that such cases are reaching court, this should be of concern because it means that the adult is in a no-win situation; she is faced with possible control by the court or control by the abuser.

In high-risk cases, social workers respond to their own lack of legitimacy by resorting to the CoP. This is reflected in case law too, with a number of decisions involving the CoP authorising coercive practices against the expressed wishes of the person and at the request of professionals such as social workers.[34] Of course, the CoP is not only, or even predominantly, coercive in its judgments. There are many cases, particularly in the High Court, where judicial scrutiny of the issues works to provide best interests authorisation for 'risky' but desired activities on the part of the person,[35] or in some cases even to find that the person has capacity to make the decision themselves, thereby upholding their autonomy.[36] When social workers 'go to law' though, they 'trade in' some of their legitimacy and in return are shielded from having to make the final decision in what they perceive to be the most challenging cases. In seeking legal legitimation, social workers' decisions are protected and reinforced whilst enabling them to deflect responsibility for any resulting coercion on to the law. However, in doing so, social workers participate in the acceptance of coercive and controlling interventions against vulnerable adults. Yet the value of social work is precisely in its holistic and supportive approach. Therefore, by participating in this process, the value of social work may be further undermined as social workers reinforce the legitimacy of the court-enforced, 'objective' intervention over more 'subjective' support-based approaches.

[34] See Lindsey, 'Protecting vulnerable adults from abuse' (2020) (n 2) for justification of this argument. In addition, see the following broad selection of cases across the spectrum of health and welfare decision-making. Of these, although in some cases I would agree that the outcome may well have been the right one on the facts, all highlight the coercive nature of the law in this area, in that they compel or prevent the person from doing something that they may otherwise wish to pursue in the absence of court intervention: *London Borough of Tower Hamlets v TB and SA* [2014] EWCOP 53; *Re AG* [2015] EWCOP 78; *Re CA* [2016] EWCOP 47; *Southend on Sea Borough Council v Meyers* [2019] EWHC 399 (Fam); *A Local Authority v JB* [2020] EWCA Civ 735.

[35] See, for example, *Re GC* [2008] EWHC 3402 (Fam) and *Wye Valley NHS Trust v B* [2015] EWCOP 60, as well as a number of cases arising from the Covid-19 pandemic where individuals who lacked capacity were permitted to return home or see loved ones where local authorities or other institutions might otherwise have been reluctant to permit such contact: *BP v Surrey County Council & RP* [2020] EWCOP 20 and *VE v AO, The Royal borough of Greenwich and South East London CCG* [2020] EWCOP 23, *Michelle Davies (by her Litigation Friend John Davies) v Wigan Council and NHS Wigan Clinical Commissioning Group* [2020] EWCOP 60.

[36] See, for example, *WBC v Z* [2016] EWCOP 4 and *Re CH (by his Litigation Friend, the Official Solicitor) v A Metropolitan Council* [2017] EWCOP 12. For an important overview of case law relating to capacity disputes see A Ruck Keene, NB Kane, SYH Kim and GS Owen, 'Taking capacity seriously? Ten years of mental capacity disputes before England's Court of Protection' (2019) 62 *International Journal of Law and Psychiatry* 56.

III. SAFEGUARDING AND SUPPORT FOR DECISION-MAKING WITH AT RISK ADULTS

Having identified the problem of social workers requiring legal legitimation of their decisions, I now turn to how the English safeguarding adults' legal framework could be improved. I argue that a new framework is necessary to limit coercive interventions authorised by mental capacity law and to empower social workers to intervene through support. I have argued elsewhere for there to be greater use of interventions which restrict perpetrators of abuse.[37] Similarly, a support-based safeguarding framework would assist in deflecting attention away from mental capacity law because social workers could have the authority to intervene without the wide-ranging interventions that result from findings of incapacity. I suggest that any amended safeguarding framework should be guided by five core principles: support; accountability; applicable to all; partnership working; and proportionate harm.[38]

A. The Provision of Support

The first principle that must underpin any change is a focus on support. The need to support decision-making is enshrined in Article 12 of the CRPD and it is now widely accepted that support should be a cornerstone principle.[39] However, what this means and how it should be implemented in practice are still subject to debate.[40] There are, for example, disagreements about the extent to

[37] Lindsey, 'Protecting vulnerable adults from abuse' (n 2), and 'Developing Vulnerability' (n 5).

[38] These criteria are different from but influenced by those set out in C Mackenzie, 'The Importance of Relational Autonomy and Capabilities for an Ethics of Vulnerability' in C Mackenzie, W Rogers, W and S Dodds (eds), *Vulnerability: New Essays in Ethics and Feminist Philosophy* (Oxford, Oxford University Press, 2014). The criteria also take into account the principles set out in similar Scottish legislation, see Adult Support and Protection (Scotland) Act 2007 s 1 which states: 'The general principle on intervention in an adult's affairs is that a person may intervene, or authorise an intervention, only if satisfied that the intervention – (a) will provide benefit to the adult which could not reasonably be provided without intervening in the adult's affairs, and (b) is, of the range of options likely to fulfil the object of the intervention, the least restrictive to the adult's freedom.' However, the principles I set out here are narrower and focused on responding to abuse rather than incorporating what is, essentially, a proportionality approach which risks overriding the wishes of the adult and coercing him/her in cases where the risks are sufficiently high.

[39] P Gooding, 'Supported Decision-Making: A Rights-Based Disability Concept and its Implications for Mental Health Law' (2013) 20 *Psychiatry, Psychology and Law* 431; E Flynn and A Arstein-Kerslake, 'Legislating personhood: realising the right to support in exercising legal capacity' (2014) 10 *International Journal of Law in Context* 81; P Bartlett and M Schulze, 'Urgently awaiting implementation: The right to be free from exploitation, violence and abuse in Article 16 of the Convention on the Rights of Persons with Disabilities (CRPD)' (2017) 53 *International Journal of Law and Psychiatry* 2; R Harding and E Tascioglu, *Everyday decisions project report: supporting legal capacity through care, support and empowerment* (University of Birmingham, 2019): http://epapers.bham.ac.uk/3067/1/Everyday_Decisions_Project_Report.pdf.

[40] A Dhanda, 'Legal Capacity in the Disability Rights Convention: Stranglehold of the Past or Lodestar for the Future?' (2006) 34 *Syracuse Journal of International Law and Commerce* 429; P Bartlett, 'The United Nations Convention on the Rights of Persons with Disabilities and Mental

which supported decision-making should replace substituted decision-making, something which others in this collection have similarly sought to consider. This debate becomes most complicated when thinking about 'risky' decisions, with the safeguarding domain considered to be the most challenging in which to fully implement supported decision-making. I argue that the provision of support for *all* decisions in relation to vulnerable adults is key, irrespective of whether that adult is ultimately found to lack the capacity to make a decision for themselves. That is not to say that the MCA ought to be repealed or is irrelevant; rather, that where safeguarding is the primary concern, then supported decision-making ought to be at the forefront of adult safeguarding practice.

As Peter Bartlett and Marianne Schulze have emphasised, the focus on Article 12 has meant that discussions about Article 16 CRPD, the right to be free from exploitation, violence and abuse, have been less developed.[41] They suggest, however, that Article 16 could be interpreted alongside other provisions to require that adults with disabilities are protected from abuse through *positive steps*. An important question therefore is *how* states take these positive steps to respond to abuse. Bartlett and Schulze argue that the CRPD not only requires an equality of approach between disabled people and others or an approach of non-interference, but that it could require giving *more protection* to people with disabilities who suffer abuse. However, the manner of that protection is key. Reading Article 16 alongside Article 12 means recognising that protection from abuse can also be achieved through supporting and empowering disabled adults to make their own decisions. A protection imperative enacted without support can lead to a return to over-protection.

A corollary of the focus on support is the need for social workers to be protected when taking risky decisions to support vulnerable adults where safeguarding concerns arise. This means that prioritising support means prioritising it in *all* cases, not solely in cases where the adult is making a seemingly 'wise' decision. This would be beneficial because of the real concern among social workers about their perceived 'duty of care'. This is a central reason why social workers are reluctant to place adults at the heart of safeguarding investigations and instead try to persuade them about a particular course of action.[42] One way that social workers can be legitimated to pursue support is through legal protection for social workers (and potentially others) who allow 'risky' decisions to be taken *where the adult has capacity to make those decisions*. There are, of course, risks in providing legal protection for social workers here; it could provide a justification for cash-strapped local authorities to withdraw support

Health Law' (2012) 75 *Modern Law Review* 752; Flynn and Arstein-Kerslake, 'Legislating personhood' (n 39); Harding and Tascioglu, *Everyday decisions project report* (n 39); Keeling, '"Organising objects"' (n 21).

[41] Bartlett and Schulze, 'Urgently awaiting implementation' (n 39).

[42] Keeling, '"Organising objects"' (n 21).

altogether on the basis of individual choice. However, this will partly depend on the framing of the protection as well as the overall substance of the safeguarding framework. That is why I frame this protection as a corollary of the provision of support. The two only work together and cannot be separated without serious risk of leaving vulnerable adults unprotected.

B. Accountability

If social workers are to be protected when taking decisions to support, particularly decisions in the most high-risk cases, then accountability for those decisions is also fundamentally important. The decision-making processes of local authorities, and more specifically actions or omissions of individual social workers need to be subject to scrutiny. There are various mechanisms through which effective accountability can be achieved. I suggest here that a combination of professional ethics and legal review would be an appropriate starting point.

First, accountability can be promoted through rigorous professional ethics standards, which hold professions to a higher standard than the civil law. Placing ethics at the heart of social work may therefore be more effective in improving safeguarding practice than the resort to law. Jonathan Montgomery makes a similar argument in relation to medicine.[43] He emphasises the value of professional ethics to healthcare practice in contrast to what he described as the 'amoral commitment to choice and consumerism' facilitated by legal activity.[44] Professional ethics therefore has an important role to play in maintaining standards. Regulation of social work has recently undergone a period of transition and Social Work England, the new regulator, has developed new professional standards for social work. Those standards include social work accountability for the quality of practice and decisions made by social workers, as well as requiring social workers to work within legal and ethical frameworks.[45] Promoting ethical practice in social work is especially important if social workers are to be given greater legitimacy to intervene, and ensuring this accountability through ethics, rather than law, has been an important step forward in the context of other care professions.[46]

There is, however, a role for law in ensuring social work accountability, particularly if social workers are given greater authority to allow risky decision-making.

[43] J Montgomery, 'Law and the Demoralisation of Medicine' (2006) 26 *Legal Studies* 185.

[44] Ibid, 186.

[45] See Social Work England (2019), *Professional Standards*: www.socialworkengland.org.uk/media/1640/1227_socialworkengland_standards_prof_standards_final-aw.pdf (accessed 9 December 2020).

[46] Such as medicine, see Montgomery, 'Law and the Demoralisation of Medicine' (n 43).

In this instance, additional review mechanisms may be warranted to ensure a public perception of fairness and accountability.[47] One suggestion in the CoP context has been incorporating a clear review mechanism for cases where the person at the centre disagrees with a decision.[48] A similar review mechanism could be contained within the amended safeguarding provisions such that the person affected by the decision has a clear route to challenge it. This level of review would require an independent body and one option would be to make it part of the role of Safeguarding Adults Boards (SABs), created under the Care Act 2014 section 43. They may be well placed to make such decisions given their statutory function to protect adults in their area, albeit their lack of independence from local authorities may be a concern.[49] Of course, this power of review would work most effectively where positive action was taken to intervene in a person's life (even in a non-coercive way). However, where a social worker takes a decision to support a risky decision, it should be possible for interested others within the vulnerable adult's life to also request a review under the safeguarding framework. Overall, rigorous professional accountability for social workers will be a central part of any amended safeguarding legislation if there is to be an expansion of powers for social workers or legal protection for them where they support risky decision-making.

C. Applicable to All

I have argued elsewhere that there is a need for safeguarding laws to apply to all, effectively arguing for a removal of the requirement for support needs as is currently required under the Care Act.[50] A non-discriminatory framework focused on safeguarding *all adults* vulnerable to abuse is likely to be more sensitive to the range of factors that make a person vulnerable. As Beverley Clough explains, the MCA creates a 'stark dividing line between those who have a cognitive impairment, who can thus be capable of being deemed to lack capacity, and those without a cognitive impairment, who cannot'.[51] This sharp distinction can lead to over-protection of those who have particular disabilities and under-protection of those who are seen as choosing to put themselves at risk, such as women in situations of domestic abuse with an intimate partner. A non-discriminatory framework would provide the opportunity for a more nuanced

[47] D Platt, 'Care or Control? The Effects of Investigations and Initial Assessments on the Social Worker–Parent Relationship' (2008) 22 *Journal of Social Work Practice* 301, 304.

[48] L Series, P Fennell, J Doughty and A Mercer, *Welfare Cases in the Court of Protection: A Statistical Overview* (Cardiff, Cardiff University, 2017): www.sites.cardiff.ac.uk/wccop/new-research-an-overview-of-welfare-cases-in-the-court-of-protection/ (accessed 9 December 2020).

[49] Sch 2, Care Act 2014.

[50] Lindsey, 'Developing Vulnerability' (n 5).

[51] Ibid, 476.

response to these issues which actually focuses on the situation and the facts that give rise to the safeguarding concern.

To some extent this is already the case, for example, the Care Act section 42(1)(a), makes clear that the safeguarding provisions apply even to those adults who are not receiving local authority support. Unlike the MCA therefore, the safeguarding provisions do not state that an impairment or disability is required for the safeguarding duty to be triggered. I do not suggest here that the MCA should be repealed or amended in this regard, although I do have some sympathy with that argument. My argument is, instead, that the safeguarding framework ought to be focused on protecting people who, for whatever reasons, are not in a position to be able to protect themselves. The Care Act currently frames this as related to support needs, but actually, there may be a much wider range of reasons as to why a person is unable to protect themselves. This would be an important way of encompassing those who might be vulnerable as a result of their disability, but it would not restrict safeguarding to that group.

D. Partnership Working

Safeguarding processes must also be carried out in partnership with the person, taking into account their experiences and wishes, rather than as 'organising objects'.[52] Failing to hear and take into account the wishes and needs of the individual is less likely to result in a successful outcome, whatever the intervention. Furthermore, there is intrinsic value in involving the person; they are valued as an individual and are encouraged to develop the capacity to make decisions about their future based on their own values. This is, to some extent, captured in the approach known as 'making safeguarding personal'.[53] However, this rhetoric needs to be strengthened within the legal framework to ensure the individual is *always* consulted and involved at every stage about decisions which will affect them. Explicitly enshrining this principle in law strengthens the discursive pressure on local authorities to translate that into their practice and strengthens social work legitimacy if they are formulating interventions in cooperation with the adult.

[52] Keeling, '"Organising objects"' (n 21).

[53] Making safeguarding personal is a Local Government Association initiative which brings together various local authorities to agree on an approach which, in essence, ensures that safeguarding is done with the person rather than following a procedural approach. See Association of Directors of Adult Social Services, *Making Safeguarding Personal* (ADASS/Local Government Association, 2017): www.adass.org.uk/making-safeguarding-personal-publications (accessed 9 December 2020).

E. No More Harm than the Adult was Already Living With

Finally, the principle that any safeguarding intervention should not result in more harm in the adult's life than they were living with before the intervention must be maintained. This is important because many of the CoP interventions noted earlier in this chapter would not fulfil this test. Protecting the person by removing them from their home and restricting their liberty could be seen as putting them at greater risk and does little to empower them as a decision-maker. State intervention can create further harm and is something we must avoid in reforming the law.[54] For example, in *In re A (Capacity: Refusal of Contraception)*[55] the High Court held that whilst it was in Mrs A's best interests to receive contraception, it should not be forced on her without her consent. Not only would this undermine her autonomy but a forcible intervention against her wishes may actually have created more harm than the intervention was designed to protect her from, for example by having to use restraint or causing distrust of, and disengagement from, healthcare professionals. Of course, calculating and weighing harms will, in some cases, be challenging in practice. However, a similar approach is already taken in mental capacity law when, for example, weighing a person's best interests.[56] Evaluating harms in a person's life is not intended to be an exact scientific measurement; rather, the requirement works to force social workers and other decision-makers to consider the nature of the intervention that they are putting forward and to carefully balance it against existing, and future, risks of harm.

IV. CONCLUSION

In this chapter I have highlighted that where social workers refer welfare cases to the CoP, this can result in controlling interventions that protect the adult at risk of abuse, but it is a form of legal coercion rather than support. This is, perhaps, understandable in high-risk cases of abuse where social workers feel caught between their duty of care to protect and wanting to empower the vulnerable adult. However, it is likely further exacerbated by social workers' limited legitimacy to intervene in supportive ways which may lack the enforceability and apparent objectivity of law's legitimacy. In light of the difficulties with resorting to legal coercion, I have argued that social workers need the legitimacy to intervene in more supportive ways, protected and backed up by adult

[54] Lindsey, 'Developing Vulnerability' (n 5).

[55] *In re A (Capacity: Refusal of Contraception)* [2010] EWHC 1549.

[56] C Kong, J Coggon, M Dunn and A Ruck Keene, 'An Aide Memoire for a Balancing Act? Critiquing the 'Balance Sheet' Approach to Best Interests Decision-Making' (2020) 28(4) *Medical Law Review* 753.

safeguarding legal frameworks. In the second half of the chapter I suggested that this could be achieved through stronger safeguarding provisions, guided by five core principles. The aim of this change would be to facilitate a move away from the MCA and to provide social workers with the protection and legitimacy to support 'risky' decision-making. Whilst the interaction of the MCA and Care Act undoubtedly provides local authorities with some flexibility and provides court authorisation to legitimate decisions in what are no doubt challenging social work cases, resorting to law can also control vulnerable victims of abuse without empowering social workers to intervene through support-based responses.

15

Putting the Pieces Together: Article 12, 'Safeguarding' and the Right to Legal Capacity

MARGARET ISABEL HALL

I. INTRODUCTION

KOFI ANNAN, THEN Secretary General of the United Nations, described the UN Convention on the Rights of Persons with Disabilities[1] (CRPD) as 'a remarkable and forward looking document' heralding the 'dawn of a new era – an era in which disabled people will no longer have to endure the discriminatory practices and attitudes that have been permitted to prevail for too long.'[2] More than 15 years later this new era has yet to be fully realised. The interpretation and implementation of Article 12 of the CRPD – 'Equal recognition before the law' – remains a point of particular controversy and debate.[3] On one side of this debate, concerns have been raised that removing the current mental capacity-based limits on the exercise of legal capacity would expose persons with mental disabilities to unjust hardship. The persistence of these concerns has hindered the full implementation of the CRPD, as reflected in Canada's ratification with the reservation that Canada may continue to use substitute decision-making even if Article 12 is interpreted as requiring its elimination.[4] On the other side of the debate, proponents of Article 12 have emphasised the harms flowing from mental capacity-based discrimination,

[1] GA Res 61/106 UN Document A/RES/61/106 (6 December 2006).

[2] A Lawson 'The United Nations Convention on Persons With Disabilities: New Era or False Dawn?' (2006–2007) 34(2) *Syracuse Journal of International Law & Commerce* 563.

[3] See, C de Bhalis and E Flynn, 'Recognising legal capacity: Commentary and analysis of Article 12 CRPD' (2017) 13(1) *International Journal of Law in Context* 6.

[4] Canada's declaration and reservations. [Accessed April 2021]: https://treaties.un.org/Pages/ViewDetails.aspx?src=TREATY&mtdsg_no=IV-15&chapter=4&clang=_en#EndDec; see, N Cavaino, 'Conceptualizing capacity: interpreting Canada's qualified ratification of Article 12 of the UN Disability Rights Convention' (2014) 4(1) *Western Journal of Legal Studies* 1.

advocating for supported decision-making as a means of enabling all persons to exercise legal capacity or for the stronger position that legal capacity should be exercised on the basis of the person's will and preferences.[5]

For critics of Article 12, the exercise of legal capacity by a person who cannot understand the nature and consequences of that exercise unfairly exposes that individual to financial, emotional, and physical harm, sacrificing the person's embodied well-being on the altar of an abstract ideal of equality. Melvyn Freeman and others have argued that legal capacity without mental capacity would effectively 'violate' other rights 'expressed and asserted' in the CRPD, including the right to enjoyment of the highest attainable standard of health, the right to liberty, and the right to justice.[6] The combination of limited comprehension, the inability to perceive and defend one's own interests, and the ability to freely transfer assets and provide other forms of material or physical benefit through the exercise of legal capacity would also create an irresistible target for predators. That targeting in and of itself enhances the risk of oppression and manipulation, separate and apart from any cognitive limitations experienced by the person who is targeted. Law's role in enforcing consequences flowing from the exercise of legal capacity also engages the broader social interest long protected by equity – that the law will not allow itself to be used as a tool for wrongdoing. Article 12's critics have not been persuaded that supported decision-making provides an adequate replacement for the protection provided through mental capacity-based limits on the exercise of legal capacity in all circumstances.[7] Other issues of concern include the sometimes murky line in practice between support, undue influence, and substitute decision-making,[8] and the impact of Article 12 on criminal

[5] J Craigie, 'Against a singular understanding of legal capacity: Criminal Responsibility and the Convention on the Rights of Persons With Disabilities' (2015) 40 *International Journal of Law and Psychiatry* 6 doi: 10.1016/j.ijlp.2015.04.002 citing M Bach and L Kerzner, *A New Paradigm for Protecting Autonomy and the Right to Legal Capacity* (Ontario, Law Commission of Ontario, October 2010): www.lco-cdo.org/wp-content/uploads/2010/11/disabilities-commissioned-paper-bach-kerzner.pdf; G Richardson, 'Mental disabilities and the law: From substitute to supported decision-making?' (2012) 65 *Current Legal Problems* 333.

[6] MC Freeman et al, 'Reversing Hard Won Victories in the Name of Human Rights: A Critique of the General Comment on Article 12 of the UN Convention on the Rights of Persons with Disabilities' (2015) 2(9) *Lancet Psychiatry* 844 at 845; J Dawson, 'A Realistic Approach to Assessing Mental Health law Compliance with the CRPD' (2015) 40 *International Journal of Law and Psychiatry* 70. See also George Szmukler, 'UN CRPD: Equal Recognition Before the Law' (2015) 2(11) *Lancet Psychiatry* 29; R Kayess and P French, 'Out of Darkness and into Light? Introducing the *Convention on the Rights of Persons with Disabilities*' (2008) 8(1) *Human Rights Law Review* 1; C Kong, 'The Convention for the Rights of Persons with Disabilities and Article 12: Prospective Feminist Lessons Against the Will and Preferences Paradigm' (2015) 4 *Laws* 709.

[7] M Dufour, T Hastings and R O'Reilly, 'Canada should retain its reservation on the UN Convention on the Rights of Persons With Disabilities' (2018) 63(12) *The Canadian Journal of Psychiatry* 809.

[8] R Gordon, 'The Emergence of Assisted (Supported) Decision-Making in the Canadian Law of Adult Guardianship and Substitute Decision-Making' (2000) 23(1) *International Journal of Law & Psychiatry* 61; T Carney, *Guardianship, Citizenship, & Theorizing Substitute-decisionmaking Law* (Sydney Law School Research Paper No 12/25 (2012), Legal Studies Research Paper Series).

law defences relating to mental disability like the defence of not criminally responsible by reason of mental disorder.[9]

On the other side of the debate, proponents of Article 12 note the significant risks and harms created by mental capacity-based limitations on the exercise of legal capacity.[10] Where persons are forced to depend on others as substitute decision-makers to exercise legal capacity on their behalf, the potential for that authority to be misused is significant.[11] Substitute decision-makers may use their authority in a way that respects and is consistent with the person's values and wishes, but they also may not (regardless of legislative direction); decision-making about how legal capacity will be exercised by the substitute almost always happens in private. Substitute decision-making has the further effect of stunting the individual's decision-making skills in relation to matters requiring the exercise of legal capacity. Nina Kohn, Jeremy Blumenthal and Amy Campbell have noted the potentially devastating consequences of this for persons with intellectual disabilities, in particular, on the death of a parent-guardian appointed during the person's youth.[12] Where a person cannot exercise legal capacity her or himself and *no* substitute decision-maker is appointed, legal capacity cannot be exercised at all in relation to the person except where provided for specifically in legislation.[13] In relation to certain exercises of legal capacity in Canada, including will-making and marriage, legal capacity cannot be exercised by a substitute, only by the person as long as they are capable of doing so. Perhaps most fundamentally, as asserted by the Committee on the Rights of Persons with Disabilities and others, the 'threshold' concept of mental capacity, which divides those able to exercise legal capacity from those who cannot, is irredeemably compromised:[14] 'highly controversial' and 'not, as is commonly presented, an objective, scientific and naturally occurring phenomenon' but 'contingent on social and political contexts, as are the disciplines, professions and practices which play a dominant role in

[9] Dufour, Hastings and O'Reilly, 'Canada should retain its reservation' (n 7).

[10] NA Kohn, JA Blumenthal and AT Campbell, 'Supported Decision-Making: A Viable Alternative to Guardianship' (2013) 117(4) *Penn State Law Review* 1111 at 1113, 1117–20. See also, L Harmon, 'Falling Off the Vine: Legal Fictions and the Doctrine of Substituted Judgment' (1990) 100(1) *Yale Law Journal* 1; K Booth Glen, 'Changing Paradigms: Mental Capacity, Legal Capacity Guardianship, and Beyond' (2012) 44(1) *Columbia Human Rights Law Review* 93; Bach and Kerzner, *A New Paradigm* (n 5).

[11] See, K Purser, T Cockburn, C Cross and H Jacmon, 'Alleged Financial Abuse of Those Under an Enduring Power of Attorney: An Exploratory Study' (2018) 48(4) *British Journal of Social Work* 887.

[12] Kohn, Blumenthal and Campbell, 'Supported Decision-Making' (n 10).

[13] See *Health Care (Consent) and Care Facility (Admission) Act* RSBC1996 c. 181, s 12 ('Exception – urgent or emergency health care').

[14] MI Hall, 'Mental Capacity in the (Civil) Law: Capacity, Autonomy and Vulnerability' (2012) 58(1) *McGill Law Journal* 1.

assessing mental capacity.'[15] That subjectivity, together with the relationship between mental capacity and mental disability (as discussed below), increases the likelihood the person with a mental disability being found to be incapable of making the decision in question, compounding the discriminatory effect.

The points raised on both sides of this debate are valid, and none can be easily dismissed. This is why the debate has remained intractable, a deadlock in which one side insists on non-interference with the exercise of legal capacity (achieved through supported decision-making) while the other insists on the unjust consequences of doing so. The purpose of this chapter is to try breaking that deadlock with a new tool – the relatively over-looked Article 12, paragraph 4 (the 'safeguarding provision'). An interpretation of paragraph 4 as calling for 'special' safeguards limiting the legal capacity of persons with mental disabilities is clearly incompatible with the overarching objective of Article 12 and of the CRPD itself. An interpretation of paragraph 4 safeguards as enforcing the unlimited expression of will and preference through the exercise of legal capacity is equally (though less obviously) out of step with the enjoyment of legal capacity on an equal basis with others guaranteed by Article 12 paragraph 2. Safeguards for the exercise of legal capacity by 'capable' persons have long been part of Anglo-Canadian law, located in rules and doctrines of the common law and equity. These safeguards are concerned with the genuine-ness of the person's exercise of legal capacity; whether the legal capacity exercised is a genuine expression of that person's autonomy. Persons lacking the 'mental capacity' required for a particular exercise of legal capacity have been excluded from the ambit of these traditional safeguards. The question of whether a person's consent is vitiated by undue influence or duress, or whether a transaction is unconscionable (and so unenforceable), will not be considered where the person has been legally constructed as mentally incapable of the legal capacity exercise in question; the mental incapacity 'finding' precludes these questions. The genuine-ness of that person's non-decision or mere choice will be legally irrelevant once the mental incapacity finding (precluding the exercise of legal capacity full stop) has been made.

Because these traditional safeguards have been created, interpreted and applied with 'capable' persons only in mind they require focused development to

[15] CRPD, *General Comment No 1 (2014) Article 12: Equal recognition before the law*, 11th Session, adopted 11 April 2014, UN Doc CRPD/C/GC/1, para 14: https://documents-dds-ny.un.org/doc/UNDOC/GEN/G14/031/20/PDF/G1403120.pdf?OpenElement. The General Comment provides an 'authoritative, if not binding interpretation'; See W Martin et al, 'Achieving CRPD Compliance: Is the Mental Capacity Act of England and Wales Compatible with the UN Convention on the Rights of Persons with Disabilities? If Not, What Next?' (2015) Report Submitted to the UK Ministry of Justice: http://repository.essex.ac.uk/13624/1/EAP-Position-Paper-FINAL-copy.pdf.

become more inclusive of all persons, including persons with mental disabilities. Inclusive development requires, in turn,

> recognition of [the person's] actual characteristics … reasonable accommodation of those characteristics … and the fine-tun[ing] of society so that its structures and assumptions do not result in the relegation and banishment of disabled persons from participation, which results in discrimination against them.[16]

The ultimate purpose of this 'fine-tuning' is an 'increasing *sensitivity*, increasing responsiveness to the needs of a larger and larger variety of people and things', defined by the philosopher Richard Rorty as 'moral progress.'[17]

Examining safeguards in relation to the exercise of legal capacity requires, as a preliminary step, an examination of the underlying concepts of mental and legal capacity, including their relationship to one another and to mental disability. Article 12 is concerned with the exercise of legal capacity rather than decision-making per se: although 'decision-making' is one essential aspect of that exercise, the concepts are not synonymous.

II. MENTAL CAPACITY, MENTAL DISABILITY, AND THE EXERCISE OF LEGAL CAPACITY

The concept of mental capacity in law (as opposed to medicine, social work, or other contexts) refers to an individual's cognitive ability to carry out the mental processes of decision-making; accordingly, a person may be considered mentally capable of making one kind of relatively simple decision, but not a decision about a different, more complex matter.[18] The law has traditionally treated the decision to marry as a relatively simple decision, for example, and a person may be considered mentally capable of deciding to marry but not capable of carrying out the more complex decision-making process required for will-making. The use of mental capacity as synonymous with decision-making ability, capability and competence is therefore consistent both with legal usage and with general or everyday usage[19] and is used here in that sense.

A finding of impaired mental capacity means that the person has been assessed as unable to make the decision or class of decisions in question. That assessment may be carried out by a physician (eg, to determine the person's capacity to consent to a medical procedure), or by a legal gatekeeper (eg, before executing a will), depending on the purpose for which mental capacity is being assessed. A decision, within this conceptual framework, is distinguished from a

[16] *Eaton v Brant County Board of Education*, [1997] 1 SCR 241, para 67.

[17] R Rorty, *Philosophy and Social Hope* (London, Penguin Books, 1999), 81.

[18] MI Hall, 'Situating dementia in the experience of old age: reconstructing legal response' (2019) 66 *International Journal of Law and Psychiatry* Article 101468.

[19] See A Buchanan, 'Mental Capacity, Legal Competence and Consent to Treatment' (2004) 97(9) *Journal of Royal Society of Medicine* 415 at 415.

mere choice. The latter is an expression of the individual's preference in favour of one alternative over another, together with the desire to actualise that alternative: to prefer living in Blackacre rather than Yellowacre, for example, and to desire *making that happen*. A decision, in contrast, is produced through a process of deliberation involving the following steps: understanding the matter in question; understanding the availability of different choices about that matter; foreseeing the consequences of making one choice rather than another; deliberating between those choices and their potential outcomes; and deciding (on the basis of that deliberation) to adopt one course of action rather than another as one's own. A choice always forms the basis for a decision (and remains part of it), but it will remain a *mere* choice unless the deliberative mental steps required of decision-making are also carried out (requiring, in turn, the cognitive ability or mental capacity to carry out those steps).

This legal idea of impaired mental capacity is not synonymous with mental disability. A person with a mental disability may nevertheless be considered mentally capable of making the particular decision in question, especially a low threshold decision such as marriage. Unless the mental capacity impairment is temporary (for example as a result of delirium) however, mental disability and mental capacity will always be inextricably intertwined. Mental disability refers to the identified *cause* (like intellectual disability, mental illness, or dementia) of a person's disordered or non-normal performance of thinking processes and is less a legal than a medical concern (eg for determining what treatment, if any, will be appropriate). Impaired mental capacity, in contrast, refers to one particular *effect* of mental disability – the inability to make a certain kind or class of decisions. A person may be assessed as able to make many or even all decisions despite having a mental disability, therefore, but impaired mental capacity that is not temporary will always be traceable to one mental disability or another (as providing the cause of that impaired capacity). Mental capacity-based discrimination comprises a form of disability-based discrimination by virtue of this connection.

Mental capacity has traditionally been a requirement for the exercise of legal capacity. Legal capacity confers the authority (and therefore the ability) to *use* the law, to carry out legal acts with legally enforceable consequences, and to consent to activities that would otherwise be illegal. Legal capacity is the instrument and mechanism through which the status of legal personhood is effected; Article 12's affirmation of legal personhood in paragraph 1 would be rhetorical only without the recognition that 'persons with disabilities enjoy legal capacity on an equal basis with others', in paragraph 2. Examples of actions requiring the exercise of legal capacity include getting married, making a will, appointing a power of attorney, selling property, defending one's self in court and bringing a legal action against another. Where legal gatekeepers involved in these acts suspect the person is not mentally capable of making the necessary decisions about them, they have a responsibility not to allow or enable the person's exercise of legal capacity. The lawyer preparing a will, or the justice of the peace officiating a marriage, should not proceed where she or he believes that the person does not have the mental capacity required for the exercise of legal capacity in question. If it is subsequently discovered that the person was not mentally capable but purported to exercise legal capacity, the act in question will be treated as void – neither recognised nor enforceable by law.

Consent to health treatment is a legal act (requiring legal capacity) because it works to legalise an interference which would otherwise be prohibited by the law of tort as a trespass to the person or battery. The medical gatekeeper in this context is charged with ensuring that the person is mentally capable of giving that consent, and therefore able to exercise their legal capacity by giving it. Once carried out, of course, medical treatment cannot be rescinded or treated as void, but the person will be entitled to damages for the battery (including any harms flowing from the battery). Consent to sexual activity functions in a similar way within the law of tort and within criminal law, authorising an interference with the body that would otherwise be illegal. The circumstances under which that consent is obtained in the medical and sexual contexts will of course be very different from one another but the underlying principle, including the intersection between mental and legal capacity, is the same.

The requirement of intent in the context of criminal law does not involve the exercise of legal capacity in this sense and, as a matter of textual interpretation, it would not appear to fall within the scope of Article 12 (although it has been interpreted otherwise).[20] Intent is a requirement for criminal responsibility, and a person may be found not to have the intent required for a particular crime for a number of reasons (including limited comprehension and understanding associated with mental disability).[21] The formulation of intent is not an exercise of legal capacity.

The exercise of legal capacity is both a powerful point of autonomous practice and a point of risk for all persons. By exercising their legal capacity to marry, for example, the individual assumes significant emotional and financial risks with potentially devastating long-term and legally enforcable consequences. At the same time, marrying is recognised as a significant and highly meaningful point of autonomous self-direction and personal enrichment. Buying a property or entering a contract are, similarly, points of both risk and (through the exercise of autonomy) opportunity and self-realisation: the house may be riddled with termites, the contract may prove to be a bad deal. The fact that these consequences are unwanted does not change the enforceability of the legal transaction (enabled through the exercise of legal capacity) in question. A person may later regret the decision to have surgery, or to engage in sexual relations with a particular individual, but so long as she or he was mentally capable

[20] See P Bartlett, 'The United Nations Convention on the Rights of Persons with Disabilities and Mental Health Law' (2012) 75(5) *Modern Law Review* 752.

[21] Craigie, 'Against a singular understanding of legal capacity' (n 5).

of giving consent the subsequent experience of regret is legally irrelevant. The risks inherent in the exercise of legal capacity can never be eliminated entirely, but the rules, processes and structures around the exercise of legal capacity by capable persons are meant to balance those risks with the autonomy interest engaged.

Life includes myriad other choice-based actions – what diet to follow, whether to move in with a friend – which generally do not engage the question of legal capacity at all.[22] So long as one is considered mentally capable of making them, these personal choices are characterised as private and outside of the law's concern, part of the vicissitudes of life. Nobody asks whether I have the mental capacity to plant a vegetable garden, for example, and I do not need to exercise legal capacity in order to do so. The effect of guardianship legislation and other kinds of substitute decision-making legislation for 'personal decisions' in Canada[23] is to re-characterise otherwise private choices as matters requiring mental capacity (bearing in mind that some personal choices also have legal dimensions such as entering into a tenancy agreement or mortgage) and to empower *other persons* to exercise legal capacity in relation to them.

This transformation of private non-legal matters into legal ones, subsequently locating legal capacity relating to those matters in another person (like a guardian), is an especially egregious instance of mental capacity-based discrimination, enabling an open-ended prospective interference with otherwise private decisions. It is nevertheless important to recognise the reasons why this particular kind of interference with legal capacity has been considered warranted: to recognise the harms that are responded to through the device of personal substituted decision-making, however problematic that device may be.

Camillia Kong uses the story of P, a young woman with intellectual disabilities living with her father, to illustrate how relationships of control can negatively impact autonomous self-direction.[24] P's father is described as distrustful of and hostile to the social workers attempting to assist P, preventing her from participating in activities the social workers have arranged (outings, going to college) – activities that P had expressed deriving great enjoyment from. P's father repeatedly told P that she could only trust and rely on him, that he was the only one who could and would take care of her, and that they did not need interference by social workers. When social workers were able to speak to P, she expressed a strong desire to resume attending activities and trying new things; '[b]ut when asked about whether she would like to live elsewhere apart from her father she

[22] See, A Arstein-Kerslake and E Flynn, 'The Right to Legal Agency: Domination, Disability, and the Protections of Article 12 of the Convention on the Rights of Persons with Disabilities' (2017) 13(1) *International Journal of Law in Context* 22.

[23] British Columbia's *Patients Property Act* RSBC 1996 c. 349 (court appointment of a personal decision-maker) and Representation Agreement Act 1996 RSBC c. 405 eg (advance planning appointment of a personal decision-maker).

[24] Kong, 'The Convention for the Rights of Persons with Disabilities and Article 12' (n 6).

says she "wishes to stay with her father since she is completely helpless without him".'[25] P's ability to see beyond life with her father and take action in her own interests (where those conflict with the interests of her father) is, in Kong's account, impacted by her intellectual disability. As P was considered mentally capable of making these personal decisions, however, they remained private and the social workers could not 'interfere'.

The question of what, if anything, could be done to help P is a difficult question for the reader, as it was for the social workers. Although P's father is not overtly abusive, it appears that he is manipulating P to serve his own needs for company, authority and control at P's expense. Because of the oppressive relationship context in which P is immersed, we see that it will be very difficult for P to make a different choice than the one her father has prescribed for her. P's intellectual disability is relevant both to the nature of her relationship with her father and to her ability to conceive of her life outside of that relationship – although, if she outlives her father, this will eventually be necessary.

Those who claim a continuing role for mental capacity-based discrimination may see in stories like P's the kind of context in which substitute decision-making is justified. Persons with mental disabilities are not the only persons vulnerable to relationship oppression of the kind experienced by P, however, and the law is evolving to recognise and respond to relationship-based harms experienced by 'capable' persons. The continuing inclusive development of these legal responses is the better avenue for safeguarding the well-being and autonomy of persons with mental disabilities in oppressive or exploitative relationship context (as discussed below).

III. DEVELOPING SAFEGUARDS FOR EXERCISE OF LEGAL CAPACITY: A WAY FORWARD

The five paragraphs of Article 12 set out a complete code for recognising and enabling equal recognition before the law without discrimination. Each paragraph must be read and interpreted as a part of that complete code, in relation to one another and in the context of Article 12 as a whole. Paragraphs 3 and 4, read together, set out a scheme for realising the legal personhood and legal capacity affirmed in paragraphs 1 and 2. That scheme has two essential and interconnected aspects or parts: support for the exercise of legal capacity (paragraph 3) and the 'safeguarding' provision set out in paragraph 4.

> States parties shall ensure that all measures that relate to the exercise of legal capacity provide for appropriate and effective safeguards to prevent abuse in accordance with international human rights law. Such safeguards shall ensure that measures relating

[25] Ibid, at 713–14.

> to the exercise of legal capacity respect the rights, will and preferences of the person, are free from conflict of interest and undue influence, are proportional and tailored to the persons circumstances, apply for the shortest time possible and are subject to regular review by a competent, independent and impartial authority or judicial body. The safeguards shall be proportional to the degree to which such measures affect the person's rights and interests.

Both paragraphs are necessary for the successful implementation of Article 12. Paragraph 5 of Article 12 calls for equal access to the exercise of legal capacity (requiring both safeguards and supports) in regards to matters of finance and property – matters from which persons with mental disabilities have been especially likely to be excluded because of the 'high' degree of mental capacity required.

A. Existing Supports for 'Capable' Decision-making

There are numerous examples of both supports and safeguards relating to the exercise of legal capacity by 'capable' persons. Supports are generally found in social structures and processes rather than legal rules, with some exceptions, for example where legislation provides that support must be required, or provides for structures and processes through which support will be provided. Legal advice is one obvious support for the exercise of legal capacity. Support programmes associated with court processes and proceedings, including accessibility supports for persons with disabilities such as hearing impairments are another. Professional advice supports decision-making in numerous areas relating to the exercise of legal capacity, like financial and tax advice about mortgages or property transfers for example. Most people, despite being 'mentally capable' of exercising their legal capacity in these ways, seek out supports of this kind prior to exercising legal capacity. The provision of medical information prior to decision-making about healthcare treatment is a context-specific form of legally required support for decision-making because informed consent is required for 'interference' that is otherwise illegal by virtue of tort law rules. Exercising legal capacity by consenting to sexual activity is, in contrast, a paradigmatically unsupported decision. Support for decision-making about marriage has become increasingly normalised in jurisdictions (such as British Columbia's) where family law legislation encourages would-be spouses to create 'family agreements' (many of which, one assumes, will be crafted on the basis of advice). Support for the exercise of legal capacity, in terms of accessing law and legal mechanisms in addition to decision-making, is also provided informally by family and friends and publicly by not-for-profit organisations and government services.

Because of the intersection between mental capacity, mental disability, and legal capacity, these generally available supports have not been crafted with mentally disabled persons in mind, perhaps on the basis that mentally disabled persons will be more likely to have legal capacity exercised by a substitute on their behalf. It is not difficult to conceptualise how generally available supports for the exercise of legal capacity can be made more inclusive, although doing so will require careful thought, social commitment and considerable resources. That work is underway, and a significant body of literature continues to grow around developing and implementing supports for the exercise of legal capacity.[26] From an inclusion perspective, one necessary change may be to require advice (including legal advice) for certain exercises of legal capacity where advice is now optional. Understanding is not synonymous with mental capacity and there may be all kind of reasons why a person has difficulty understanding and foreseeing the consequences of a particular matter relating to the exercise of legal capacity. This more inclusive approach to support for the exercise of legal capacity would benefit all persons, and not just those identified with a mental disability. Structures and processes for delivering this support would then need to be developed. Requiring each individual to consult with and pay for a lawyer would clearly be prohibitive, for example; online resources, while providing useful support for some, would be of little use to others. In addition to the inclusive development of these generally available supports, the development of new or special supports for persons with mental disabilities is also consistent with the overall scheme of Article 12 and with the principle of reasonable accommodations. The question of who would be entitled to these supports, in the absence of a mental capacity-like metric, would however remain open.[27]

B. Existing Safeguards for 'Capable' Decision-making

In many instances the line between support and safeguarding for the exercise of legal capacity will be more blurry than bright. An exercise of legal capacity

[26] See eg, R Harding and E Tascioglu, 'Supported decision-Making From Theory to Practice: Implementing the Right to Enjoy Legal Capacity' (2018) 8 *Societies* 25: doi:10.3390/soc8020025; 'Canadian Centre for Elder Law, *Inclusive Investing: Respecting the Rights of Vulnerable Investors through Supported Decision Making* (May 2021): https://www.bcli.org/project/inclusive-investing-respecting-the-rights-of-vulnerable-investors-through-supported-decision-making; Canadian Centre for Elder Law, *Understanding the Lived Experience of Supported Decision-Making in Canada* (March 2014): https://collections.ola.org/mon/28004/326452.pdf; G Davidson, B Kelly, G Macdonald, M Rizzo, L Lombard, O Abogunrin, V Clift-Matthews and A Martin, 'Supported decision-making: a review of the international literature' (2015) 38 *International Journal of Law and Psychiatry* 61; C Bigby, J Douglas, T Carney, S-N Then, I Wiesel and E Smith, 'Delivering decision-making support to people with cognitive disability – what has been learned from pilot programs in Australia from 2010 to 2015' (2017) 52 *Australian Journal of Social Sciences* 22; L Penzenstadler, A Molodynski and Y Khazal, 'Supported decision making for people with mental health disorders in clinical practice: a systematic review' (2020) 24(1) *International Journal of Psychiatry in Clinical Practice* 3; UN Committee on the Rights of Persons with Disabilities, 'Chapter Six: From provisions to practice: implementing the Convention, Legal Capacity and Supported Decision-Making' in *UN Handbook for Parliamentarians on the Convention on the Rights of Persons with Disabilities* (Geneva, United Nations CRPD, 2007): www.un.org/development/desa/disabilities/resources/handbook-for-parliamentarians-on-the-convention-on-the-rights-of-persons-with-disabilities/chapter-six-from-provisions-to-practice-implementing-the-convention-5.html.

[27] Bartlett, 'The United Nations Convention on the Rights of Persons with Disabilities and Mental Health Law' (n 20) at 762.

that is supported by professional advice and talked over with friends and family members interested in the person's welfare will tend to be more reflective of that person's interests, needs and expectations than one that is unsupported. This is the case for all persons, regardless of mental disability. The 'best interpretation of will and preferences' approach (as opposed to best interests) – to be applied where will and preference in relation to the exercise of legal capacity cannot be communicated – is both support and safeguard. This is because it both enables the exercise of legal capacity through the act of interpreting the person's will and preference, and precludes the need to fall back on a best interests approach.[28]

Other safeguards applying to the exercise of legal capacity are entirely disconnected from support, however, and work to restrict rather than enable the exercise of legal capacity. These safeguards are located in legal rules and doctrines rather than social structures and processes. Legal safeguards for the exercise of legal capacity by capable persons are located primarily in the doctrines and rules of common law and equity; specific pieces of legislation (such as consumer protection legislation) also contain safeguards pertaining to the specific matters dealt with within that legislation. The flexibility of common law and equity makes those rules and doctrines more useful than legislation as a site and source for the inclusive development of legal capacity safeguards, and they are the focus here, although statute-specific safeguards could also be revised to become more inclusive.

The traditional safeguards applying to the exercise of legal capacity include coercion, duress, mistake, *non est factum* (requiring a fundamental misunderstanding as to the nature of effect of the document in question), resulting trust, knowledge and approval (in the context of wills), insane delusions (also in the wills context), unconscionability, and undue influence. The purpose of these safeguards is to protect against the 'abuse' of legal capacity in two ways: first, by precluding the exercise of legal capacity where circumstances would make that exercise unfair, where those circumstances are discovered prior to legal capacity being exercised; secondly, where those circumstances are discovered after the exercise of legal capacity, by voiding the legal act in question (where possible) and providing compensation for any consequent harm. Abuse of legal capacity is not synonymous with abuse more generally, but refers specifically to the exercise of legal capacity in the circumstances.

The kinds of circumstances that create unfairness or 'abuse' for this purpose are described within each doctrine and rule; each is distinct from the others, responding to different incidents of legal capacity abuse. The common law doctrines of coercion and duress, for example, recognise and explain how and why the conduct of others may impact the choice of a person to undertake a particular course of action through the exercise of legal capacity, in a way that

[28] General Comment No 1 (n 15), para 21.

would make it unfair to enforce that choice.[29] It would also be unfair (for different reasons) to enforce an exercise of legal capacity predicated on mistake.[30] The doctrine of *non est factum* allows for a signed contract to be treated as void and unenforceable where a party to it fundamentally misunderstands the nature of the agreement for reasons other than the person's own negligence.[31] The doctrine of resulting trust creates a presumption that, where something of value is transferred legally but for no or very little consideration, the transferor intended to retain a beneficial interest in that thing.[32] That presumption can only be displaced by affirmatively establishing the person's actual intent – that she or he intended to make a gift. 'Knowledge and approval' in the law of wills refers to the requirement that, in order to make an effective testamentary gift, the person must have 'knowledge and approval' of what they are giving. This includes the general contents of their estate in relation to gifts made and the recipients of those gifts.[33] The doctrine of 'insane delusions', also in the context of wills, refers to a fixed belief in a false state of affairs that motivates the person to make a gift they would not have made in the absence of that delusion. Despite its name, 'insane delusions' do not depend on or flow from 'insanity' in a more general sense.[34] The equitable doctrine of unconscionability applies where one person (the 'stronger') has been enriched through the exploitation of a power imbalance vis-à-vis another (the 'weaker').[35] The doctrine of undue influence in Anglo-Canadian law describes the circumstances in which one person's exercise of legal capacity, including legal capacity exercised through consent, is primarily directed by the influence of another and is not, therefore, the person's own choice.[36]

All of these legal safeguards applying to the exercise of legal capacity are concerned with different aspects of the exerciser's state of mind, and the relationship between that state and the fundamental legal principle of fairness, including the equitable principle that law cannot be used to achieve unfair outcomes (unfairness here being conceptually distinct from unwanted or disliked). This concept of fairness mediates between the risk and the opportunity for autonomous practice inherent in the exercise of legal capacity by all persons. There are many reasons why the person may not have the knowledge required by a safeguarding rule, or be under a mistaken belief impacting the exercise of legal capacity in question, or be experiencing undue influence, coercion or duress, or be the target of unconscionability. An inclusive approach to

[29] *R v Ruzic* 2001 SCC 24.

[30] *Canada (Attorney General) v Fairmont Hotels Inc* 2016 SCC 56.

[31] *Marvco Colour Research Ltd v Harris*, [1982] 2 SCR 774; *Servello v Servello* 2015 ONCA 434.

[32] *Pecore v Pecore* 2007 SCC 17.

[33] *Russell v Fraser* (1980) 118 DLR (3d) 733 (BCCA); *Calderaro v Meyer* 2011 ONSC 5395.

[34] *Banks v Goodfellow* (1870) LR 5 QB.

[35] *Uber Technologies Inc v Weller* 2020 SCC 16.

[36] *Geffen v Goodman Estate*, [1991] 1 SCR 353.

developing these safeguards would recognise that the actual characteristics of an individual with a mental disability may be relevant within the analysis required by any of these doctrines or rules, but it will not be determinative.

Inclusive development will also involve looking carefully at the circumstances in which these safeguards apply, understanding that any re-drawing of scope should apply to these doctrines and rules generally, and not only in relation to persons with mental disabilities. Coercion and duress have always applied to marriage, for example; undue influence traditionally has not. The inclusive development of the rule may involve extending it to marriage, an extension that some have also called for in relation to 'capable persons'.[37] This kind of rule development is consistent with the location of legal safeguards in the flexible and inherently evolutionary rules and doctrines of common law and equity, which need not remain frozen in time or locked within particular contexts. In the case of *Norberg v Wynrib*[38] for example, the Supreme Court of Canada drew on the conceptual framework of unconscionability, originating in the law of contract, to inform the analysis of consent to an interference with the person or consent to battery. That case involved a series of sexual encounters between a woman addicted to prescription drugs and the doctor who supplied them to her. The plaintiff's mental capacity to consent was not in issue as her addiction was found not to interfere with her cognitive ability to give consent. Her consent was not, however, genuine because it was given in the context of an imbalanced power relationship, involving a high degree of trust and confidence. Here, the 'justice factor' of unconscionability in the law of contract provided insight into the issue of 'genuine consent' in the law of tort.[39]

The application of these legal safeguards to all persons, including persons with mental disabilities, is consistent with the overarching objective of Article 12, the language of paragraph 4, and the context in which it is situated (paragraphs 1, 2, 3 and 5). This approach is consistent with the interpretation of paragraph 4 provided in General Comment No 1 at paragraphs 20–23.[40] The General Comment describes paragraph 4 as 'requir[ing] States parties to create appropriate and effective safeguards for the exercise of legal capacity' with the 'primary purpose of these safeguards' being 'to ensure the respect of the person's rights, will and preferences. In order to accomplish this, the safeguards must provide protection from abuse on an *equal* basis with others' (emphasis added).[41] The general reference to safeguards against the abuse of legal capacity is sufficient to capture all generally applicable rules that work to this effect.

[37] *Banton v Banton* (1998) 164 DLR (4th) 176 (ONSC).
[38] *Norberg v Wynrib*, [1992] 2 SCR 226.
[39] Ibid.
[40] General Comment No 1 (n 15), para 20.
[41] Ibid.

In relation to undue influence (the legal safeguard referenced specifically in paragraph 4), the General Comment includes the following statement (at paragraph 22):

> All people risk being subject to 'undue influence', yet this may be exacerbated for those who rely on the support of others to make decisions. Undue influence is characterised as occurring, where the quality of the interaction between the support person and the person being supported includes signs of fear, aggression, threat, deception or manipulation. Safeguards for the exercise of legal capacity must include protection against undue influence; however, the protection must respect the rights, will and preferences of the person, including the right to take risks and make mistakes.[42]

This characterisation of undue influence is much narrower than the equitable doctrine of undue influence within the Anglo-Canadian legal tradition, which includes undue influence arising through relationship dynamics where the potential for domination is inherent in the nature of the relationship itself (giving rise to a presumption of undue influence).[43] Incorporation of this more nuanced approach within Canada's implementation of Article 12 is consistent with paragraph 7 of the General Comment No 1, which provides that 'States parties must holistically examine all areas of law to ensure that the right of persons with disabilities to legal capacity is not restricted on an unequal basis with others'.

The inclusive development of these legal safeguards applies not just to the rules/doctrines themselves, but to the application and availability of those safeguards at different points in the exercise of legal capacity. Legal safeguards may be implemented after the exercise of legal capacity as a means of providing remedy. Legal gatekeepers enabling the exercise of legal capacity are obliged not to facilitate that exercise where circumstances indicate that one of the safeguards applies. Increasing the sensitivity of gatekeepers to existing safeguards – for example, knowing and recognising the circumstances constituting duress – and ensuring that knowledgeable gatekeepers are involved in the exercise of legal capacity across contexts will be key to the inclusive development of these safeguards.

Where a problematic exercise of legal capacity is caught in this way the gatekeeper should be obliged (consistently with Article 12 paragraph 3) to facilitate supports for the purpose of overcoming the problem in question, if possible, to enable the exercise of legal capacity. Most exercises of legal capacity either require a gatekeeper of some kind or provide for the option of gatekeeper involvement. Gatekeepers include the physician obtaining informed consent, the person authorised to perform marriage, and the lawyer or notary documenting or executing transactions. Where gatekeepers are currently optional (as in the case of wills), safeguards could be strengthened by making the involvement of

[42] Ibid, para 22.
[43] *Geffen v Goodman Estate* (n 36).

gatekeepers a requirement and building the legal infrastructure to ensure that this increased role does not create new barriers of expense. Ensuring access to knowledgeable gatekeepers will make the exercise of legal capacity significantly less risky for all persons.

Where problems identified by gatekeepers cannot be overcome with supports – for example where legal capacity cannot be exercised without abuse, or where the exercise of legal capacity is necessary (perhaps if the sale of property is needed to provide for a person's care) – the exercise of legal capacity by another may be justified on the basis of the common law doctrine of necessity. Like the other common law doctrines discussed here, necessity does not apply only or in any particular way to persons with impaired mental capacity. It would not be coherent, within the overall structure of Article 12, to allow for the exercise of legal capacity despite the detection of abuse that cannot be resolved through support. To allow that exercise on the basis that it nevertheless reflects that person's will and preference would require tossing away safeguards of general application that have long played an important role in Anglo-Canadian law as a means of ensuring fairness and facilitating genuine decision-making.

The question of safeguards in relation to otherwise personal and private decisions for which legal capacity *becomes* necessary through impaired mental capacity is more complicated. Buying a house, getting married, making a will, consenting to medical treatment are all recognisable exercises of legal capacity for all persons to which legal safeguards apply; personal decision-making is not. The legal safeguard in this context is substitute decision-making itself: the transformation of personal decisions into decisions requiring legal capacity and the location of that capacity in the substitute decision-maker. In practice, this legal capacity is most likely to be used as the exercise of legal capacity only in relation to certain kinds of personal matters. These may include decisions about where and/or with whom to live (including residential care); who to associate or engage in romantic or sexual relationships with; whether to participate in educational or employment opportunities; whether to engage with social services. Because these choices are especially vulnerable to oppressive relationship contexts (as illustrated by the story of P, above) supported decision-making may not always be an adequate replacement. For example, the 'stronger' party may block access to support and/or provide ostensible support for the person that advances their own interests.

Some commentators have interpreted the safeguards in paragraph 4 as allowing for some mode of substitute decision-making 'that should kick in when decision-support proves to be of no avail.'[44] This interpretation would allow for substitute decision-making in oppressive relationship contexts with

[44] M Scholten and J Gather, 'Adverse consequences of Article 12 of the Convention on the Rights of Persons with Disabilities and an alternative way forward' (2018) 44 *Journal of Medical Ethics* 226, 228.

respect to personal decisions (to which traditional safeguards for the exercise of legal capacity do not apply), but is fundamentally inconsistent with the overarching purpose of Article 12 and the interpretation provided by General Comment No 1.

An inclusive approach to this issue starts with re-conceptualising the problem to be resolved in terms of an oppressive relationship and coercive control rather than the impaired mental capacity of the person within that relationship. The kind of relationship-based control described in P's story is not exclusive to persons with intellectual or mental impairments, and many persons with mental disabilities do not experience oppressive relationship context of any kind. The reluctance to acknowledge these kinds of relationship-based harms for persons without mental disabilities has meant in the past that substitute decision-making has provided the only available mechanism for response, requiring a 'finding' of impaired mental capacity. It has been harder to ignore or explain away relationship-based harms impacting persons with mental disabilities for a number of reasons. The personal pathology rationalisation for justifying relationship-based harms (the 'she wants it' or 'she's asking for it' narrative) is less tenable in relation to persons with disabilities, the relationship is more likely to be subject to public scrutiny and the person is likely less adept at hiding the circumstances from others.

The development of new legal responses to relationship-based harms in recent years outside of the substitute decision-making framework has changed this landscape. These include development of the inherent jurisdiction in England and Wales[45] and the development of domestic violence legislation, adult protection legislation and the criminal law, to recognise and respond to coercive control. The post-CRPD world calls for these new legal responses to be constructed and applied in a way that is inclusive of persons with mental disabilities (and not exclusive to them) in a way that respects the genuine autonomy of all persons. That work will ultimately support the vision of Article 12 and the CRPD.

IV. CONCLUDING REMARKS

Protection, associated with *parens patriae* and the state's obligations towards vulnerable populations, is not a legal principle. Protection is the straw man in any legal contest between protection and the fundamental legal values of autonomy and legal equality; it wins only by constructing the person in need of

[45] J Lindsey and R Harding, 'Capabilities, capacity and consent: sexual intimacy in the Court of Protection' (2021) 48(1) *Journal of Law & Society* 60–83: DOI: 10.1111/jols.12278; J Lindsey, 'Protecting Vulnerable Adults from Abuse: Under-protection and Over-protection in Adult Safeguarding and Mental Capacity Law' (2020) 32(2) *Child and Family Law Quarterly* 157–75; MI Hall, 'The Vulnerability Jurisdiction: Equity, *Parens Patriae*, and the Inherent Jurisdiction of the Court' (2016) 2(1) *Canadian Journal of Comparative and Contemporary Law* 185.

protection as 'lesser-than', leading in turn to further harm. In this chapter, I have proposed understanding concerns about and resistance to Article 12 as rooted in concerns about fairness (as opposed to the need to protect): that it is unfair to fix persons with consequences they could not comprehend or foresee, and that it is inequitable for the law to be used, through the exercise of legal capacity, for this purpose. My re-conceptualisation, from protection to fairness, makes visible the significance of traditional fairness-based legal safeguards to the exercise of legal capacity enjoined by Article 12 and in doing so situates Article 12 within the broader context of Anglo-Canadian tradition, 'grafting itself then upon the ancient body of truth, which thus grows much as a tree grows by the activity of a new layer of cambium.'[46] That interconnected growth is necessary for the core idea of Article 12 to become a taken-for-granted legal 'truth': that mental capacity-based limits on the exercise of legal capacity cause more harm than good, and that legal capacity can be exercised by all persons in a way that is consistent with fairness, justice, and equity.

[46] W James, *Pragmatism* (Cambridge MA, Harvard University Press, 1975), 35, cited in M Radin, 'The Pragmatist and the Feminist' (1990) 63(6) *Southern California Law Review* 1699, 1709.

16

Supporting Everyday Legal Capacity: Navigating the Complexities of Putting Rights into Practice

ROSIE HARDING[1]

I. INTRODUCTION

SINCE THE UN Convention on the Rights of Persons with Disabilities (CRPD) came into force, the question of how a commitment to supporting legal capacity can be translated into effective, person-centred law has become a topic of significant academic, legal and policy debate. This debate has been particularly intense since the Committee on the Rights of Persons with Disabilities (CommitteeRPD) published their first general comment on Article 12 of the CRPD. In that General Comment, the CommitteeRPD interpreted the CRPD to require the abolition of substitute decision-making frameworks (like guardianship and objective best interests decisions), and their replacement with (appropriately safeguarded) support frameworks.[2] Translating the CommitteeRPD's interpretation of Article 12 CRPD into effective law is, however, proving particularly difficult and remains controversial.[3]

[1] I'd like to thank the International Institute for the Sociology of Law, Oñati, for hosting our workshop, all of the workshop participants for their thoughtful contributions, and Mary Donnelly and Ezgi Taşcıoğlu for being such fabulous collaborators. The research on which this contribution is based has been funded by the British Academy (MD150026); the Leverhulme Trust (PLP-2017-184); and the University of Birmingham ESRC Impact Acceleration Account. I am extremely grateful to all of these funders for their support.

[2] R Harding, 'The Rise of Statutory Wills and the Limits of Best Interests Decision-Making in Inheritance' (2015) 78 *Modern Law Review* 945–70.

[3] A Dhanda, 'Legal Capacity in the Disability Rights Convention: Stranglehold of the Past or Lodestar of the Future?' (2006–2007) 34 *Syracuse Journal of International Law & Commerce* 429–62; A Dhanda, 'Conversations between the proponents of the new paradigm of legal capacity' (2017) 13 *International Journal of Law in Context* 87–95.

As contributions to this collection show, few jurisdictions have mental capacity law frameworks that can be considered fully compliant with the CommitteeRPD's approach to Article 12. Sweden's longstanding system of the 'god man' (limited guardian) seeks to minimise the use of guardianship, and is a longstanding example of a legal system that ensures that people retain full legal capacity.[4] Similarly, the system of Representation Agreements in British Columbia pre-dates the CRPD, and provides access to a self-nominated supported decision-making framework.[5] In both of these jurisdictions, however, substituted decision-making frameworks are still available as an alternative to support frameworks, and many of the challenges associated with balancing support and protection remain.[6] Ireland's Assisted Decision Making (Capacity) Act 2015, which was not in force at time of writing, sets out a comprehensive and graded scheme for supported decision-making in Irish law.[7] Once this new scheme is fully implemented, evaluation of it will be vital to assess how well it works, and to what extent it complies with Article 12 CRPD.[8]

In 2017, the Law Commission of England and Wales proposed that a regulatory power to set up a supported decision-making scheme should be included in amendments to the Deprivation of Liberty Safeguards under the Mental Capacity Act 2005.[9] In 2018, the UK Government's final response to this proposal was that despite general agreement with the principles of supported decision-making, 'it is not clear at this stage whether a new regulatory scheme is an appropriate response'.[10] No such regulatory power was therefore included in the Mental Capacity (Amendment) Act 2019, and the case remains to be made as to whether a formal supported decision-making scheme should be developed. In this chapter, which draws on my empirical research about everyday decision-making by people

[4] AF Johns, 'Person-Centered Guardianship and Supported Decision Making: An Assessment of Progress Made in Three Countries' (2016) 9 *Journal of International Ageing Law & Policy* 1–32; SS Herr, 'Self-determination, Autonomy and Alternatives for Guardianship' in SS Herr, LO Gostin and HH Koh (eds), *The Human Rights of Persons with Intellectual Disabilities: Different but equal* (Oxford, Oxford University Press, 2003); Mattsson, Chapter 13, this volume.

[5] K James and L Watts, *Understanding the Lived Experiences of Supported Decision-Making in Canada: Legal Capacity, Decision-Making and Guardianship* (Law Commission of Ontario, March 2014); Hall, Chapter 15, this volume.

[6] R Harding, E Taşcıoğlu and M Furgalska, *Supported Will-Making: A Socio-Legal Study of Experiences, Values and Potential in Supporting Testamentary Capacity* (University of Birmingham, 2019); See also Mattsson, Chapter 13, this volume and Hall, Chapter 15, this volume.

[7] Flynn, Chapter 7, this volume.

[8] Other jurisdictions that have introduced legal change in this area since the CRPD include Victoria, Australia; Austria; and Peru. There is not space here to describe all of these frameworks in detail; see further Harding, Taşcıoğlu and Furgalska, *Supported Will-Making* (n 6).

[9] Law Commission, *Mental Capacity and Deprivation of Liberty* (Law Com No 372) (London, Law Commission of England and Wales, March 2017).

[10] www.parliament.uk/business/publications/written-questions-answers-statements/written-statement/Commons/2018-03-14/HCWS542/.

with intellectual disabilities,[11] I explore how the current, stratified, approach to supported decision-making in English law works in practice. I argue that the current regulatory framework around decision-making in England and Wales implicitly holds a set of problematic assumptions about who should support disabled people and what kinds of decisions are appropriate for supported decision-making, and ultimately prioritises a paternalistic, substitute decision-making framework. Through empirical analysis, I will show that there are conceptual, practical and legal issues with how supported decision-making happens in practice. I conclude that substantive legal reform that combines greater access to support with more supervision of supporters would be the most appropriate response to the challenges posed by support for legal capacity as mandated by Article 12 of the CRPD.

I begin with a brief methodological note, outlining the socio-legal, empirical research on which this chapter rests. I then provide an overview (in section III) of the current socio-legal context of support for decision-making in English law. In section IV, I argue that the current approach is plagued with conceptual, practical and legal issues, which I explain through analysis of my empirical data. Through exploring the multiple challenges presented by the current legal framework, I demonstrate the difference a nominated supporter scheme could make both in supporting the enjoyment of legal capacity by intellectually disabled people[12] and in putting in place effective safeguards against abuse (section V).

II. METHODOLOGICAL NOTE: THE EVERYDAY DECISIONS RESEARCH

The analysis that follows draws on data from the Everyday Decisions qualitative interview study[13] and a follow-up study on supported will-making.[14]

[11] R Harding and E Taşcıoğlu, *Everyday Decisions Project Report: Supporting Legal Capacity through Care, Support and Empowerment* (University of Birmingham, November 2017); R Harding and E Taşcıoğlu, 'Supported Decision-Making from Theory to Practice: Implementing the Right to Enjoy Legal Capacity' (2018) 8 *Societies* 25; Harding, Taşcıoğlu and Furgalska, *Supported Will-Making* (n 6).

[12] A quick note on terminology: in this chapter, I generally use the terms 'intellectually disabled people'. I intend this term to be broad, inclusive, and to cover a range of cognitive disabilities, including learning disabilities, acquired brain injuries, neurodiversity, and degenerative neurological conditions like dementia. I have used 'intellectually disabled people' rather than 'people with disabilities' to signify my conceptual and political orientation towards the social model of disability.

[13] Harding and Taşcıoğlu, *Everyday Decisions Project Report* (n 11); Harding and Taşcıoğlu, 'Supported Decision-Making from Theory to Practice' (n 11); R Harding and E Taşcıoğlu, '"That's a bit of a minefield": Supported decision-making in intellectually disabled people's intimate lives' in C Ashford and A Maine (eds), *Research Handbook on Gender, Sexuality and Law* (Cheltenham, Edward Elgar, 2019); R Harding, '"He got down on one knee": Intellectual disability, intimacy and family law' in B Clough and J Herring (eds), *Disability, Care and Family Law*, 1st edn (London, Routledge, 2021) pp 156–81.

[14] Harding, Taşcıoğlu and Furgalska, *Supported Will-Making* (n 6).

Taken together, these projects included interviews with 25 care and support professionals, 19 intellectually disabled people, and six supporters chosen by the disabled participants to help them with participation. See Tables 1 and 2 for demographic information. Ethical approvals were provided by the University of Birmingham Humanities and Social Sciences Ethical Review Committee. In line with the requirements of the Mental Capacity Act 2005, all participants had capacity to consent to participate in the research. Accessible participant information sheets and consent forms were used to facilitate participation by intellectually disabled participants. Interviews were recorded to enable verbatim transcription, and all names and potentially identifying information were changed as part of the transcription process. Interviews with intellectually disabled participants were also video recorded, to enable additional analysis of body language and assist in accurate transcription where verbal expression was unclear.

Table 1 Demographic Information – Care Professionals

Age		**Gender**	
18–24	16% (n=4)	Male	12% (n=3)
25–34	4% (n=1)	Female	88% (n=22)
35–44	24% (n=6)	**Race/Ethnicity**	
45–54	32% (n=8)	Black African	4% (n=1)
55–64	16% (n=4)	Black Caribbean	4% (n=1)
65–74	8% (n=2)	Mixed (White/Black Caribbean)	12% (n=3)
Highest Qualification		White British	80% (n=20)
Unknown	8% (n=2)	**Occupation**	
NVQ Level 2	4% (n=1)	Housekeeping	8% (n=2)
NVQ Level 3	24% (n=6)	Frontline Care Worker	20% (n=5)
NVQ Level 4	4% (n=1)	Team Leader/Co-ordinator	12% (n=3)
NVQ Level 5	12% (n=3)	Care Manager/Deputy Manager	16% (n=4)
Professional qualifications	4% (n=1)	Brain Injury Case Manager	32% (n=8)
Degree (undergraduate)	16% (n=4)	Mental Capacity Assessor	8% (n=2)
Higher Degree	32% (n=8)	Best Interests Assessor	4% (n=1)

These data were analysed thematically, using a range of deductive (researcher driven) and inductive (data driven) codes. Thematic analysis offers a flexible approach to qualitative data analysis, which is not grounded in a particular

Table 2 Demographic Information – Intellectually Disabled Participants

Age Group		**Gender**	
18–24	5% (n=1)	Male	37% (n=7)
25–34	21% (n=4)	Female	63% (n=12)
35–44	21% (n=4)	**Impairments**[15]	
45–54	21% (n=4)	Learning difficulty	79% (n=15)
55–64	21% (n=4)	Sensory impairment	21% (n=4)
65–74	11% (n=2)	Physical impairment	47% (n=9)
Living Arrangements		Acquired Brain Injury	11% (n=2)
With Family	3	Autism Spectrum Disorder	11% (n=3)
Supported Living	6	**Supported at Interview**	
Independent	9	Supporter present	63% (n=12)
Care Home	1	No Supporter	37% (n=7)

conceptual approach.[16] Conceptually, critical discourse analysis[17] guided the close analysis of these qualitative data. Critical discourse analysis looks at text and talk with a particular focus on and attentiveness to relationships of power, dominance, and social inequality.[18] In this chapter, the critical discourse analysis begins from the emancipatory potential of the CRPD 'paradigm shift',[19] and in particular the importance of appropriately safeguarded support frameworks that are attentive to the will, preferences, beliefs and values of intellectually disabled people.

III. SUPPORTING LEGAL CAPACITY IN ENGLISH LAW

English law does not currently make provision for a formal, nominated supporter scheme. There are, however, a wide range of informal, quasi-formal and formal support frameworks that have been created by the Mental Capacity Act 2005,

[15] Totals do not add up to 100% as several participants had multiple impairments.

[16] V Braun and V Clarke, 'Using thematic analysis in psychology' (2006) 3 *Qualitative Research in Psychology* 77–101.

[17] TA van Dijk, 'Principles of Critical Discourse Analysis' (1993) 4 *Discourse & Society* 249–83; N Fairclough, 'Critical discourse analysis and critical policy studies' (2013) 7 *Critical Policy Studies* 177–97.

[18] van Dijk (n 17).

[19] See further Dhanda, 'Legal Capacity in the Disability Rights Convention' (n 3); Dhanda, 'Conversations between the proponents of the new paradigm' (n 3); K Booth Glen, 'Changing Paradigms: Mental Capacity, Legal Capacity, Guardianship, and Beyond' (2012) 44 *Columbia Human Rights Law Review* 93–169.

the Care Act 2014 and through other legislation[20] and case law[21] that interact to provide the legal framework for supporting legal capacity in England.[22] Informal support mechanisms are also formally recognised for some limited purposes.

Table 3 Supported and Substitute Decision Frameworks in English Capacity Law

Support Framework	**Source**	**Scope**	**Supported or Substituted?**	**Safeguards**
Informal Support	MCA 2005, s 1	Entitlement in all decisions whether or not the person has capacity.	Supported	No formal safeguards
Best interests decisions	MCA 2005, s 4	Best interests decisions require consideration of the wishes and feelings of the person.	Substituted	No formal safeguards
General defence	MCA 2005, s 5	Acts in connection with care or treatment where reasonable belief that the person lacks capacity and the act is in their best interests.	Substituted	No formal safeguards
Lasting Power of Attorney (Health and Welfare)	MCA 2005, s 9	Health and welfare decisions only; only valid if the person lacks capacity.	Substituted	Must be registered with the Office of the Public Guardian; subject to supervision.

(continued)

[20] There are additional frameworks in the Mental Health Act 1983 (as amended), but consideration of these is outside the scope of this chapter.

[21] Of particular note are *Aintree v James* [2013] UKSC 67 and *Briggs v Briggs and Others* [2016] EWCOP 53.

[22] Note that there are four legal jurisdictions in the UK, and capacity law is an area where there is increasing divergence between England, Wales, Scotland and Northern Ireland: see further Harding, Taşcıoğlu and Furgalska, *Supported Will-Making* (n 6); W Martin and others, *The Essex Autonomy Project Three Jurisdictions Report: Towards Compliance with CRPD Article 12 in Capacity/Incapacity Legislation across the UK* (June 2016); Stavert, Chapter 10, this volume.

Table 3 *(Continued)*

Support Framework	Source	Scope	Supported or Substituted?	Safeguards
Lasting Power of Attorney (Property and Affairs)	MCA 2005, s 9	Financial decisions only; while the person has capacity can act with the person's consent. Can act without consent if the person lacks capacity.	Either supported or substituted	Must be registered with the Office of the Public Guardian; subject to supervision.
Deputy (Health and Welfare)	MCA 2005, s 19	Health and welfare decisions only; may be consulted on other matters.	Substituted	Appointed by the Court of Protection; supervised by the Office of the Public Guardian; must keep records.
Deputy (Property and Affairs)	MCA 2005, s 19	Financial decisions only; may be consulted on other matters.	Substituted	Appointed by the Court of Protection; supervised by the Office of the Public Guardian; financial bond required; must keep accounts.

(continued)

Table 3 *(Continued)*

Support Framework	Source	Scope	Supported or Substituted?	Safeguards
Advance Decisions to Refuse Treatment	MCA 2005, s 24	Advance decisions to refuse specific kinds of medical treatment, including clinically assisted nutrition and hydration.	Supported	Advance refusals must comply with the rules in the MCA to be valid. Additional steps required to refuse life-sustaining treatment.
IMCA (Independent Mental Capacity Advocate)	MCA 2005, s 35	Serious medical treatment; placement in long term care; care reviews; safeguarding.	Supported	No formal safeguards
Enduring Power of Attorney	Enduring Powers of Attorney Act 1985	Financial decisions only; no new EPAs since 2007.	Substituted	Must be registered, but less supervision than LPA.
Consultee	MCA 2005, s 32	Substitute consent to participate in research.	Substituted	No formal safeguards
Relevant Person's Representative (RPR)	MCA 2005, Schedule A1, Part 10	Maintain contact with the relevant person, and to represent and support the relevant person in all matters relating to the Deprivation of Liberty Safeguards (DoLS).	Supported	No formal safeguards

(continued)

Table 3 *(Continued)*

Support Framework	Source	Scope	Supported or Substituted?	Safeguards
Appropriate Person (Care Act)	Care Act 2014	Same role as Care Act Advocate, but informal and removes entitlement to independent advocacy support.	Supported	No formal safeguards
Care Act Advocate	Care Act 2014	Needs assessments, care and support plans and revisions. Also available to support carers in certain circumstances.	Supported	No formal safeguards
Appropriate Person (LPS)	Mental Capacity (Amendment) Act 2019	Liberty Protection Safeguards, not yet in force, but when implemented will replace the RPR under the DoLS framework in the Mental Capacity Act 2005.	Supported	No formal safeguards
Appointee	Social Security Administration Act 1992 (as amended)	Claiming state benefits on behalf of another person.	Substituted	No formal safeguards

As Table 3 shows, the key piece of capacity legislation in England and Wales is the Mental Capacity Act 2005 (MCA). The MCA governs 12 of 16 decision-support frameworks in English capacity law, and takes a functional approach to mental capacity,[23] which considers capacity to hinge on the ability to make

[23] Mental Capacity Act 2005, s 3.

specific decisions at particular times. If a person is found to lack capacity to make that decision, the decision can be made for them by another person, under the 'best interests' framework. This decision-specific basis for determining whether or not a person has capacity rests on five core principles, which cover a presumption of capacity, support for decision-making, unwise decisions, best interests and a preference for the least restrictive option. For present purposes, principle 2 (A person is not to be treated as unable to make a decision unless all practicable steps to help him to do so have been taken without success)[24] is the most important, as this is the key legal basis for supporting legal capacity under the MCA.

Unfortunately, principle 2 of the MCA does not set out a clear right to decision-making support. The phrase 'all practicable steps' is vague, and it is not obvious what 'without success' means. The MCA also does not specify whose responsibility it is to take these 'practicable steps', nor does it state who is responsible for providing support, what qualifications (if any) they need to have to do so, or who has the responsibility for funding any support that is provided by a professional. The lack of specificity in the MCA is a product of the far-reaching form of the statute, which is, in turn, grounded in the overarching purpose of the MCA: to provide a legal basis for (substitute) best interests decision-making in almost all decisional contexts.[25] Some decisions, particularly those relating to family law (eg, consent to sex, marriage, divorce or adoption),[26] are excluded from the best interests framework, but remain included in the decision-specific capacity assessment approach of the MCA. In practice, this means that if a person is found to lack the mental capacity to consent to sex, for example, then they will be prevented from engaging in intimate relationships.[27] The only decisions that sit completely outside the MCA are decisions about mental health treatment that fall under the Mental Health Act 1983,[28] and the right to register to vote, which is not limited by the functional mental capacity test under the MCA[29] or by any common law rule.[30]

In practice, for most everyday choices, 'support' provided under the MCA takes the form of informal support from a family member, friend, carer, or personal assistant. Where the decision in question falls to be made in the context of the provision of social care, then support may be provided by a social care worker. Similarly, legal professionals may provide support to make decisions relating to legal matters; and doctors or allied health professionals may provide support to help a patient make medical decisions. In some circumstances,

[24] Mental Capacity Act 2005, s 1(3).

[25] Law Commission, *Mental Incapacity* (London, HMSO, 1995).

[26] Mental Capacity Act 2005, s 27.

[27] J Lindsey and R Harding, 'Capabilities, Capacity and Consent: Sexual Intimacy in the Court of Protection' (2021) 48 *Journal of Law and Society* 60–83.

[28] Mental Capacity Act 2005, s 28.

[29] Mental Capacity Act 2005, s 29.

[30] Electoral Administration Act 2006, s 73.

a statutory advocate must be appointed to support and advocate on behalf of the person,[31] though these are limited to particular kinds of decisions.[32] There are various types of statutory advocacy available for different kinds of decisions: Independent Mental Capacity Advocates (IMCA) support decisions about long-term changes in accommodation, including deprivations of liberty, or serious medical decisions; Independent Mental Health Advocates (IMHA) help people understand their rights under the Mental Health Acts; and Care Act Advocates support people to understand their rights under the Care Act 2014, supporting involvement in decisions about care assessments, reviews, care planning and safeguarding. Importantly, however, statutory advocates will generally not be appointed where the person has someone else who can support them. For IMCAs, this includes a court appointed deputy, a donee of an Enduring or Lasting Power of Attorney (LPA),[33] or an informal carer/supporter who the person with impaired capacity identifies 'as a person to be consulted in matters affecting his interests.'[34] Formal support from a statutory advocate is therefore limited in situations where the person has informal carers, even though carers often struggle to navigate the complexities of the health and social care systems.[35]

Where a person creates a financial LPA, they can consent to this power being used by their attorney while they have capacity to make decisions about financial matters. Financial LPAs can, therefore, be lawfully used as a formal support scheme, if both donor and attorney wish to do so. In contrast, health and welfare LPAs can only come into force if the donor loses capacity to make the decision in question. This means that in health and welfare matters there is less flexibility to use an LPA as a nominated support framework for a person who retains capacity.[36] If a person is deprived of their liberty under the Deprivation of Liberty Safeguards[37] then they will have a 'Relevant Person's Representative' (RPR), which is a formal advocacy and support role that is sometimes filled by a volunteer (family member, friend, carer, etc) and sometimes by a paid representative. In the new 'Liberty Protection Safeguards'[38] the relevant person's

[31] Mental Capacity Act 2005, ss 35–41; Care Act 2014, s 67.

[32] Mental Capacity Act (Independent Mental Capacity Advocates) (General) Regulations 2006 (UKSI 2006/1832); Mental Capacity Act (Independent Mental Capacity Advocates) (Expansion of Role) Regulations 2006 (UKSI 2006/2883).

[33] Enduring Power of Attorney was abolished by the MCA, but enduring powers created before the MCA came into force remain valid. Enduring powers are only available for property and financial affairs.

[34] Mental Capacity Act (Independent Mental Capacity Advocates) (Expansion of Role) Regulations 2006 (UKSI 2006/2883), regulation 3(1)(d).

[35] E Peel and R Harding, '"It's a huge maze, the system, it's a terrible maze": Dementia carers' constructions of navigating health and social care services' (2014) 13 *Dementia* 642–61.

[36] For more detail on powers of attorney in English law, see R Harding and E Peel, 'Polyphonic Legality: Power of Attorney Through Dialogic Interaction' (2019) 28 *Social & Legal Studies* 675–97.

[37] Mental Capacity Act 2005, Schedule A1.

[38] Mental Capacity (Amendment) Act 2019, due to come into force in 2022.

representative has been replaced by the 'appropriate person' which can only be a voluntary role. Where the person deprived of their liberty does not have anyone willing to be an appropriate person, they will instead (usually) have access to an IMCA.

Appropriate persons and statutory advocates are also available under the Care Act 2014. Advocacy under the Care Act is only available where the person 'would experience substantial difficulty' in one of the areas of the capacity test under the MCA (understanding, retaining, using or weighing relevant information, communicating their decision).[39] Care Act advocates are, as with IMCAs and IMHAs, only available in certain circumstances, and for particular decisions. If the person has an 'appropriate person' then no independent advocacy entitlement arises. This suggests that independent statutory advocacy is constructed as equivalent to, and a formal replacement for, informal support from family and friends. Yet all of the different forms of statutory advocates have greater rights to access records about the person than informal/family supporters, or appropriate persons, which creates potential for tensions and for inequity between those who have an independent or statutory advocate, and those who are supported only by family members, friends, or paid personal assistants.[40]

Supported decision-making is not, currently, a significant component of the mental health legislative regime in England and Wales. There is not space in this chapter to go into detail in relation to the technicalities of the Mental Health Act 1983, as amended (MHA).[41] Suffice to say, the MHA is a system that authorises treatment without the patient's consent. As a consequence, it is far from compatible with the CRPD.[42] It is possible that supported decision-making and advance expressions of choices may form a greater part of the MHA if recommendations from the Wessely Review[43] are implemented.

Finally, it is worth mentioning the place of support for legal capacity in the best interests test, under section 4 MCA. Case law has confirmed that best interests is a subjective assessment of what is best for that particular person, rather than an objective assessment of the optimal outcome for the reasonable person in a similar position.[44] This subjective appraisal should include evaluation of the person's wishes, feelings, beliefs and values.[45] This interpretation of best interests under the MCA arguably brings that legal framework closer to compliance with Article 12 of the UN CRPD, as interpreted by the Committee on the Rights

[39] Care Act 2014, s 67(4).

[40] See eg, Mental Capacity Act 2005, s 35(6).

[41] For a detailed overview of the English system, see P Bartlett and R Sandland, *Mental health law: policy and practice*, 4th edn (Oxford, Oxford University Press, 2014).

[42] T Minkowitz, 'CRPD and transformative equality' (2017) 13 *International Journal of Law in Context* 77–86.

[43] S Wessely, *Modernising the Mental Health Act: Increasing Choice, Reducing Compulsion* (Final Report of the Independent Review of the Mental Health Act 1983, December 2018).

[44] *Aintree v James* [2013] UKSC 67.

[45] Mental Capacity Act 2005, s 4(6).

of Persons with Disabilities (CommitteeRPD).[46] Since *Aintree* there appears to have been a shift towards somewhat more person-centred decision-making in the Court of Protection, but the extent to which the person's views can shape the outcome remains unclear.[47]

In summary, current frameworks for supporting legal capacity in English law are multiple and complex. Looking across these different provisions, there are three significant points to note. First, the legislative regime creates a false equivalence between formal independent advocacy and informal support from family members, friends and informal carers. Second, the multiplicity of legislative rules, different entitlements, and different powers that different classes of supporter have makes the system particularly difficult for intellectually disabled people and their family members and informal carers to navigate. Third, the legislative framework, whilst including some formalised elements of support, is primarily a substituted decision regime. This stratified approach furthermore generates a number of tensions, which work together to produce uneven effects on those using capacity law support frameworks.

IV. TENSIONS IN THE STRATIFIED APPROACH TO SUPPORTING LEGAL CAPACITY

There are three types of tension apparent in the stratified approach to supported decision-making outlined above: conceptual, practical and legal. In this section, I consider each of these in turn, using data from the Everyday Decisions research to explore how these tensions play out in the lives of intellectually disabled people.

A. Conceptual Tensions

The current stratified, piecemeal approach to support under the MCA holds within it some problematic conceptual assumptions about supporting decision-making. First, the MCA framework assumes that decision-making support is easy to provide, and that anyone can and should be able to provide support to any intellectually disabled person who needs to make a decision. Yet in the Everyday Decisions project, we found that the MCA approach really only works well for straightforward everyday choices about what to wear, what to do that day, or what to eat. Disabled participants all reported good support with making these kinds of choices, and care professional participants were

[46] Committee on the Rights of Persons with Disabilities, *General Comment No 1 on Article 12: Equal recognition before the law* (April 2014) UN Doc CRPD/C/GC/1.

[47] M Donnelly, 'Best Interests in the Mental Capacity Act: Time to say Goodbye?' (2016) 24 *Medical Law Review* 318.

universally confident in supporting everyday decisions, using a range of tools like pictures and objects of reference.[48] In contrast, more complex life choices and decisions require nuanced, ongoing and consistent support to help people to realise their life goals, and this kind of support was not always available. Where high-quality support is available to people, then it can be transformational, but even that is not without challenges in the complex, relational lives of intellectually disabled people.

Eva, a care co-ordinator within a case management company,[49] told a story about how one of her clients had been facilitated to develop much better communication skills, using eyegaze technology. This client, who was born with cerebral palsy, has 'really limited speech, like two or three words she could say' and lived at home with her family.

> Recently she got a new … speech and language therapist who's given her an eyegaze … and they've been working with her on how to use that. And over the last two years she's gone from somebody that didn't have any kind of input into what happened to her, to somebody that's just gone and made her own will. Because with the therapist's help and the right technology she's actually been able to express an opinion and it's been clear to everybody [that] she's a really intelligent young lady. The trouble is that her mum doesn't think that she has got all this ability. She doesn't think the therapist and her staff know her daughter as well as she does. […] So mum is being very resistant and not letting her make her own decisions, and the staff are really stuck in the middle. […] They've been told, and the therapist agrees that she can make all these decisions for herself. She's even planning a weekend break away and she's done it all herself just on the eyegaze. But mum said 'don't be ridiculous, she doesn't know what she's doing, you can't let her do that' and has stopped it all (Eva, CP_18, Care Co-ordinator).

As well as highlighting the importance of high-quality support, this story speaks to a second conceptual tension in the current system: the presumption that it does not matter who provides support to an intellectually disabled person. In telling this story, Eva places the 'blame' for tensions in providing support firmly with the client's mother. She continued, by saying what the client's staff and therapists were trying to do to resolve the tensions:

> So we're trying to work with mum, and the therapists are trying to work with her so that she actually can communicate to her daughter the same way that everyone else seems able to, to try to improve her opinion so that she might gradually start to step back. Because in theory in law she's an adult, this young lady, so she should

[48] Harding and Taşcıoğlu, *Everyday Decisions Project Report* (n 11); Harding and Taşcıoğlu, 'Supported Decision-Making from Theory to Practice' (n 11).

[49] Case management companies provide support and services to people with acquired brain injuries who have funds to pay for their services, usually as a consequence of a financial settlement in a personal injury/medical negligence case. In the Everyday Decisions project, it seemed that intellectually disabled people who have access to case management seem to have much greater levels of personalised support than those who do not.

> be allowed to make her own decisions. But she's living in the family home, with her mum who's always been the primary carer who's got a big influence on what decisions get made. ... So it's [easy] to say, 'well, just ignore her mum and do whatever she wants you to do.' But actually if [the staff] do that mum gets really upset and angry. There's a lot of phone calls, a lot of arguments, and it just upsets the client. So she tends to just let mum get her own way, which is really sad to see (Eva, CP_18, Care Co-ordinator).

These kinds of tensions between different supporters are not unique. Reported case law from the Court of Protection often demonstrates how the different people that surround and support an intellectually disabled person (eg, family members, carers, friends, and professionals) can have very different views about what would be best for that person, what that person would want, or the care they should receive.[50] If these supporters have different opinions they may each try to use their role as a supporter to influence that person to choose the option that aligns most closely with their view. The forms of informal supported decision-making that exist in the MCA, alongside the stratified nature of support, when combined with these different views, can mean that the person at the heart of the decision becomes pushed and pulled in different directions, can become more confused, and less able to make their own decisions, particularly when it comes to difficult decisions and life choices. This can, in turn, lead to disagreements between different parties, and escalating tensions between the disabled person and their formal and informal support networks, which require careful management.

Consider this example from Lucy, a day service manager, who facilitated an advocate to support one of their service users to move out of her family home and into her own place:

> In the past we had ... a service user who continued to say they wanted to live on their own. And that was a very difficult time for family, because this service user continued to come to staff at day centre because she felt comfortable to do that. [...] I spoke to an advocacy agency and got someone involved to be able to speak to my service user, to be able to follow that decision and the opportunity to be able to live on her own. [...] She was quite able – she'd got a mild learning disability, she had got some sort of capacity to understand – this person, the advocate was here to support her in what she wanted to do. The advocate got involved and obviously made regular visits, built that friendship up. We needed to remain impartial from all that, the decision making, because although we were a support person if you like as a day centre, we wanted to

[50] Recent examples in the Court of Protection include disputes between family and health and social care providers about the withdrawal of life-sustaining treatment, *Re TW* [2021] EWCOP 13, *Re NZ* [2021] EWCOP 16; the vaccination of care home residents against the wishes of their family members, *Re V* [2021] EWCOP 4, *NHS Tameside & Glossop CCG v CR (by his litigation friend, CW) v SR* [2021] EWCOP 19; and more complex cases like *A Local Authority v TA, XA, GA (by her litigation friend, The Official Solicitor), SR (GA's deputy for property and affairs)* [2021] EWCOP 22, where the son of an elderly woman with severe dementia was removed from her home and served with a civil restraint order following his abusive and controlling behaviour.

> remain a support for the family as well, because that's who we are and that's what we do. So we didn't want to be directly involved in that, but we supported the individual to maintain the friendship with the advocate. We gave them time, we gave them space, we gave them opportunities to meet and we'd all support that. This service user then was identified living arrangement for them to go and live if you like. We supported in transition, so we gave the information to the staff identified to work in that area. We supported them to tea visits … Unfortunately, a few months down the line, she left us as day care, because she went on to pursue other things. She wanted to look at voluntary work, and she'd found a new lease of life basically (Lucy, CP_1, Day Centre Manager).

This story from Lucy encapsulates many of the conceptual tensions in supported decision-making under the MCA. As we see at the beginning of Lucy's story, the disabled person at the heart of the story had expressed a consistent view that she wanted to live a more independent life. This is discursively expressed through 'continued to say'. Yet rather than this expression of wishes and desires translating into immediate support from the formal service, because, as Lucy says, her service has an ethos of support for both the disabled person and their family carers, an independent source of support was brought in to help the disabled person mediate between her wishes, and those of her family. In many respects, this is a 'good news' story – the disabled person's expressed will and preferences translated into a positive change in her life. The final sentence of Lucy's story, beginning with 'unfortunately', however, hints at a different set of tensions related to the financial side of social care: by supporting this person to lead a more independent life, the day care centre lost her as a service user. The particular service Lucy works for was highly committed to supporting intellectually disabled people to live as independently as possible, but this is not necessarily the case for all services, or even for family members (as the above story from Eva demonstrates).

Finally, there is a potential conceptual tension between independent advocacy and informal supported decision-making. In Lucy's story (above), the advocate was a positive source of support for the disabled person, able to successfully negotiate potential conflicts of interest between her and her family. In contrast, under the MCA and Care Act, informal family support and independent advocacy are generally positioned as being interchangeable roles. If a person has a family carer that can act as an 'appropriate person', they are not always entitled to statutory advocacy, leaving a potential support gap for the intellectually disabled person.[51] Whereas independent advocates may be experienced in dealing with and supporting people with decisions across a wide range

[51] There are no limits, of course, on when a person can access independent or charity advocacy, but eligibility criteria for an IMCA are governed by ss 35–40 of the Mental Capacity Act 2005 and associated regulations, and for a Care Act advocate, by ss 67–68 of the Care Act 2014.

of areas, family members may not have had training in mental capacity law, or have access to quality information about navigating the health and social care system.[52]

Furthermore, a statutory advocate, whilst generally 'person-centred' in their practice is often a systemic insider, whereas an informal (family/friend) supporter chosen by the intellectually disabled person is *their* insider. This distinction may not always (or even often) lead to problems, but it has the conceptual potential to do so. A professional advocate will have the ingrained habits, skills and disposition to be an insider in the social care field. Advocates with wide experience in the field may have institutionalised cultural capital through advocacy qualifications, experience and credentials which mean they are taken more seriously than informal supporters. This means they may become habituated into the social care system, developing awareness of the unwritten rules about how decisions are made, or how things are done. This then potentially puts those who are *not* entitled to a statutory advocate (because they have an informal supporter/RPR/appropriate person) at a disadvantage. Conversely being a systemic insider might limit the options that some independent advocates see in a particular case, because their experience tells them that one or other course of action is unlikely to be successful because it has failed in their previous experience in the field.

There does not, however, need to be an either/or approach to advocacy and support. Combining both formal and informal support for decision-making is likely to give intellectually disabled people the best chance to make decisions that are well-informed, and in line with their will, preferences, beliefs and values. Disabled participants in this research often expressed a preference for support from someone that they had a longstanding relationship with. So, for example, when Penny was making a new will after her husband died, she went to a solicitor, but also had support from her son, and from an advocate that had known her for a long time:

> I made it with the solicitor. But I had, my stepson was there helping me as well. And we had another lady that was helping me. I used to work, I used to do a lot with [charity] and she used to be my support on [charity]. … She was our advocate. … you don't want to start with someone afresh and tell them, because it would take ages wouldn't it? (Penny, IDP16_SWM1)

Penny's story shows how supported decision-making can work well. In her case, she was able to make a new will by combining specialist input from a solicitor, practical support from her family, and independent support from an advocate. Rather than considering advocacy and professional support as an alternative to family support, being attentive to the relational contexts that people live in can help intellectually disabled people to make more complex everyday legal

[52] See further, Peel and Harding, '"It's a huge maze, the system"' (n 35).

decisions. Unfortunately, and perhaps in part because of the way that advocacy has been constructed through the regulatory framework as only needed when a person does not have a family carer, there are also issues with access to statutory advocates. As Alice (a case manager with a background in occupational therapy) said: 'ideally I'd like to see every person have, I know you're meant to have IMCAs, but trying to get an IMCA is a nightmare' (Alice, CP_20).

In this section, I have highlighted three conceptual problems with how supported decision-making is currently constructed in English law: that the regulatory frameworks assume that support is easy to provide, and therefore anyone can do it; that it does not matter who provides support, despite the complex relational lives of intellectually disabled people; and that fundamentally different kinds of support are conflated in the regulatory frameworks. The stratified nature of the regulatory frameworks around supported decision-making create these conceptual tensions. Hierarchies between different supporters are at least partly to blame for the way that these conceptual tensions impact the everyday lives of intellectually disabled people.

B. Practical Challenges

In addition to these important conceptual issues, there are practical challenges that emerge in the context of these stratified regulatory frameworks, around whether a disabled person's wishes or preferences are taken seriously, and whether their choice of supporter is always respected. Despite the fundamentally supportive and collaborative ethos of the MCA, many cases that are heard in the Court of Protection get to that point as a consequence of disagreements between the person, and/or their family members and the professionals involved in the person's care.[53]

For some of the care professionals who participated in the Everyday Decisions project, other parts of the regulatory regime, like the Deprivation of Liberty Safeguards (DoLS), could be used to force engagement from other parts of the system:

> I can give an example of a lady who had suffered a brain haemorrhage, and she'd gone into hospital for treatment, and then was discharged to a nursing home. And her husband and children remained living in the family home, and she very much expressed a wish to return home. And I established that that was potentially the plan at the initial admission to the nursing home; however, it never came about, and two

[53] See, for example, recent cases like *A Clinical Commissioning Group v AF and Others* [2020] EWCOP 16, where there was a dispute between P's daughter and the clinicians treating her father about whether or not to continue with Clinically Assisted Nutrition and Hydration (CANH) via a PEG tube; or *A County Council v LW and Another* [2020] EWCOP 50, which concerned a dispute between P and the local authority responsible for her care about where and with whom she should reside.

> years later she's still in the nursing home. … And the husband was really struggling to fight to have his wife home, and to have her being nursed at home so she can see her children grow up. So really it was quite frustrating for them because they're not being supported, and the council was not taking any action to enable this woman to go home with a package of care. They weren't going to look at the house to see if they could make adaptations. So I'd seen that she'd been subject to the best interests DoLS process, and nothing was coming about. So it was about using that as a lever to try and effect that wish for her and that decision. So that's one example I can think of where I feel it's worked, because I concluded it wasn't in her best interests. Now unfortunately I never found out whether she went home, but it had to go to court. (Judith, CP_12, Best Interests Assessor)

There are also practical issues about continuity of support under the stratified framework set out in the MCA. If the supporter is different for every decision (which is possible under the s. 4 best interests framework because responsibility for making a decision if the person lacks capacity varies depending on the decision to be made) then there can be a relative lack of continuity, awareness of a person's wishes and feelings or any mutual understanding. Whilst anyone making best interests decisions under the MCA is required to have regard to the Code of Practice, there is no legal requirement for supporters and decision makers (whether formal or informal) to have training in how to support people to make their own decisions or to express their views about what should happen to them.

Legal professionals, for example, may be tasked with supporting people to make decisions about powers of attorney, wills or advance decisions to refuse treatment, but may not have had any formal training on how to support decision-making, or even any disability awareness training to help them to serve intellectually disabled clients. Consider this example from Gareth's interview, where he was talking about his most recent experience of making a will, with his supporter, Catherine:

> *Gareth*: Well that's why when I say about having good support with me. Having people that know me well and know how, they know when they talk to me. Like Catherine … So if I didn't understand [the solicitor] Catherine was picking it up and she–
>
> *Catherine*: It's a bit like translating wasn't it. So it's –
>
> *Gareth*: – she would explain it much better in a simple term.
>
> *Catherine*: Yeah. I mean I would say to them, you know, I would say 'sorry, can you simplify it?' And then I would, if Gareth was still struggling, I would simplify it to how I thought he would best understand it. And that's how we got on didn't we? So it was a bit of them. A bit of it they could have done better. But what they couldn't explain I went over.

There is now a duty on health and social care services to provide accessible information,[54] but no similar duty arises in the context of legal or other

[54] NHS England, *DCB1605 Accessible Information: Specification v1.1* (August 2017).

professional services for intellectually disabled people, despite general rights to reasonable adjustments under the Equality Act 2010. Providing extra support to help intellectually disabled people make complex decisions may also take longer than providing services to non-disabled clients. Without training, and readily available easyread and accessible resources, this may mean that legal and professional services that are charged by the hour (like legal services) are more costly for disabled clients, leading to discrimination.

C. Legal Issues

Finally, there are several legal issues that come up in the context of providing support to a disabled person, depending on the status of their supporter. These include different regulatory frameworks, gaps in access to advocacy, and issues around how and whether different kinds of supporters are supervised. Whereas statutory advocates have a legal right and duty to access a wide range of information about the person they support,[55] family carers and informal supporters have no such right of access. This can lead to challenges in accessing information and records because different interpretations of confidentiality and data protection can be an excuse for not sharing information with informal supporters and family carers.[56]

The shift from independent advocacy, provided through charitable organisations and self-advocacy groups, towards statutory advocacy under the relatively narrow MCA and Care Act criteria has also created practical challenges for some disabled people. Consider, for example, this story told by Luke, who described himself as having Asperger's syndrome, ADHD, PTSD and depression. He was struggling to understand changes to the support he received through direct payments, and his advocate was off work sick:

> [The local authority are] taking advantage of the fact that my advocate is now off ill. So they're now doing it now without my advocate – which is apparently not a legal requirement for the things that they want to do. I'm not legally required to have an advocate there so therefore they're moving ahead with things that they don't need to have an advocate for – which is the financial side of things, so they're now taking all the money back again.
>
> Everything that was agreed is 'oh, did we agree to that?' and things like that, and I'm like, 'you know full well that's what you agreed to.' And it's 'oh that's not how we see it, we'll have to come around and talk to you and discuss it with you.' And I've said that [my advocate is] off, [but they say] 'You don't need an advocate to be there for these things. It's not a legal requirement for you to have an advocate so therefore we can come around with your permission.' … And each time they've done that I've just– I don't know what my rights are. (Luke, IDP_19)

[55] Mental Capacity Act 2005, s 35(6).

[56] R Harding, *Duties to Care: Dementia, relationality and law* (Cambridge, Cambridge University Press, 2017).

Here, we see Luke report that his local authority used the lack of statutory entitlement to advocacy for particular decisions to limit his access to support. In this short snippet, he uses the formulation 'not a legal requirement' twice when telling his story. By drawing the narrow statutory rules around access to advocacy into the story, he is reflecting how his social workers have translated the lack of a statutory requirement to provide access to an advocate into a limit on his right to have support.

The stratified support framework also means that there are very different levels of supervision, and legal checks and balances in respect of different kinds of supporter (see Table 3, above). The vast majority of supported decision-making discussed by participants in the Everyday Decisions project was informal support, often in the context of best interests decisions, but also decisions supported by personal assistants and family carers. Sometimes, unfortunately, the lack of supervision of informal support can contribute to problems for intellectually disabled participants. Consider, for example, the story Gareth (an older man with learning difficulties and hearing and visual impairments) told about experiencing financial abuse by his (former) personal assistant who, when confronted, resigned from her role:

> After a while when that was all going on, being financially abused, which I didn't totally understand what was happening. … a very good friend of mine, … he had the same [PA]. Coincidence. And he just come up to me one day, he goes, 'Have you had any problems lately?' And he didn't tell me straight off why, he didn't say why at that time, 'have you had any problems lately?' I goes, 'no not quite,' but then the alarm bells started to ring. And he said, he just said to me then, 'well yeah I mean something's been happening to me as well.'
>
> I thought right OK, thank you for that, I've been warned, I've been told, I'm happy. Unless the person that had the same person, PA, had told me this was happening, I'd have been none the wiser. And he told me. Of course then he went and organised a meeting for this person to go to a meeting in [city] right, this is before me. And you know what? She resigned from her job, guilty conscience. She just walked. So when I got in touch with the people who had helped to fund me … I said, 'well look, yes I'm having this problem as well, right.' And of course then right, we'll send a letter out, we'll talk to the person, and then they'll arrange a meeting. Of course they did, they set up a meeting, again second time around she resigned rather than face the music. (Gareth, IDP_3, SWM4)

Of most concern in this story from Gareth is that there is no suggestion that the personal assistant who financially abused him and his friend was subject to any form of prosecution or censure. This suggests that the current frameworks surrounding safeguards against wrongdoing by supporters of intellectually disabled people are not currently working as well as they should. These conceptual, practical and legal issues, when considered alongside the remarkable levels of complexity in the law relating to supported decision-making, combine to suggest that a different approach to supporting legal capacity is needed in English law.

V. THE POTENTIAL BENEFITS OF A FORMAL NOMINATED SUPPORTER SCHEME

Given the difficulties with the current approach, it is clear that reform is needed to better embed support for the enjoyment of legal capacity in everyday life. In this chapter, I have shown that the complexity and stratification of support frameworks in English law leads to conceptual, practical and legal issues in supported decision-making, and current safeguards for intellectual disabled people are generally insufficient to protect their enjoyment of legal capacity.

As discussed above, jurisdictions that offer nominated supporter frameworks often do so alongside a functional assessment of capacity, and most retain the potential, as a last resort, to make essentially substitute decisions that prioritise the wishes and preferences of the person. A nominated supporter framework can also operate alongside other frameworks (like the MCA) as an alternative to them. For example, in both British Columbia, Canada and Victoria, Australia, support frameworks sit alongside power of attorney and guardianship provisions.

Experience from other jurisdictions suggests that there can be significant benefits deriving from a nominated supporter scheme, in addition to offering greater compliance with obligations under the UN CRPD. A pilot study in Bulgaria, for example, concluded that supported decision-making improves the quality of life of intellectually disabled people and has positive effects on self-determination, personal development, inclusion in the community and independent living, as well as offering significant economic benefits.[57] Evaluation of a supported decision-making pilot scheme in South Australia noted similar benefits to supported persons, and additional benefits to supporters.[58] Benefits to supporters included changes to the ways they thought about decision-making with the person they supported, and 'positive improvements in the nature and quality of their interpersonal relationships'.[59]

Given the importance of safeguarding in the context of support, it is vital that supporters, particularly those who support financial decisions, are subject to appropriate levels of supervision by a public body. Supervision of supporters offers the most effective way to provide appropriate and effective safeguards to prevent abuse, as required by Article 12(4) CRPD.[60] One way of achieving this in England without costly system re-invention could be to extend the system of Court of Protection visitors,[61] set up to supervise Deputies appointed by the Court of Protection and attorneys appointed through registered Enduring and Lasting Powers of Attorney. Additional supervision would generate additional

[57] Bulgarian Centre for Not-for-Profit Law, *Cost Benefit Analysis of Supported Decision-Making* (Sofia, BCNL, 2014).

[58] M Wallace, *Evaluation of the Supported Decision-Making Project* (South Australia, Office of the Public Advocate, 2012).

[59] Ibid.

[60] UN CRPD Article 12(4) See further, Hall, Chapter 15, this volume.

[61] Mental Capacity Act 2005, s 61.

costs, but the potential savings that arise from formally recognising supported decision-making, such as were noted in the case studies in Bulgaria and Australia, in combination with modest registration, reporting and supervision fees, could off-set these costs.

The key difference that a nominated supporter scheme could make is, however, that instead of safeguards being focused on the functional capacity of the disabled person, safeguards are directed at third parties in the process who have the potential or opportunity to perpetrate abuse. A formal nominated supporter scheme is likely to offer the greatest potential benefits for intellectually disabled people, and could replace some of the substituted decision-making frameworks in the MCA (see Table 3, above). This would help to tip the balance of that legislation away from substituted decision-making, which is not compatible with the right to enjoy legal capacity under Article 12 CRPD, towards greater respect and support for supported decision-making, which prioritises the preferences of disabled people.

VI. CONCLUDING REMARKS

In this chapter, I outlined the complex and stratified approach to supporting legal capacity in English law, before putting forward a set of conceptual, practical and legal critiques of the current position, grounded in socio-legal, empirical research. I have argued that reform of the MCA away from the current model, which prioritises substitute decision-making and unsupervised support, towards a nominated supporter scheme might offer positive benefits to intellectually disabled people, as well as refocusing safeguards on those most likely to perpetrate abuse. For reasons of space, I have not set out here precisely what any such nominated support system might look like.

Multiple examples of legislation in force and being implemented in other jurisdictions are detailed elsewhere in this volume. Whilst it remains the case that no jurisdiction has yet created a system that fully operationalises the right to enjoy legal capacity without recourse to any substituted decision-making, we can learn from each other in developing CRPD-compatible approaches to supporting legal capacity. By thinking through the constraints and challenges of supported decision-making, we can test the boundaries of what is possible and what is desirable in the context of real-world decisions.

Given recent reforms to the MCA through the Mental Capacity (Amendment) Act 2019, it seems unlikely that there is the political appetite for significant reform of English mental capacity law in the immediate future. Yet by offering carefully constructed alternatives to the current best interests and substitute decision-making models that permeate English law, as well as demonstrating the limitations of the current framework, as I have sought to do in this chapter and others have done in their contributions to this volume as a whole, we can help to make the case for positive legal and social change.

Index

Lightning Source UK Ltd.
Milton Keynes UK
UKHW020018060722
405441UK00003B/131

9 781509 940349